Innovation and Incentives

Innovation and Incentives

Suzanne Scotchmer

The MIT Press
Cambridge, Massachusetts
London, England

MIT Press books may be purchased at special quantity discounts for business or sales promotional use. For information, please email special_sales@ mitpress.mit.edu or write to Special Sales Department, The MIT Press, 5 Cambridge Center, Cambridge, MA 02142.

This book was set in Sabon by SNP Best-set Typesetter Ltd., Hong Kong.

Printed and bound in the United States of America.

Library of Congress Cataloging-in-Publication Data

Scotchmer, Suzanne.
Innovation and incentives / Suzanne Scotchmer.
    p. cm.
Includes bibliographical references and index.
ISBN 0-262-19515-1 (alk. paper)
1. Research—Economic aspects. 2. Intellectual property. 3. Research.
4. Research—Finance. I. Title.

HC79.R4S26 2005
338′.064—dc22

2004053094

10 9 8 7 6 5 4 3 2

Contents

Preface

Creation and discovery are mysterious processes. But whatever else is required, economists are reasonably certain that incentives matter. In this book I discuss some of the incentive systems that our societies have created, and their potential for spurring technological or scientific advance.

This book is written for nonspecialists, at the level of upper division undergraduates and beginning graduate students studying economics. It supposes that the reader is grounded in intermediate-level microeconomics, although most of the book can be understood without it. My own teaching materials, as well as useful links, can be found at http://socrates.berkeley.edu/~scotch/innovation. If used for a graduate course, the book should be supplemented with readings from the extensive bibliographies at the ends of the chapters. A course based on this book might have as its goal the task of explaining how the creation of knowledge fits into a competitive, capitalist economy, and how institutions create incentives to encourage research. It has a largely normative focus: What should those institutions look like?

Although I have cited a large number of works, the book is not organized as a review of the economics literature. I have given short shrift to topics for which other authors have given accessible, integrated treatments (see the footnotes and references), and I have emphasized certain areas because I hope to nudge readers in that direction. Areas that I have not emphasized include how investments play out in patent races, how market structure affects incentives to innovate, the open-source movement, and the details of how patent law might be reformed in the face of growing discontent. Areas that I emphasize include the role of public funding, the hybridization of public and private incentive mechanisms, the necessary link between incentive mechanisms and the scarcity of research "ideas," the cumulative nature of research, and globalization.

My treatment departs from other treatments in its premise that ideas for R&D investments are scarce, and the scarcity of ideas constrains progress, just as a reluctance to invest resources can. An innovation requires both an idea and an incentive to invest in it.

Government funding of almost anything, including R&D, can be vilified as ineffective, too costly, and likely to produce bad outcomes. However, patents and other intellectual property mechanisms are often vilified in exactly the same way. This book does not add to the many lamentations that have been written about both the public and private systems, but instead tries to give a systematic treatment of what our choice among such mechanisms should depend on. The analysis begins with an articulation of the problem to be solved and tries to discover which incentive mechanism is most suited to the problem. For many creative environments, intellectual property in any of its forms may be inferior to some form of procurement or public sponsorship. One of the main questions is when that is likely to be so.

For teaching purposes, the book uses the tools of economics. I have tried to use those tools to shed light on current controversies, such as the patenting of genetic sequences, business methods, and computer software; the difficulty in enforcing copyrights in the digital age; the role of technical protection systems; and the antitrust and innovation issues that surround network industries. I have also tried to give students a nontechnical overview of current legal rules, especially those legislated in the last ten years.

The book reflects my collaborations in teaching and writing at Berkeley and elsewhere. Among the coteachers, collaborators, friends, and previous students who have indirectly contributed to this book are Pamela Samuelson, Mark Schankerman, Jerry Green, Nancy Gallini, Ted O'Donoghue, Deborah Minehart, Richard Gilbert, Jacques Thisse, Peter Menell, Rob Merges, Mark Lemley, and Hal Varian. I have been surrounded at Berkeley by a large community of scholars in the Economics Department, Boalt School of Law, the Goldman School of Public Policy, the Haas Business School, and the Department of Agricultural Economics, who have collectively supported and informed this work. I hope I have thanked them in the way they like best, by citing their works. Parts of this book were read and improved by Bronwyn Hall, John Covell, Mark Schankerman, Manuel Trajtenberg, Neil Gandal, Thomas Coupé, Joseph Farrell, and Jean Lanjouw. My largest debt is to Stephen Maurer, who coauthored three chapters, but also read and improved the others. As the reader can see from the references, I have also read widely in the works of my colleagues elsewhere. This has been a great pleasure.

Institutions that have hosted me during the preparation of this manuscript include the Court of Appeals for the Federal Circuit, University of Auckland, Institute of Economics at the University of Copenhagen, UCLA, Universitá Autonoma di Barcelona, and of course UC Berkeley, where the students have seen several drafts. Students who assisted in this work include Yooki Park, Kevin Schubert, Taehee Woo, and Stylianos Tellis.

1 Institutions: A Brief Excursion through History

with Stephen M. Maurer

The United States currently devotes about 2.6 percent of GDP—$264 billion—to research and development.[1] Of this, the federal government pays more than a quarter, a fraction that was much larger for most of the twentieth century after World War II. Some federally funded research is done in-house (27%) and in national laboratories (13%), but more than half is given to industry and universities, which receive similar amounts. Looked at from the other side, about 10 percent of industry's R&D effort and 60 percent of universities' R&D effort are funded by the federal government. Foundations and lower levels of government also make important contributions to research, mostly by giving research funds to universities, private firms, and individuals.

The numbers mask a bewildering array of funding schemes and incentives. Most R&D investments made by private firms are aimed at securing a market advantage. Market advantage is often, but not always, given as intellectual property, mostly patents and copyrights. Firms also compete for contracts to carry out government research agendas and can even receive grant funding, under the federal Small Business Innovation Research Program (SBIR). They receive research funding for military hardware and space exploration as well. Universities receive direct grants from industry, often in return for promised intellectual property rights, and also from government. Some government funding, such as that for the human genome project, carries an obligation to put the resulting knowledge in the public domain (available for free access). The output of other government funding can be patented.

---

1. Unless otherwise noted, the data quoted in this chapter refer to the year 2000 and were compiled by the National Science Foundation. See, generally, the statistics available at www.nsf.gov/sbe/stats.htm, and more specifically *Science and Engineering Indicators 2002.*

All forms of funding are implicitly incentive schemes, since they set the direction of research and encourage people to do it. Some funding is given ex ante, such as grants, whereas other funding is given ex post, such as patents and prizes. Prizes were eclipsed by patents during the Industrial Revolution, but they have never vanished as an incentive mechanism. For example, the Defense Advanced Research Projects Agency (DARPA), which is the research arm of the Department of Defense, has offered a $1 million prize to elicit a fortyfold improvement in robotic vehicles for rough terrain (Defense Advanced Research Projects Agency, 2003; Holden 2003).

Research, like art, has always relied on wealthy patrons. In the modern world, this fact is evident in the names Stanford, Ford, Rockefeller, Carnegie, Mellon, and so forth, that are attached to universities and grant-giving foundations. Government funding, whether for military purposes, pure science, or targeted industrial objectives, has also been a common thread, although the nature of the governments providing the funds has changed, as has the process by which they are given. Government funding in modern democracies arises from a more inclusive political process than that used by the Greeks or medieval monarchies, and might therefore be more directed to creating knowledge or technology with widespread benefits. In many of its current forms, it has the advantage of peer review by fellow scientists. Some government funding has always been mission-directed, often in search of better war machines. Archimedes was supported for such purposes, and so was Robert Oppenheimer, director of the Manhattan Project in World War II.

The only fundamentally new incentive scheme of the past 400 years is intellectual property. Whereas wealthy benefactors and governments can indulge in basic science and curiosity-driven research, a research agenda driven by patents is hostage to the market and to consumer sovereignty. The consumers who are sovereign are those with resources.

The tale told in this chapter is one of institutions in flux. Before R&D could arise as an organized activity, societies needed both the ability and incentive to fund it. The *ability* to fund research requires command over resources. Governments, with their ability to tax, and private concentrations of wealth emerged some time after farming appeared in Mesopotamia (modern Syria and Iraq) around 8000 BC. Innovation also requires an *incentive* to fund research. If research leads to widespread benefits for citizens, governments may have an incentive to invest as part of their legitimate missions. Wealthy individuals may invest in R&D for many reasons, including philanthropy, curiosity, or a desire for acclaim. Inventors who are not wealthy need a means to appropriate the benefits they create for others. As we will see, innovation has always been spurred by governments and wealthy individuals, but the main means of appropriating benefits—intellectual property—developed much later. One of the ways that governments have spurred invention in recent eras is through what is sometimes called "regulatory pull," namely, creating commodity standards that can only be met with some new innovation.

Appropriability follows both from the nature of the knowledge and from the institutions that support discoveries. When we make a distinction between pure science and technology, we are often distinguishing knowledge that is not appropriable (such as the knowledge that planets orbit the sun) from knowledge that could have commercial value (such as engineering discoveries). To the extent that this distinction relies on institutions such as markets, and on preferences, it is not fundamental.[2]

1.1   The Ancients

The story begins much earlier than the written record—without innovation, it is difficult to make a record.[3] We can guess that invention in prehistoric societies was haphazard and unplanned. Although prehistoric societies made some clever inventions like the boomerang and Eskimo toggle-joint harpoon, the archeological evidence suggests that they were technologically conservative. Artifacts like flint tools and pots remained essentially unchanged for centuries. If invention was slow to take off, one explanation can be found in a dearth of social institutions to support research. People who spent their time improving the technology of subsistence might improve the well-being of the community as a whole, but could put their own survival at risk. There were presumably no social

---

2.   Nevertheless, many scholars have made distinctions of this type. Schumpeter (1942) distinguished between "invention" and "innovation." Mokyr (2002) distinguishes between "propositional knowledge" and "technological knowledge." Such distinctions are not central in this book, because the relevant aspects of knowedge are revealed in economic models. This book uses words like *technology* and *engineering* because they are the English-language words for certain kinds of knowledge, but it does not rely on any precise definition.
3.   Our discussion of prehistoric and ancient technology in section 1.1 is largely drawn from De Camp 1980 and Finley 1973. The emphasis here is on the institutions in which these technologies developed, as a prelude to our later discussions of incentives.

institutions like intellectual property or funding agencies to compensate them for their efforts.[4]

The first known inventor was a "government employee," Imhotep, who lived in Egypt about 2650 BC. He built the first pyramid, and was probably a Da Vinci–like genius who also served as a priest, scholar, sculptor, carpenter, poet, and doctor. Greek and Roman writers continued to revere him, albeit as an exaggerated, wizard-like figure, well into the Christian era. Imhotep's innovations were steadily eclipsed by later pyramid builders, all "government employees." Within a few decades, other government employees working for Khufu (aka "Cheops": d. 2613 BC) figured out how to move 50-ton granite slabs. Fourteen hundred years later, workers for Ramses II (d. 1212 BC) moved 1,000-ton statues routinely. In modern terms, all of these achievements amounted to direct government procurement of R&D.

The Greek city-states produced a golden age of science and technology between 600 and 300 BC. Along the way, the Greeks added new institutions of research and discovery to the direct government procurement model of Cheops. First, Greek culture accorded respect and reputation to wealthy individuals who devoted their time and resources to science. Examples include the astronomer Anaxagoras (d. fifth century BC); the engineer Archytes (d. fifth century BC), who worked out the theory of the pulley and built toys powered by compressed air; and the mathematician and inventor Archimedes (d. 212 BC).

Second, Greek city-states purchased research. In one famous example, Dionysius, the tyrant of Syracuse, hired Archimedes as a consultant to determine whether a crown was really made from pure gold. The task led to the buoyancy principle that bears Archimedes' name. Dionysius also pioneered the use of what would now be called large research teams. In 399 BC, he used a combination of conscription, high wages, and bonuses to attract skilled workers from all over the Mediterranean to work on military technologies such as giant warships and missile weapons. This early experiment led, among other things, to the catapult.

Third, the Greeks introduced a new type of self-funding research institution: schools organized around one or more great teachers. As in

---

4.   Macroeconomists speculate that invention was slow to take off because there was only a small population generating new ideas; see Romer 1996 for a summary. Although mathematical treatments of the hypothesis date from the 1990s, this insight was anticipated by De Camp forty years earlier. See Finley 1973, 6.

modern universities, the ancient schools created a powerful incentive for would-be academics to build their reputations through research and publication. Still, the scientific and technological benefits were limited. Socrates (d. 399 BC), Plato (d. 347 BC), and Aristotle (d. 322 BC) all belonged to schools, but only Aristotle was a scientist.

Finally, the Greeks' scientific tradition led to the establishment of the Library of Alexandria. When Alexander the Great transplanted Greek culture to Egypt, he found himself in what seemed to him an intellectual wasteland. Alexander's successors Ptolemy I (d. 283 BC) and Ptolemy II (d. 246 BC) built the library to remedy this problem. In a book-starved world, the library's core asset, 750,000 papyri purchased all over the world, was a unique resource. The Library of Alexandria foreshadowed modern research facilities like Princeton's Institute for Advanced Study. It included facilities for housing specimens, conducting experiments, delivering lectures, and storing library books. An endowment recruited scholars from throughout the known world to study, write, and teach.

Both basic science and engineering flourished as never before. Resident scholars prepared star charts of unprecedented accuracy (Hipparchus (d. 120 BC)), measured the size of the earth to 15 percent (Eratosthenes (d. ca. 194 BC)), invented the heliocentric theory of the solar system (Aristarchus of Samos (d. 230 BC)), and formalized geometry (Euclid (fl. ca. 300 BC)). The library also produced two first-rate engineering-type inventors. The first, Ctesibius (ca. 270 BC) is sometimes referred to as the "Edison of the Ancient World." His inventions included improved water pumps, the first metal spring, the first pneumatic pipe organ, the first keyboard, and an improved water clock. He also built a compressed air catapult that failed because no one could machine adequate parts. The library's other most noteworthy inventor was Hero of Alexandria (d. AD 62) In addition to publishing works on mathematics and physics, Hero invented improved gearing, a surveying instrument, an air-driven fountain, and a famous engine driven by jets of steam.

After Greek hegemony declined, the Romans created an empire across Europe. They are not remembered for as much inventiveness as the Greeks, nor did they improve memorably on the institutions of research and learning, but they did contribute to technology. Like large corporations today, the Romans' huge administrative machine was large enough to capture the positive externalities associated with innovation. State ambition was a powerful incentive for engineering feats like building aqueducts. Roman innovation also benefited from a second practice, in which successful inventors routinely petitioned the emperor for rewards. This allowed inventors to recover at least some of the benefits that their work conferred on society. Examples of government-sponsored innovators include Sergius Orata, a building contractor who invented central heating (ca. 75 BC) and Marcus Vipsanius Agrippa, a Roman statesman and military commander who designed novel siege weapons and catapults (d. 12 BC).

Assessing the performance of ancient institutions is a messy business. For example, we do not know what R&D rate would have been optimal, or whether more resources would have accelerated technological development. There is no evidence that the ancients themselves thought very systematically about how to organize incentives. Even an experienced engineer like Vitruvius (d. 25 BC) seems to have viewed innovation as a series of accidental discoveries and frivolous projects. His writings never argue that a more systematic inquiry could accelerate progress or benefit the economy through cost-savings. Despite these ambiguities, most scholars share a lingering suspicion that the ancient world should have done better. In the words of one classicist, "Great things emerged from the [Alexandria] Museum, in military technology and ingenious mechanical toys. But no one, not even the Ptolemies themselves, who would have profited directly and handsomely, thought to turn the energy and inventiveness of a Ctesibius to agricultural or industrial technology. The contrast with the Royal Society in England is inescapable" (Finley 1973, 148).

There is some evidence that modern institutions like intellectual property would have helped matters, at least at the margin. We know that the ancient world repeatedly discovered and forgot the same inventions, such as central heating and the arch. Partly these failures were due to the absence of printing, without which the recording and dissemination of knowledge is difficult. However, inventors also tended to keep their discoveries secret, so that inventions sometimes died with their inventors. Available evidence suggests that secrecy was especially prevalent in shipbuilding. A modern system of patents would have ameliorated the problem by providing an economic reward for disclosure. However, this is far from saying that modern institutions would have accelerated classical innovation in any substantial way. In the end, all institutions are limited by factors in the broader society. First, ancient societies tended to look down on engineering as a subject not fit for gentlemen. This was notoriously true of Plato and Socrates, and according to Plutarch, even of Archimedes. Second, most ancient societies were more interested in preserving the existing social order than adopting potentially subversive innovations. When a mechanical engineer found a better way to move heavy columns, the Emperor Vespasian (d. AD 79) gave him a reward but refused to adopt the technology. Said the emperor, "You must let me feed my poor commons." A similar but less heartwarming story is also told about the Emperor Tiberius (d. AD 37), who supposedly met the inventor of plastic ("unbreakable glass"). Tiberius had the man beheaded, lest, he said, "gold be reduced to the value of mud" (Finley 1973, 149; see also De Camp 1980, 178).

1.2   In Between: Monasteries, Guilds, and Universities

After the fall of Rome, most ancient texts were lost, and so far as we know, basic science stagnated. Nevertheless, a modest interest in engineering continued throughout the so-called Dark Ages.[5] In the East, citizens of Antioch produced the first artificial streetlights (ca. AD 350) and improved water-clock designs (ca. AD 450). Even in the West, government patronage remained important. When the Goth Theodoric (d. 526) conquered Rome, he hired the philosopher Boethius as a minister. Among his other duties, Boethius built advanced sundials and water clocks as gifts for adjacent rulers.

Europe emerged from the Dark Ages with important new institutions. It was not their stated purpose to foster innovation, but they nevertheless did so. The new Church monasteries combined practical economic activity with increasingly sophisticated research. After AD 500, monasteries started operating small libraries so that monks could learn to read. For the next 600 years, monasteries and cathedral schools were Europe's main centers of learning. Monasteries also operated some of the most technologically advanced mills, factories, and farms in Europe. In the process, they overcame the traditional prejudice against mere technology (Mokyr 1990, 203–204).

Meanwhile, in the secular world, craftspeople organized themselves into guilds. Guilds passed strict laws against revealing their secrets to outsiders, but encouraged members to share innovations among themselves. Potentially, the guilds' market power gave them the ability to capture the positive externalities associated with innovation. However, this same cartel-like character proved their undoing. Mokyr (1990,

---

5.   This discussion of medieval technology in section 1.2 is largely drawn from Gimpel 1977.

178–179, 258–259) tells how Dutch guilds opposed progress in ship-building, Swiss printers obtained laws to bar an improved printing press, and French paper producers used sabotage and arson to block machines that would have speeded up pulp production. Even if the guilds had been a force for innovation early on, they had become a net drag by the time they mostly vanished in the eighteenth century.

On the institutional side, the rise of universities created still more incentives for scholars to perform and publish research. Prior to 1100, learning had been limited to monasteries and cathedral schools. Beginning in the twelfth century, Europeans rediscovered mathematics and the classics, which were taught in the new universities along with medicine and natural science. Medieval teachers organized guilds to decide who would be entitled to earn student fees by lecturing. This led to diplomas and the first formal institutions of higher learning. By 1450, Europe hosted eighty universities. The new system also encouraged R&D. Roger Bacon (d. 1292), who discovered the formula for gunpowder and speculated on visionary technologies, taught at Paris and Oxford. In 1348, Giovanni Di Dondi built one of the first mechanical clocks while working as an astronomy professor in Padua.

Together, the new institutions unlocked medieval creativity. Thirteenth- and fourteenth-century writers marveled at the rate of invention and treated the engineers as heroes. Furthermore, the engineers themselves developed confidence. Surviving notebooks are filled with ideas for novel power sources and machines. Contemporary accounts describe how clockmakers had agreed on needed improvements and were working to achieve them in a systematic way.

1.3   Early Modern Europe: Patents, Prizes, and Patrons

Science grew explosively from the beginning of the Renaissance (in fourteenth-century Italy) through the Industrial Revolution (ca. 1750–1850). The growing realization that innovation could lead to prosperity persuaded European governments to make unprecedented efforts to promote it. In the process, they developed the first systems of intellectual property rights and reinvigorated existing institutions based on prizes, patronage, and other rewards.

Medieval monarchs had long rewarded supporters by giving them patents—legal monopolies over the right to provide particular goods and services. By the fifteenth century, rulers were also offering patents to foreigners who agreed to import new technologies. By the sixteenth century, French local authorities were using a similar system to encourage domestic inventors. Eventually, patents became a reward for innovation.

In the beginning, patents were given at the discretion of the ruling authority. Since they were not routinized under the authority of a disinterested administrative body, they were subject to abuse. People complained that rulers created patent monopolies too lightly or too arbitrarily, or for corrupt reasons. The patent system was formalized largely as a remedy.[6] The first formal patent statute was in Venice in 1474, and in 1623, the English Parliament passed the Statute of Monopolies. The Statute specified appropriate circumstances in which patents could be used to reward inventors, and was mainly aimed at limiting monopolies, rather than facilitating them.

The origins of copyright can also be found in the Crown's right to hand out monopolies.[7] The Stationers Company in England, a guild, had been given a monopoly on printing. The system gave the guild the power to limit competition much as copyright does today. Because the guild needed a government license to print books, the system also served as a form of censorship. Eventually, however, the authorization for this licensing relationship expired, and when Parliament failed to renew it, the Stationers' interests became allied with authors rather than the Crown. They now petitioned Parliament for a copyright act, which resulted in the Statute of Anne, the first copyright law, in 1710. The copyright law provided for a limited term, similarly to patents.

Lucrative early patents include those on the pendulum clock (1657), the torsion pendulum clock (1675), the steam powered pump (1698), the first modern ("regenerative") steam engine (1767), and punch card–controlled looms (1802).

Prizes also became an important device for stimulating both basic science and technological innovation. Sometimes a challenge was posted without a prize, since winning it added to reputation and could attract a patron. Newton solved the era's most important challenge in 1697 by calculating the path that a ball should take for the fastest descent to a point not directly beneath it. The solution opened the way to multivariate calculus. In a later period, prizes led James Maxwell (d. 1879) to devise a mathematical theory of Saturn's rings and Heinrich Hertz

6.   For a more complete account, see Ryan 1998, chap. 2.
7.   This discussion follows chap. 2 of Goldstein 1994, which should be consulted for more details. Ryan (1998) tells a similar story for the abortive history of copyright in Venice, much earlier.

(d. 1894) to detect radio waves. Prizes were also offered for technological contributions, as opposed to basic science. Some are mentioned in chapter 2.

Finally, governments reinvigorated the ancient practice of patronage. An important example was the Danish king's support of Tycho Brahe (d. 1601), who made the astronomical observations that underlie the conclusion (together with his assistant Johannes Kepler, d. 1630) that the earth revolves around the sun. This laid the groundwork for Newton's physics. Sometimes support was offered ex post, after the researcher had demonstrated his worth, in which case patronage also acted as a prize. In England, George III gave the astronomer William Herschel (d. 1822) a stipend of £200 a year after he discovered Uranus. Herschel used the money to build the biggest telescope in Europe. Similarly, Frederick the Great (d. 1786) lured Leonhard Euler (d. 1783) and Joseph-Louis Lagrange (d. 1813) to Berlin after declaring that "the greatest mathematicians in Europe should reside at the Court of the greatest king in Europe." When Frederick died, Lagrange considered offers from Naples and Spain before joining the ill-fated Louis XVI in Paris.

The widespread reliance on prizes and patrons had several drawbacks. The first was secrecy. Many mathematicians kept their techniques secret in order to win as-yet-unannounced challenges. When Scipione del Ferro died in 1526, he passed the secret of solving a special case of the cubic equation to just one student. In contrast, modern institutions are designed to overcome the urge to secrecy. Scholars in modern universities must publish in order to achieve advancement or acclaim, and patents are public by their very nature.

A second maladaptive feature, emphasized by Rosenberg and Birdzell (1986), is that systems of patronage and prizes are too centralized. An advantage of intellectual property is that responsibility for innovation is decentralized among the citizens. However, we will argue in chapters 2 and 8 that prize and grant systems can be equally decentralized, and can mimic the advantages of patents. Such prize systems were presaged by institutions that emerged in the Industrial Revolution. In the silk-weaving industry of Lyons in the late eighteenth and early nineteenth centuries, self-motivated inventors could apply for rewards to a central prize authority, without the innovation having been commissioned in advance (Foray and Hilaire-Perez, forthcoming; Foray 2004). This system is decentralized in much the same way as patents.

A third maladaptive feature was that, to compete for a prize, the researcher had to fund the effort himself or find backers. Even if this only required subsistence levels of funding, as with mathematical prizes, it could be a deterrent. Universities ameliorated this problem by giving scholars the time, funding, and incentive to pursue self-motivated research, rather than the research agendas chosen by patrons. Copernicus (d. 1543), Galileo (d. 1642), Isaac Newton (d. 1727), John Dalton (d. 1844), Alessandro Volta (d. 1827), André-Marie Ampère (d. 1836), and James Maxwell (d. 1879) all spent at least part of their careers as university professors. Newton's predecessor resigned from his endowed chair so that the twenty-four-year-old genius could devote himself to full-time research. University staff jobs supported still more scientists, including James Watt (d. 1819) and Michael Faraday (d. 1867). Our modern universities are similar in many respects.

1.4   Patents Come into Their Own

The last half of the nineteenth and early twentieth centuries were a golden age of invention.[8] The era brought electric lights, movies, phonographs, radio, telephones, airplanes, and automobiles. Inventors were admired as never before or since.[9] The lure of patents played a central role in this transformation.

The period also illustrated the defects of patents, prefiguring debates that still rage today.[10] One unavoidable difficulty is that patents reward inventors ex post, which leaves them the problem of funding their research up front. Many of the era's most prominent inventors dodged this problem by working in basements and garages until they were established. Thomas Edison (d. 1931), Gottlieb Daimler (d. 1900), John Dunlop (d. 1921), Alexander Graham Bell (d. 1922), George Eastman (d. 1932), and Guglielmo Marconi (d. 1937) all obtained their first patents while working in modest home laboratories in their spare time. But this model was not sustainable. Most of the twentieth century's hallmark inventions required large design teams and

8.   The discussion of modern scientific and technological history in section 1.4 is largely drawn from Strandh 1979, Newhouse 1988, and Jeans 1967. Detailed descriptions of leading scientists are also found in Gillespie 1970.

9.   Henry Ford received 5,000 fan letters and nearly ended up in the U.S. Senate. Journalists talked about "The Ford Craze" and claimed that a better public speaker could have been elected president.

10.   Machlup and Penrose 1950 describe the debates of the nineteenth and early twentieth centuries. The arguments are marvelously similar to those in the current literature.

laboratories.[11] This technological imperative put innovation beyond the reach of basement tinkerers.[12]

Inventors reacted by developing three broad strategies to obtain financing. The first solution, prefiguring Silicon Valley, was to become an entrepreneur. Many of the era's foremost inventors traded on their reputations to hop from one start-up to the next. In the process, they structured remarkably sophisticated venture capital deals based on a mix of private stock offerings, joint ventures, spin-off companies, revenue sharing, and stock options.[13] Some companies took off and made investors rich. Others ended in stock swindles and vaporware.[14]

The second solution was to turn the activity of invention into a business in its own right. In the 1870s, Edison founded an "invention factory" entirely devoted to R&D. The factory followed a bewildering variety of business models including performing contract research for

---

11.   By the 1920s, companies in the high-technology industries of that era (e.g., aircraft or gyroscope manufacturers) typically employed about a dozen engineers. By midcentury, a product like the V-2 missile contained 90,000 parts. Designing and building such a weapon required 1,960 scientists, engineers, and technicians; this did not include the 3,852 people who served as support staff. Large design teams proved indispensable for such twentieth-century innovations as airplanes, automobiles, computers, microelectronics, and large software development.

12.   There were still solitary geniuses, but they seem like escapees from the nineteenth century. Albert Einstein (d. 1955) discovered special relativity while working alone in a Swiss patent office. Edwin Land (d. 1991) broke into a Columbia University laboratory night after night so that he could work on his Polaroid filter. David Williams (d. 1975) worked out key elements for the U.S. Army's revolutionary M-1 carbine while serving time in a North Carolina penitentiary.

13.   The case of Elmer Sperry (d. 1930) was fairly typical. In 1882 he and his former employer started a spin-off company to manufacture arc lights and generators. In 1888 Sperry launched a second company based on his patents for streetcars and electric automobiles. In 1890 he organized a syndicate to develop streetcars. The enterprise's stated purpose was to obtain patents that could either be sold off or used to start a manufacturing company. In 1903, Sperry persuaded a wealthy capitalist to join him in a joint venture to develop new batteries and electroplating methods. Finally, in 1910, he persuaded a small group of capitalists to fund the Sperry Gyroscope Company. Sperry received stock, salary, and a percentage of revenues.

14.   In 1902 a group of investors hired Lee deForest as a front man for a chain of radio stations. The company had no stations and a minuscule R&D budget. It was, however, extremely good at persuading investors to part with their money. See Lewis 1991, 39–41.

others, providing consulting services, selling patents for cash and stock, participating in joint ventures, and spinning off discoveries into Edison-controlled manufacturing businesses. Edison believed that this mix of strategies was the key to managing risk. In his view, routine contract R&D was just as important as high-profile inventions like the lightbulb.

The third solution was for established companies to develop innovations in-house.[15] The first modern industrial laboratories were in the German chemical industry (Mowery and Rosenberg 1998). In the 1850s, chemical research moved out of the university and into industrial laboratories organized by firms like Bayer, BASF, Hoechst, Casella, and AGFA. Around 1900, similar industrial laboratories started to proliferate in the United States. Early examples included General Electric (1900), Dow (1901), DuPont (1902), AT&T (1908), Goodyear (1909), and Eastman Kodak (1912). Most of the new laboratories were concentrated in the electrical and chemical industries. By 1910, 300 laboratories had been founded. By 1940, industry was operating 13,500 laboratories at a combined annual budget of $200 million.

The other big problem that patents presented was how to cash out. The simplest model was for inventors to sell their patents and leave development and manufacturing to others. The problem, as Edison pointed out (and it is still true today), was that inventors and investors seldom agreed what a particular innovation was worth.[16] In such cases the inventor had little choice except to become a manufacturer. When Charles Hall (d. 1914) discovered a cost-effective way to refine aluminum, existing manufacturers spurned his patents. He succeeded in finding venture capitalists to buy stock in what later became Alcoa Aluminum. Similar stories produced Ford Motor Company, RCA, Eastman Kodak, and other twentieth-century giants.

These problems would have occurred even if the patent system was perfect. In fact, the nineteenth-century patent system—like the current

---

15.   Schumpeter (1942) early saw the trend away from individual inventors to formal institutions, and gives an interesting account. See also Mowery and Rosenberg 1998.

16.   Sometimes the disagreements were technical. When the telephone was invented in the 1870s, most people thought that television would follow within a few months. In fact, it took sixty years. People also disagreed about what kind of inventions consumers needed or would find useful. After Hertz demonstrated the existence of radio waves in 1889, building a crude wireless telegraph was technically straightforward. In fact, it took five more years for Marconi to realize that consumers might want such a thing.

one—was very far from perfect. First, patent applications were complicated and usually required multiple approvals. This kept transaction costs high well into the nineteenth century. Second, enforcement costs were often ruinous. During his lifetime, Charles Goodyear (d. 1860) spent far more on his lawyer, the aging Daniel Webster, than he ever made from patenting vulcanized rubber. Third, patent litigation created uncertainty and slowed the growth of industry. Contemporary observers blamed patent litigation for stifling development of the telephone, movies, automobiles, radio, television, and airplanes, rather than serving their intended purpose of stimulating discovery. Some scholars also blame excessive patent litigation for the slow progress of early photographic processes in England compared to that in France. Finally, some inventors used patents to impose their own technological prejudices on competitors. This happened repeatedly in the case of the steam engine.[17]

1.5   Modern Patrons: Foundations

Prior to 1900, university science budgets were not much larger than those in the humanities.[18] The rise of big science in the twentieth century required huge expenditures.[19] One immediate consequence was that

---

17.   Thomas Savery (d. 1715) used his overbroad patent for a steam-powered mine pump to stop Thomas Newcomen (d. 1729) from manufacturing the first true steam engine in 1712. The impasse was only resolved when Savery died and his heirs agreed to a license. Later in the century, James Watt (d. 1819) used his patents to block high-pressure improvements that he considered dangerous and technically complex. Watt's refusal to license competitors froze steam-engine technology for two decades. Finally, George Corliss (d. 1888) revolutionized efficiency by adding slide valves to pistons. Despite their evident superiority, competitors did not try to extend the idea until Corliss's patents expired in 1876. For an interesting discussion of this, see Scherer 1984. Surprisingly, some disputes had a silver lining. Watt designed his celebrated "sun-and-planets" gear in order to design around a previously patented crank.

18.   During the 1880s, Albert Michelson (d. 1931) measured the speed of light using only a modest grant from the U.S. National Academy of Sciences. Soon afterward, Heinrich Hertz (d. 1894) and an assistant built enough equipment to demonstrate radio. Existing university endowments were more than enough to cover these needs.

19.   Big science was not just expensive; it also forced administrators to create "institutional memories" for experiments that might take decades. Perhaps the most extreme example is NASA's Gravity Probe B project, an experiment designed to test the general theory of relativity from space (Reichhardt 2003). Stanford physicists first proposed the project in 1960. After forty years and more than one-half billion dollars, the satellite was scheduled for launch in 2004.

funding decisions could no longer be made in ad hoc contacts between individuals. The era of big science was ushered in with astronomy, where state-of-the-art telescopes were too expensive for any individual university and also generated more data than a single university could analyze. This led to large, semiautonomous observatories, even in the 1800s.[20] Similar research institutes were built around specimen collections and other special-purpose facilities, often funded by wealthy individuals. In the twentieth century, such institutes were largely funded at taxpayer expense.

The Gilded Age (late nineteenth century) put unprecedented fortunes into private hands.[21] About seventy foundations were established between 1900 and 1930. Like the federal government in later years, the foundations were so rich that they often ended up setting R&D priorities for the country as a whole. For example, the first Carnegie and Rockefeller institutions each had $10 million endowments, a figure equivalent to the total annual operating budgets of the country's top fifteen research universities and also commensurate with the total federal research budget around the turn of the century. Foundation resources continued growing until the Depression. By the late 1930s, foundations were spending about $80 million per year, including $40 million in research grants. At the time, only six U.S. universities spent more than $2 million per year (including faculty salaries) on R&D.

The foundations needed new strategies to spend such sums productively. For the first thirty years or so, they searched for ways to keep decision making in their own hands. Their first initiatives centered on identifying and attacking problems that universities and government had ignored. Beginning in 1901–1902, the Rockefeller and Carnegie foundations created a host of new institutes dedicated to medicine, geophysics, botany, and astronomy. By World War I, these were the strongest sectors in American science. When these opportunities were exhausted, the foundations began identifying and eliminating bottlenecks in particular fields. This typically involved long-term investments in physical capital (e.g., large telescopes, university laboratories, and atom

20.   California's Lick Observatory was an early example. During the 1870s, scientists persuaded real estate magnate James Lick that a 36-inch telescope would preserve his memory more effectively than his original choice, a pyramid to be built in downtown San Francisco. The facility was completed in 1880 at a cost of $700,000. Lick's body is interred inside the pier that supports the telescope.

21.   Our discussion follows Geiger 1993.

smashers) and human beings (e.g., research fellowships). This strategy deserves much of the credit for propelling United States science, particularly physics and astronomy, into rough parity with Europe.

By the early 1930s, these opportunities had also been exhausted. Even the largest foundations discovered that researchers were proposing more projects than they could possibly evaluate. At this point, foundations did the only thing they could do: give money to trusted researchers or departments, and hope for the best. This type of benevolence started prior to World War I and accelerated during the 1930s. Over time, foundations refined these arrangements into a formal peer review system. After World War II, the federal government adopted more or less the same process, namely, to solicit open-ended research proposals and fund the best ones (see chapter 8).

For all practical purposes, the scientific community ended up regulating itself, even though the money came from wealthy patrons. This is a major departure from previous eras, when patrons either chose the research agenda or delegated that authority to the inventors themselves but did not use peer review. Of course, peer review has an upside and a downside. It can weed out duplicative efforts or inquiries that are known to be unpromising, but it can also institutionalize groupthink.[22]

Foundation spending declined rapidly during the Depression. Despite creation of the massive new Ford Foundation in 1950, foundations never recovered their prewar share dominance. That said, they continue to be major players in such diverse niches as university infrastructure, medicine, large telescopes, and social science research.

1.6   Big Science and the Growth of Government Funding

In the end, an intellectual property system supplies what markets want. By contrast, patrons can make judgments and choices. In the twentieth century, "patron" has come to mean "government." Since the 1930s, the U.S. federal government has launched repeated, high-profile initiatives to develop new technologies for aviation, space, nuclear energy, electronics, and health care. The current research establishment institutionalizes those long-ago choices.

---

22.   An example of groupthink on an international scale was the development of civilian supersonic transport in the 1960s. See the discussion in chapter 2.

Government Laboratories In the opening years of the twentieth century, much of the R&D performed by government employees was military. Government armories and design bureaus produced astonishingly sophisticated technologies, particularly for naval weapons like torpedoes and battleships.[23] By 1918, battleships were firing 1,400-pound projectiles at ranges up to 12 miles. Achieving that kind of performance required concurrent advances in multiple unproven technologies, including gyroscopes, analog computers, electric data transmission, turbine propulsion, and large castings. Government bureaus continued to play a major role in building new weapons systems throughout the twentieth century.

In the civilian world, the most ambitious nineteenth-century projects were run by the U.S. Geological Survey and the Department of Agriculture. Government efforts to map and explore North America made geology one of the first sciences where Americans could compete with Europe. Following the Civil War, the Department of Agriculture purchased substantial contract research from the country's land grant universities. Most other government efforts were modest and focused on practical problems like mine safety. As a result, government R&D had relatively little impact on universities or industry. In-house government R&D increased dramatically in the first decades of the twentieth century as agencies moved from studying society's problems to regulating them. By the late 1930s, total federal R&D spending had increased about tenfold from the turn of the century, although it was still small by today's standards. Government scientists also remained focused on practical problems like agriculture, geology, meteorology, and conservation.

We have already noted how twentieth-century technologies shifted inventive activity from individuals to large research institutions. Within the federal government, the earliest example of big science was the National Committee for Aeronautics (NACA). NACA began as an emergency measure during World War I to promote industry/academic/government coordination on war-related projects. By the early 1920s, it had adopted a new and more ambitious mission: to promote military and

---

23. Researchers did receive valuable input from civilian scientists and engineers. Both the self-propelled torpedo (1866) and steam-turbine propulsion in warships (1897) were completed without official support or interest. Once demonstrated, government design bureaus enthusiastically developed both technologies.

civilian aviation through applied research that looked beyond current needs. NACA's researchers pursued this mission through the agency's impressive collection of in-house wind tunnels, engine test stands, and flight test facilities. Commercial and military clients were also permitted to use NACA's facilities on a contract basis.

In 1922, NACA had 100 employees. By 1938, it had 426. In addition to formal assignments, staff were encouraged to pursue unauthorized "bootleg" research, provided that it was not too exotic. The result was a long string of fundamental breakthroughs, including the "NACA engine cowl" (1930s), the "NACA wing" (1940s), and the "area rule" for supersonic aircraft (1950s).[24] The NACA experience provided a powerful model for World War II research, the postwar government laboratories, and NACA's successor, the National Aeronautics and Space Administration (NASA).

Modern government laboratories are a product of World War II. During World War I, the United States had drafted thousands of scientists into government laboratories. Twenty years later, U.S. academics persuaded the government to follow a different strategy. It created the Office of Scientific Research and Development (OSRD) to run military research. Unlike earlier initiatives, OSRD did not try to micromanage research. Instead, it limited itself to setting priorities and identifying problems that could be solved in time to affect the war. After that, bureaucrats stayed out. Implementation was delegated to self-governing laboratories composed of academic researchers from around the country. The largest OSRD laboratories were located at Los Alamos, New Mexico (atomic weapons research), and MIT (radar). Each employed about 1,200 civilians.[25]

---

24. NACA's aircraft were the first to break the sound barrier and eventually flew to the edge of space. The story is told by Wolfe 1979.

25. The army's atomic bomb project eventually cost $2 billion. OSRD spent $1.5 billion on radar. Smaller groups included the Applied Physics Laboratory at Johns Hopkins (advanced artillery fuses), the Jet Propulsion Laboratory at Cal Tech (rockets), the Harvard Underwater Sound Laboratory (torpedoes), Penn State's Moore School (the ENIAC computer), Columbia (operations research for bombing), and Harvard (sonar and radar laboratories). Universities provided management and, in most cases, facilities under "no loss and no gain" contracts. Additional work was done at research institutes and industrial laboratories. In at least one case, a particularly urgent problem—finding an industrial-scale process for making RDX explosive—was sent to several different competing laboratories at Michigan, Cornell, and Penn State.

OSRD's wartime laboratories were so successful that Congress preserved the Los Alamos facility and created additional atomic facilities at Brookhaven, NY, and Argonne, IL. These became the nucleus for the current network of national laboratories. Congress also extended the OSRD model to biology by founding the National Institutes of Health (NIH).[26] The second wave of national laboratories came during the Korean War and was designed to accelerate electronics and nuclear technology. These early-1950s institutions included the Lincoln Laboratory, Lawrence Livermore National Laboratory, and the Applied Electronics Laboratory. The final wave of OSRD-style laboratories came in the 1960s and was dedicated to big science. Most of these institutions were focused on physics (Stanford Linear Accelerator, Fermilab) and astronomy (National Radio Astronomy Observatory, National Astronomy and Ionosphere Center, National Optical Astronomy Observatories).

The end of the Cold War (1989) eliminated the threats that justified big physics research. Managers of national laboratories responded with more or less frantic efforts to find new missions to justify their continued existence. These included technologies for simulating nuclear weapons ("stockpile stewardship"); applying atom-smasher technologies to molecular biology; advanced computing initiatives; and gene sequencing. More than ten years later, their missions were still in flux.[27]

Government Grants Nineteenth-century governments did not solicit grant applications, did not promise to make funds available, and made no particular effort to choose the best proposals. If funds were made available, they went to whichever scientists mounted the most persistent lobbying efforts. Having an ally in government also helped. In England, the British government funded Charles Babbage's famous Difference Engine—predecessor to the computer—in 1823 (Newhouse 1988). Similarly, the British Admiralty paid for a wave tank so that William Froude could conduct his pioneering studies of boat hulls, leading to modern

---

26.   Anomalously, medical research had not followed the same model as OSRD and national laboratories in World War II. Instead, most life scientists spent the war working in their own labs. There they produced important breakthroughs, including penicillin and blood plasma.

27.   Lawrence Berkeley Laboratory, always on the short list of possible closures, made the biggest effort to reinvent itself. By 2000, 17 percent of the lab's funds came from private sources. The lab also redirected its traditional focus on physics to include life sciences (22%) and computing (17%).

hydrodynamics (Porter 1994). In the United States, Congress financed Samuel Morse's experimental telegraph between Washington, DC, and Baltimore. Morse later patented the technology. The U.S. and British governments also subsidized a transatlantic telegraph cable owned by financier Cyrus W. Field (Standage 1998).

The first steps to formalize government-funded research took place in Germany. In 1884, electrical magnate William Siemens (d. 1892) persuaded the German government to set up the Imperial Physical and Technical Institute to attack problems in applied physics. The Kaiser Wilhelm Institute for Chemistry followed in 1910 (reorganized as the Max Planck Society after World War II).

In America, government support for universities remained minuscule until the 1940s. At the end of the Depression, universities, like the rest of the U.S. economy, were operating far below capacity. World War II changed that. By 1944, government contracts accounted for three times the R&D that universities had performed before the war. Wartime success permanently changed the landscape. During the early postwar period, universities continued to support themselves by maintaining or extending wartime programs aimed at developing particular weapons or technologies. However, academics worried that these programs would damage research by skewing work toward a handful of militarily useful disciplines, promoting classified work that had limited value to science and to the university's mission of disseminating knowledge, and exhausting the store of basic knowledge on which wartime successes had been built.[28] Congress agreed. Over time, new institutions like the National Institutes of Health (1946), the National Science Foundation (1950), and even the Office of Naval Research (1946) shifted federal support back to the kind of curiosity-based research that foundations had pioneered in the 1930s. Although slow to get started, the budgets of the new agencies rose steeply after 1950. By 1958, NIH and NSF accounted for 40 percent of the federal government's $219 million budget for university R&D.

Basic research got a further boost after the Soviet Union shocked the West by launching the first artificial satellite in 1957. Over the next ten years, university R&D rose from 0.1 to 0.2 percent of GNP, and

---

28. The most famous statement of this view is found in Vannevar Bush's *Science: The Endless Frontier* (1946). Despite initial indifference, the report eventually became the cornerstone of postwar science policy.

shifted toward curiosity-driven basic research.[29] By 1970, total university R&D budgets had reached $2.3 billion, and almost four-fifths was devoted to basic research. Federal spending paid for 70 percent of this effort. But this happy expansion of federal R&D funding could not survive budget pressures from the Vietnam War and the economic downturn that followed. Between 1968 and 1974, spending in universities by the NSF and Defense Department fell by 50 percent in real terms. Budgets remained tight for the rest of the 1970s. Since then, real growth has rarely exceeded 1 or 2 percent, although funding remains much higher than before the expansion.

1.7   Modern Hybrid Institutions

The U.S. research establishment has very few research laboratories or funding mechanisms that are purely public, purely academic, or even purely industrial. Hybrid institutions, blending public funding with intellectual property, were the twentieth century's "new idea" about research funding.

The Military-Industrial Complex   Society devotes enormous resources to weapons procurement.[30] Since World War II, at least half of federal R&D spending has been directed to military wares, and usually more.[31] During the twentieth century, military research increasingly moved from government armories and ordnance bureaus to the national laboratories and private firms. President Dwight Eisenhower called this fusion of military objectives and private interests the "military-industrial complex." Whatever its drawbacks and dangers, there is no denying that the system produced breathtaking technological leaps. Successful megaprojects

---

29.   Between 1957 and 1968, NSF spending expanded from $40 million to $480 million. NIH spending went from $85 million to $722 million during this period.

30.   In some sense, most military R&D does not quality as "innovation" at all. Except for spin-offs, Pentagon spending is pure economic waste. Furthermore, the benefits of weapons research are largely nullified by the fact that the antagonist is also doing weapons research. Antagonists would be much better off if they could agree not to waste research funds on weapons, but they face the classic "prisoner's dilemma." If they agree to cut back, each side will have an incentive to cheat.

31.   See chap. 2 of Mowery and Rosenberg 1998 for a more complete account.

included atomic reactors (1942), atomic bombs (1945), hydrogen bombs (1952), nuclear-powered submarines (1954), intercontinental ballistic missiles (1959), and missile-firing submarines (1960).

Given the sums involved, the Pentagon has had ample opportunities to experiment with different incentive systems. Most basic research is funded by targeted grants and contract research. Since the 1950s, DARPA has been particularly innovative. DARPA's most important invention, little noticed at the time, was the Internet (1969); see chapter 10.

Aircraft procurement is fairly typical. During the 1960s, the Pentagon's attempts to purchase aircraft based on paper studies produced cost overruns and disappointing performance. Since then, the Pentagon has experimented with various incentive schemes in which companies build prototypes for competitive "fly-offs." Particularly in recent years, government has rarely covered more than a fraction of the companies' development costs. Instead, parties compete for contracts that typically offer profits significantly higher (4.4%) than normal returns to capital. Conceptually, this very complicated system combines aspects of matching grants, prizes, and contests. We discuss these models further in chapters 2 and 8.

NASA provides a civilian counterpart to this basic Pentagon model. NASA's greatest successes included the Apollo moon landing (1969), weather and communication satellites (ca. 1964), and unmanned probes to Venus, Mars, and the outer solar system (1970s). All of these programs involved lavishly funded, military-style R&D with well-defined goals. Later projects such as the Space Shuttle (1980s), Hubble Space Telescope (1990s), and Space Station (2001) were notably less successful. Since the 1980s, NASA has suffered a troubling string of procurement failures, including two Shuttle disasters and billions of dollars spent on failed technologies designed to achieve low-cost access to space (the National Aerospace Plane and the X-33). Some of NASA's difficulties are probably inherent in trying to do directed research in an era of small budgets and poorly defined goals. Nevertheless, critics have widely criticized the agency's incentive structures and called for fundamental changes, including a return to prizes.

Basic Research by Industry   At the beginning of the twentieth century, industry specialized in development and left basic research to academics. Shareholders no doubt approved, since basic discoveries rarely had any appropriable commercial value. By the 1920s, industry laboratories had outgrown the universities that had been feeding them with scientific discoveries. Industrial laboratories spent six times more on R&D than universities did in 1930 and ten times more in 1940. These trends accelerated after World War II. Between 1953 and 1999 there was about a twelvefold increase in real R&D spending by industry, while real GDP increased less than fivefold. The fastest annual growth rates took place during the 1950s (18%).[32]

Industrial laboratories ended up pursuing basic research in-house rather than depending on academic research. During the 1930s, Bell Labs launched a solid-state physics program that led to the transistor, won a Nobel Prize, and opened the door to modern electronics. In the late 1930s, DuPont lured chemist Wallace Hume Carothers away from Harvard by promising to fund any polymer-related research that he wanted to do. Carothers invented nylon.

Postwar industry achieved breakthroughs in basic research such as the transistor (1948), the integrated circuit (1958), the laser (1960), high-temperature superconductivity (1986), and even relict radiation from the Big Bang (1965). These achievements required lavish R&D expenditures that could not be sustained after AT&T was broken up in 1974 and IBM lost its near monopoly over computer markets in the 1980s. By the mid-1980s, both laboratories had started to downsize and to refocus on explicitly commercial projects. It is unclear how to assess this development. On the one hand, Bell Labs' shareholders gained little or nothing when their company discovered the Big Bang. On the other hand, Bell Labs' other big postwar discovery, the transistor, made the current digital revolution possible. Will Bell Labs' diminished successors make similar transformative discoveries?[33]

The Academic-Industrial Complex   Patents invaded the academy in the 1890s, largely due to the activities of Michael Pupin (d. 1935) at Columbia University, who became wealthy by patenting improvements to radio, telephones, and X-rays. Most scientists disapproved. One

---

32.   Most of this growth was fueled by increases in federal funding for research performed in private firms, which rose from 40 percent of industrial laboratory budgets in 1953 to 57 percent 1960. Thereafter, federal support became less important, and by the end of the century, the federal government was only funding about 10 percent of industrial research.

33.   These observations hark back to Schumpeter (1942), who argued that R&D is much more likely to come from large firms with market power than from small firms.

British journal summarized prevailing sentiment this way: "Working as he does with public funds, directing as he does the minds and hands of students, it is, to say, scarcely honest [for a professor] to go with the results of such work to the Patent Office."[34]

One natural way to avoid these ethical dilemmas was to use patents to support the research program itself. In 1914, a Berkeley chemistry professor named Frederick G. Cottrell founded the Research Corporation to patent university discoveries. He hoped for an endless cycle in which the corporation's patents would fund research in universities that produced still more patents. Despite its quasi-academic mission, the corporation maximized profits as ruthlessly as any business. In particular, it did not hesitate to use its patents to create cartels (to the extent of provoking an antitrust investigation), to rank research proposals according to their moneymaking potential, and to browbeat faculty into taking out patents and spending more time on applied research. During the 1930s, the corporation devoted most of its efforts to funding atom smashers at Berkeley and half a dozen other institutions in a vain attempt to corner the medical isotopes market.[35]

Such excesses made many academics nervous. The Wisconsin Alumni Research Fund (WARF) tried to bridge the gap between academic and commercial mores through socially responsible investing that balanced dissemination against "reasonable royalties." Success was hard to measure. Nevertheless, WARF managed to avoid cartels and other offensive tactics.

When foundation support for university research fell during the Depression of the 1930s, faculty began to reevaluate industry support. By 1936, nine other universities had imitated WARF's model. By midcentury, individual scientists' attitudes toward patents were shifting. While the average scientist still frowned on patents, this did not keep Robert Goddard (rocketry), Enrico Fermi (medical isotopes), and Leo Szilard (atomic energy) from patenting their work. Conversely, other scientists resisted patenting or else filed patents for the sole purpose of preventing others from doing so. Today, this strategy would be called "copylefting."[36]

---

34.   The remarks were published in 1884. See Heilbron and Seidel 1989.
35.   The Research Corporation would probably have succeeded if World War II had not intervened. Nuclear reactors developed for the U.S. atomic bomb project drastically reduced the cost of making medical isotopes.
36.   See Heilbron and Seidel 1989. In theory, patenting should not be necessary since publication bars any subsequent patent application. However, this notion has slippage.

Academic interest in industry support faded after federal funds became plentiful during World War II. Nevertheless, some postwar universities took advantage of military research to reap both scientific and industrial benefits. The principal innovator was Stanford University, which used military electronics research contracts to develop technologies that were later used in magnetic resonance and atom-smasher experiments. The work produced several Nobel Prizes and a world-class physics program. Stanford's electronics programs also spawned several start-up companies that donated money to the university.[37] Stanford's leaders could rightly claim that the triangular relationship between university, industry, and the military had made each partner stronger.[38] In 1970, Stanford University improved on the WARF model by opening a new kind of licensing office that specialized in marketing technologies to industry.

The Bayh-Dole Act of 1980, which authorized the patenting of federally funded innovations, signaled a return to corporate alliances. University interest in patents was further accelerated by the biotechnology boom that followed shortly afterward. The Reagan administration also took steps to promote closer academic-industry cooperation as a way of promoting U.S. competitiveness in electronics and other technologies.[39] By decade's end, most universities had opened licensing offices on the Stanford model.

University research was a natural investment for industry. In the last half of the twentieth century, U.S. companies used between 2 and 3 percent of their R&D budgets to fund academic research. The resulting contacts helped industry monitor emerging frontiers, kept its own scientists current, and provided useful advice when in-house projects hit snags. For their part, universities created Organized Research Units to attract commercial funds, often by promising intellectual property rights to resulting discoveries. This was particularly trendy in hot new technologies like biotechnology, microelectronics, manufacturing, materials

---

37.   Stanford also invented the concept of a university research park. By the early 1950s, Stanford spin-offs like Varian and Hewlett-Packard were leasing space from the university. Ten universities opened research parks between 1950 and 1975. In addition to making money, the parks were supposed to promote closer interactions with industry.

38.   The Stanford Research Institute was an interesting variation on this theme. Founded to do contract research that Stanford's faculty were not interested in, it became more or less self-supporting by the 1960s.

39.   NSF created fourteen Engineering Research Centers by 1987. Industry contributed about one-third of the funds; the balance came from NSF. By the late 1980s the centers accounted for 3 percent of NSF's budget.

science, and artificial intelligence. Universities also signed massive research contracts with industry.[40] In most of these deals, industry received generous promises of intellectual property that was at least partly funded by federal sponsors.

Observers blame these deals for making academic science (and particularly biology) more secretive and patent conscious. Oddly, university patenting has not been particularly lucrative. Even a successful research institution like the University of California earned only $13 million from patent licenses in 1999, net of licensing costs. This was less than 1 percent of the $1.5 billion that UC researchers received from the federal government.

In retrospect, the most striking legacy of the late twentieth century was to blur the line between industry and academia. There were hundreds of start-up companies during the 1980s, such as Chiron and Genentech, which arose from university innovations. Unlike earlier generations, the faculty who founded start-ups in the 1980s and 1990s seldom left the university. Universities blurred the line further by taking equity stakes in the new companies. At the same time, the new companies focused far more on research than traditional firms did, and retained some of the character of university laboratories. By the late 1980s, most biotech firms had evolved into research boutiques where scientists pursued patentable discoveries in campus-like settings.

---

40.   The experience in biotechnology is particularly instructive. In 1974, Monsanto contributed $23 million to two Harvard scientists in return for patent rights. Besides bringing in patents, the deal strengthened Monsanto's in-house laboratories and allowed the company to move its old-fashioned chemical business into pharmaceuticals and agriculture. Hoechst signed a similar $70 million deal with the Harvard Medical School in 1984. Hoechst used the deal to strengthen its in-house biotech capabilities and to influence Harvard's research agenda in directions that favored the company. In the 1990s, Novartis gave $25 million to UC Berkeley in return for an option on patent rights in agricultural research.

During the 1990s, large pharmaceutical companies went beyond deals with individual universities and began offering money to entire academic communities. The largest of these grant programs, a $50 million program called The SNP Consortium, paid academics to put gene sequences in the public domain. Apart from promoting basic knowledge, the program prevented small biotechnology companies from patenting the information, which made it less likely that pharmaceutical companies would have to pay extortionate royalties if a particular sequence later turned out to be valuable.

1.8   Conclusion

One of the questions that arises in this chronology is whether the historical development of institutions was in any sense inevitable. As suggested by North (1981), institutions are driven by technological imperatives, but technology is also driven by institutions. Without the large federal commitment to space exploration in the twentieth century, we could not have contemplated the far side of the moon. No commercial enterprise would embark on such a thing because that type of pure science has no obvious commercial value.

The financial requirements of big science that emerged in the past century afflicted both private industry and public institutions. In such an environment, a funding mechanism like patents, which reimburses the inventor ex post, must do its work within institutions that can also marshal funds ex ante. But there is also a question of sensible decision making. Those who put up the funds have a large impact on the direction of research. Especially for science that has no commercial value, whose values should govern the expenditure of resources? For that matter, whose views on the prospects for success should be heeded? And at the political level, was it sensible for the United States to devote such a large amount of resources to space exploration when the Germans or Japanese or French might otherwise have done it? We turn to international issues in chapter 11.

References and Further Reading

Bush, V. 1945. *Science: The Endless Frontier.* Washington, DC: U.S. Government Printing Office.

Casson, L. 2002. *Libraries in the Ancient World.* New Haven, CT: Yale University Press.

Cohen, W. 1995. "Empirical Studies of Innovative Activity." In P. Stoneman, ed., *Handbook of the Economics of Innovation and Technological Change*, 182–264. Oxford: Basil Blackwell.

Cohen, W., and R. Levin. 1989. "Empirical Studies of Innovation and Market Structure." In R. Schmalensee and R. Willig, eds., *Handbook of Industrial Organization*, vol. 2, chap. 3, 1060–1107. New York: Elsevier Science Publishing Co. (North-Holland).

De Camp, L. S. 1980. *The Ancient Engineers.* New York: Ballantine Press.

Defense Advanced Research Projects Agency. 2003. "DARPA Grand Challenge." Available at www.darpa.mil/grandchallenge/.

Finley, M. I. 1973. *The Ancient Economy*. Berkeley, CA: University of California Press.

Flatow, I. 1992. *They All Laughed . . . From Light Bulbs to Lasers: The Fascinating Stories Behind the Great Inventions that Have Changed Our Lives*. New York: HarperCollins.

Foray, D. 2004. *The Economics of Knowledge*. Cambridge, MA: MIT Press.

Foray, D., and L. Hilaire-Perez. Forthcoming. "The Economics of Open Technology: Collective Organization and Individual Claims in the 'Fabrique Lyonnaise' during the Old Regime." *Research Policy*.

Geiger, R. L. 1986. *To Advance Knowledge: The Growth of American Research Universities, 1900–1940*. New York: Oxford University Press.

Geiger, R. L. 1993. *Research and Relevant Knowledge: American Research Universities Since World War II*. New York: Oxford University Press.

Gillespie, C. C., ed. 1970. *Dictionary of Scientific Biography*. New York: Scribner.

Gimpel, J. 1977. *The Medieval Machine: The Industrial Revolution of the Middle Ages*. New York: Penguin.

Goldstein, P. 1994. *Copyright's Highway: The Law and Lore of Copyright from Gutenberg to the Celestial Jukebox*. New York: Hill and Wang.

Heilbron, J. L., and R. W. Seidel. 1989. *Lawrence and His Lab: A History of the Lawrence Berkeley Laboratory*. Berkeley, CA: University of California Press.

Jeans, J. 1967. *The Growth of Physical Science*. Greenwich, CT: Fawcett.

Lewis, T. 1991. *Empire of the Air: The Men Who Invented Radio*. New York: HarperCollins.

Machlup, F., and E. Penrose. 1950. "The Patent Controversy in the Nineteenth Century." *Journal of Economic History* 10:1–29.

Mokyr, J. 1990. *The Lever of Riches: Technological Creativity and Economic Progress*. Oxford: Oxford University Press.

Mokyr, J. 2002. *The Gifts of Athena*. Princeton, NJ: Princeton University Press.

Mowery, D., and N. Rosenberg. 1998. *Paths of Innovation*. New York: Cambridge University Press.

Nelson, R., ed. 1962. *The Rate and Direction of Inventive Activity*. Princeton, NJ: Princeton University Press for the National Bureau of Economic Research.

Newhouse, E. L., ed. 1988. *Inventors and Discoverers: Changing Our World*. Washington, DC: National Geographic Society.

North, D. 1981. *Structure and Change in Economic History*. New York: Norton.

Peebles, C. 1995. *Dark Eagles: A History of Top Secret U.S. Aircraft Programs*. New York: Ballantine.

Perret, G. 1991. *There's a War to Be Won: The United States Army in World War II.* New York: Random House.

Porter, R. 1994. *The Biographical Dictionary of Scientists.* New York: Oxford University Press.

Prager, F. D. 1944. "A History of Intellectual Property from 1545 to 1787." *Journal of the Patent Office Society* 26:711–760.

Reichhardt, T. 2003, November 23. "Unstoppable Force." *Nature* 426:380–381.

Romer, D. 1996. *Advanced Macroeconomics.* New York: McGraw-Hill.

Rosenberg, N. 1982. *Inside the Black Box: Technology and Economics.* New York: Cambridge University Press.

Rosenberg, N. 1994. *Exploring the Black Box.* Cambridge, UK: Cambridge University Press.

Rosenberg, N., and L. E. Birdzell Jr. 1986. *How the West Grew Rich: The Economic Transformation of the Industrial World.* New York: Basic Books.

Scherer, F. M. 1984. *Innovation and Growth: Schumpeterian Perspectives.* Cambridge, MA: MIT Press.

Schumpeter, J. A. 1942. *Capitalism, Socialism, and Democracy.* New York: Harper & Row.

Standage, T. 1998. *The Victorian Internet.* New York: Berkley Books.

Strandh, S. 1979. *A History of the Machine.* New York: A&W Publishers.

Wolfe, T. 1979. *The Right Stuff.* New York: Bantam Books.

2　Investing in Knowledge

In the digital age, it has become fashionable to speak of "information goods." By information goods, we usually mean computer software and entertainment products stored in digital form, such as music. Information goods have a feature that sets them apart from ordinary private goods. They are public goods in the technical sense meant by economists: use by one person does not preclude use by any other person and does not cost additional resources, except the small cost of distributing them. That is, the use of such a good is nonrival. Further, it is difficult to exclude unauthorized users from using such a product once it exists. Intellectual property rights, usually copyrights, are the means by which society tries to create a workable market in information goods.

Knowledge has the same property. Once there is a known technique for efficiently coding information in microwaves, or it is known that DNA is a double helix, or someone has published the proof of Fermat's last theorem, then everyone can use that knowledge simultaneously without incurring additional costs of discovery. Knowledge and information goods share the property of nonrivalness.

In other ways, of course, information goods and knowledge can be quite different. For information goods, the emphasis is on creativity. For knowledge, the emphasis is on discovering useful information that exists in nature. Information goods are generally protected by copyright, and knowledge, at least knowledge that is technically useful, is generally protected (if at all) by patents. However, to a first approximation, the rationale for copyrights and patents is the same, and in this chapter we will think of information goods and knowledge as having the same essential property of nonrivalness.

Intellectual property law often seems to protect objects that are very tangible, like clocks, rather than ethereal things like poems or knowledge. However, it is the knowledge of how to make a clock that is nonrival, not generally the clock itself.[1] What an intellectual property right protects is not the clock as an object, but rather the template for producing it. For information goods, the template is the information itself, for example music, which may involve the contributions of a composer (a musical score) or the contributions of both a composer and a performer (a performance stored on a CD).

The difference between private goods and knowledge is illustrated by a controversy that arose in the eighteenth century, recounted entertainingly by Dava Sobel (1995). In 1714, the English Parliament had offered a prize of £20,000 for solving the problem of determining longitude. This sum would be equivalent to millions in today's currency.

The problem was that mariners had no way of knowing how far east or west they had sailed. There was a famous naval incident in which an English fleet was grounded on a shoal that could have been avoided if only the navigators had known their longitude. Two thousand sailors were lost, along with four warships. In another tragic incident, an expedition rounded South America, looking for a fertile island known to offer water and scurvy-curing plants. The ship sailed north to the latitude of the island, but then did not know whether to go west or east to find it. They first sailed west. After some days the captain lost faith and turned around, only to come upon the inhospitable coast of South America. They then had to sail west again to find the island. By that time, hundreds of sailors had died of scurvy.

The prize committee, named the Board of Longitude, was largely composed of astronomers looking for an astronomical solution analogous to how sailors use the pole star to find latitude. The eventual solution was not so elegant, at least in concept. Instead of referring to the stars, the solution was a clock that could faithfully keep London time. It had long been understood that, by comparing the time at a fixed location with the local time at the ship, as judged by the sun, the mariner could discern what "time zone" he was in, which is essentially longitude. The contribution of the claimant John Harrison was to build a clock that could withstand storms, changes in temperature, and salt air.

The Board of Longitude was reluctant to recognize the clock as a solution to the problem they had posed, and refused to give the prize.[2]

---

1.   Actually, the clock itself can be a nonrival public good if mounted on a public monument for use by an entire community.

2.   The lesson that some scholars emphasize is that prize authorities cannot be trusted. That is not the emphasis here, although there are other examples of

Eventually the English Parliament intervened at the behest of King George III and awarded a prize over the board's objections. Sobel gives the impression that the board's reluctance was rooted in human foible. The board consisted mostly of astronomers looking for an astronomical solution, not the mechanical solution they received.

However, there is a more sympathetic reading. What Parliament had solicited was knowledge. What it got were four clocks, all different. Compare Harrison's clocks with the astronomical algorithm that the board had hoped for. Such an algorithm did, in fact, materialize. The so-called lunar method used observations of distance between the moon and the stars to infer longitude. The lunar method had the essential feature of a pure public good: the tables that linked the observations to longitude were costly to compile in the first place, involving countless calculations, but once this was done, anyone could use the template at only the additional cost of owning the tables. The knowledge was nonrival.

In contrast, each of Harrison's four clocks took many years to produce, nineteen years in the case of the third one. Unlike pure knowledge, it would not be efficient to make such clocks freely available, since each is costly to produce. Users should only have access if they are willing to pay that cost. Further, the Board of Longitude could not be sure that the clocks could be reproduced at all.

The Board of Longitude did not have the language of rival and nonrival, or of private goods and public goods. Nevertheless, they recognized that in the clocks, they had not gotten the knowledge template they were looking for. It was only after several decades of wrangling that they arrived at a solution. In 1765, they asked Harrison to dedicate to the public both the clocks and a written description of how to make one, so that others could replicate it. That is, to earn the prize, Harrison had to hand over a template. He was also asked to make two replicas of the most developed clock, using only his written and published description and not having access to his original clock.

---

prize authorities reneging on prizes. In 1787, Nicholas Leblanc solved the problem of deriving soda from sea salt in response to a prize of 100,000 francs offered by the French Academy. The prize was refused, and the patent that Leblanc was later awared was annulled (Mokyr 1990, 107). In 1903, Alberto Santos-Dumont thought he was entitled to a prize offered by the private Aero Club in Paris for making an airship that could fly around the Eiffel Tower in 30 minutes. They kept changing the rules, and he never received the prize (Hoffman 2003).

The disclosure had its intended effect. In 1737 there was just one clock capable of discerning longitude, but by 1815 there were approximately 5,000, produced by many other clockmakers (Sobel 1995, 163).

This, of course, is similar to how patent law works. In applying for a patent, the applicant must disclose the template. In the case of a patent, there is no prize. Instead, payment is made by sheltering the inventor from competition. The inventor gets an exclusive right to use the template for a limited period of time, after which it is dedicated to the public.

Once the template is made public, there is no natural barrier that excludes users from using it. An intellectual property right is a legal barrier, created so that the inventor can be compensated. It is a tortured solution to the problem of providing a public good. The objective of this chapter is to consider and compare alternative solutions. We begin, however, by explaining why a competitive market may not give enough incentive to invest in knowledge.

2.1   Intellectual Property: Tolls on the Information Highway

The virtue of the competitive market is that it ensures the efficient production and distribution of private goods. When economists say that the competitive market is efficient, they mean two things. First, once goods are produced, they go to the consumers who value them most. Everyone who is willing to pay at least the market price of a clock gets a clock. Second, if the market is perfectly competitive, the price of a good is the opportunity cost of the (marginal) resources required to produce it. A clock will only be produced if its value to the consumer is greater than the opportunity cost of the clockmaker.

These points can be seen in the most familiar demand-and-supply diagram, in figure 2.1. When each user buys at most one unit of the good, the demand curve can be represented as a willingness-to-pay curve, shown in figure 2.1. The consumers are ranked on the horizontal axis by inverse willingness to pay for a clock. If the consumers are named $n = 1, 2, 3, \ldots$, the height of the demand curve at the nth clock represents the willingness to pay of the nth user. Then, if the marginal cost of producing clocks is the horizontal line, and if clocks are supplied in a competitive market, the market price will be p. Everyone with willingness to pay higher than p will buy a clock. The marginally excluded consumer would impose an incremental resource cost equal to the area with diagonal shading, which is higher than his or her willingness to pay for the clock, and this is why the exclusion is efficient. (The reasoning is

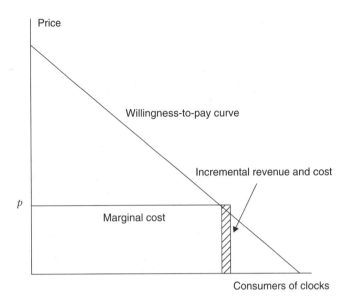

Figure 2.1
Market for clocks

more complicated, but carries the same message, if there are fixed costs to production or increasing marginal costs.)

Try to apply the same reasoning to information goods such as computer software or knowledge, such as the lunar method of determining longitude. Depriving a user of access is efficient if depriving him frees up the good for another user who values it more, or if depriving him saves resources that are more valuable than giving him access. But this is where nonrivalness matters. Depriving a user does not free it up for another user, since the other user could use it simultaneously, and it does not free up resources, since the investment in a given software application is made only once. There is no efficiency reason to deprive anyone of use. Indeed, if the software were provided by a competitive market with many suppliers, the competitive price would have to be zero. Everyone would be served, and access would be efficient.

However, the efficient competitive price, zero, will not cover the costs of developing the software, and therefore the market will not work. This is a variation on the usual economists' argument for why nonrival (public) goods should be provided at public expense, with free access assured. It is the same as the argument for why environmental quality, lighthouses, and legal structure should be provided at general taxpayer expense and not be charged to users on a per-use basis. It is the same argument for why knowledge is produced in public institutions like universities and then made freely available to all users.

A similar argument may also apply to clocks. If it was costly to develop the template for producing the clocks at the marginal cost shown in figure 2.1, then the competitive market for clocks will have the same problem as the competitive market for software. Competition in the market will not allow the inventor of the template to be compensated.

Intellectual property protection is a solution to the problem of covering the development cost of the software or of the template for clocks. Intellectual property rights make the proprietor a monopolist.

But the problem with monopoly pricing is deadweight loss. Deadweight loss occurs when people are excluded from using the good even though their willingnesses to pay are higher than the marginal cost. In figure 2.2, the area under the demand curve is v. This is the consumers' surplus that would be provided at the competitive price, zero, namely the sum of all the users' willingnesses to pay. If competitively supplied, the social value of the innovation over its entire lifetime is v/r. The parameters m, π, and ℓ are fractions, and $m + \pi + \ell = 1$. The per-period profit at the proprietary price is πv, and the value of the patent over its (discounted) life T is $\pi v T$. (For an explanation of discounted time, see technical note 2.8.1.) The area ℓv, called "deadweight loss" in figure 2.2, is the per-period loss in consumers' surplus due to the users who are

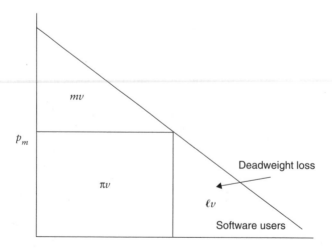

Figure 2.2
Market for software

excluded through proprietary pricing during the life of a patent. The area mv is the consumers' surplus that remains, despite the proprietary price. It accrues to the consumers who are in the proprietary market, each of whom receives less consumers' surplus than he would with a competitive price, which would be zero.

Deadweight loss is the main defect of intellectual property as an incentive mechanism. However, there is an important caveat to this argument, namely, price discrimination. The deadweight loss imposed by a monopolist can be mitigated, and possibly eliminated, if the monopolist can discriminate on price. Figure 2.3 shows the willingness to pay of two different users, one of whom is excluded by the proprietary price. Surely the proprietor would be better off selling to that user at a price equal to the user's willingness to pay (which is still higher than marginal cost), and also charging a higher price to the nonexcluded user, who otherwise retains some surplus. A monopolist that can discriminate on price has an incentive to serve the whole market, charging each user his or her willingness to pay. With perfect price discrimination, serving the users with low willingness to pay does not jeopardize the monopolist's ability to extract profit from users with high willingness to pay.

Price discrimination can go a long distance toward redressing the inefficiency of deadweight loss, but it is hard to implement. The main difficulty is in preventing the users with high willingness to pay from exploiting the price intended for users with low willingness to pay. It is

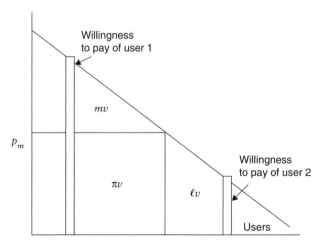

Figure 2.3
Price discrimination

also necessary to prevent arbitrage. Arbitrage means that a user with access to a low price buys it and resells it in the market with the high price.

The arguments we have made so far are ex post arguments, in the sense that they pertain to efficient distribution of the good once it has been invented. The ex post perspective is not very favorable to intellectual property protection, due to deadweight loss. If the avoidance of deadweight loss were the only criterion for choosing between intellectual property protection and public sponsorship, the share of public spending would probably be even larger than it is currently in the Western world. It currently ranges from about one-fourth to one-half of total R&D spending.

Despite its ex post defects, the main justification for intellectual property protection is made from the ex ante perspective. Intellectual property protection gives innovators an incentive to invest in new knowledge. However, intellectual property protection is not the only way to do that. The remainder of the chapter considers alternatives that avoid the deadweight loss of monopoly pricing. Before doing so, we consider two virtues of intellectual property rights that offset the deadweight loss.

The first virtue is decentralization. The incentive operates without the inventor having to negotiate with an invention authority. Probably the most important obstacle to effective public sponsorship is in tapping ideas for invention that are widely distributed among firms and inventors. The lure of intellectual property protection does that automatically. This is especially important if it is a private inventor and not a public sponsor who is likely to think of a good idea for an innovation. The following sections propose a model of the creative process, and investigate more systematically how public sponsors might also harness that widely dispersed creative genius.

The second virtue is that intellectual property rights impose the cost of an invention on its users, and not more generally on taxpayers. Each innovation is paid for voluntarily through proprietary prices. When innovations are funded out of general revenue, there is no guarantee that the benefits received by any individual taxpayer outweigh that taxpayer's share of the cost. This argument in favor of intellectual property protection is particularly convincing for innovations with a narrow clientele, such as computer games or other whimsical things, but has less force for innovations with widely dispersed benefits. All taxpayers benefit from services provided by satellite imaging for better navigation, sensing stations for weather forecasts, and the development of vaccines. For such goods, public sponsorship with free access is probably a good idea. Where it gets murky is in that vast arena of competing uses for public funds where different constituencies argue for different R&D projects.

The next sections compare intellectual property protection with forms of public sponsorship, with a view toward trying to understand which incentive system is the better one, or in what circumstances.

2.2   Ideas and Innovations

Many discussions of R&D incentives begin from the premise that intellectual property is the solution to the incentive problem. The objective of such inquiries is to evaluate the design of intellectual property incentives, or to suggest modifications. However, in this book, we will start from the problem, rather than starting from the solution, and ask whether there are other incentive mechanisms that are superior. There are clearly reasons to be skeptical of intellectual property, in particular, the problem of deadweight loss.

If we start from the problem rather than the solution, then we must first formulate the problem. That is, we need a model of the creative environment in which the incentive system operates. The model here follows Green and Scotchmer (1995) and O'Donoghue, Scotchmer and Thisse (OST, 1998) in making a clean separation between an exogenous process that generates ideas for innovations, and the decisions whether to invest in them. An innovation requires both an idea and an investment in it. The notion of the "efficient investment" in R&D must obviously be tied to some notion of what the investment displaces. In considering what efficient investment means, section 2.6 compares this model to some others that have been proposed by economists.

We describe an idea by a pair (v, c). The variable v represents the per-period consumers' surplus with competitive supply, as in figures 2.2 and 2.3, and c represents the cost of developing the idea into an innovation. If the social value lasts forever and the product is competitively supplied, then the discounted social value is v/r. (See technical note 2.8.1.) We will assume that, if the invention is marketed by a proprietary firm, the per-period profit is πv, where π is a fraction less than one. Then the proprietary profit available under a patent that lasts for discounted length T is $\pi v T$. We assume that the associated deadweight loss is ℓv per period, so that the associated deadweight loss is $\ell v T$.

The advantage of prizes over patents is that they can avoid the deadweight loss of proprietary pricing. Suppose, in particular, that the prize is set equal to the patent value, $\pi v T$. Then the prize gives the same incentives to invest in the idea as the intellectual property system, but with less deadweight loss, assuming that the innovation goes into the public domain. When is such an alternative possible?

To set a prize equal to the value of a patent right, the prize giver must observe the value v. This may be impossible. But even if the prize giver can observe v, the researcher may fear that the prize giver will renege, or try to give a smaller prize than he or she deserves. The prize system will work best if the value v is also verifiable by a court, so that the prize giver can be sued for any attempt to cheat.

But even if the two conditions, observability and verifiability of v, are met, a prize equal to the patent value may not be the best option. In fact, it might seem natural to base the prize directly on the R&D cost c instead of v, since that would enable a sponsor to minimize the amount of money that must be raised for rewards. In practice, however, this would not work—how would the cost be observed? First, a sponsor cannot observe cost by consulting the researcher's accounting data. The economic definition of cost is the minimum cost required to achieve the result. If the sponsor simply reimbursed the accounting costs, the researcher might, for example, be given an incentive to go to the beach under the guise of attending research conferences. Second, in most research endeavors, the laboratories and researchers' time are spread among many research projects. Overhead costs must be apportioned among the projects. No one except the researcher, and possibly not even him or her, can know how to apportion the costs.

Perhaps most importantly, some research efforts do not pay off with certainty, and then cost has an ambiguous meaning. PhRMA, the trade organization of the pharmaceutical firms, estimates that fewer than one in five drug-development efforts results in a successful drug. The failures obviously cannot be identified in advance, or the drug companies would avoid them. If only the successful drugs result in profitable intellectual property rights or prizes, the cost being covered by the intellectual property rights or prizes would have to include the cost of failures as well as successes. If only the successful drugs are rewarded, they must be rewarded at least five times more than the average cost per drug-discovery effort.

In some cases the prize giver can observe something about v so the prize can depend on v. We shall refer to the size of the prize as $\rho(v)$. Even though the prize giver cannot make the prize depend directly on cost an optimally chosen prize should reflect some subjective notion of its distribution. If costs for ideas with value v are lower on average for some types of innovations, then presumably the prize $\rho(v)$ should also be lower. For other types of innovations, the expected costs might be higher on average, and the prize should be higher. In making these judgments, the sponsor recognizes that, since the cost c is unobservable, a prize $\rho(v)$ smaller than the social value v/r may not cover cost, and a prize larger than the cost may attract too many competitors. The benefit of giving lower prizes must be balanced against the possibility of discouraging some innovations.

The examples of incentive mechanisms in this chapter address two types of creative environments: those where the creation of knowledge addresses a known need, and those where the need had not been identified, or at least articulated by a sponsor, prior to someone thinking of the idea. In the latter context, it is natural to call the idea scarce, in the sense that the idea also identifies the economic need.

The distinction between ideas that address well-known needs and ideas that are scarce has implications for what types of mechanisms can be used. If the need is known in advance, then it makes sense for a sponsor to post a prize to address it, or otherwise to solicit solutions ex ante. The prizes would typically be contingent on some performance standard dictated by the need. In contrast, an incentive system to reward scarce ideas could not very easily be established in advance, at least with a performance standard. The terms of the reward must be established ex post.

The distinction between well-known needs and scarce ideas is, of course, fuzzy. A need can have varying degrees of specificity, from "demonstrate that Maxwell's equations are correct" to "improve the efficiency of harnessing water power."

2.3 Prizes

We will discuss two types of prizes, those directed at well-known needs known to sponsors and those directed at scarce ideas that originate with innovators. *Targeted prizes* are posted ex ante. They reward solutions to needs that originate with sponsors, and the sponsor's needs are formalized in performance standards that must be met to claim the prize. The inventor's idea is a solution to the sponsor's stated need.

Such prizes do not tap all the creativity that is widely dispersed in the population. What happens if someone thinks of a great idea for which no reward has been posted? As we saw in chapter 1, potential innovators have frequently gone to legislatures to wheedle funding, both ex ante and ex post. The possibility of getting rewards ex post is sometimes institutionalized as *blue-sky prizes*. These are prizes offered for innovations that are not identified in advance. Instead, judges are allowed to "know it when they see it." (For blue-sky prizes, "the sky is the limit.") Blue-sky prizes must be tailored ex post to the value of the innovation. Since the nature of the innovation is not stated in advance, there are no prespecified performance standards. This creates a problem, which also carries over to contests: the innovator must trust that an appropriate prize will be given.

We illustrate two methods that have been used to ensure that a prize reflects the value v, namely, making the prize conditional on a verifiable performance standard, and giving the inventor the option to choose intellectual property protection instead. Performance standards can be specified ex ante for targeted prizes, but they must be specified ex post for blue-sky prizes. If the inventor has the option to choose intellectual property instead of the prize, the prize effectively becomes a patent buyout. The inventor will not agree unless the prize is at least as large as the patent value $\pi v T$. By accepting the prize, the innovator renounces the patent right and puts the innovation in the public domain. But he or she will only do this if the prize is at least as large as the value of the patent, and in this sense, the prize is constrained to reflect the value.

An example of how the buyout works occurred when the French inventors of photography, Louis Daguerre, and the heir, Isidore Niépce, of his co-inventor sold their rights in an ex post negotiation in 1839. The inventors received pensions totaling 10,000 francs per annum in exchange for revealing the secrets of the process at a joint meeting of the French Academies of Art and Science. Afterward, the process was put in the public domain (Newhouse 1988). We can only presume that the French inventors received value commensurate with their invention, since they would not have accepted a prize less than the patent value.[3]

In contrast, John Hyatt chose patent protection over a prize for inventing celluloid in the nineteenth century (Porter 1994). Hyatt had originally invented celluloid in order to compete for a prize posted by a manufacturer of billiard balls who wanted to replace ivory. However,

---

3.   Contemporary observers contrasted this procedure with what happened in England, where a better process was stifled by patent litigation (Newhouse 1988).

when Hyatt realized that his invention had wider applicability, he chose patent protection instead, apparently judging the value of the patent to be greater than the prize.

Michael Kremer (1998) suggests a direct way to buy out the patent at a price that reflects the full social value. Since the value of the invention is likely to be observable by rival firms after the invention has been made, the patent authority can turn the patent into a prize as follows. The invention authority appropriates the patent, and auctions it to rival firms. With small probability the sponsor delivers the patent to the highest bidder in return for the bid price, and otherwise puts the innovation in the public domain. The rivals will bid the same as if the high bidder would receive the patent with probability one, and they therefore reveal their valuations. The winning bid should be (close to) the private value $\pi v T$. The sponsor can divide the winning bid by πT to get an estimate of the value v. Kremer suggests that the sponsor pay the inventor a prize equal to the estimated social value, v/r, from general revenue. This scheme is enforceable, provided the parameters πT are specified in advance, so that a court could enforce it.

Patent buyouts allow the government to confiscate inventions with high public consequences, such as pharmaceuticals, without hurting the innovator. If anything, the Kremer scheme increases the incentive to invest, since the innovator's reward v/r is larger than the value of the patent $\pi v T$. However, such a high prize also leads to social waste if it incites rival firms to duplicate each other's costs in a wasteful race (see chapter 4). Under these circumstances, it may be better to choose a prize $\rho(v)$ below the social value, as discussed in the previous section.

An example of linking the prize to verifiable performance standards occurred in the Lyonnaise silk-weaving industry. Members of the Fabrique Lyonnaise could make improvements to weaving on their own initiative and then petition a prize committee for remuneration. It is unclear whether most of these improvements would alternatively have been patentable, but the terms of the ex post reward evidently did not rely on that alternative. Often the prize committee set the terms of the reward based on performance criteria, such as the number of weavers who adopted the innovation (Foray 2004; Foray and Perez, forthcoming). Such terms had the effect of ensuring that the prize was given only in return for value.

Targeted prizes were common in France along with blue-sky prizes. In 1795 a prize was offered for a means to preserve food to feed Napoléon's vast armies and navy. The prize was awarded in 1810 to

Nicolas Appert on condition that he publish the technique and put it in the public domain (Porter 1994, 16). His technique, which involved heat sterilization of food packed in bottles, is still in use. (If the solution seems obvious, we should remember that the causes of spoilage were not understood.) Other targeted prizes led to improvements of the steam engine (Porter 1994) and also water power, which led to the first water turbine (Strandh 1979).

One of the most famous targeted prizes was the longitude prize discussed earlier. By the time the English prize was posted in 1714, similar prizes in other countries had gone unclaimed. The failure to determine longitude was the principal cause of a large and growing number of naval and commercial catastrophes. No one disputed the high value of a solution, but mariners despaired of finding one.

There also seems to be a renaissance of prize giving in our own era. For example, the X Prize Foundation was established in 1996 with a $10 million prize for the first private firm to carry three passengers to a suborbital height of 100 km twice within a single two-week period.[4] To date, twenty-three teams representing seven countries have entered (X Prize Foundation, 2003). Observers report that at least three teams are likely to produce actual hardware. One effort has reported that it plans to spend $5–$7 million in the effort. Some commentators believe that several teams have a reasonable chance of claiming the prize before it expires (Hoffman 2003).

Another modern targeted prize was $30 million announced in 1992 to develop a new "super efficient refrigerator" (Penn 1993; Zuckerman 2003). To receive payment the winner had to sell 250,000 copies of the new refrigerator by 1997. Although Whirlpool won the contest, they did

---

4.   Long-distance fight has traditionally been supported by prizes. Famous examples include the first flight across the English Channel in 1909 ($5,000), the first flight across the North Atlantic in 1919 (£10,000), and the first nonstop flight from New York to Paris in 1927 ($50,000). The 1927 contest, which resulted in Lindbergh's flight, is particularly interesting. The prize was originally offered in 1919 for the first flier to accomplish the feat before 1924. This incentive may have been insufficient given the technologies of the time; in any case, there were no takers. The prize was then renewed for an additional five-year period, drawing a total of nine teams into the race, although at least one of these efforts failed to obtain adequate financing. The remaining teams spent a total of $400,000 in the effort. Seven of these aircraft either crashed on takeoff or disappeared. Lindbergh's successful effort cost $25,000 (X Prize Foundation, 2003; Jablonski 1972).

not meet the performance standard, selling only 200,000 units, and the prize was not paid.

Finally, we mention two targeted prizes with performance standards that have been offered for inventions with great value to the sponsor or to society but no commercial value. The first was a German prize for demonstrating that Maxwell's equations of electromagnetism were correct. The prize was offered by the Berlin Academy in 1879, and the feat was accomplished by Heinrich Hertz, albeit long after the prize expired (Bryant 1988).

A modern prize with similar character is the RSA Factoring Challenge, which offers $250,000 for the first team to factor a specified 2048-bit integer. Rewards for smaller specified numbers start at $10,000 (RSA Security, 2003). RSA sells a commercial implementation of public key encryption whose security rests on the computational difficulty of factoring large numbers. If the prize goes unclaimed, RSA has more confidence in the security of its system. This is a case where the sponsor is better off if it does not get what it is looking for. The successful claimant cannot profit from the discovery in any way other than by winning the prize.

These examples show that prizes can be linked to value by (1) administering prizes in a legal environment where intellectual property protection is also available and (2) making the prize contingent on a performance standard. These techniques can apply to either targeted prizes or blue-sky prizes, although patent protection is probably a more important backup for blue-sky prizes, as a way to avoid ex post holdup.

So far these arguments have been entirely about the feasibility of linking prizes to the value of the innovation. They do not inform us about the optimal size of the prize. If costs are "expected" to be much lower than value, then it is sensible to set a prize much lower than the social value, even if the social value can be observed. The appropriate size of a prize should also be tailored to the number of participants that the sponsor wishes to attract.

In the simple ideas model so far considered, it is desirable to avoid duplication of costs. When ideas are scarce, this is not a problem—scarcity means that only one inventor can fill the market niche defined by his or her idea. In that case, the size of the prize should simply balance the possibility of giving up the innovation (when the prize turns out to be less than cost) against the social cost of overrewarding the innovator.

Such a balancing must be done by reference to a subjective distribution of costs, conditional on value.

For targeted prizes, ideas are typically not scarce. There are typically several ideas that could fill the targeted need. In such an environment, simple prizes share a defect of intellectual property protection, even if the prize can depend on the value. Since there is no one to aggregate the information and make an efficient choice, there is no way to ensure that only the agent with the best idea invests, or even that a single agent invests. Those problems can be partly addressed by the contests we discuss in the following section.

2.4   Choosing among Ideas

Suppose that two firms have substitute ideas (v_i, c_i), $i = 1, 2$, for how to serve the sponsor's need. Firm 1's idea is the better one if

$$\frac{1}{r}v_1 - c_1 \geq \frac{1}{r}v_2 - c_2,$$

Otherwise the sponsor will prefer the idea of firm 2. To identify the better idea, information about both ideas, (v_1, c_1) and (v_2, c_2), must be aggregated and compared. Without aggregating the information, no one in the economy knows which idea is better. Firm 1 does not know because it does not know the parameters of firm 2's idea, and firm 2 does not know because it does not know the parameters of firm 1's idea. And the sponsor knows neither.

How do patent incentives perform in this situation?

A patent system will not generally aggregate the information, and will not necessarily limit investment to the best idea. Suppose that the ideas are similar enough so that only one of the ideas can be patented—the other would infringe. For a patent of length T, the firms' prospective patent rewards are $\pi v_1 T$ and $\pi v_2 T$. There are two possible outcomes in this situation, both of which may be inefficient. If the patent values are high enough—that is, if $c_1 \leq (1/2)\pi v_1 T$ and $c_2 \leq (1/2)\pi v_2 T$—both firms may enter a patent race, each winning with probability one-half. In that case, costs are inefficiently duplicated. If the patent values are relatively low—that is, if $c_2 > (1/2)\pi v_2 T$ and $c_1 > (1/2)\pi v_1 T$—then it may be that only one firm enters the race, but there is no guarantee that it will be the right firm. Indeed, the firm that enters cannot evaluate whether its prospective innovation will provide more surplus than that of the rival, because it does not know the other firm's idea.

Thus, from the point of view of aggregating information, patents are a very imperfect incentive mechanism. Can a sponsor do better?

2.5   Contests

To some extent, a sponsor can solve the problem of finding the best idea for a targeted objective by setting up contests. The efficacy of these contests will depend on what the contract payments can depend on (this is where verifiability is important), and in general, the contests will not achieve the first best. That is, they may not ensure that the best idea is selected, or that it is implemented at minimum cost.

A Simple Commitment to Pay   The first commitment device is extremely simple and also very common. The sponsor sets a prize and commits only to give it away. He or she does not make the payment conditional on any specified performance, but rather announces an objective. Ex post the sponsor will choose the contestant who comes closest to meeting the objective. There is no reason for an enforcement body to be involved, except to make sure that the prize money is actually paid to someone. The sponsor cannot renege on paying the prize and has no reason to pay it to any contestant other than the one who comes closest to the stated objective.

The problem with this simple mechanism is the same one that arises with patents. There is no guarantee that only the firm with the best idea invests, and indeed, there may be an inefficient duplication of costs, especially if the prize is large. It improves on patents by avoiding deadweight loss, but it would be nice to do better.

We now discuss two contest-like mechanisms that are more complicated than a simple commitment to give away the money. Suppose, in particular, that two firms have substitute ideas (v_i, c_i), $i = 1, 2$, for how to serve the sponsor's need. We assume that, if the sponsor could observe these values, the most attractive idea would be the one providing the greatest social surplus. The sponsor would choose firm 1's idea if $(1/r)v_1 - c_1 \geq (1/r)v_2 - c_2$, and pay c_1, and would otherwise choose firm 2's idea. The problem is that the sponsor cannot observe (v_1, c_1), (v_2, c_2). The firms may have an incentive to lie about them if they think that lying will garner a profitable government contract. Solving this problem will involve waste.

A Vickrey Auction   The Vickrey auction goes some distance toward eliciting efficient investment but only works if the value can be verified ex post.[5] So far as the author knows, this has not been used in practice. In the second-price (Vickrey) auction, the sponsor asks each prospective innovator $i = 1, 2$ to report the social surplus $s_i = (1/r)v_i - c_i$ that it could provide. The firms report some values s_1, s_2. Of course the sponsor cannot verify that either firm is reporting s_i honestly. However, this will not matter because the promised payments will give the firms an incentive to be honest.

The sponsor chooses the firm that reports the highest net surplus. Suppose that this is firm 1. The sponsor promises a payment to the winning firm, firm 1, that is equal to $(1/r)v_1 - s_2$. Notice that the payment depends on the other firm's bid s_2, not on the winning bidder's bid s_1. The sponsor then asks firm 1 to invest. After paying its own costs c_1, firm 1 ends up with the payment $[(1/r)v_1 - s_2 - c_1] = s_1 - s_2$.

The second-price auction has the following properties: assuming that the firms report their respective surpluses honestly, then (1) the payment to the winning firm, say firm 1, will be close to (but no smaller than) the cost c_1 if s_1 is close to s_2, and (2) the winning firm makes nonnegative profit by delivering the innovation in return for the specified payments.

We can now ask whether the premise is valid: Does either firm have anything to gain by misrepresenting its net surplus to the sponsor? In the case that $s_1 < s_2$, does firm 1 want to overstate s_1? Unless its lie causes firm 1 to win the bid instead of losing it, the lie has no effect, since firm 1's payment does not depend on its own bid s_1. If the lie is large enough to change the outcome, then firm 1's profit is $s_1 - s_2$, which would be negative. Firm 1 is better off losing the bid and making zero profit.

In the case that $s_1 > s_2$, does firm 1 want to understate the surplus s_1? Unless its lie causes firm 1 to lose the bid instead of winning it, the lie again has no effect. If the lie is large enough to change the outcome, then firm 1 makes zero profit by losing the bid instead of earning

5.   It is named after economist William S. Vickrey, who first exposited its remarkable properties in his 1961 paper. The simplest example is where an auctioneer wants to transfer an object to the agent with the highest valuation but cannot observe the valuations. The auctioneer asks each bidder to state a valuation, then gives the object to the highest bidder, but only charges a price equal to the second highest bid. In that situation, nothing needs to be observed ex post. In the version given here, each agent has two unknown variables, cost and value. The value must be observed ex post, but not the cost.

$s_1 - s_2$, which is positive. Thus, firm 1 has no incentive to lie about s_1. The same argument applies to firm 2.

Thus, the most important feature of the second-price auction is that each firm has an incentive to report faithfully on the net surplus it can deliver, and the sponsor can safely pick the firm that claims the highest surplus.

The second-price auction is particularly attractive if the surplus available from the two rivals is expected to be similar. In that case, the payment to the winning bidder will be close to the winning bidder's cost, and equal if $s_1 = s_2$. In general, however, a sponsor would care about the size of the transfer that must be paid to the winning bidder. The social cost of raising funds for general revenue may be smaller than the social cost of taxing a single market but is still not zero. The second-price auction yields an efficient outcome in the sense that the high-surplus firm is asked to invest, and there is no duplication of cost.

The second-price (Vickrey) auction assumes that the ex post payment can depend on the delivered value. But that is the difficulty we would like to avoid. The contest we now discuss, following Che and Gale (forthcoming), is a hybrid between the commitment prize and the Vickrey auction.

A Prototype Contest   The ex ante problem of the sponsor is to elicit investment in the best idea, given that payment cannot be conditioned on the value of the delivered innovation. Another possibility is to let the firms demonstrate their ideas by developing prototypes, and then choose between them ex post. This is obviously costly, but may be the best option in an environment where value delivered is not verifiable to a court.

But to elicit investment, the sponsor still needs a commitment to pay ex post, avoiding the temptation to negotiate a low price once the prototypes are delivered. If the sponsor cannot commit to pay a price above development cost, the innovators will not invest.

The prototype contest solves this problem by allowing the firms and the sponsor to make contingent contracts before any investments are made. The contracts specify what price the sponsor will pay to each innovator, contingent only on buying that firm's innovation. The sponsor's observation of quality is reflected only in the decision to buy. The only enforcement problem is to make sure that if the inventor is chosen, the price will be as specified in the contract written before the innovator invested. Each firm would like to get a high price if its innovation is chosen, but a high price increases the chance of not being chosen ex post. This constrains the prices demanded by the firms in negotiating the contracts ex ante. On the other hand, since the contingent contracts are negotiated before costs are sunk, the firms will not offer prices so low that they do not cover costs.

To see this mechanism more explicitly, suppose the two potential innovators have ideas (v_1, c_1), (v_2, c_2).[6] Suppose, for concreteness, that $v_1 > v_2$. If v_1 is very close to v_2, then in an ex post auction, the winning bid would be close to zero, and neither bidder would be likely to cover its expected cost. This is remedied in the following contest by letting the firms bid ex ante, before they sink their costs. For simplicity, assume that the qualities v_1, v_2 are known to all parties, even if they cannot be verified in court. Thus, all the parties know what qualities of innovations will be delivered ex post. The firms will announce ex ante the prices (ρ_1, ρ_2) at which they are willing to sell their innovations ex post. Each firm will receive this price, but only if chosen by the sponsor ex post.

Our objective is now to characterize the firms' equilibrium bids. These are bids such that neither firm has an incentive to revise its bid, assuming that the other firm's bid is fixed. An oddity of the equilibrium is that the contingent bid prices cannot be deterministic. That is, neither bidder will bid a single price. If they are constrained to do so, the scheme will not work. This is evidence of how difficult it is to solve the problem.

To see that the prices cannot be deterministic, suppose that $v_1 = v_2$ and $c_1 = c_2 = c$, and consider what prices the firms will demand. A natural guess is $(\rho_1, \rho_2) = (2c, 2c)$. These are the minimum prices the firms could demand and still cover their costs in expectation, assuming that the tie-breaking rule is to randomize evenly between the firms. Since each firm would win the bid with probability 1/2, the revenues would be $(1/2)\rho_1 = (1/2)\rho_2 = c$.

However, these prices are not an equilibrium. If firm 2 demands price $2c$ in the event that it is chosen, then firm 1 can improve profit by reducing its own demand to $\rho_1 = 2c - \varepsilon$, where ε is a small positive number. With prices $(\rho_1, \rho_2) = (2c - \varepsilon, 2c)$, the sponsor will choose firm 1, and firm 1 will make profit $\rho_1 - c = c - \varepsilon$ instead of 0. This shows that the zero-profit prices $(\rho_1, \rho_2) = (2c, 2c)$ are not an equilibrium. Of

---

6.   The discussion here tailors the model to the ideas context. Che and Gale use a more standard model in which there is a known function that yields quality in return for investment effort. The firms announce their qualities in advance, coupled with a random distribution on prices.

course there are no lower prices that are an equilibrium either, since at least one firm would then not cover cost in expectation.

The solution to this problem is so-called mixed strategies. Instead of choosing a deterministic price, each firm chooses a probability distribution over prices, and the price actually offered to the sponsor is a random draw from this distribution.

An equilibrium will have the property that the firms randomize on whether they develop the innovation, as well as on the price. With some probability each firm will drop out, which means that it does not innovate and demands a zero price. If both firms drop out, the sponsor fails to procure the innovation.

Denote the cumulative distributions on price by

$$F_1, F_2 : \left[0, \frac{v}{r} \right] \to [0,1]$$

For each $\rho \in [0, (v/r)]$, the probability that the firm chooses a price no larger than ρ is $F_i(\rho)$, for $i = 1, 2$. The firm will never choose a price larger than (v/r) because the sponsor would never pay a price greater than the value of the innovation. The price $\rho = 0$ will imply that the firm does not innovate, and a positive price will imply that the firm does innovate. Thus $F_1(0)$, $F_2(0)$ are the probabilities that the two firms do not innovate.

The firms' decisions whether to innovate and what price to demand will be made independently of each other, not observing each other's choices. Their choices are commitments in the sense that they cannot change the contract ex post if, for example, the other firm's price turns out to be lower.

For the example with symmetric ideas $(v_1, c_1) = (v_2, c_2) = (v, c)$, there is an equilibrium in which the firms drop out with probabilities $F_1(0) = F_2(0) = c/(v/r)$, and the cumulative distributions on prices are $F_1 = F_2 = F$, defined as follows:

$$F(\rho) = \begin{cases} \dfrac{c}{(v/r)} & \text{if } 0 \le \rho < c \\[2ex] 1 - \dfrac{c}{\rho} + \dfrac{c}{(v/r)} & \text{if } c \le \rho \le \dfrac{v}{r} \end{cases}$$

This implies that $F(0) = c/(v/r)$. With probability $c/(v/r)$ the firm drops out and asks for price $\rho = 0$. The firm never chooses any price between 0 and c. For prices between c and v/r, the probability distribution has density function $F'(\rho) = c/\rho^2$. That is, conditional on innovating, the firm puts most of its probability weight on a price near the cost c, with the probability weight declining to the maximum (v/r).

This is an equilibrium because each price in the support of the distribution yields the same expected profit as any other price, namely zero, and no other price would yield greater profit. If firm 1 drops out (chooses price $\rho = 0$), it makes zero profit. If firm 1 develops the innovation and demands any price ρ in the interval $[c, (v/r)]$, firm 1's expected profit is $\rho[F_2(0) + 1 - F_2(\rho)] - c = \rho[c/\rho] - c = 0$. The term $[F_2(0) + 1 - F_2(\rho)]$ represents the probability that firm 1 wins the bid ex post. With probability $F_2(0)$ firm 2 drops out, and with probability $1 - F_2(\rho)$ firm 2 innovates but demands a higher price than firm 1's price.

These strategies hold the firms to the lowest possible expected profit that will induce them to invest, given that two of them are asked to innovate. However, it is important to notice that, aside from the oddity of random prices, the investment decisions are inefficient. With some probability, the sponsor does not get the innovation, and even if the sponsor gets it, there is a large probability that the costs will be duplicated. Allowing duplication is how the sponsor induces rivalry to keep the procurement price down.

The reader can work out how this mechanism must be modified if the firms' ideas (v_1, c_1), (v_2, c_2) are different. In that case, the random prices, conditional on both firms innovating, may have the consequence that the sponsor does not always choose the highest-value innovation. Instead, the innovator chooses the innovation that generates the highest surplus, which will be the lower-value innovation if the innovator also demands a very low price.

The main example of prototype competition has occurred in military procurement. Prior to the 1970s, the U.S. Air Force usually acquired prototypes from a single vendor after a contest to choose the best written proposal, and then decided whether to accept it. That procedure led to widely criticized cost overruns in the 1960s. In the 1970s the air force moved to a system where two rival companies received contracts to build prototypes followed by a flight competition to demonstrate quality. This process led to the F-16 and F-18 fighter jets (Sweetman 1991).

While these contracts do not exactly mirror the mechanisms we have discussed, they show that the sponsor can use prototype competition to keep quality high and costs low, at least relatively. Rogerson (1994) points out that the payoff to winning the prototype competition is a lucrative production contract. According to Rogerson, such procurement can be viewed as a three-stage process consisting of (1) a design phase in which multiple firms pursue competing designs, (2) a selection phase in which a limited number of firms compete to produce prototypes and/or a final design, and (3) a production phase, typically involving production by a single firm. He argues that the production phase allows the Department of Defense to "award larger prizes to more important innovations, at least in a rough sense" as well as providing ongoing incentives to improve the product after initial adoption. Firms that reach the production phase typically enjoy economic profits (above the normal return to capital) amounting to 4.4 percent. The super-normal rate of return can be viewed as a prize.

It is important to notice in the prototype mechanism that a high social price is paid for the inability to observe or verify value. The prototype contest may involve duplicated costs, and there is also some probability that the inferior product will be chosen. Indeed, both firms may drop out so that no prototype materializes. In the case where a prototype is chosen, the price may be very high. These are all phenomena that we observe in practice.

2.6   Efficient Investments in Knowledge

To compare incentive schemes from a normative point of view, we must have some notion of an efficient investment plan. Which ideas should elicit an R&D investment? We cannot understand the efficiency of any incentive mechanism unless we have a model of how technological opportunities arise, and a standard by which to know whether investing in them is efficient.

A much-discussed puzzle is why technological progress was so rapid in the twentieth century. Real output per capita in the United States grew about 1.75 percent per year in the twentieth century, a much higher rate than previously. In attempting to measure the source of growth, economists have concluded that much of it was due to technological advance (see chapter 9). The premise of this book is that there is a relationship between R&D spending and growth, but how should we evaluate the following type of statement? "Humans would have been better off if they had made earlier investments in technological progress, and thus accelerated the growth spurts, such as those that occurred in the Industrial Revolution and the twentieth century. Consumers would then have had modern technologies much sooner."

By what standard could such a statement be true or false? Notice that the statement has both normative and positive elements. It asserts that such an acceleration would have been possible, and asserts further that such an acceleration would have been an economic improvement. To evaluate such a statement, we must understand to what extent technological growth is exogenous, and to what extent it can be influenced by incentives and rates of R&D spending. The ideas model used in this chapter has both an exogenous part, the occurrence of ideas, and an endogenous part, the incentive to invest in them. Progress is limited by human imagination, and in some historical periods or geographic locations, by an inability or unwillingness to marshal resources.

Not all economic models of technological advance are set up to evaluate efficiency in investment, or to compare incentive mechanisms. For example, the evolutionary model of Nelson and Winter (1982) (see also Mokyr 1990, chap. 11) is a positive model of technical change, rather than a normative model. Regardless of the incentive mechanisms in place, firms are assumed to invest in R&D when profit falls below a certain level. There is no notion of rationality that drives investment decisions.

In the model of factor-price induced technical change originating with Hicks (1932) (but see Ruttan 2001 for a summary and applications), changes in factor prices drive technological progress. Innovators exploit the profit opportunities that arise when this happens. There is no explanation for why factor prices change, and no explanation for which technological opportunities are sitting around waiting for the environment to change. If a given opportunity to improve technology is available, why isn't an even better opportunity available?

Economists have also developed a large literature, mostly concerned with patent races, based on what we might call the "production-function" models of R&D investment. In the production-function models, there is a commonly known function that specifies the cost of achieving an innovation, either with given probability or at a given expected time. The patent-race models using the Poisson process for time of discovery fall in to this category (for a review see Reinganum 1989), as do the probability-of-discovery models (Wright 1983; Tandon 1982, 1983; Shavell and van Ypserle 2001). However, these models do not say how the investment opportunity arises in the first place. The implicit premise is that, by investing enough resources, all progress could happen tomorrow. There are no limits on human imagination. Like the induced-change model, the production-function model is an incomplete model of technical change.

Much of the endogenous-growth literature (see Romer 1996 for a summary) also relies on a production function for knowledge, and shares the limitations of that model. However the production function is for "aggregate" knowledge. The aggregation might conceivably mask a process of investment in ideas, but since there is no separation between the occurrence of an idea and the creation of an innovation, efficiency of the disaggregated investments cannot be evaluated.

The ideas model proposed in this book achieves a balance between limits on human imagination and the incentive problem of marshaling resources. The notion of efficiency here is a standard one, namely, that investment in an idea is efficient if it provides positive (discounted) consumers' surplus net of costs, at least in expectation. This is a definition that takes account of how investments in knowledge are funded. If investments are funded by intellectual property protection, then they generate less consumers' surplus (or more deadweight loss) than if they are funded by public sponsors and put in the public domain.

However, the notion of efficiency also has nuances, of which we consider three.

First, ex post regret does not mean that an investment was ex ante inefficient. In the 1960s and 1970s, a worldwide race was on to develop supersonic civilian transport, an effort that turned out to be very expensive and that ultimately failed. England and France jointly developed the Concorde; Russia developed a version dubbed "Concordski" by the Western press; and the United States also wanted to join the fray with the "SST." Congress offered subsidies to design such an airplane, and eventually the competition was between Boeing and Lockheed. Boeing proposed to reduce drag by using an adjustable wing, called the swing wing. Lockheed insisted loudly that it would not work, and after considerable public debate, Boeing jettisoned it. In the face of growing opposition by environmentalists due to the sonic boom and other impacts, Congress took the opportunity to shut down the project. This was after more than a billion dollars had been invested in design efforts (Hansen 1995). Supersonic transport more generally came to a lusterless end. The Concorde lost money for its entire flying career. It was retired in 2003. The SST was aborted after a huge investment but before development was completed, and the Concordski crashed.

Should we conclude that the investments in supersonic transport were misguided in the first place? The problem with such a conclusion is that the outcome of an R&D project is almost always uncertain.

Failures are inevitable. Ex post failure does not necessarily mean that the investment should not have been undertaken—good bets can have bad outcomes. In any case, the test of ex post success is not useful, because the investment decision must obviously be taken before success or failure can be known. The best that can be done here is to use decision mechanisms or incentive mechanisms that are likely to lead to good decision making, and to recognize that failures are possible.

The second nuance concerns the problem of battling experts. This one is fundamental and calls into question the whole notion of efficiency. Economists have competing definitions of efficiency for the case that experts disagree when faced with the same information. (See technical note 2.8.3.) In the R&D context, such disagreement seems likely.

If two experts disagree about the prospects for success due to different information, they may nevertheless come to agreement if they share all the information possessed by the two of them. The convenient thing about agreement is that it gives a benchmark for what is efficient. If all the agents, using all the information, agree that investment is efficient, then presumably it is. There is no reason to think that they are collectively deluded. The difficulty is that experts may disagree even after sharing their information. This was probably the case of Lockheed and Boeing in the SST example, although their public proclamations may also have been tainted by self-interest.

The assumption that underlies agreement is that all the agents begin from a common prior belief about the true efficiency of the investment, and their initial disagreement is due only to asymmetric information. This is why they can resolve their disagreement by sharing information. The assumption of common priors underlies an extensive economics literature on asymmetric information, and it is therefore elaborated in technical note 2.8.2, which is an example.

The third nuance concerns the endogeneity of development paths, so-called path dependence. There are different notions of what path dependence might mean and how it arises (see, e.g., David 2000). Here we mean that not all ideas for innovations are known when investment decisions must be taken, and thus there can be regret. Any investment has the potential to set in motion a whole sequence of related investments that will entrench a technology; see the model of cumulative innovation in chapter 5. The right interpretation of efficiency must account for options on expected future development. Since the future path of development has a stochastic element, the decision maker must have a subjective view of what is likely to happen, and with what probabilities, and then calculate economic welfare as an expected value. If this seems too demanding, try to formulate an alternative. Compared to what?

In the case of technology paths, the problem of ex post regret is, if anything, compounded. Efficiency may require cautiousness in investment, perhaps even delay, in order to preserve options for choosing other technology paths if other ideas come along.

Consider, for example, the reciprocating-piston internal combustion engine. The violence of reciprocating motion dissipates energy through heat and stresses the engine in other ways. Many alternatives have been suggested, one of which is not only viable but is thought by some commentators to be superior. This is the Wankel rotary engine. (For a complete history, see Norbye 1971.) The rotary engine has a more direct link to the drive shaft and avoids much of the inefficiency involved in translating the up-and-down motion of pistons. The rotary apparatus is much simpler. It occupies half the space for the same power, has more or less half the moving parts, and costs about half as much per unit horsepower as a typical American V8 piston engine.

Despite its attractions, the rotary engine lagged the reciprocating-piston engine by decades, and has never come close to displacing the piston engine in automobiles. If the reciprocating-piston engine and the rotary engine had been placed side by side on the drawing board when internal combustion engines were first developed, it seems possible that the rotary engine would also (or exclusively) have been developed. It seems a pure accident of history that the piston assembly was already known. Development of the rotary engine only began in the 1930s after large cumulative investments had already been made in the design of piston engines. Playing catch-up at that point was probably doomed to failure. Nevertheless, the rotary engine was promising enough that in 1970, General Motors bought a nonexclusive, worldwide license for the technology, with total payments coming to about $50 million (1970 dollars). Rotary engines have been sold by American, Japanese, and European manufacturers, but they have always been relatively pricy and have not challenged in any serious way the commercial dominance of the reciprocating-piston engine. Rotary engines pretty much vanished from automobiles by the 1990s.

Since the piston engine was developed and refined, while the rotary engine was not, we cannot know whether it would have been better to start down that path earlier. Suppose we take on faith that, from an even start, the rotary engine would have developed to be competitive with, or even superior to, the reciprocating-piston engine. Would the ascendancy of the reciprocating-piston engine necessarily be inefficient? Even if everyone agreed that a better idea such as the rotary engine would eventually come along, delay is costly. If the delay is predicted to be long, then the better idea is not worth waiting for. And of course there is no way to predict the delay with certainty. If the competing idea has not yet been had, it is difficult to be confident that such an idea is likely.

Regret is inevitable if the better idea comes along too late for adoption—for example, because the other technology is already highly developed. That may well be the case with the Wankel engine.

But to repeat, regret does not mean that investment in the first technology was inefficient. Its efficiency can only be addressed by reference to expectations about the rate at which competing ideas are likely to occur, and whether they are likely to be better. These are the matters on which experts may easily disagree, which casts us back to our previous discussion. When experts disagree for reasons other than asymmetric information, economists have no satisfying definition of efficiency.

2.7   Summary

In this chapter, we have seen that a competitive market may not give enough incentive to invest in knowledge and have argued that there are several solutions to this problem, all imperfect. Intellectual property is just one incentive mechanism, in which rewards are given as limited market power.

As an incentive mechanism, intellectual property has the following virtues:

1.   The reward is linked to the social value of the invention, so that firms will, to some degree, compare social value and social cost when deciding whether to invest.
2.   Users of the intellectual property voluntarily pay the costs, so no one objects to its development.

The defects of intellectual property protection are easiest to see by listing the virtues of other well-designed incentive mechanisms:

1.   Innovations that are paid for out of tax revenue can be put in the public domain, which involves less deadweight loss than intellectual property rights.
2.   A well-designed incentive mechanism can better aggregate the private information of firms, to make better investment decisions and to delegate research efforts more efficiently.

3.   In a well-designed incentive mechanism, rewards can be tailored to expected costs.

This book does not argue that intellectual property incentives are always better or worse than public sponsorship, but rather that the choice between them should depend on the research environment. The strongest case for patents is when research ideas are "scarce," but even then, a prize system can dominate a patent system if the prize can be made to depend on the value of the invention. With intellectual property, it is automatic that the value of the reward depends on the social value of the innovation.

In the case that a sponsor can set up rivalry between potential innovators, intellectual property seems less attractive. Even when the value of the delivered innovation is unverifiable ex post, the sponsor can choose the best offering, while at the same time holding the innovators to a payment that is commensurate with their costs. The mechanism involves duplicated costs but so can intellectual property.

2.8   Technical Notes

2.8.1   Discounted Time

In the expression $\pi v T$ for the present value of the patent, the variable T represents discounted time from the present until the expiration of the right at some time τ that satisfies

$$T = \int_0^\tau e^{-rt} dt \cong \sum_{t=1}^\tau \frac{1}{(1+r)^t}$$

where r is the discount rate. "Ordinary time" runs from $\tau = 0$ to $\tau = \infty$, and "discounted time" runs from $T = 0$ to $T = 1/r$, since $1/r$ is the maximum T in the preceding equations, corresponding to $\tau = \infty$. If time is continuous, we use e^{-rt} for discounting, and if time is counted in years or other integral units, we use $1/(1 + r)^t$. To see that one approximates the other, take a Taylor expansion.

2.8.2   Battling Experts and Common Priors

If two firms have different private information about the value of a research program, but a common prior, then sharing their information will bring them into agreement about the prospects for success. However, their disagreement will persist if they start from different priors.

Suppose that the project has a true value v, which is random, and that experts have private signals v_1, v_2 of the value. For simplicity, suppose that the true value v takes two values, $v = 0$ and $v = 100$. Suppose that the distribution of the signal v_1, conditional on v, is given by $Q(\cdot|v)$, and that Q is also the conditional distribution of v_2.

Using Bayes' rule we can compute each firm's posterior probability that $v = 100$, where the prior probability of $v = 100$ is given by the prior belief. If the prior belief is $\hat{P}$, call the posterior probability distribution $\hat{Q}$. Firm 1's posterior probability of $v = 100$, knowing only its own signal, v_1, is

$$\hat{Q}(100|v_1) = \frac{Q(v_1|100)\hat{P}(100)}{Q(v_1|100)\hat{P}(100) + Q(v_1|0)\hat{P}(0)}$$

where the denominator is the probability of firm 1 observing signal v_1. Similarly, if firm 1 knows both signals, the posterior probability of $v = 100$ is

$$\hat{Q}(100|v_1,v_2) = \frac{Q(v_1|100)Q(v_2|100)\hat{P}(100)}{Q(v_1|100)Q(v_2|100)\hat{P}(100) + Q(v_1|0)Q(v_2|0)\hat{P}(0)}$$

where the denominator is the probability that firms 1 and 2 will observe (v_1, v_2).

Suppose now that firm 2 has a different prior probability than firm 1. Suppose that firm 2's prior probability is $\tilde{P}$, where $\tilde{P}(100) > \hat{P}(100)$. Then firm 2's posterior probability of $v = 100$, after observing both signals (v_1, v_2), is

$$\tilde{Q}(100|v_1,v_2) = \frac{Q(v_1|100)Q(v_2|100)\tilde{P}(100)}{Q(v_1|100)Q(v_2|100)\tilde{P}(100) + Q(v_1|0)Q(v_2|0)\tilde{P}(0)}$$

Clearly $\tilde{Q}(100|v_1, v_2) > \hat{Q}(100|v_1, v_2)$. Firm 2 will be more optimistic than firm 1, even though they share the information (v_1, v_2). The optimism is due to the prior belief and not to their different information. If they shared a common prior, $\hat{P} = \tilde{P}$, then sharing their information v_1, v_2 would bring them into agreement about the probability that $v = 100$.

2.8.3   Subjective Probabilities and Cost-Benefit Analysis: A Paradox

When agents have different subjective probabilities of success, the cost-benefit criterion for investment may conflict with a notion of Pareto improvement based on idiosyncratic beliefs. Suppose there are two risk-neutral agents, $i = 1, 2$, who place probabilities $q_1 = 0.4$, $q_2 = 0.6$ on success of the project. The agents have willingnesses to pay w_1, w_2 in case of success, and they have endowments $e_1 = e_2 = 10$. The cost of the research project is $c = 1$. We will say that the investment project passes the cost-benefit test if $q_1 w_1 + q_2 w_2 \geq c$. Suppose, however, that the investment is worthless, $w_1 = w_2 = 0$, so that the cost-benefit test fails. Neverthelesss, the investment can make the agents better off in an ex ante sense because they can "bet" against each other using their idiosyncratic beliefs on the state space {success, failure} created by the investment. An optimal allocation, conditional on investment, is to let agent 2 consume all nineteen remaining units of the private good in case of success, and otherwise to let agent 1 consume all nineteen units. The expected utility of agent 1 is then $(1 - q_1) * 19 = 11.4 > e_1 = 10$, and the expected utility of agent 2 is $q_2 * 19 = 11.4 > e_1 = 10$. This shows that the ex ante expected utilities of the agents can be larger with investment than without, even if the research output has no intrinsic value and the investment is costly.

References and Further Reading

Anton, J. J., and D. A. Yao. 2002. "The Sale of Ideas: Strategic Disclosure, Property Rights and Contracting." *Review of Economic Studies* 69:513–531.

Arrow, K. 1962. "Economic Welfare and the Allocation of Resources for Invention." In R. Nelson, ed., *The Rate and Direction of Economic Activities: Economic and Social Factors*, 609–626. National Bureau of Economic Research Conference Series. Princeton NJ: Princeton University Press.

Barton, J. H. 1997. "Patents and Antitrust: A Rethinking in Light of Patent Breadth and Sequential Innovation." *Antitrust Law Journal* 65:446–449.

Bryant, J. H. 1988. *Henrich Hertz: The Beginning of Microwaves*. Piscataway, NJ: Institute of Electrical and Electronics Engineers, Inc.

Che, Y.-K., and I. Gale. Forthcoming. "Optimal Design of Research Contests." *American Economic Review*.

David, P. 2000. "Path Dependence, Its Critics and the Quest for 'Historical Economics.'" In P. Garrouste and S. Ionnides, eds., *Evolution and Path Dependence in Economic Ideas: Past and Present*. Cheltenham, UK: Elgar Publishing.

Davis, L., and J. Davis. 2004. "How Effective are Prizes as Incentives to Innovation? Evidence from Three Twentieth-Century Contests." Paper presented at the conference "What Motivates Inventors to Invent." Pisa: The Network on European Policy for Intellectual Property at Scuola Superiore Sant-Anna.

De Laat, E. A. 1996. "Patents or Prizes: Monopolistic R&D and Asymmetric Information." *International Journal of Industrial Organization* 15:369–390.

Eisenstein, E. L. 1983. *The Printing Revolution in Early Modern Europe.* Cambridge, UK: Cambridge University Press.

Foray, D. 2004. *The Economics of Knowledge.* Cambridge, MA: MIT Press.

Foray, D., and L. Hilaire-Perez. Forthcoming. "The Economics of Open Technology: Collective Organization and Individual Claims in the 'Fabrique Lyonnaise' during the Old Regime." *Research Policy.*

Gallini, N., and S. Scotchmer. 2001. "Intellectual Property: When Is It the Best Incentive Mechanism?" *Innovation Policy and the Economy* 2:51–78.

Green, J., and S. Scotchmer. 1995. "On the Division of Profit in Sequential Innovation." *RAND Journal of Economics* 26:20–33.

Hansen, J. R. 1995. "What Went Wrong: Some New Insights into the Cancellation of the American SST Program." In W. M. Leary, ed., *From Airships to Airbus,* vol. 1, 168–189. Washington, DC: Smithsonian Institution Press.

Hicks, J. R. 1932. *The Theory of Wages.* London: P. Smith.

Hoffman, P. 2003. *Wings of Madness: Alberto Santos-Dumont and the Invention of Flight.* New York: Hyperion Books.

Jablonski, E. 1972. *Atlantic Fever.* New York: Macmillan.

King, G. J. 1978. "Army Flying Machine." Case 9-578-711. Boston: Intercollegiate Case Clearing House.

Kremer, M. 1998. "Patent Buyouts: A Mechanism for Encouraging Innovation." *Quarterly Journal of Economics* 113:1137–1168.

Laffont, J.-J., and J. Tirole. 1986. "Using Cost Observation to Regulate Firms." *Journal of Political Economy* 94:614–641.

Laffont, J.-J., and J. Tirole. 1987. "Auctioning Incentive Contracts." *Journal of Political Economy* 95:921–937.

Maskin, E., and J. Riley. 1980. "Auction Design with Correlated Reservation Values." Mimeograph. Princeton, NJ: Department of Economics, Princeton University.

Maurer, S., and S. Scotchmer. 2004. "Procuring Knowledge." In G. Libecap, ed., *Advances in the Study of Entrepreneurship, Innovation and Growth,* 1–31. Amsterdam: JAI Press.

Mokyr, J. 1990. *The Lever of Riches: Technological Creativity and Economic Progress.* Oxford: Oxford University Press.

Nelson, R. 1959. "The Simple Economics of Basic Scientific Research." *Journal of Political Economy* 67:304.

Nelson, R., and S. Winter. 1982. *An Evolutionary Theory of Economic Change.* Cambridge, MA: Harvard University Press.

Newhouse, E. L., ed. 1988. *Inventors and Discoverers: Changing Our World.* Washington, DC: National Geographic Society.

Norbye, J. P. 1971. *The Wankel Engine: Design, Development, Applications.* Philadelphia: Chilton Book Co.

O'Donoghue, T., S. Scotchmer, and J.-F. Thisse. 1998. "Patent Breadth, Patent Life and the Pace of Technological Progress." *Journal of Economics and Management Strategy* 7:1–32.

Penn, C., 1993. "Super Efficient Refrigerator Finalists." *Home Energy Magazine.* Available at hem.dis.anl.gov/eehem/93/930305.html.

Porter, R. 1994. *The Biographical Dictionary of Scientists.* New York: Oxford University Press.

Reinganum, J. 1989. "The Timing of Innovation: Research, Development and Diffusion." In R. Schmalensee and R. D. Willig, eds., *Handbook of Industrial Organization*, 849–908. Amsterdam: Elsevier.

Rogerson, W. P. 1994. "Economic Incentives and the Defense Procurement Process." *Journal of Economic Perspectives* 8:65–90.

Romer, D. 1996. *Advanced Macroeconomics.* New York: McGraw-Hill.

RSA Security. 2003. "Cryptographic Challenges." Available at www.rsasecurity.com/rsalabs/challenges/index.html.

Ruttan, V. W. 2001. *Technology, Growth and Development: An Induced Innovation Perspective.* Oxford: Oxford University Press.

Sappington, D. 1982. "Optimal Regulation of Research and Development under Imperfect Information." *Bell Journal of Economics* 13:354–368.

Shavell, S., and T. van Ypserele. 2001. "Rewards versus Intellectual Property Rights." *Journal of Law and Economics* 44:525–547.

Sobel, D. 1995. *Longitude: The True Story of a Lone Genius Who Solved the Greatest Scientific Problem of His Time.* New York: Walker.

Strandh, S. 1979. *A History of the Machine.* New York: A&W Publishers.

Sweetman, W. 1991. *YF-22 and YF-23 Advanced Tactical Fighters: Stealth, Speed and Agility for Air Superiority.* Osceoloa, WI: Motorbooks.

Tandon, P. 1982. "Optimal Patents with Compulsory Licensing." *Journal of Political Economy* 90:470–486.

Tandon, P. 1983. "Rivalry and the Excessive Allocation of Resources to Research." *Bell Journal of Economics* 14:152–165.

Vickrey, W. 1961. "Counterspeculation, Auctions, and Competitive Sealed Tenders." *Journal of Finance* 16:8–37.

Wright, B. 1983. "The Economics of Invention Incentives: Patents, Prizes and Research Contracts." *American Economic Review* 73:691–707.

X Prize Foundation. 2003. Available at www.xprize.org/.

Zuckerman, S. 2003. "New Wave of Energy Efficient Refrigerators." Available at www.ecomall.com/greenshopping/icebox2.htm.

3   A Primer for Nonlawyers on Intellectual Property

with Stephen M. Maurer

Intellectual property (IP) law is not a single subject. It embraces a half dozen protection regimes including patents, copyright, and trade secrets, as well as sui generis laws like the Europeans' Database Directive of 1996, and special statutes for plants. For the most part, formal protections cover different types of innovation, although this principle has been breached in the case of computer software, to which patents and copyright both apply. Trade secrecy applies to any subject matter that can be kept secret.

Legal scholars draw clear distinctions among the branches of IP law, whereas economists tend to focus on the policy levers they all share—length, breadth, the required inventive step, and exemptions—without tying their analysis to any specific body of law. The legal approach is messier. This chapter provides a quick overview of IP as lawyers conceive it, and motivates the stylized economic models found later in the book. Except as noted, we focus on American law. Most countries follow broadly similar rules, especially after the comprehensive worldwide TRIPS treaty was enacted in 1994. TRIPS is discussed in chapter 11.

After laws are enacted by the U.S. Congress, they are codified into a set of books, the *United States Code*, where they are organized by topics. The U.S. patent law is in volume 35, referred to as 35 USC, and copyright is in volume 17. Sometimes we will refer to a particular law by the name of the original legislation (e.g., "Semiconductor Chip Protection Act") and sometimes by the code section (e.g., "17 USC §901").

Both patent law and copyright law incorporate many amendments that have accumulated over the years by acts of Congress. Both have also been clarified and changed by court decisions. We refer to important court opinions in footnotes, in case the reader wants more detail. Readers who want to do their own legal research should consult section 3.8.

Most intellectual property statutes and court cases are federal. The U.S. Constitution grants the right to create patents and copyrights to Congress, and the states cannot create conflicting rights. For example, states cannot trump Congress's decision to leave certain knowledge unprotected by creating their own intellectual property laws. States also cannot increase protection beyond that provided by Congress.[1]

At the administrative level, patents are the only form of intellectual property screened by a government agency before the right is granted. The U.S. Patent & Trademark Office (PTO) decides whether applicants have met the legal and factual standards required for a patent.

3.1   Patents

A patent gives its owner the right to sue for infringement if anyone tries to make, use, sell, offer, import, or offer to import the invention into the country issuing the patent (35 USC §154). It thus grants a legal monopoly. In addition to infringement, there is also a concept of contributory infringement. This lets patent holders sue to stop third parties from knowingly selling inputs that are "especially adapted" for use in patented combinations or processes (§271(c)).

Patents are the gold standard of intellectual property protection. With other forms of protection, if a third party duplicates the protected innovation independently, he or she can use it. The absence of this independent-invention defense makes patent law uniquely powerful.

Covered Subject Matter   To be patentable, an invention must meet four basic requirements: patentable subject matter, utility, novelty, and non-obviousness. The first two requirements focus on technology. An invention satisfies the patentable-subject-matter requirement if it is (1) a machine, (2) a manufactured product, (3) a composition made from two or more substances, or (4) a process for manufacturing objects. In practice, the PTO and courts almost always stretch these categories to encom-

---

1.   *Sears, Roebuck & Co. v. Stiffel Co.*, 376 U.S. 225 (1964); *Compco Corp. v. Day-Brite Lighting, Inc.*, 376 U.S. 234 (1964); *Bonito Boats, Inc. v. Thunder Craft Boats, Inc.*, 489 U.S. 141 (1989). An apparent exception involves trade secrets, which are created by State law. However, for these purposes, trade secrecy is not a form of intellectual property protection; federal policy lets inventors can keep their work secret if they want to (*Kewanee Oil Co. v. Bicron Corp.*, 416 U.S. 470 (1974)).

pass new technologies. For example, in 1980 the U.S. Supreme Court narrowly upheld a patent on a genetically engineered bacterium that eats oil slicks, thus ruling that life forms can be patented.[2] This decision opened the door to a broad range of other life forms. Famous biological products that were later patented included a reproducible cell line, the Moore line, and the Harvard Medical School oncomouse, both used in cancer research. The cell line was controversial not because of its patentability, but rather because of who owned it. The eponymous patient, John Moore, claimed that he himself should own it, since the cell line originated in his body.[3] The oncomouse, being a mammal, was a particularly charming life form, which helped to revive the moral debate about whether life forms should be patentable.[4] The oncomouse has also been patented in Europe, Japan, and Australia, but not in Canada.

These subject matters are controversial mainly for philosophical reasons. Since this is an economics book, we will put aside the moral and philosophical issues and stick to incentives. Would the incentives to develop and use the Moore line be different if John Moore had a blocking right in the cell line, while the researchers had a blocking right in their development of it? Is there anything fundamentally different about bacteria and mice from, for example, computer software? To the extent that they are different in germane ways, is patent law set up to accommodate those differences? Those are the types of issues that the rest of the book will equip us to address.

Another furor over subject matter arose in 1998 when the Court of Appeals for the Federal Circuit clarified the status of business-method patents. It upheld a patent for a method of calculating and managing the net value of mutual funds, using strong affirmative language that any "method" that "produces a useful, concrete and tangible result" was patentable even if not dependent on a particular device.[5]

---

2. *Diamond v. Chakrabarty*, 447 U.S. 303 (1980).

3. *Moore v. Regents of the University of California*, 793 P.2d 479, 271 Cal. Rptr. 146 (1990). The cell line was developed by researchers at UCLA and assigned to the University of California. The court rejected the theory that Moore should own the cell line, while acknowledging complications due to a physician's obligation to disclose his or her intentions.

4. You can visit the mouse at www.hms.harvard.edu/news/images/onco_mouse.jpg.

5. *State St. Bank & Trust Co. v. Signature Fin. Group, Inc.* 149 F.3d 1368 (Fed. Cir. 1998).

Business-method patents have been particularly criticized for issuing on trivial or well-known methods. U.S. patent 5,794,207 describes a method for conducting a Dutch (descending-bid) auction. This selling technique has been in use for centuries. Since the Dutch auction was well known, why did it merit a patent? A legal response may be that the use or implementation of the Dutch auction meets the requirements of patent law. However, an economic inquiry would ask whether the requirements of patent law make sense. Is the patent necessary to elicit this implementation? If not, doesn't the patent on a well-known method hurt consumers rather than help them, as well as being an affront to common sense? How should the requirements of novelty and nonobviousness be interpreted to avoid mistakes? We return to business methods below, and to the more general questions in chapters 4 and 5.

The second requirement for patentability is utility—that is, an invention must offer some positive benefit to society (§101). Historically, this requirement was usually invoked against devices that either did not work (e.g., perpetual-motion machines) or were against public policy (e.g., gambling devices). Today, the rule is mainly used to deny patents to drugs that have not been shown to be safe and effective or to chemical compounds whose only known use involves research and experimentation. It has also been used to rein in the patenting of gene sequences, where utility is interpreted to mean that the function of the DNA fragment must be known.[6] A related requirement (§112) is that the invention must be "enabling" and, according to the Supreme Court, "reduced to practice."[7]

The remaining two requirements withhold protection from inventions that produce only trivial or nonexistent advances over existing knowledge. Novelty asks whether the patent's teaching has been previously used or described in a single publication (§101). Similarly, nonobviousness asks whether the invention differs from the "prior art" in ways that would not have been obvious to somebody who had "ordinary skill" in the technology. During the 1940s, the U.S. Supreme Court set a very restrictive standard by declaring that inventions could only be

---

6. *Ex Parte Deuel* 27 USPQ2d 1360 (Bd. Pat. App. & Inf. 1993).
7. The Supreme Court ruled in *Reed v. Cutter* 1 Story 590 (1841) that "an imperfect and incomplete invention . . . not actually reduced to practice and embodied in some distinct machinery, apparatus, manufacture, or composition of matter, is not, and indeed cannot be, patentable under our patent acts."

patented if they evidenced a "flash of creative genius."[8] Congress overruled this interpretation by statute in 1952. Today, even trivial inventions qualify, but even current standards ignore the costs of invention.[9]

Duration All statutory intellectual property rights eventually expire. The maximum duration of a patent is twenty years from the date of filing, although patent life can be truncated earlier by a failure to pay maintenance fees (called renewal fees in Europe).[10] The property right that lasts twenty years is in the knowledge needed to make and use the protected object, as opposed to the object itself. The patent holder's right to control individual objects that embody the invention expires as soon as he or she sells them. This doctrine is called the first-sale rule.

Breadth As a formal legal matter, infringement must be established with respect to one of the several "claims" in the patent document. Claims are chosen by the applicant and patent examiner as minimal combinations of elements that qualify for protection, and any missing element saves the offending product from infringement. To infringe, the accused product must embody every element of at least one claim.

The patent monopoly would be meaningless if limited exactly to the original invention. In that case, even trivial changes would allow competitors to appropriate the patent's insights without paying royalties. Although breadth is not a legal term of art, patent law implicitly creates such a concept in the "doctrine of equivalents,"[11] by which the patent claim is deemed to cover any product that "does the same work in substantially the same way to accomplish substantially the same result." As we will see in chapter 4, economists have defined breadth in ways that do not always track legal concepts and court decisions.

Exemptions and Defenses If the rightholder asserts rights that do not meet the foregoing requirements, a defense to infringement might be that the patent is invalid. Beyond this, there are five basic groups of defenses.

---

8.   *Cuno Engineering Corp. v. Automatic Devices Corp.*, 314 U.S. 1 (1941).
9.   *Graham v. John Deere Co.*, 383 U.S. 1 (1966).
10.   35 USC §154(c). Prior to 1994, the maximum patent life was seventeen years after the date of issue. Congress changed the rule in accordance with the TRIPS treaty discussed in chapter 11.
11.   *Graver Tank & MFG Co. v. Linde Air Products Co.* 339 U.S. 605, 70 S. Ct. 854, 94 L.Ed. 1097 (1950). *Autogiro Co. of America v. United States*, 181 Ct. Cl. 55, 384 F.2d 391 (Ct. Cl. 1967).

The first group of defenses make sure that patent monopolies only go to inventors who make full and timely disclosures. For example, the originality requirement (§116) says that applicants cannot receive a patent on someone else's invention. Similarly, the abandonment, on-sale bar, and first-use rules, in §102, force inventors to file their applications (if at all) within one year after they start to exploit the invention. Finally, the enablement requirement states that the patent application must describe the invention clearly enough so that somebody "with ordinary skill in the art can make and use it without undue experimentation."[12] Despite this requirement, most patents are obscure and hard to read. Empirical studies show that corporations rarely bother to monitor—much less learn from—newly issued patents.

The second group of defenses applies when patent holders "misuse" their patents. The misuse defense is often used in conjunction with an alleged antitrust violation. However, courts also apply the misuse concept to practices that extend the patent holder's rights beyond the "careful balance between monopoly and free usage" set by Congress.[13] Trying to interpret this language is a lawyer's and economist's nightmare, but examples may include patent licenses that require the licensee to pay royalties for unpatented products; licenses that require royalty payments after the patent expires; and licenses that require the licensee to grant back intellectual property rights to any improvements.[14] At least in theory, a misuse defense is not permanent. Instead, patent holders can change their conduct and wait for the effects to dissipate.

---

12.   Scarce inputs (e.g., microorganisms) needed to practice the invention must also be made public (*In re Wands*, 858 F.2d 731 (Fed. Cir. 1988)). There are several repositories where patented microorganisms are stored.

13.   *Brulotte v. Thys*, 379 U.S. 29 (1964).

14.   See, for example, *Zenith Radio Corp. v. Hazeltine Rsch., Inc.* 395 U.S. 100 (1969) (contract requiring licensee to pay royalties based on total sales regardless of whether patent was actually used constitutes "misuse"); *Brulotte v. Thys*, 379 U.S. 29 (1964) (contract requiring licensee to pay royalties after expiration of the patent constitutes "misuse"); *Morton Salt Co. v. G.S. Suppiger Co.*, 314 U.S. 488 (1942) (contract requiring licensee to purchase unpatented salt tablets for use in patented machine constitutes "misuse"); *Transparent-Wrap Mach. Corp. v. Stokes & Smith*, 329 U.S. 637 (1947) (license-back provision is not per se illegal, but may be unacceptably anticompetitive depending on the circumstances). A license agreement can provide for perpetual royalties if the licensed technology contains both patented and trade-secret information. This is because trade-secret protection can theoretically last forever (*Aronson v. Quick Point Pencil*, 440 U.S. 257 (1979)).

The third group of defenses consist of judge-made exemptions in cases where the infringer's conduct is socially beneficial. The repair exemption lets customers maintain patented machinery.[15] In the past there has also been a restricted research exemption, allowing researchers to use patented inventions for noncommercial research or experimentation. Even for commercial research, the extent to which innovators should control the innovations that build on their contributions is a deep policy question; see chapter 5. In the case of research tools, some ability to collect royalties is obviously necessary, or there would be no incentive to create them (Eisenberg 1989). According to nineteenth-century case law, the research exemption only applied "for amusement, to satisfy idle curiosity, or for strictly philosophical inquiry." The main users of this exemption have been universities. In the growing climate of commercialization of university research (see chapters 1 and 8), the boundary between commerce and philosophical inquiry has become blurred, and the research exemption has largely been abolished.[16]

The fourth group of defenses is designed to keep patent owners from playing fast and loose with the federal court system and PTO. For example, the doctrines of laches and estoppel prevent patent holders from deferring enforcement or making misleading assurances that encourage infringers to run up more damages. Similarly, the statute of limitation (§286) requires patent owners to bring suit (if at all) within six years. Patent applicants must also meet minimal standards of honesty vis-à-vis the PTO. For example, file-wrapper estoppel prevents patent holders from reinterpreting ambiguous patents in ways that contradict previous statements to the PTO. Similarly, the duty of candor requires applicants to volunteer information about facts (e.g., prior art) that might make their patents unenforceable. Applicants who actively mislead examiners are also subject to a fraudulent procurement defense. Many scholars complain that the last two defenses have been counterproductive, since they encourage patent applicants to avoid research that might uncover inconvenient facts. In theory, the PTO could fix the problem by

---

15. *FMC Corp. v. Up-Rights, Inc.*, 21 F.3d 1073 (Fed. Cir. 1994).

16. In 2002, the Court of Appeals for the Federal Circuit ruled that the research exemption did not depend on whether a particular institution "is engaged in an endeavor for commercial gain, so long as the act is in furtherance of the alleged infringer's legitimate business" (*Madey v. Duke*, 307 F.3d 1351 (Fed. Cir. 2002)). In this case, the court found that Duke's legitimate business was education and research, which apparently disqualifies universities whether or not they reserve the right to earn revenues from research.

requiring inventors to conduct reasonable searches before they apply for a patent.

Finally, it sometimes happens that two inventors apply for, and even receive, separate patents for the same invention. When the telephone was invented, an independent inventor, Elisha Gray, arrived at the patent office with his application a mere two hours after Alexander Graham Bell filed his application on February 14, 1876. As related by Flatow (1992), if Gray had believed in the commercial value of his device, he could have written an application earlier and preempted Bell. But even after Gray lost the race to the patent office, the commercial value was unclear and his attorneys advised him not to pursue a priority dispute. Suppose, however, that he had done so; how would (or should) the priority dispute have been resolved? This is an area where U.S. law differs from that of most of the rest of the world. In the United States, priority is given to the first inventor, and elsewhere to the first inventor to file an application.[17]

Under most patent laws, governments can suspend rights during times of national need. During World War I, the U.S. military browbeat airplane companies into cross-licensing each other and suspended all radio patents. The United States also seized 5,000 German chemical patents, including aspirin, and licensed them to American manufacturers.[18] This right to nullify or modify patent rights when necessary for the public interest is also preserved in the TRIPS agreement discussed in chapter 11.

Relief   The rights conferred by intellectual property are only valuable if exclusive use of the intellectual property can be enforced. The main tools that courts use to punish infringers are money damages, paid by the infringer to the rightholder, and injunctions, which are court orders against further infringement.

---

17.   As we have mentioned, it is only patent law that works against independent inventors, and it is not obvious that the rule against independent invention is the optimal one; see Maurer and Scotchmer 2002. The difference between the first-to-file and first-to-invent rules is particularly important in cases of cumulative invention; see Scotchmer and Green 1990. The first-to-file rule can encourage inventors to choose patents over trade secrecy.

18.   After the war, Germany's patents were used to establish a Chemical Foundation to advance science and industry. In 1932, the foundation earned almost $9 million in royalties.

Courts have used two calculations for money damages, investigated further in chapter 7. The concept currently in favor is "lost profit," the idea being restoration.[19] Where the invention has been widely licensed, restoration means paying the standard royalty rate. The calculation is harder if the rightholder had no intention of licensing, or if licenses were intended but no licensing contracts had been made. In the latter case, courts must try to construct a "reasonable royalty" that willing parties would have agreed to in the course of a hypothetical negotiation.[20] In theory, courts can increase damages up to three times the actual injury if the infringer acted intentionally or in bad faith.[21] In practice, potential infringers can usually immunize themselves by obtaining competent legal advice before they use the invention.[22]

Patent holders can also obtain court orders against infringement before or after trial (§283). Courts grant preliminary injunctions where there is (1) a strong probability of success on the merits, and (2) a likelihood of "irreparable injury" if no injunction is granted.[23] In theory, courts will not grant a preliminary injunction if the defendant is likely to suffer "disproportionate hardship."[24] When preliminary injunctions are granted in high fixed-cost industries, such as semiconductors, they create a danger of bankruptcy. Observers claim that plaintiffs who obtain preliminary injunctions frequently extract much larger settlements than they would ever receive in damages. Fear of injunctions has produced

---

19.   35 USC §284; see also *SmithKline Diagnostics, Inc. v. Helena Labs. Corp.*, 926 F.2d 1161, 1163 (Fed. Cir. 1991).

20.   See *Georgia-Pacific Corp. v. United States Plywood Corp.*, 318 F.Supp. 1116 (S.D.N.Y. 1970). *Georgia-Pacific* tried to make the analysis more predictable by recommending ten "factors" (e.g., remaining patent life; the invention's advantages over rival technologies) that courts should consider before arriving at an estimate. Despite this, analyses of reasonable royalties remain inconsistent from case to case.

21.   35 USC §284; see also *Roberts v. Sears, Roebuck & Co.*, 723 F.2d 1324 (7th Cir. 1983).

22.   *SRI International, Inc. v. Advanced Technology Labs., Inc.*, 127 F.3d 1462 (Fed. Cir. 1997); *Kalman v. Berlyn Corp.*, 914 F.2d 1473 (Fed. Cir. 1990).

23.   *GenDerm Corp. v. Ferndale Labs., Inc.*, 32 USPQ 1567 (E.D. Mich. 1994). The concept of "irreparable injury" does not seem useful to many economists, since most harms can be compensated by enough cash. Courts usually issue injunctions when either the patent holder is about to go out of business, or damages are likely to be late, uncertain, or difficult to prove.

24.   *PPG Indus., Inc. v. Guardian Indus. Corp.*, 75 F.3d 1558 (Fed. Cir. 1996) (preliminary injunction withheld where plaintiff would not lose significant revenues and defendant's business would be shut down).

socially wasteful arms races in which companies acquire massive patent portfolios for the sole purpose of deterring each other (Hall and Ziedonis 2001).[25]

Patent holders who win at trial can obtain permanent injunctions.[26] Courts are usually willing to grant this relief because it encourages licensing talks and also makes future damages estimates unnecessary. Nevertheless, courts sometimes refuse to issue an injunction where there are broader public interests at stake.[27]

Quality of Patents   In the beginning of the U.S. patent system, Thomas Jefferson examined patent applications in his role as secretary of state. When his duties regarding foreign policy became more onerous, the examination system lapsed into a registration system. Patents were issued to anyone who could pay the $35 application fee (Ryan 1998, 32). Critics complained that the system produced low-quality patents that encroached on the public domain, encouraged baseless litigation, and defrauded investors. In the 1830s, Congress created the PTO to screen patents before they issue. Today, quality is controlled by professional examiners. Examiners are always scientists or engineers; they may also be attorneys. Among other things, examiners are supposed to search the literature to make sure that the invention is actually new, examine the application to make sure it meets the legal requirements for patentability, and ask the applicant to answer questions or amend the application to surrender overbroad claims.

Many scholars have criticized the examination system based on the suspicion that examination has been captured by industry, that examiners are rewarded for approving as many applications as possible, and that examiners have a poor track record of finding relevant prior art. On the other hand, there is a question as to how much examination is optimal. (See, e.g., Merges 1999 and Lemley 2001.)

---

25.   Even then, deterrence can break down if one side—usually called a "troll"—does not operate an active business. Trolls do not care whether they are enjoined or not.

26.   *Kearns v. Chrysler Corp.*, 32 F.3d 1541 (Fed. Cir. 1994).

27.   *Datascope Corp. v. Kontron, Inc.*, 786 F.2d 398 (Fed. Cir. 1986) (refusing to grant permanent injunction in medical-device case where practicing physicians preferred to use infringing product); see also *Jenn Air v. Modern Maid Co.*, 499 F.Supp. 320 (D. Del. 1980) (courts may withhold preliminary injunctions where infringing product relates to health care, environment, or other critical public interests).

In the 1990s, the PTO and courts expanded patentable subject matter to include computer software,[28] which then became controversial largely because of what were perceived as "low-quality patents" (Barton 2000; Lemley 2001; Hall 2003). "Low quality" refers to the PTO's failure to screen out applications that do not meet the requirements for patentabilty, especially as to prior art. Since patents on computer software emerged rather precipitously (software had previously been protected by copyright), most of the prior art was not in the main database consulted by patent examiners, which is prior patents. Instead the prior art was largely to be found in industry practice, in existing computer programs, and to some extent in academic publications. All of these are harder to search than prior patents.

In principle, a rival inventor or other member of the public can file a protest if he believes that the PTO is about to issue a defective patent. Because PTO proceedings tend to be invisible, this rarely happens. After the patent issues, reexamination can be requested by any member of the public at any point in the life of the patent. This is an area where the United States and Europe differ. The analogous proceeding in Europe is an "opposition" to the patent, which must be filed in the European Patent Office (a consolidated patent office discussed in chapter 11) within nine months after issuance. The opposition is a more adversarial proceeding than reexamination in the United States. In the United States close to half of reexaminations are initiated by the patentees themselves, whereas in Europe this almost never happens (Graham et al. 2003). European oppositions are more frequent and more often result in modification or revocation of the patent.[29]

---

28. During the 1970s, the U.S. Supreme Court suggested that computer software was a "mathematical algorithm" that could not be patented (*Gottschalk v. Benson*, 409 U.S. 63 (1972)). However, lower-court decisions have pointed out that a computer running software is akin to a physical machine. Today, most software can be patented if it produces a "tangible, useful result" (*In re Alappat*, 33 F.3d 1526 (Fed. Cir. 1994)).

29. Merges (1999) estimates from 1995 data that about 7 percent of European patents trigger opposition proceedings, and only about 0.3 percent of U.S. patents trigger reexaminations. Graham et al. (2002) show a slightly greater discrepancy, 8 percent and 0.2 percent. The latter also find that the opposition and reexamination rates are substantially lower than average in the semiconductor, software, and computing industries, and higher in biomedicine. Both these studies find that patents are much more likely to be revoked in an opposition proceeding (between 35 percent and 50 percent) than in a reexamination proceeding (roughly 10 percent).

3.2   Copyright

Copyright gives rightholders the exclusive right to copy, reproduce, distribute, adapt, perform, or display their works. The right is much narrower than a patent, because copyright only protects expression.[30] For example, you cannot copy *Gone with the Wind*, but you can write a book about a Southern belle, her roguish lover, and the Burning of Atlanta. More precisely, copyright does not protect ideas, procedures, discoveries, or methods of operation (17 USC §102(b)).

Covered Subject Matter   Copyright law protects "original works of authorship fixed in any tangible medium of expression" (§102(a)). Examples include literature, music, drama, dance, pantomime, graphics, sculpture, movies, sound recordings, and architecture. Copyright also extends to anthologies and other compilations (§103(a)). Unlike patent law, copyrighted works do not have to meet the so-called novelty standard.[31] They must, however, show minimal creativity. This means that simple databases (e.g., telephone directories) cannot be copyrighted under U.S. law.[32]

Breadth and Duration   In general, copyright breadth is set by the doctrine of "comprehensive nonliteral similarity." This prevents an infringer from avoiding liability by making mechanical changes to a short story, such as changing the names of the characters, or arbitrary changes to software code, such as renaming the variables or reordering the pieces.[33] Congress has also expanded breadth to include so-called derivative works that exploit preexisting publications. The concept includes, inter alia, sequels and translations (§103(a)).

Copyright makes up for its narrow breadth by having an exceptionally long duration. Protection starts when a work is published and continues until seventy years after the author's death (§302). Like patent holders, copyright owners cannot assert rights in particular physical copies after the first sale, although this too is changing as vendors have started to license the use of copies rather than sell them (see chapter 6).

---

30.   *Whelan Assocs., Inc. v. Jaslow Dental Lab., Inc.,* 799 F.2d 1222 (3rd Cir. 1986).
31.   *E. Mischan & Sons, Inc. v. Maycana, Inc.,* 662 F.Supp. 1339, 1340–43 (S.D.N.Y. 1987).
32.   *Feist Publications, Inc. v. Rural Telephone Service Co., Inc.,* 499 U.S. 340 (1991).
33.   See, for example, *Castle Rock Enter. v. Carol Pub. Group, Inc.,* 150 F.3d 132, 140 (2d Cir. 1998).

Exemptions and Defenses   Courts have recognized a "fair-use" defense to a charge of copyright infringement since the 1840s, and it is codified in the Copyright Act of 1976. This doctrine extends to comment, criticism, news reporting, scholarship, research, parody, library photocopying, and reverse engineering. Fair use is a common defense against infringement. For example, in the 1990s someone wrote a takeoff called *The Wind Done Gone*, written from the perspective of a slave, using the characters developed in *Gone with the Wind*. The heirs of the author of *Gone with the Wind* sued for infringement. The defense was fair use, and after various legal wranglings, the case settled.

Congress has told judges to consider four factors in deciding whether a use is fair or infringing: (1) the purpose and character of the defendant's use, (2) the nature of the copyrighted work, (3) the amount and substantiality of the materials copied, and (4) the effect of the copying on the plaintiff's potential market (§107). (Congress did not tell judges the objective, but only what to consider.)

In addition to defining fair use, Congress has also created exemptions for certain types of socially useful conduct. Typical examples include library patrons' right to make limited photocopies, computer users' right to archive software, and cable TV providers' right to retransmit commercial broadcasts (§111(f)). The right to rebroadcast is only available where the cable TV provider agrees to pay royalties under a compulsory license.

Defendants can also assert a defense if the copyright holder fails to satisfy certain formalities. These used to include placing a printed notice on copyrighted works and depositing copies in the U.S. Library of Congress. Most formalities were abolished after the U.S. joined the Berne Convention in 1989 (see chapter 11). However, copyright owners must still register their works with the government before filing suit for infringement (§412).

Finally, copyright shares various defenses with patent law. Examples include abandonment,[34] misuse,[35] and unclean hands.[36]

---

34.   *Pacific & S. Co. v. Duncan*, 572 F.Supp. 1186 (N.D. Ga. 1983).

35.   *Lasercomb America, Inc. v. Reynolds*, 911 F.2d 970 (4th Cir. 1990) (software contract that prohibited purchaser from creating a competing product was an unacceptable restraint of trade).

36.   See, for instance, *Rosemont Enters., Inc. v. Random House, Inc.*, 366 F.2d 303 (2d Cir. 1966) (litigant who purchased rights to infringing book in order to suppress a new biography was guilty of "unclean hands").

Relief   Copyright holders can seek actual damages based on the higher of their own lost profits or the infringer's earnings (§504). Alternatively, copyright owners can seek statutory damages of up to $30,000 for each infringement, or $150,000 if the infringement is willful. Statutory damages allow owners to enforce their copyrights where damages would be minimal or hard to prove. Courts can also issue preliminary and permanent injunctions to prevent future copying. (The publisher of *The Wind Done Gone* was initially enjoined by a district court from distributing copies, but the preliminary injunction was overturned by a higher court before the case settled.)

Finally, copyright infringers are subject to criminal penalties. The maximum for first-time offenders is $25,000 in fines and one year in jail. Until fairly recently, these penalties were limited to infringement done for "commercial advantage or private financial gain." Congress changed the rule in 1996 after ideologically motivated hackers began to distribute stolen software over the Internet free of charge.[37] Today, criminal penalties are available against anyone who reproduces or distributes more than $1,000 worth of copyrighted works within a single 180-day period (§102(a)). Copyright owners can also ask the court to impound or destroy infringing items.

Variations   Copyright has less of a one-size-fits-all character than patents do. Congress has periodically created industry-specific statutes featuring one-of-a-kind breadth, duration, and/or defenses. Examples of this sui generis approach include statutes protecting analog sound recordings, semiconductor chips, and boat hulls. Unlike normal copyright, protection under the last two statutes expires after ten years.[38] The Semiconductor Chip Protection Act also has a special, fair-use-type exemption that permits reverse engineering for the purpose of developing an improved chip, but not for the purpose of cloning the original chip. The Boat Hull Protection Act contains a similar exemption for "teaching."

Congress has also experimented with legislation that sets royalty rates and forces companies to adopt technical safeguards against unauthorized copying. For example, the Audio Home Recording Act (1992) requires any company that manufactures, distributes, or imports digital

---

37.   *U.S. v. LaMacchia*, 871 F.Supp. 535 (D. Mass. 1994).
38.   17 USC §904(b) (Semiconductor Chip Protection Act); 17 USC §1305(a) (Boat Hull Protection Act).

recorders to pay a 2 percent royalty on each unit (3 percent for tape manufacturers). Industry members are supposed to split the proceeds through voluntary agreements and must defer to the Librarian of Congress if they cannot agree (§1007). (The Librarian of Congress plays a similar role under various copyright statutes.) The act also supports technical protections by requiring manufacturers to install a Serial Copy Management System (SCMS) in each unit shipped. SCMS examines each piece of music to see whether it contains a copyright notice; if so, it attaches a digital notice telling other SCMS machines not to make further copies. This keeps consumers from making copies of copies.[39]

Finally, under the Digital Millennium Copyright Act (1998), §1002(c), copyright owners can collect damages from manufacturers who fail to pay royalties or sell circumvention technologies. This is discussed in chapter 7.

3.3   Trade Secrets

Trade-secret law protects individuals and businesses against the "misappropriation of trade secrets by improper means." It is state courts, not Congress or federal courts, that created the law of trade secrecy as an extension of traditional contract and tort principles. To rationalize the resulting inconsistencies, thirty-four state legislatures have passed some version of the Uniform Trade Secrets Act (UTSA), designed to summarize, and in some cases change, judge-made case law. In general, our discussion follows UTSA.

Covered Technologies   A trade secret can include any information that (1) derives economic value from not being readily known to, or ascertainable by, others, (2) whose owner has taken reasonable steps to keep it secret, and (3) is not publicly available. Unlike patents, a trade secret does not have to be novel or even relate to a particular technology.[40]

---

39.   17 USC §1002(a)(2). The statute does not even try to describe the complicated SCMS system. Details can be found in *Recording Indus. Assn. of America, Inc. v. Diamond Multimedia Systems, Inc.* 29 F.Supp. 2d 624 (C.D. Cal. 1998).

40.   *Sinclair v. Aquarius Electronics, Inc.* 42 Cal.App.3d 216, 184 USPQ 682 (1974) (trade secrets need not be patentable); *Choisser Rsch. Corp. v. Electronic Vision Corp.*, 173 USQPQ 234 (Cal. Super. 1972) (trade secrets include "slight advances").

Almost any information, including financial data and customer lists, qualifies.

Duration and Breadth   In principle, a company can keep anything secret, potentially forever. Some secrets, such as the formula for Coca-Cola, have demonstrated remarkable longevity, even if not yet infinite. In practice, most secrets leak out after a few years. This is particularly true of product designs, which usually become obvious once a device is displayed, advertised, or sold to consumers.

Defenses and Exemptions   Trade-secret law recognizes three broad groups of defenses to a charge of misappropriating a trade secret. First, defendants can claim that the information they took was not a trade secret and/or that the owner did not take reasonable steps to protect it. In practice, this usually means showing that the owner failed to adopt normal precautions like nondisclosure agreements, physical security, and computer passwords.

Second, the defendant may argue that he or she received the secret by means that were not improper. If Claude receives the secret from Blair who stole it from Alan, but Claude does not know that it was stolen, then Claude is not liable and cannot be enjoined from using the secret. Improper means of receiving the secret include criminal conduct (e.g., theft, bribery, espionage, fraud, or electronic surveillance), torts, and other noncriminal acts like breaching contracts, violating confidential relationships, or persuading others to do so.

Finally, courts sometimes refuse to enforce trade-secret claims on public-policy grounds. For example, competitors can reverse engineer products to find out how they work,[41] although they can waive this right by contract.[42] Courts also invoke public policy to limit the enforcement of trade secrets against former employees. This usually means that agreements to protect the secret cannot unreasonably restrict the employee's right to earn a living. Instead, restrictions must be limited as to both time and geography.

---

41.   *Acuson Corp. v. Aloka Co.*, 209 Cal.App.3d 425, 10 USPQ2d 1814 (1989); *Futurecraft v. Clary Corp.*, 205 Cal.App.2d 279 (1962).

42.   Manufacturers can also discourage reverse engineering by using technical measures. Common examples include encasing key electronic components in epoxy, shipping software without human-readable "source code," and retaining physical control over leased equipment in the field.

Relief   Trade-secret owners are entitled to damages for past injury. These are usually based on the higher of the owner's lost profits or defendant's earnings as a result of his or her misappropriation.[43] Punitive damages are also available.[44]

Trade-secret owners can also seek preliminary and permanent injunctions against future use of the secret. Generally speaking, such injunctions must terminate as soon as the secret becomes public. However, courts sometimes allow the injunction to continue for a "limited, reasonable period" if stealing the secret gave the defendant a head start in using the technology.[45]

Effects on Commerce   Unlike all other forms of intellectual property, trade-secret law allows owners to suppress knowledge. Nevertheless, the law encourages the sharing and sale of secrets. For example, owners can share the secret with potential buyers under a nondisclosure agreement.

3.4   Miscellaneous Rights

Design Patents   Traditional patents must show utility—that is, they have to produce tangible results in the physical world. In 1842, Congress created a second statute to protect purely decorative products. This design-patent statute covers any product that is new, original, nonobvious, and ornamental (35 USC §171). Design patents expire after fourteen years (§173).

Unfair Competition   Federal courts sometimes use the doctrine of unfair competition to block copying that would destroy the incentives for producing a given product in the first place.[46] The main strength of this approach is that—unlike most forms of intellectual property—it invites judges to apply economic reasoning.

Plant-Protection Statutes   The Plant Patent Act (1930), 35 USC §163, extends patent protection to anyone who discovers and asexually

---

43.   See, for example, *Morlife, Inc. v. Perry*, 56 Cal.App.4th 1514 (1997).
44.   See, for instance, *Robert L. Cloud & Associates, Inc. v. Mikesell*, 69 Cal.App.4th 1141 (1999). UTSA limits punitive awards to two times actual damages.
45.   See, for example, *USM Corp. v. Mason Fastener Corp.*, 467 N.E.2d 1271 (1984).
46.   *International News Service v. Associated Press*, 248 U.S. 215 (1918); *National Basketball Assn. v. Motorola, Inc.*, 105 F.3d 841 (2d Cir. 1997).

reproduces new types of plants. Similarly, the Plant Variety Protection Act (1970), §2321 et seq., gives breeders the exclusive right to sell, market, or offer sexually reproduced plants for a period of twenty years. The act also contains a broad exemption for private, noncommercial use (§2541).

Database Rights   Databases are becoming increasingly central to both science and commerce, especially in the Internet age. Almost every query to an Internet website retrieves data from a database. U.S. copyright law does not protect databases that are deemed "noncreative."[47] However, the European Union has adopted a sui generis copyright law for databases[48] and has pressed the United States to follow suit. Although for a time it seemed likely that Congress would pass some type of database legislation, the debate has quieted as of this writing. One policy question is whether protection should require creativity, since the costliness of assembling a database may not depend on its creative content. On the other hand, there are many informal ways to protect databases—for example, by restricting how much information a user can download, or by updating the database at regular intervals. In practice, there is little or no evidence that lack of protection has impeded the creation of new databases.

3.5   The Problem of Disclosure

Chapter 2 stressed the public-goods nature of knowledge. To get the full benefits from new knowledge, the knowledge must be used. Knowledge has two main uses: to end users, usually through new products, and as a foundation for future discoveries. That is, knowledge can be used for consumption or research.

In the case of patents, where independent invention is not a defense to infringement, the patented technology must be disclosed so that rivals and courts know what is protected. Disclosure also ensures that the knowledge enters the public domain when the patent expires. Lawyers refer to the knowledge that is thus provided as the "teaching" of the patent. While patents are in force, patent holders have an almost absolute

---

47.   *Feist Publications, Inc. v. Rural Telephone Service Co., Inc.*, 499 U.S. 340 (1991).

48.   Council Directive No. 96/9/EC, O.J.L 77/20 (1996). For a discussion of the issues here, see Maurer and Scotchmer 1999.

right to control uses of the knowledge they have created. In contrast, for traditional copyrighted works, there has been no need for a disclosure requirement, since written expression is self-disclosing.

The patent holders' rights to control the new knowledge they disclose is hard to enforce. The underpowered airplane designed and patented by the Wright brothers (U.S. patent 821,393) could only fly because they had figured out that propellers work on an airfoil principle, like wings. Using the data they had derived for the wing in windtunnel experiments, they were then able to optimize the shape and position of the propeller (Wainfan 2003). If the Wright brothers had claimed all uses of the knowledge in their patent, and if the PTO had granted the claim, they would have had an easier time enforcing their patent against other patent holders and airplane designers. However, it is hard to protect a physical principle such as the knowledge that a propeller works as an airfoil, even if claimed. The airfoil principle is at work in every propeller, and propellers had long been in use, even if the physical principle that makes them work was not well understood.

A design invention such as how to position a propeller on an airplane is also difficult to protect as a trade secret. Nevertheless, inventors generally prefer to avoid disclosure, because it is difficult to protect all of the knowledge disclosed in a patent. Trade secrecy is especially attractive if the inventor thinks that the trade secret would never leak out and never be rediscovered independently by someone else. However, choosing trade secrecy undermines the well-thought-out objectives of the patent system. The invention will not become public in the timely manner contemplated by the designers of the patent statute, and the knowledge may not be used to further the research of rivals in the meantime.

Many innovations can be protected alternatively as trade secrets or by patents. However, computer software has the distinction of having three types of protection available: trade secrecy, patents, and copyright. The system seems incoherent in that the three types of protection demand different disclosures. The most anomalous of these is copyright. When programmers register their code at the copyright office, they are allowed to suppress large amounts of it—that is, the intellectual property right provides for secrecy rather than disclosure. In contrast, patents require disclosure, although typically not of code. The disclosure would typically concern structural aspects of the program, but even there, critics complain that the disclosure is insufficient. And, of course, if programmers rely on trade secrecy, distributing the program in compiled form, they disclose nothing. They may be vulnerable to reverse engineering, which is possible from the compiled program, but that is costly and unreliable for complicated programs.[49]

Congress has occasionally recognized that sharing knowledge should be an explicit policy goal. The Semiconductor Chip Protection Act of 1984, which creates a sui generis form of protection for computer chips, grants a right to reverse engineer the circuitry on chips to get at the embodied knowledge, but prohibits the use of that knowledge for cloning. The knowledge can be used to make improved chips, with the required improvement left for interpretation by the courts. As we will see in chapter 5, these provisions operate very much like the economists' interpretation of breadth.

3.6   Breadth and the Required Inventive Step

In anticipation of the models and incentive issues to be investigated in chapters 4 and 5, we draw attention to two particularly important policy levers of intellectual property law, which we will call the required inventive step, and the breadth of the right. The required inventive step governs which innovations are protectable, and the breadth governs how different another product must be to avoid infringement. In chapter 5 we will sort out their respective economic roles. Many discussions of patent incentives conflate these two policy levers into one lever, assuming that an innovation that has a large enough inventive step to be protected will automatically escape infringement, and an invention that escapes infringement has a large enough inventive step to be patentable. This is incorrect as a matter of law, at least for patents, and has economic implications.[50]

In patent law, the required inventive step and the breadth follow from the requirements of novelty and nonobviousness, as interpreted in

---

49.   For general and comprehensive discussions of how computer software is protected, see Samuelson et al. 1994 and Menell 2002. For the role of reverse engineering, see Samuelson and Scotchmer 2002.
50.   When first studying these issues, Scotchmer and Green (1990) assumed that the two criteria—noninfringement and patentability—coincide. Subsequent inquiries, such as Green and Scotchmer 1995, and especially Scotchmer 1996 and Denicolò 2002, make a clear distinction between these two policy instruments. Scotchmer (1996) argues that in the donut of case B in figure 3.1, where a new product is infringing, the owner of B is better off if the new product is not patentable because that increases B's bargaining power in the licensing negotiation. See Lemley 1997 for a discussion of how patents and copyrights differ as to blocking possibilities.

case law. The required inventive step must be such that the innovation is not obvious to one skilled in the art. The breadth is governed by the doctrine of equivalents.

In copyright law, particularly as it relates to the traditional subject matter of literary works, paintings, and other art, almost any work is protectable—the requirement of inventive step is not onerous. However, the property right is also narrow. Copyright protects against copying, and, aside from the fact that the copyright protects against mechanical changes, there is no notion of equivalents that extends the breadth beyond the expression.

Comparing patent law to copyright (to the extent that they can be compared, since they cover different subject matters), patent law imposes a more serious requirement as to inventive step, grants more breadth, and is shorter than copyright.

Figure 3.1 shows two different patents, for products A and B, each understood to be at the center of a product space. Each point in the surrounding territory represents a different substitute product. The inner sphere around product A encloses the substitute products that are infringing due to supposed "equivalence"—it represents the patent's breadth. The outer sphere encloses the substitute products that have become "prior art" due to their similarity to A and that do not embody an inventive step necessary to receive a patent. The donut represents products that are noninfringing but also unpatentable, which will presumably be supplied by a competitive fringe, constraining the profit earned by the owner of product A.

For product B, the spheres are reversed. The inner circle encloses the substitute products that are barred from patentability by prior art,

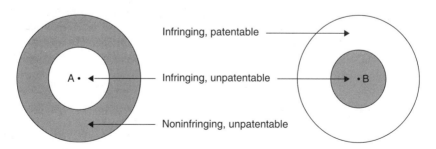

Figure 3.1
Patent A: Narrow; large required inventive step
Patent B: Broad; small required inventive step

whereas the outer circle encloses the products that are infringing. In example B, there will be products that are infringing but patentable, which means that so-called blocking patents may occur. A patent received by another innovator will be blocked by the owner of B, since it infringes the patent on B. A license is required to market it.

To illustrate these ideas, consider the laser. As described by the inventor Charles Townes (1999), there were two related technologies, the maser and the laser, which use the same principle to create coherent electromagnetic waves, microwaves in the case of the maser or light waves in the case of the laser. Coherence means that all the photons have the same direction and frequency, and is the property that concentrates energy. Laser technology grew out of the maser technology but presented different technical difficulties.

The patent on the maser was deliberately written broadly enough to include all similar means of creating coherent electromagnetic waves, including light waves. Townes did the work leading to the maser at Columbia University and assigned the patent to the Research Corporation, described chapter 1. After doing additional work, he obtained a patent on the laser and assigned it to Bell Labs. The Research Corporation later sued Bell Labs for infringement, when they used the laser without a license on the maser. The case was eventually settled, granting royalties from Bell Labs to the Research Corporation. The settlement was based on the assumption that the Research Corporation and Bell Labs had blocking patents on the laser. The laser infringed the maser patent, but was itself a patented invention, since it solved technical difficulties not described in the maser patent. In figure 3.1, the patented technology B would be the maser, and the laser would fall in the donut.

Which of the two patents in figure 3.1 implies a better incentive system? We have not equipped ourselves to answer that question, because we have said nothing about the costs of innovation or the welfare of consumers or the degree to which the innovator enables follow-on discoveries (but see chapter 5). However, even in this very simple model, it is possible to contemplate what we might mean by the "strength" or "protectiveness" of the patent.

A rightholder mainly gets protection by preventing rivals from marketing close substitutes. The right of rivals to market close substitutes is governed by breadth. However, the required inventive step also matters. For substitutes that are infringing, the patent holder will typically be better off if they are not patentable. He or she then controls the pricing of infringing substitutes and does not have to negotiate with another patent holder who has a blocking patent. For substitutes that are non-infringing, the patent holder will typically be better off if the substitute is supplied by another patent holder than if it is supplied by competitors, since prices will generally be higher if the market is controlled by two oligopolists. Thus, the arrangement that is best for the rightholder is a very broad patent so that close substitutes are infringing, and an inventive-step requirement that is coextensive with breadth. The patent holder's best position is when all infringing substitutes are unpatentable, and when all noninfringing substitutes are patentable.

How do these observations apply to business-method patents? The question should be posed from the society's perspective, not from the patent holder's perspective, and we are not yet ready to consider the question in its entirety. In the case of the Dutch-auction patent described earlier, critics pointed out the absurdity of allowing the patentee to restrict use of a well-known idea. It is presumably a mistake to give patents on technologies that the applicant did not invent, since the patents serve no incentive purpose. On the other hand, what if the patent is narrow? Narrow patents are not very harmful to competition, regardless of the required inventive step. Even if all the rival implementations are patented, the market for using Dutch auctions will be competitive if the patents are very narrow.[51]

This is not to argue that a low bar to patentability (low inventive step) is always harmless. In the Dutch auction, the patented products would be substitutes. In another famous example, that of semiconductor chips, the patented technologies are typically complements. Every innovator in the industry must obtain licenses from hundreds of previous rightholders. Merely as a matter of transaction costs, if nothing else, the need to license all these pieces may deter innovation. The transactions not only are expensive but take time and create uncertainty. This problem of many patented complements goes by various names,

---

51. Another example concerns insulating sleeves for paper cups that protect users from burning their fingers. Barton (2003) describes how minor changes in the pattern of dimples stamped into the sleeves have received patent protection. Indeed, it may be an affront to common sense that such insulating sleeves are patentable. However, it is hard to find the threat to competition unless the sleeves are mutually infringing. Similarly, there has been a proliferation of patents on paper clips throughout the twentieth century, continuing to the present (Petroski 1996). Does anyone feel unduly burdened by the high price of paper clips? Competition is saved by the fact that they are noninfringing.

including patent thickets and the anticommons.[52] We discuss it further in chapters 5 and 6.

3.7 Intellectual Property and Antitrust

For most practical purposes, U.S. antitrust law is found in sections 1 and 2 of the Sherman Act. Section 1 prohibits two or more competitors from forming "contracts, combinations or conspiracies in restraint of trade" (15 USC §1). Since 1911, courts have interpreted section 1 according to the "rule of reason." Section 2 applies to unilateral acts instead of conspiracies, and prohibits firms from acquiring or keeping a monopoly by improper means.

The main implication of section 1 is that business arrangements must promote competition, usually by creating technical efficiencies, more than they restrict it.[53] This is the rule-of-reason analysis. However, courts have also held that certain practices are clearly destructive and should always be illegal under section 1. These "per se" violations include horizontal price-fixing agreements, vertical agreements to set minimum prices, and geographic allocation of markets.

Section 2 does not make monopoly illegal but outlaws "wrongful acts" to maintain monopolies.[54] A section 2 violation can arise from attempted monopolization that falls short of its goal. A monopoly created by intellectual property is not illegal in itself. However, patents may offer tempting opportunities to engage in wrongful acts.

Courts have had a hard time reconciling the Sherman Act's hostility to cartels with the legal monopolies created by intellectual property. Nevertheless, firms cannot use their intellectual property any way they want to. As a judge has remarked, "That is no more correct than the proposition that use of one's personal property, such as a baseball bat, cannot give rise to tort liability."[55] The basic point is that sections 1 and 2 both require wrongful acts. Courts have been trying to define the dif-

---

52.   The term *anticommons* is a play on words and refers to the "tragedy of the commons," which is usually taught in freshman economics. In the tragedy of the commons, peasants in early modern Britain overgrazed shared pastures ("the commons") because the absence of private ownership eliminated incentives to conserve. The "anticommons" hypothesis holds that property rights can also destroy assets by promoting friction and deadlock.

53.   *Standard Oil Co. v. United States*, 221 U.S. 1, 31 S.Ct. 502 (1911).

54.   *United States v. Aluminum Co. of America*, 148 F.2d 416 (2d Cir. 1945).

55.   *United States v. Microsoft Corp.*, 253 F.3d 34, 63 (D.C. Cir. 2001).

ference between normal and wrongful uses of intellectual property since the 1920s.

As we will discuss more fully in chapter 6, licensing is generally considered a pro-competitive practice. First, it allows rightholders to share their intellectual property with others. Second, licenses are often needed to resolve so-called blocking patents—cases where several patent holders can keep a particular product or technology from being used. However, licensing also creates opportunity for wrongful acts, usually as a section 1 violation. Since intellectual property rights are designed to create legal monopolies, some restraints are legal. For example, courts have repeatedly held that intellectual property owners can refuse to license anyone at all.[56] Similarly, intellectual property owners can require the licensee to charge a particular price, restrict output, stay within a particular geographic territory, or limit use of the license to a particular field of use.[57] Courts generally also uphold nonexclusive licensing (that is, licensing to several licensees simultaneously), and even exclusive licensing, between companies that are not normally rivals (see chapter 6).

The analysis is harder in cases involving an exclusive license between competitors. According to the rule of reason, such agreements can be beneficial if they promote competition by encouraging the licensee to invest in the technology, realizing economies of scale, or allowing the licensor and licensee to integrate complementary R&D, production, or marketing efforts. On the other hand, these factors may not be enough if the exclusive license significantly reduces competition in a market.

---

56. *Image Technical Services, Inc. v. Eastman Kodak*, 125 F.3d 1195 (9th Cir. 1997); accord, U.S. Department of Justice and Federal Trade Commission, *Antitrust Guidelines for the Licensing of Intellectual Property* (April 6, 1995) (antitrust law does not require an IP owner to set up competition in its own technology). *Image Technical Services* leaves open the possibility that section 2 might require a monopolist to offer nonexclusive licenses where would-be entrants cannot otherwise compete.

57. *United States v. General Elec. Co.*, 272 U.S. 476 (1926) (price restrictions upheld); *General Talking Pictures Corp. v. Western Elec. Co.*, 304 U.S. 175 (1938) (field-of-use restrictions upheld); *United States v. E.I. DuPont de Nemours & Co.*, 188 F.Supp. 41 (D. Del. 1953) (output restrictions upheld); *Miller v. Institutform, Inc. v. Institutform of North America, Inc.*, 605 F.Supp. 1125 (M.D. Tenn. 1978) (territory restrictions upheld). The U.S. Department of Justice has traditionally argued that patent holders should not be allowed to restrict the prices charged by licensees. An evenly divided Supreme Court declined to change the rule in *United States v. Huck Mfg. Co.*, 382 U.S. 197 (1965).

Finally, some licenses are inherently suspect. Examples include provisions that keep the licensee from using or developing other technologies, licenses that fix prices between firms that would otherwise compete with one another, and licenses that fix the price at which licensees can resell patented goods.[58]

In addition to licensing, parties frequently trade intellectual property rights through cross-licenses and patent pools. In general, courts try to balance the "dominant purpose" of the patent pool against its "likely effect on competition."[59] Courts usually approve arrangements that remove blocking patents so that firms can bring technologies to market. Conversely, they are suspicious of pools that encourage participants to reduce R&D expenditures, or limit competition between different technologies. In general, pool members are free to exclude competitors. However, courts sometimes make an exception where pool members have substantial market power and nonmembers cannot compete effectively.

So-called sham licenses present a recurring danger. Suppose A, B, and C compete in the same market. According to section 1, they cannot agree to fix prices or divide the market into geographic territories. What would happen, though, if they disguised their transaction as a series of licenses with D? A, B, and C could then separately agree to restrictions that required them to maintain minimum prices, divide geographic markets, or otherwise coordinate their actions. Such an agreement has potential to be collusive and is illegal.[60]

Finally, intellectual property owners can run afoul of the antitrust laws under section 2 without entering into licenses or agreements at all. Courts agree that merely applying for intellectual property rights or suing to enforce them is never by itself illegal, since federal intellectual property law expressly authorizes these acts. However, section 2 may be triggered if a firm performs other acts that have a "dangerous probability"

---

58.   *United States v. Univis Lens Co.*, 316 U.S. 241 (1942); *Ethyl Gasoline Corp. v. United States*, 309 U.S. 436 (1940).

59.   *Standard Oil Co. v. United States*, 283 U.S. 163 (1931).

60.   *United States v. U.S. Gypsum Co.*, 333 U.S. 364, 400 (1948). Sham agreements are also a problem for intellectual property litigation. Courts usually encourage parties to settle their differences through cross-licensing. Such agreements may be unlawful if they are part of a broader scheme to exclude competitors. See, for example, *United States v. Singer Manuf. Co.*, 374 U.S. 174 (1963).

of acquiring or maintaining a monopoly. Finding instances of such a thing is clearly tricky, since the patent itself grants market power. Examples of acts that have been deemed illegal include purchasing patent portfolios in order to exclude competitors from a particular technology;[61] requiring purchasers to buy unpatented goods or services in order to obtain a patented product;[62] requiring would-be licensees to purchase multiple patents in a package;[63] or requiring parties to do all of their business with the patent holder.[64] Section 2 also prevents firms from obtaining intellectual property—and the market power it confers—by fraud. Examples include misleading the PTO about one's eligibility for a patent, trying to enforce a patent after learning that it is invalid, and conducting "sham" litigation against competitors.[65]

It is apparent from the historical hints in this chapter that intellectual property evolves along with technology, and indeed it must do so in order to be effective. In fact, the importance of intellectual property in the industrial landscape has varied widely. Antimonopoly judges have been the least supportive of intellectual property. For example, during the 1880s, the U.S. Supreme Court complained that Congress was trying to "grant a monopoly for every trifling device." Similarly, New Deal justices went out of their way to restrict patents during the 1930s and 1940s. Since then, the pendulum has swung back. In 1952, Congress passed a new patent statute that overruled several New Deal decisions. More recently, the PTO has expanded the subject matter of patents, such as to semiconductor chips, computer software, and business methods. Many commentators think that intellectual property protection was much strengthened in the 1990s.

---

61.   *SCM Corp. v. Xerox Corp.*, 463 F.Supp. 983, 1007 (D.Conn. 1978); but see *Image Technical Services, Inc. v. Eastman Kodak Co.*, 125 F.3d 1195 (9th Cir. 1997).

62.   *Morton Salt Co. v. G.S. Suppiger Co.*, 314 U.S. 488 (1942).

63.   *Zenith Radio Corp. v. Hazeltine Rsch., Inc.*, 395 U.S. 100 (1969). However, parties can "voluntarily" bundle IP rights for mutual convenience. The distinction between "voluntary" and "mandatory" bundling tends to confuse economists, who see all contracts as voluntary.

64.   *Tampa Elec. Co. v. Nashville Coal Co.*, 365 U.S. 320 (1961).

65.   See, for example, *Walker Process Equip. v. Food Machinery & Chem. Corp.*, 382 U.S. 172 (1965) (fraudulently procured patent); *Handgards, Inc. v. Ethicon*, 601 F.2d 986 (9th Cir. 1979) (baseless litigation after owner discovered that patent was invalid); *Argus Chemical Corp. v. Fibre Glass-Evercoat, Inc.*, 812 F.2d 1381 (Fed. Cir. 1987) (fraud on the PTO).

3.8   Technical Note: Doing Legal Research

This chapter provides enough legal background to understand the current book and, in most cases, the professional economics literature. That said, some readers may want to learn more about particular issues. Fortunately, almost all research universities host large, well-stocked law libraries. Furthermore, publishers have produced streamlined tools that make finding the law easier than almost any other kind of library research. This section lists the major resources.

Primary Sources   Finding statutes is easy if you already have a formal citation like 35 USC §163. For example, federal statutes are collected in a series of volumes called *United States Code*. If not, most statute books are also indexed by subject matter ("copyright") and popular name ("Digital Millennium Copyright Act"). Court opinions are collected in bound volumes called "Reporters." Among U.S. federal courts, the main case reporters are *The Supreme Court Reporter, Federal Reporter* (U.S. Court of Appeals decisions), and *Federal Reporter Supplement* (U.S. District Court decisions). Some intellectual property cases are also found in the *United States Patent Quarterly* (USPQ), which contains an extensive index of patent, trademark, copyright, and other intellectual property cases. Additional case reporters exist for each of the fifty states. Case reporters are almost always published in chronological order and have no obvious structure. If the citation is already known, they are easy to use. If only the name of a party is known, it may be necessary to consult a digest or search through an online service.

Secondary Sources   Economists can usually rely on what legal scholars have written instead of reading case law or statutes for themselves. For important subjects, multivolume treatises are often the best place to start. Some leading examples include treatises by Milgrim (trade secrets), Chisum (patents), Nimmer (copyright), and Areeda (antitrust). Even if it does not provide the answer directly, a good treatise usually provides plenty of leads for further research. The problem may also have been discussed in a law review. These can be searched through online indexes and full-text services like LEXIS. A good law review article will mention every possible case or statute that bears on the problem.

Many commercial publishers offer digests that collect and sort the main points of each published case under headings like "Patent Law" or "Copyright." The largest and oldest digests are produced by the West

Publishing Company. These provide a more or less complete guide to all of the case reporters mentioned above. Cases that happen to mention a particular statute are also digested in USC (supra) and other annotated codes.

Electronic Services   Almost all of the primary and secondary sources already listed can be searched through the online services LEXIS/NEXIS[66] or WESTLAW. Both services offer Boolean, full-text searches of case law, statutes, law reviews, and treatises. Furthermore, WESTLAW allows readers to search its copyrighted "key note" index. In addition to offering LEXIS/NEXIS and WESTLAW, some vendors provide smaller but still useful collections on CD-ROM. Boolean searches can be a frustrating way to learn about a general concept like "copyright" or "restitution." Here, traditional paper resources like digests and treatises are still the best option. Boolean searches are ideal for finding cases that involve certain rare situations. Examples include finding all patent cases that interpret particular words in a statute; that mention a particular technology or brand name; or that involve a particular company, court, judge, or law firm.

Finally, the PTO maintains a searchable online database that contains most patents. You can access the database by visiting www.uspto.gov. There is no comparable service for copyrights, which do not need to be registered.

References and Further Reading

Allison, J. R., and M. A. Lemley. 2002. "The Growing Complexity of the United States Patent System." *Boston University Law Review* 82:77–145.

Anton, J. J., and D. A. Yao. 1994. "Expropriation and Inventions: Appropriable Rents in the Absence of Property Rights." *American Economic Review* 84:190–209.

Areeda, P. E., and H. Hovenkamp. 1985. *Economics and Federal Antitrust Law*. St. Paul, MN: West.

Barton, J. 2000. "Intellectual Property Rights: Reforming the Patent System." *Science* 287:1933–1934.

Barton, J. 2003. "Nonobviousness." *IDEA: The Journal of Law and Technology* 43:475–508.

---

66.   LEXIS/NEXIS is typically available to law school personnel and—on occasion—other university patrons. LEXIS/NEXIS also offers free access to selected online files—including recent federal cases—at www.lexisone.com.

Chisum, D. S. 2001. *Chisum on Patents: A Treatise on the Law of Patentability, Validity, and Infringement*. San Francisco: Bancroft-Whitney.

Cowan, R., and P. A. David. 1999. "The Explicit Economics of Knowledge Codification and Tacitness." Working Paper 99-027. Stanford, CA: Department of Economics, Stanford University.

Denicolò, V. 2002. Two-Stage Patent Races and Patent Policy." *RAND Journal of Economics* 31:488–501.

Eisenberg, R. 1989. "Patents and the Progress of Science: Exclusive Rights and Experimental Use." *University of Chicago Law Review* 56:1017–1055.

Flatow, I. 1992. *They All Laughed . . . From Light Bulbs to Lasers: The Fascinating Stories Behind the Great Inventions that Have Changed Our Lives*. New York: HarperCollins.

Graham, S., B. H. Hall, D. Harhoff, and D. Mowery. 2003. "Patent Quality Control: A Comparison of U.S. Patent Reexaminations and European Patent Oppositions." In W. Cohen, ed., *Intellectual Property in the Knowledge-Based Economy*. Washington, DC: National Academies Press.

Green, J., and S. Scotchmer. 1995. "On the Division of Profit in Sequential Innovation." *RAND Journal of Economics* 26:20–33.

Hall, B. H. 2003. "Business Method Patents, Innovation and Policy." Working Paper 9717. Cambridge, MA: National Bureau of Economic Research.

Hall, B. H., and R. H. Ziedonis. 2001. "The Patent Paradox Revisited: An Empirical Study of Patenting in the U.S. Semiconductor Industry, 1979–1995." *The RAND Journal of Economics* 32:101–128.

Lemley, M. A. 1997. "The Economics of Improvement in Intellectual Property Law." *Texas Law Review* 75:989–1083.

Lemley, M. A. 2001. "Rational Ignorance at the Patent Office." *Northwestern University Law Review* 95:1495–1532.

Maurer, S. M. 2003. "New Institutions for Doing Science: From Databases to Open Source Biology." Paper presented at the conference "European Policy for Intellectual Property." Maastricht, the Netherlands: Maastricht Economic Research Institute on Information and Technology. Available at www.merit.unimaas.nl/epip/papers/maurer_paper.pdf.

Maurer, S. M., and S. Scotchmer. 1999, May 14. "Database Protection: Is It Broken and Should We Fix It?" *Science* 284:1129–1130.

Maurer, S. M., and S. Scotchmer. 2002. "The Independent Invention Defense in Intellectual Property." *Economica* 69:535–547.

Menell, P. 1989. "An Analysis of the Scope of Copyright Protection for Application Programs." *Stanford Law Review* 41:1045–1104.

Menell, P. 2002. "Can Our Current Conception of Copyright Law Survive the Internet Age? Envisioning Copyright Law's Digital Future." *New York Law School Law Review* 46:63–199.

Merges, R. 1994. "Intellectual Property Rights and Bargaining Breakdown: The Case of Blocking Patents." *Tennessee Law Review* 62:75–106.

Merges, R. 1997. *Patent Law and Policy*. Charlottesville, VA: Michie.

Merges, R. 1999. "As Many as Six Impossible Patents Before Breakfast: Property Rights for Business Concepts and Patent System Reform." *Berkeley High Technology Law Journal* 14:577–615.

Merges, R., P. Menell, M. A. Lemley, and T. Jorde. 1997. *Intellectual Property in the New Technological Age*. New York: Aspen.

Milgrim, R. M. 2001. *Milgrim on Trade Secrets*. San Francisco: Bancroft-Whitney.

Miller, A. R., and M. H. Davis. 1990. *Intellectual Property: Patents, Trademarks, and Copyright*. St. Paul, MN: West.

Nimmer, M. B., and D. Nimmer. 2001. *Nimmer on Copyright*. San Francisco: Matthew Bender.

Petroski, H. 1996. *Invention by Design: How Engineers Get from Thought to Thing*. Cambridge, MA: Harvard University Press.

Poyago-Theotoky, J., J. Beath, and D. S. Siegell. 2002. "Universities and Fundamental Research: Reflections on the Growth of University-Industry Partnerships." *Oxford Review of Economic Policy* 18:10–12.

Ryan, M. P. 1998. *Knowledge Diplomacy*. Washington, DC: Brookings Institution Press.

Samuelson, P., R. David, M. Kapor, and J. H. Reichman. 1994. "A Manifesto Concerning the Legal Protection of Computer Programs." *Columbia Law Review* 94:2308–2431.

Samuelson, P., and S. Scotchmer. 2002. "The Law and Economics of Reverse Engineering." *Yale Law Journal* 111:1575–1663.

Scotchmer, S. 1996. "Protecting Early Innovators: Should Second-Generation Products Be Patentable?" *RAND Journal of Economics* 27:322–331.

Scotchmer, S., and J. Green. 1990. "Novelty and Disclosure in Patent Law." *The RAND Journal of Economics* 21:131–146.

Townes, C. H. 1999. *How the Laser Happened: Adventures of a Scientist*. Oxford: Oxford University Press.

Wainfan, B. 2003, December. "Wright Flyer Aerodynamics." *Flight Journal* 8:58–61.

Walsh, J. P., A. Arora, and W. M. Cohen. 2003. "Research Tool Patenting and Licensing and Biomedical Innovation." Paper presented at the conference "European Policy for Intellectual Property." Maastricht, the Netherlands: Maastricht Economic Research Institute on Information and Technology. Available at www.merit.unimaas.nl/epip/papers/walsh_paper.pdf.

4 On the Optimal Design of Intellectual Property

A virtue of intellectual property as an incentive mechanism is that it decentralizes decision making. Anyone with a good idea can invest in the idea in the hope of a payoff, without negotiating with an invention authority. Since the profit available from exclusive control of the innovation will be correlated with its social value, intellectual property encourages potential innovators to screen their ideas by comparing cost to some measure of expected social value. If innovators make mistakes, it is mainly they who suffer, possibly in the company of their backers. If they guess correctly, they and their backers are the main beneficiaries. No one should begrudge them their successes or failures, because no one is taxed without voluntarily buying the fruits of their new knowledge.

These are powerful endorsements even though, as stressed in chapter 2, other mechanisms share some of the same virtues, and can avoid some of the defects, such as deadweight loss. Nevertheless, intellectual property is an important incentive mechanism. Both lawyers and economists have spilled a lot of ink on the question of how it should be designed. That is the subject of this chapter.

All branches of intellectual property have certain features in common, as discussed in chapter 3: a stipulated duration, a notion of "breadth" (usually not established by statute, but rather in case law), a notion of the minimum protectable inventive step, and some "fair-use" exemptions (with the exception of patents).

These policy levers operate differently, and have different importance, in different models of the creative environment. Many of the arguments in this chapter, especially those related to patent races, are more suited to patents and patentable subject matter than to copyrights and creative works. Patent races can only occur if the targeted idea is known to several rivals, and if the intellectual property right will only be available to the winner. For the most part, it is hard to conceive of copyright races, at least for creative works. Authors writing novels will not be racing for a prize available to only one of them, and the novels they produce will not typically be perfect substitutes. Indeed, to the extent that the novels of two authors are similar in style or content, each reader will typically want to buy both novels or neither, but typically not just one. The same is true of music.

The most important decision made by a creator of copyrighted works is not whether to pursue a given "idea," but whether to become an author rather than, for example, a carpenter. The margin at which incentives operate is in nudging potential creators toward a life of creativity, rather than in eliciting investment in any particular novel or symphony. The length and breadth of the intellectual property right, together with the fair uses that are granted, determine how profitable these creations are, and influence how many people become creators of copyrighted works.[1]

For industrial inventions, however, the incentive system operates more at the level of ideas for innovations than at the level of lifestyle choices. That is mostly the focus of this chapter.

4.1   How Profitable Should Intellectual Property Rights Be?

It is tempting to think that strengthening intellectual property rights is always a good idea if it leads to more innovation. That view is short-sighted for at least two reasons. Strong intellectual property rights increase the deadweight loss on innovations that would be forthcoming even with weaker rights, and strong intellectual property rights can lead to an inefficient duplication of R&D costs, as firms vie for possession of those rights.

Figure 4.1 depicts a space of "ideas," as described in chapter 2. Each idea (v, c) can be represented as a point in the space. As in chapter 2, the variable v represents the potential value provided to consumers by the innovation. In particular, v is the per-period consumers' surplus that would be available with competitive supply, as depicted under the demand curve in figure 2.2 of chapter 2. For the moment assume that the only policy lever of interest is the (discounted) duration of protec-

---

1. See section 8.5 for a model in which agents self-select to become creators, depending on the rate at which they have good ideas and on the rewards for implementing those ideas. The model is used to describe grant rewards but could equally well describe copyright rewards to authors.

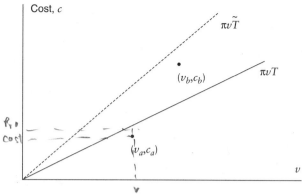

Figure 4.1
Ideas, innovations, and length of protection

tion, T. (Discounted time is clarified in technical note 2.8.1 at the end of chapter 2.) The intellectual property protection then provides profit in amount $\pi v T$.

The profit obviously depends on v, the size of the market. Figure 4.1 shows the profit, as it depends on v, for two different patent lives, T and $\tilde{T}$, where $T < \tilde{T}$. The longer patent life $\tilde{T}$ provides more profit for each idea. Increasing the strength of protection will lead to more innovation. For example, the idea represented by (v_b, c_b) would be profitable enough for investment with the longer protection, but not with the shorter protection, since

$$\pi v_b T < c_b < \pi v_b \tilde{T}$$

As was originally pointed out by Nordhaus (1969), increasing the duration of protection may not be beneficial from a social point of view, due to deadweight loss. For investments in ideas such as (v_a, c_a), which would be made with the shorter intellectual property rights, the lengthening of protection increases deadweight loss and reduces the social value of the innovation. If the deadweight loss is ℓv per period, $\ell < 1$, and the patent life lasts for duration T, the social value of investing in the idea (v_a, c_a) is

$$(v_a/r) - \ell v_a T$$

where r is the discount rate. The social value is therefore larger with shorter protection than with longer protection, provided the innovation gets made. At some point, lengthening rights in order to stimulate innovation becomes so costly in terms of deadweight loss that any incremental innovation is not worth it.

The second social loss that may arise from strong protection is duplicated costs. Suppose that, for some research objective, many different firms have ideas for achieving it—ideas are not scarce. For a commonly known and relatively cheap idea such as (v_a, c_a), several firms may invest, inefficiently duplicating costs.

However, the ideas model has so far not accounted for the fact that research projects have uncertain outcomes. The notion of duplication is imprecise if research outcomes are uncertain, especially if the successes and failures of different firms are independent. If several researchers attempt a project, it may turn out ex post that all fail, or that several succeed. However, we cannot infer from either of these outcomes that, from an ex ante perspective, the research plan was either deficient or duplicative.

Suppose, in particular, that each idea for the targeted objective is risky in its own idiosyncratic way, as assumed by Tandon (1983). Modify the notion of an idea so that it can be represented as a triple (v, c, p), where v is the value of achieving the specified objective, c is the cost of the research approach, and p is the probability that the approach fails. For simplicity, assume that firms have ideas with the same costs and value but that the approaches are different, so that the successes and failures of different approaches are independent. If n approaches are taken, the probability that all of them fail is p^n, so that the probability of at least one success is $1 - p^n$, which we will denote by $P(n)$.

$$P(n) = (1 - p^n)$$

In this environment, the main efficiency question is how many approaches will be taken, and which ones. Since the approaches to the problem are different and their successes and failures are independent, they are not entirely duplicative. One firm may succeed where others fail. One of the objectives of patent incentives is to govern the number of attempts.

Let S represent the social value of a specific targeted objective, and let Π represent the profit available from winning the intellectual property right. The profitability of the intellectual property right obviously depends on the length of protection and the size of the market; in the preceding notation, $\Pi = \pi v T$. However, as we will see in the remainder of this chapter, the patent value also depends on other aspects of the intellectual property right. It is the level of profit, and not specifically the patent life, that matters for the argument here, so we use the more general notation Π.

It will generally hold that $S \geq \Pi$, since it is difficult for an innovator to collect more than the social value of the innovation. In the simple model of section 2.2, the per-period social value while the innovation is protected is $(\pi + m)v = (1 - \ell)v$, where $\ell = 1 - \pi + m$, which is larger than per-period profit πv. The discounted social value is

$$S = \left(\frac{1}{r} - T\right)v + (1 - \ell)vT = \frac{1}{r}v - \ell v T$$

which is the maximum potential consumers' surplus minus the deadweight loss.

Our objective is to compare the optimal number of participants in the research effort with the equilibrium number that will enter in a race. This will also guide us in how to choose the best patent value, Π. We will use figure 4.2 to investigate the optimal number of entrants, called n^*, and the equilibrium number of entrants, called n^e, and how these depend on S and Π. For the moment we will ignore the fact that the policy levers that affect Π, such as the duration T of protection, also affect the social value S.

For each n, the expected per-firm profit is $(1/n)\Pi P(n)$. Per-firm profit is greater than the per-firm cost c for all n such that the function $\Pi P(n)$ lies above the total cost line. Firms will enter up to the point where the additional firm would not make profit, that is, n^e satisfies

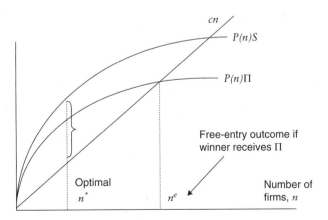

Figure 4.2
Equilibrium and optimal number of entrants

$$\frac{1}{n^e} \Pi P(n^e) = c$$

Thus, the entrants dissipate the expected profit in equilibrium. This determines how many firms will enter the patent race.

However, the equilibrium number is not the optimal number. The social value provided by the nth entrant is

$$S[P(n) - P(n-1)] - c$$

The optimal number of participants, n^*, can be described as the number where the marginal entrant would add as much social value as social cost c, but his or her successor would not:

$$S[P(n^*) - P(n^* - 1)] \geq c \geq S[P(n^* + 1) - P(n^*)]$$

The optimal number n^* can be seen in figure 4.2 as the place where the distance between $P(n)S$ and cn is maximized. It is marked by a bracket.

The optimal number of participants n^* can be either larger or smaller than the equilibrium of the race, n^e, depending on the patent value, Π. If the private value of the intellectual property right Π is relatively high, as shown, then the equilibrium number of participants n^e may be too large. If Π is relatively small (not shown), then the total-profit curve is shifted down at every point, and the equilibrium number of participants will be too small. The intersection that defines n^e will lie to the left of n^*.

Suppose, for example, that the winner collects the entire social value as profit, $\Pi = S$. Then the curves $P(\cdot)S$ and $P(\cdot)\Pi$ coincide, and there will be too much entry, $n^e > n^*$. The intuitive reason is that the marginal entrant receives the average profit rather than the marginal profit, but it is the marginal profit that determines the optimal number of participants.[2]

---

2.   This is a well-known problem, usually discussed as the problem of the commons. On a common grazing land, the marginal animal eats some grass that other animals would otherwise eat, thus reducing their value by enhancing its own. An owner of the commons would graze fewer animals on the common than will graze with free entry, and would earn more profit than the joint profit with free entry. For a history of the application of this idea to patent races, see Reinganum 1989. Reinganum reviews models going back to Loury (1979) and Lee and Wilde (1980). In their models the probability of discovery is converted to a time of discovery, by assuming that failure by all the firms leads to another round of attempts until someone wins. The equivalence is shown in technical note 4.7.1. The version used here was also used by Wright (1983) to compare prize and patent systems.

Due to the concavity of $P(\cdot)$, the average profit is greater than the marginal profit. Each entrant imposes a cost on previous entrants that is not taken into account. By entering the race, the entrant reduces the probability that another firm will win. This reduction provides private value to the entrant, but no social value—it is a transfer among the firms. The private value of entry can be positive even if the social value of entry is negative.

If the patent value Π could be chosen separately for each market, then it should be chosen so that $P(n^*)\Pi = cn^*$, where n^* is the socially optimal number of researchers. The value Π should be reduced in figure 4.2 so that the curve $P(\cdot)\Pi$ intersects the total cost curve at n^*. (If the policy levers that affect Π also affect S, then n^* also shifts as Π is reduced.)

Echoing chapter 2, the value Π can equally well be interpreted as a prize. There is, however, an important difference between prizes and intellectual property rights, which leads to the conclusion that the optimal value of a prize is greater than the optimal value of a patent. Raising money for a prize imposes less deadweight loss. If there is literally no deadweight loss to raising money to fund a prize, then the social value of the innovation S is equal to v/r instead of $v/r - \ell v T$.

Just as with patents, very large prizes for targeted objectives may incite a race. To govern the number of entrants, the prize should be chosen such that $P(n^*)\Pi = cn^*$, except that the optimal n^* is larger due to the larger social value S (the curve defined by $P(n)S$ is higher if S is larger). The optimal number of participants is smaller if the reward is given as a patent than if given as a prize, and the private value of the patent should be smaller than the value that would be offered as a prize.

In section 4.4 this probability-of-success example is modified so that a failure in one period leads to a renewal of efforts in the next period, until at least one of the approaches succeeds.

4.2   Breadth as a Policy Lever

Although length of protection is the most obvious policy lever for governing the profitability of an intellectual property right, it is not the instrument that shows up in patent disputes. Patent disputes almost always revolve around either validity of the patent in the first place, or the subtle question of how different another product must be in order not to infringe. The latter notion is colloquially known as the "breadth" of the property right. The property right will obviously be more profitable if the rightholder can exclude substitutes from the market.

Once we admit breadth as another policy lever, the innovation no longer determines a fixed demand curve, as we have so far assumed. The demand curve will be more elastic, and generally lower, if close substitutes are allowed in the market.

Consider, for example, the insulating sleeves for paper cups that are mentioned in footnote 51 of chapter 3. If one looks closely, almost all of these mundane conveniences display patent numbers, which suggests that the first patent was narrow rather than broad. If it was broad, the first patentee could have kept all the other variants out of the market and made some profit. As it is, the patentee cannot charge a high price, because a high price will cause customers to flee to another vendor. The demand curve for the patentee's particular version of the insulating sleeve is presumably very elastic, as are the rivals' demand curves, even if the sleeves are slightly different. Competition will thus keep the price down.

An example of a broad patent is U.S. patent 4,736,866 (1988) on the Harvard oncomouse, also mentioned in chapter 3. This transgenic creature came into existence when two researchers infused a fertilized mouse egg with genetic material associated with cancer. The resulting mouse and its progeny are very cancer prone and are thus good research animals. However, instead of claiming only the process of transforming the fertilized egg, or the specific mouse line itself, the patent claims all "non-human transgenic mammals" created using their method (Merges and Nelson 1990). Under such broad claims, later researchers will not be saved from infringement even if their own efforts to create a transgenic walrus require large costs and extraordinary expertise, and the walrus is used to study obesity rather than cancer.

As mentioned in chapter 3, the legal notion of patent breadth arises from the claims of the patent and the doctrine of equivalents, by which courts can give the patentee exclusion rights beyond the literal claims. However, these categories do not map very conveniently onto economic ideas, so economists have suggested their own notions of breadth, which may apply to intellectual property other than patents. They have modeled breadth in two ways: in "product space," defining how "similar" a product must be to infringe a patent, and in "technology space," defining how costly it is to find a noninfringing substitute for the protected market. Further, economists have studied breadth in two types of innovative environments: where an innovation is threatened by horizontal competition, and where an innovation might be supplanted by an improved innovation. The discussion of improvements is left to chapter 5 on cumulative innovation.

In the first notion of breadth, the size of the market for the patented product depends on the closeness of noninfringing substitutes. Figure 4.3(a) shows how demand for a proprietary product shifts when the price of a substitute changes. (For simplicity in figure 4.3, the marginal cost of producing both goods is assumed to be zero.) The lower demand function, $x_1(\cdot, \tilde{p}_2)$, represents demand for the proprietary good when the patent is narrow, so that the substitute is available at the competitive price $\tilde{p}_2 = 0$. The higher demand curve, $x_1(\cdot, \hat{p}_2)$, applies when the patent is broad, so that the substitute good is supplied at a proprietary price, either by the patent holder or by a licensee.

Thus, the narrow patent is much less profitable than the broad patent. Under the narrow patent, the proprietor only earns profit $\tilde{\pi}_1$ per period. Under a broad patent, the proprietor earns profit $\hat{\pi}_1 + \hat{\pi}_2$ per period; he or she has rights in both markets. The demand curve for the patented good is even higher under a broad patent if the substitute is not supplied at all. But the substitute market will presumably be supplied, since the patent holder can generally make more profit by supplying both markets.

The second interpretation of breadth (Gallini 1992) is that breadth governs the cost of inventing around the patent, and thus of legally

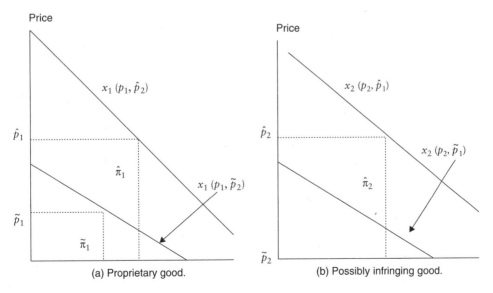

(a) Proprietary good.

(b) Possibly infringing good.

Figure 4.3
Proprietary and possibly infringing goods

entering the protected market. The product sold by each entrant is a perfect substitute for the proprietary product, but since entry is costly, there will only be a limited number of entrants and the market will not be perfectly competitive. Entry will lead to a proprietary price lower than the monopoly price, to an extent that depends on the cost of entry.

To see this, suppose that the price in the proprietary market is governed by a function $p(\cdot)$, where $p(n)$ is the price with n suppliers. The price $p(\cdot)$ falls with n. This reflects the idea that if there are more suppliers in the market, there will be more competition. In figure 4.4, $p(1)$ is the monopoly price and $p(\infty) = 0$ is the competitive price. (For simplicity, the marginal cost of producing this product is assumed to be zero, so that the competitive price is zero.) For a number of suppliers n such that $1 < n < \infty$, the price will be between the monopoly price and the competitive price. The total profit in the market with n suppliers is then $p(n)x(p(n))$, and each supplier receives a fraction $1/n$ of this profit.

Suppose that the cost of entry through duplication is K. Entry will stop at the number of market participants n that solves

$$\frac{1}{n+1}[T\,p(n+1)\,x(p(n+1))] < K \leq \frac{1}{n}[T\,p(n)\,x(p(n))] \tag{4.1}$$

These inequalities mean that the final entrant makes nonnegative profit, but that an additional entrant would make negative profit. Thus, the rightholder also earns profit approximately equal to K, as governed by (4.1).

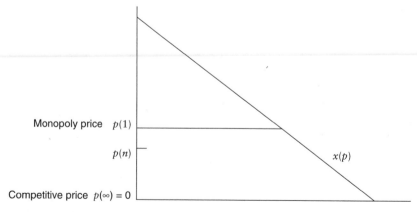

Figure 4.4
Price as it depends on the number of entrants

In fact, the patent holder can earn more profit than K by licensing entrants instead of tolerating entry through duplicative costs. The costs of entry, K, are pure social waste, and the firms should be able to profit by avoiding these costs. Licensing is the obvious solution. The simplest licensing option is to offer entry at a license fee K to as many firms as want to enter, using the patent holder's technology. Entrants then have the same profit options as they had without the licensing offer. Licensing leads to the same number of entrants and same market price, but enriches the patent holder by Kn if there are n entrants. In general, the patent holder can do even better by licensing with royalties. Whether there is licensing or not, both the patent holder's profit and the price of the proprietary good will be determined by the cost of entry K. Lower costs of entry, K, lead to a lower price in the protected market and also to lower profit for the proprietor, but never less than K.[3]

Thus, even though the statutory life of all formal intellectual property is fixed without reference to the nature of the innovation, there is room for fine-tuning the innovator's profit through the breadth of the right. We caution, however, that courts and the PTO do not generally grant or interpret claims with a view toward fine-tuning profit. These arguments are more germane to trade-secret protection, where entry is always possible at the cost of reverse engineering the protected product. If the cost of reverse engineering is commensurate with the cost of invention, then licensing can lead to a price lower than the monopoly price, and will keep the inventor's profit commensurate with costs.

4.3 Structuring the Profit: Length and Breadth

Section 4.1 investigated how large a patent reward should be, given that patents generally lead to deadweight loss, and given that patents may incite too much or too little rivalry in a patent race. Section 4.2 showed that breadth is a policy lever for fine-tuning the value of a patent, just as the duration of the right is. In this section, we assume that the correct value of the patent right has been determined, say Π, and ask how the value should be structured as a policy matter. To provide profit in amount Π, should patents be broad and short or narrow and long? Structuring the intellectual property right will have an impact on the deadweight loss.

---

3.   This is the argument of Maurer and Scotchmer (2002). The argument that price falls gradually with the number of entrants depends on the nature of competition in the market. The hypothesis about how price depends on n is consistent with Cournot competition.

We reconsider the two notions of breadth discussed in section 4.2. First, suppose that breadth determines the cost, K, of entering the patent holder's market. The cost K must be of similar magnitude to Π to ensure that the patent holder earns Π. As argued previously, the patent holder's profit is determined by K whether the patent holder tolerates entry or licenses to prevent it. With licensing, the profit will be somewhat greater than K but still determined by K. We will assume that K is large enough to ensure that the patent holder covers cost.

Given the required entry cost K, however, the patent can be structured with a short patent life or a long patent life. Let T^* be short enough so that even a single entrant is deterred and long enough so the patent holder can cover cost by charging the monopoly price, earning discounted profit $p^*x(p^*)T^*$ that is no smaller than Π. This should be possible due to the choice of K.

However, the patent could alternatively be made to last longer, say $\tilde{T} > T^*$. Then there may be a threat of entry, resulting in a market price lower than p^*, as discussed in section 4.2. The lower price, say $\tilde{p}$, will be determined by the cost of entry K, which determines the number of entrants or licensees. The patent holder's profit is again determined by K.

Our objective is to compare the policies (T^*, K), $(\tilde{T}, K)$ from the consumers' point of view. From the innovator's point of view, the two policies are (more or less) equivalent, since they provide (more or less) the same profit, determined by the cost of imitation, K. With the shorter patent life T^*, the innovator's profit is earned by charging the monopoly price for a relatively short period, and with the longer patent life $\tilde{T}$, by charging a lower price for a longer period and possibly by collecting license fees.

The relative merits of the policies (T^*, K) and $(\tilde{T}, K)$ depend on whether price-eroding entry occurs through imitation or licensing. The option to invent around the patent at cost K will reduce price whether or not firms license, as already described. However, licensing changes the social calculus. If firms would actually spend the resources to invent around a patent, then it is probably best to structure patent law to avoid that waste. The better policy is (T^*, K) (Gallini 1992).

On the other hand, licensing is more profitable for the patent holder than tolerating entry.[4] If the patent holder licenses to prevent rivals from

4.   See Aeppel 2004 for a discussion of whether rivals actually design around patents. In some cases they do, but in at least one case, the patent holder dropped the price to avoid that outcome, as suggested here.

inventing around the patent, then the market price will be reduced without wasting resources. In that case, the best combination of length and breadth turns out to be a very long (infinite) patent life. There will be many licensees, and the price will be close to the competitive price but high enough so that the discounted value of profit over the life of the patent covers the cost of innovation.

The argument can be understood by examining figure 4.5, and it is given more formally in technical note 4.7.1. The argument comes down to a ratio test.[5] If the ratio of per-period profit to per-period dead-weight loss is smaller with the monopoly price p^* than with the lower price $\tilde{p}$, then $(\tilde{T}, K)$ is the better policy. Deadweight loss is the consumer cost of proprietary pricing. Hence the lower ratio means that the consumer cost of creating a given amount of profit is higher. Higher consumer loss means lower consumers' surplus. As can be seen in figure 4.5, with linear demand the ratio test supports the longer patent life with lower price.

Second, we revisit the first definition of breadth, defined by whether the good described by figure 4.3(b) infringes the patent on the good described by figure 4.3(a). The prescription for how to structure protection is less definitive in this case.

Let $\hat{T}$ and $\tilde{T}$ be the lengths of broad and narrow protection, respectively, that generate the same profit for the proprietor. That is,

$$\hat{T}(\hat{\pi}_1 + \hat{\pi}_2) = \tilde{T}\tilde{\pi}_1 \tag{4.2}$$

The duration of narrow protection, $\tilde{T}$, must be considerably longer than the duration of broad protection, $\hat{T}$, especially if the two goods are close substitutes. By looking at figure 4.3, it is impossible to tell which of the regimes is better. However, there are at least two cases where the best regime is clear.

The best regime depends on the elasticities of substitution between the patented good in figure 4.3(a) and its kin in figure 4.3(b), and elasticities of substitution between those two goods together and all other

---

5.   The ratio test developed in technical note 4.7.1 originates with Tandon (1982) and Kaplow (1984), and is used by Gilbert and Shapiro (1990), who argue that substituting lower prices for longer protection is socially beneficial. Maurer and Scotchmer (2002) explain how breadth can be used to achieve that result. Klemperer (1990) applies a similar ratio test in another model. Ayres and Klemperer (1999) make a similar argument that monopoly power in each period should be restrained, and Denicolo (1996) investigates the robustness of all these arguments.

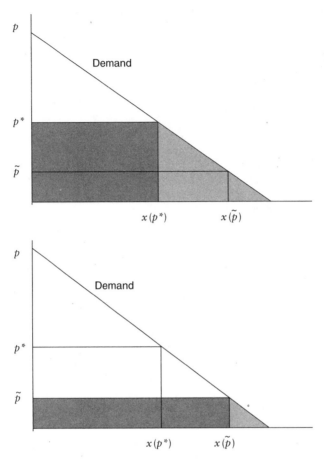

Figure 4.5
The ratio test

goods.[6] With narrow protection, demand will be displaced from the market in figure 4.3(a) to the market in 4.3(b), as well as to other goods more generally. With broad protection, there will be less displacement of demand between the two markets in figure 4.3, and more displacement to other goods. This is because, with broad protection, both goods in figure 4.3 will have proprietary prices.

The first example where the best regime is clear is when the demand for the patented good and its substitute as a group is very inelastic. Suppose, for example, that the patented good is a text-editing program and the substitute is a similar text-editing program. If the substitute is infringing, both will be sold at proprietary prices. If the prices are similar, a consumer will choose between them on the basis of their idiosyncratic differences. If the substitute text editor were competitively supplied, some consumers would buy the substitute even though they prefer the patented one at a similar price. If the overall demand for text editors is very inelastic—everyone will choose one text editor or the other—then it is sensible to have a broad, short patent, because monopoly pricing becomes similar to a lump-sum tax on text editing, and lump-sum taxes avoid distortion.

A second example where the best regime is clear is when the two goods are not substitutes at all, but the potential infringement is by a different use of the same technology, serving different users entirely. For example, the patent might be on a chemical used for a particular purpose, and the second market might be for a second use of the same chemical. Then the two demand curves in figure 4.3(a) coincide and $\hat{\pi}_1 = \tilde{\pi}_1$. If the ratio of deadweight loss to profit is the same in each use, both regimes lead to the same deadweight loss.

Here we again use ratio test. If the ratio of profit to deadweight loss is the same in both uses, both regimes lead to the same deadweight loss. If the ratio of deadweight loss to profit is, for example, smaller in figure 4.3(b), then the broad, short patent is better because it reduces total deadweight loss.

These arguments bring us back to the realization that intellectual property rights create taxes on markets. The problem of structuring these

---

6.   Of special relevance to this discussion is the 1990 paper of Paul Klemperer, who studies breadth in a model with more structure and focuses on the displacement of consumer demand from the proprietary product to a competitive fringe. He mostly assumes that the infringing substitutes will not be supplied. The alternative assumption is made here because the proprietor will typically find it profitable to supply infringing substitutes at proprietary prices.

taxes is related to the problem of choosing optimal commodity taxes more generally. Which commodities should be taxed in order to raise a given amount of money while minimizing distortions? The answer is, those for which demand is inelastic. Of course, in the intellectual property context, the taxes must be related to the invention. If the revenue is divorced from the invention, the incentive purpose of the intellectual property system fails.

4.4   Some Virtues and Defects of Patent Races

A patent race occurs when two or more firms pursue the same targeted objective and only one will receive the intellectual property right. The virtues of patent races are of particular relevance to competition policy, as discussed further in chapter 6. We have already alluded to some virtues of patent races in section 4.1, which pointed out that patent races can increase the probability of innovation when inventors have different ideas for how to solve a targeted problem.[7]

It is sometimes the case that with enough attempts, any approach can be made to succeed. Then a second virtue of patent races emerges: patent races can accelerate progress. This section shows how that occurs, but also elaborates a defect of patent races as incentive mechanisms, namely, that they do not aggregate information in the economy efficiently and do not necessarily lead to efficient investment decisions.

Following the interpretation in section 4.1, let $P(n)$ be the probability that at least one firm succeeds in each period when there are n firms participating. Suppose further that firms will continue to race in successive periods until one succeeds, and that the cost in each period is the same. Then, with n firms participating, the probability of success in each period is $P(n)$, and the expected time to discovery is $1/P(n)$. The calculation behind this assertion is given in technical note 4.7.2, but it is intu-

---

7.   There is a large literature on strategic interaction among firms vying for intellectual property rights. Patent races may lead to deficient incentives or excessive incentives, to too much product proliferation or to too little. The interested reader should see, for example, Loury 1979; Lee and Wilde 1980; Reinganum 1981, 1982, 1989; Wright 1983; Judd 1985; Harris and Vickers 1985a, 1985b; Dasgupta and Stiglitz 1980a, 1980b; Fudenberg et al. 1983; Dasgupta and Maskin 1987. Most of these papers study R&D contexts where there is a "production function" for knowledge. Instead of being scarce, ideas are common knowledge, and all progress could occur instantly if enough resources were devoted to it.

itively clear that the time to discovery will be shorter if the probability of discovery is greater in each period.

The value of the discovery, whether from a private point of view or social point of view, must be discounted from the time it occurs. With no discounting, the private value would be Π and the social value would be S, regardless of when they occur. However, as shown in technical note 4.7.2, the discounted expected value of the total profit is $\Pi P(n)/(P(n) + r)$ and the discounted expected value of the total social surplus is $S(n)/(P(n) + r)$. This, too, is intuitive. The expected discounted value of, say, Π is close to Π itself if either the probability of discovery $P(n)$ is large in each period or the discount rate r is close to zero.

The firms accrue costs in each period until the research program is successful. Without discounting, the expected cost of the n firms would be $nc/P(n)$ (the per-period cost times the expected length of the race), but with discounting the expected discounted cost is $nc/(P(n) + r)$. This too is shown in technical note 4.7.2.

The per-firm expected profit is thus

$$\frac{1}{n} \frac{\Pi P(n) - cn}{P(n) + r} = \frac{\frac{1}{n} \Pi P(n) - c}{P(n) + r}$$

Assuming that firms compete away all the profit, there will be entry until $\Pi P(n^e) - n^e c = 0$, as in the one-period race.

Since $P(n^e) > P(1)$, the times to discovery satisfy $1/P(n^e) < 1/P(1)$. Thus, a patent race accelerates innovation.

In this simple model, each firm invests at a fixed rate, which costs c per period. However, the same result is true if the firms can increase the rates at which they invest in R&D. If two firm are racing for a patent, they will invest more money per unit time than if their efforts are combined in a single enterprise. See technical note 6.7.2.

Previewing the discussion in chapter 6, United States competition policy makes much of the salutary effects of patent races and promotes them. As a counterweight to this optimistic view, we point out some inefficiencies that can arise. Chapter 2 already alluded to the fact that patent races (and simple prize systems) do not aggregate the firms' private information and do not use their information efficiently. Patent races do not necessarily promote investments by the firms with the best ideas, even though patent incentives will eliminate the firms with truly worthless ideas or truly exorbitant costs. Nevertheless, if it is possible to find the firms with the best ideas, it is preferable to do so, and the contests discussed in chapter 2 may perform better than patent races.

Another defect of patent races arising from different information is as follows. Sometimes firms have private information directly relevant to other firms, in the sense that the private information of firm 1 would change firm 2's subjective valuation of its prospect for success. For example, each of two pharmaceutical firms in pursuit of a therapy or vaccine might realize that rivals have different experience with and information about similar research projects. Each firm might therefore want to know how optimistic the rival is. The firms will be watching each other's investments closely. If the rival is investing in the same project, that is bad news from the perspective that the rival might win, but good news from the perspective that the rival thinks the investment is worthwhile. If the rival is investing, the firm has a reason to stay in, but also a reason to drop out. Of course, this also works in reverse. The firm is being watched by the rival, and knows that the rival's own investment strategy depends on its own. This example is continued in technical note 4.7.3, showing how the firms can get locked in an equilibrium in which each invests solely because the other is investing, or can alternatively get locked in an equilibrium in which each stays out of the race solely because the other has stayed out. Only one of the equilibria is efficient, which shows again that the patent race need not aggregate and use information efficiently.

4.5   The Role of Exemptions

An intellectual property right allows the rightholder to exclude others from making or using the protected invention. However, the right to exclude is limited in many ways. Perhaps most importantly, intellectual property rights are limited as to length and breadth, as discussed earlier. Other limitations include:

- Fair use (of copyrighted works)
- Independent invention or reverse engineering
- Research exemptions

Different exemptions have different rationales. Commentators sometimes argue that exemptions are prima facie unfair, since they impinge on the innovator's or author's right to control the use of his or her work. That is more akin to a "moral rights" argument than to the incentives-based arguments used in this book. If Congress is authorized to grant intellectual property rights for the purpose of creating incentives, then it can surely create limitations on those rights.

Some exemptions are not directed at incentives at all. Fair uses of copyrighted works include the right to parody, the right to review, and the right to excerpt in small amounts. These rights have an obvious public-policy rationale, in that they support First Amendment rights to free speech. It is hard to discuss First Amendment values in purely "economic" terms. However, there are also purely economic considerations. The transaction costs of licensing copyrighted works for incidental use would be prohibitive and would probably result in infringement instead of licensing (Gordon 1982).

For copyright, the biggest set of "exemptions" arises through the fact that copyright only protects expression, not ideas or functionality. This has important implications for computer software. Since interfaces between hardware and software (or operating systems and software) are functional, there is a legal argument for allowing interfaces to be reverse engineered. For the economics of interoperability, see chapter 10.

The defense of "independent invention" is one of the primary differences between patent law and other types of protection. In patent law, protection does not depend on how a suspected infringer achieves the infringing product; the infringement only depends on whether the infringing product is covered by a claim in the patent, as interpreted by a court. But in trade-secret law, the suspected infringer is exempt from liability if he or she independently discovers the protected knowledge or reverse engineers it. Similarly, in copyright, the structure of a computer program is not protectable. If a rival programmer independently duplicates the same structure (and it is not also patented), that programmer is exempt from liability.[8]

These legal differences do not seem rooted in economics, and our goal is not to explain them in terms of legal doctrine, but rather to explain the economic effects.

Actually, we have gone a long distance toward analyzing the independent-invention defense in our discussion above of breadth. The economic effects of entry depend on the relative costs of the original innovator and each entrant. It does not matter whether these costs are incurred to circumvent a patent, to reinvent the product independently, or to reverse engineer it. In each case, entry erodes the innovator's profit to an extent that depends on the cost of entry, K. The threat of entry

---

8.   See Samuelson and Scotchmer 2002 for a legal and economic analysis of reverse engineering. See Menell 2002 for discussion of how protection of computer software has developed.

will only kill innovation if the cost of entry is low relative to the cost of innovation. In general, a threat of independent invention can have the salutary effect of keeping rewards commensurate with costs (Maurer and Scotchmer 2002; Ottoz and Cugno 2004).

However, an independent-invention defense can be harmful where an important part of the cost is in discovering "dry holes." By some counts, only one in five efforts to develop a new drug succeeds. If so, the cost of each successful drug must be recovered five times in order to keep the pharmaceutical companies in business and give them an incentive to attempt drug discoveries. In fact, PhRMA, the trade organization of the U.S. pharmaceutical firms, estimates that fewer than 30 per cent of new drugs (those actually brought to market) produce revenues that exceed R&D costs, and that the cost of each new drug brought to market is $800 million.[9] Reverse engineering or other independent invention could be so corrosive to the market prospects of the successful firm that it stifles the development of drugs. We hasten to add, however, that it is not obvious, based on the arguments of chapter 2, that pharmaceuticals should be funded with IP incentives rather than public sponsorship. For drugs that are clearly "necessary," such as vaccines and antibiotics, there is a strong case for public sponsorship.

Finally, we turn to research exemptions. As mentioned in chapter 3, these have been largely abolished for patents but may apply to other types of intellectual property. Under the Semiconductor Chip Protection Act of 1984, rival chip manufacturers are allowed to reverse engineer and otherwise experiment with chips for the purpose of creating improvements, although they are prohibited from entering the market with clones. To enter the market, reverse engineers must use the chip to create an improvement. Similarly, under the Plant Variety Protection Act for protecting hybrid seeds, purchasers of crop seeds are allowed not only to save seed for planting, but also to use the seeds for their own experimentation in creating new hybrids (Moschini 2003). These provisions are designed to strike a balance between protecting innovators and promoting follow-on innovation. That balance is further discussed in the next chapter.

---

9.   PhRMA, 2003. This number is obviously very large, partly because, at a minimum, it includes the costs of "dry holes," and it is also inflated for the opportunity cost of research funds tied up in the long period of drug discovery and clinical trials.

4.6   The Problem of One-Size-Fits-All

There are two important defects of general-purpose intellectual property regimes such as copyrights and patents that arise from the fact that "one size fits all" within the classes of covered technologies. First is the simple fact that the rights cannot be modified according to the protection actually needed. The length of protection is set by statute, and breadth of patents is under the control of the PTO and courts, who have no mandate to make decisions based on economic reasoning. It is almost inevitable that some classes of innovations are underrewarded and others are overrewarded relative to the costs of invention.

The second defect is that the reward structure cannot be modified according to the market structure in which the innovator operates.

The dangers of a one-size-fits-all system can be seen in the much vilified business-method patent, U.S. patent 5,960,411, issued to amazon.com on its one-click method of checking out of the virtual store. The click carries information about the buyer's payment and shipment information, so that it need not be entered again. As is true of many business-method patents, this technology seems obvious to many people. Even if there is a modest invention, the patent seems like a disproportionate reward. Can this concern be addressed within the one-size-fits-all paradigm of patent law?

First, does the one-click technology embody the minimum inventive step needed for a patent? What was invented? Surely the idea of using information gathered in previous purchases is not new, at least to a vendor skilled in the art of being a vendor. And on the buyer's side, finding a way to give the information efficiently is also not new, or at least is obvious to someone skilled in the art of being a buyer. Even if some part of the one-click technology is truly new, one could argue that the standard of patentability, or minimum inventive step, should be such that the invention does not qualify for a patent. This is not a very satisfactory approach, though, because it is too binary. Either the innovator is very much overrewarded, or the innovator is not rewarded at all.

Then what about breadth? Perhaps the one-click patent is simply too broad. The breadth of a patent is determined by the claims that were granted, as interpreted by courts. Claims that go beyond what was invented can overreward the inventor, and that may be the problem with the one-click patent. One could argue that the claims should not include the general idea of preserving information on either the user's computer or the vendor's server, and that any other means of transferring that data to an order form—for example, by dragging an icon rather than by clicking—should escape the patent. If the claims were interpreted in that way, the protection would be much more similar to copyright protection than patent protection, since the idea is not protected. Narrow claims of that type would have the same virtue as narrow protection for methods of implementing the Dutch auction, discussed in chapter 3. The proliferation of patents would be of only limited concern, since their narrow breadth would protect competition.

Finally, we consider the problem of market structure. In a very famous book, Joseph Schumpeter (1942) hypothesized that large, monopolistic firms are more innovative than small, competitive firms. The hypothesis has led to a large but inconclusive empirical and theoretical literature asking whether it is true. The inquiry is mostly directed at competition policy, in particular whether merger of firms should be tolerated because it leads to innovation.

That market structure can change the incentive to innovate was shown theoretically by Arrow (1962).[10] Suppose that the innovation in question is a cost-reducing innovation, and suppose that the cost reduction is so large that the innovator will become a monopolist even if the market was previously competitive. Compare the following two situations. Prior to the innovation, the innovator operates in a perfectly competitive market, or, prior to the innovation, the innovator is already a monopolist. Then, contrary to Schumpeter's hypothesis, the incremental profit earned by the innovator is larger if the innovator begins as a competitor than if he or she begins as a monopolist. This is because, as a monopolist, he or she would have earned some profit in any case.

On the other hand, the gain in consumers' surplus is larger if the innovator starts as a monopolist, since consumers then started with already high prices. Thus, when the innovator begins as a monopolist rather than a competitor, innovation creates less profit and more consumers' surplus. As a consequence, it may be optimal to offer greater profit incentives—for example, through patent life—but there is no way to achieve that, since intellectual property rights cannot depend on market structure.

---

10.   See also the discussion in chap. 2 of Blair and Kaserman 1985, which shows this graphically and describes extensions.

4.7   Technical Notes

4.7.1   The Ratio Test: Profit to Deadweight Loss

Suppose the duration and price that result from the two policies (T^*, K^*), $(\tilde{T}, K)$ are (T^*, p^*), $(\tilde{T}, \tilde{p})$, where $T^* < \tilde{T}$ and $p^* > \tilde{p}$. If the two policies generate the same profit for the innovator and the ratio (4.4) holds, then the policy $(\tilde{T}, \tilde{p})$ (a lower price for a longer duration) generates more discounted consumers' surplus. Both policies are equally profitable if

$$p^* x(p^*) T^* = \tilde{p} x(\tilde{p}) \tilde{T} \tag{4.3}$$

where $x(p)$ is the quantity demanded at price p.

For each price p, let $s(p)$ represent the consumers' surplus, namely, the area under the demand curve above the price. Then consumers are better off with the policy $(\tilde{T}, \tilde{p})$ than with the policy (T^*, p^*) if

$$\tilde{T}s(\tilde{p}) + \left(\frac{1}{r} - \tilde{T}\right) s(0) > T^* s(p^*) + \left(\frac{1}{r} - T^*\right) s(0)$$

where $s(0)$ is the consumers' surplus at the competitive price $p = 0$. On each side of the inequality, the first term is the consumers' surplus during the life of the patent, and the second term is the consumers' surplus after the protection ends. The inequality can be written

$$\tilde{T}[s(0) - s(\tilde{p})] < T^*[s(0) - s(p^*)]$$

The loss in consumers' surplus by imposing a price higher than the competitive price can be written as the profit $\tilde{p} x(\tilde{p})$ plus deadweight loss, say $d(\tilde{p})$ (the lighter shaded area in figure 4.5):

$$s(0) - s(\tilde{p}) = \tilde{p} x(\tilde{p}) + d(\tilde{p})$$

The policy $(\tilde{T}, \tilde{p})$ is therefore better for consumers than (T^*, p^*) if

$$\tilde{T}[\tilde{p} x(\tilde{p}) + d(\tilde{p})] < T^*[p^* x(p^*) + d(p^*)]$$

Using $\tilde{T}\tilde{p} x(\tilde{p}) = T^* p^* x(p^*)$, the inequality holds if and only if

$$\frac{\tilde{p} x(\tilde{p})}{d(\tilde{p})} > \frac{p^* x(p^*)}{d(p^*)} \tag{4.4}$$

This is the ratio test alluded to in section 4.3. That is, the better policy is the one for which, in each period of protection, the ratio of profit to deadweight loss is greater. If demand is linear as in figure 4.5, then this inequality holds, so the policy with lower price and longer duration, $(\tilde{T}, \tilde{p})$, is better than the policy with higher price and shorter duration, (T^*, p^*).

4.7.2   Patent Races: Probabilities of Success and Time to Completion

We revisit the simpler patent race described above, where each firm has an "idea" (v, c, p), and assume that if all firms fail in a given period, they will renew their efforts in the next period, at the same cost. This will lead to the same dynamics as a model based on a "Poisson" process of discovery, as discussed by Loury (1979), Lee and Wilde (1980), and Reinganum (1989). The version of the model given earlier is that of Tandon (1982, 1983) and Wright (1983).

Let $P(n)$ be the probability that at least one firm succeeds when there are n firms participating. The time to discovery can be any of $i = 1, 2, 3 \ldots, \infty$. The probability of having the first success in period i is the probability that there is a success in period i but no success in any previous period, namely, $P(n)(1 - P(n))^{i-1}$. Thus the expected number of periods until success can be calculated as

$$\sum_{i=1}^{\infty} i P(n)(1 - P(n))^{i-1} = P(n)\sum_{i=1}^{\infty} i(1 - P(n))^{i-1} = -P(n)\sum_{i=1}^{\infty}\frac{d}{dP(n)}(1 - P(n))^i$$

$$= -P(n)\frac{d}{dP(n)}\sum_{i=1}^{\infty}(1 - P(n))^i = -P(n)\frac{d}{dP(n)}\left[\frac{1}{P(n)} - 1\right]$$

$$= \frac{1}{P(n)}$$

The firms accrue costs in each period until the research program is successful, but the costs must be discounted, so they are less than $c/P(n)$. The discounted cost of n firms that accrue costs until period i is $\sum_{t=1}^{i} nc/(1+r)^t$. Thus, the expected cost to n firms that remain in the race until there is a success is

$$nc\sum_{i=1}^{\infty}\left[\sum_{t=1}^{i}\left(\frac{1}{1+r}\right)^t\right]P(n)(1 - P(n))^{i-1} = nc\sum_{i=1}^{\infty}\frac{1}{r}\left[1 - \left(\frac{1}{1+r}\right)^i\right]P(n)(1 - P(n))^{i-1}$$

$$= \frac{nc}{r}\left[1 - \frac{P(n)}{r + P(n)}\right] = \frac{nc}{r + P(n)}$$

The value of the intellectual property right must also be discounted from when it is achieved. With probability $P(n)(1 - P(n))^{i-1}$, the value must be discounted i periods. The expected discounted value of Π is thus

$$\Pi \sum_{i=1}^{\infty} \left(\frac{1}{1+r}\right)^{i} P(n)(1-P(n))^{i-1} = \Pi \frac{P(n)}{1+r} \sum_{i=1}^{\infty} \left(\frac{1-P(n)}{1+r}\right)^{i-1} = \Pi \frac{P(n)}{P(n)+r}$$

Hence the total expected profit to all firms together is

$$\frac{\Pi P(n) - nc}{P(n)+r}$$

Each firm receives a share $1/n$ of this expected profit. Thus, there will be entry until $\Pi P(n^e) - n^e c = 0$, as in the one-period race.

4.7.3   Patent Races: Aggregating Correlated Information

Assume that the firms are pursuing an innovation of unknown value but that each firm has a private "signal" of the eventual value. We show that the patent race can have an equilibrium in which the firms reinforce each other in error, each carrying out the same investment strategy as the other, in particular, an inefficient one.[11]

Let the signals be v_1, v_2 for firms 1 and 2 respectively. The targeted objective has a common value given by nature, and the signals are correlated with that value (hence the signals are correlated with each other). For example, suppose that the targeted research objective is to use a genetic target to find a drug. Then it is either true or not that there is a chemical in the chemical libraries that will bond with that target. Firms might have different optimism or pessimism based on their other drug research. A high signal v_1 will be interpreted to mean that researcher 1 is optimistic. That optimism would be reinforced if researcher 1 knew the other firm also had a high signal, and would be tempered if the other firm had a low signal. Thus, each firm would also like to know the signal (information) possessed by the other firm. Although the signals do not completely resolve the uncertainty, they contain information in the sense that they shift beliefs. For example, if both firms have low signals, the observer will think it more likely that the value will be low, or that the probability of success is low, and may scuttle the project.

This is a situation where patents can perform quite badly, while a sponsored attempt to aggregate the information can perform reasonably well.

---

11.   This discussion follows Minehart and Scotchmer (1999), although they considered the pure problem of information revelation and not the additional complexity of rivalry in a patent race.

To be concrete, suppose that the true value of the innovation is a random variable v, and that éach firm, $i = 1, 2$, has a private signal $v_i \in \{L, H\}$ (low or high) of the innovation's value, and the same cost, c. If firm 1 knows only its own signal, then the expected value that it places on the innovation can be written $E(v|v_1)$, where the expectation is taken with respect to the posterior distribution of v, knowing v_1. For example, if firm 1 has a signal $v_1 = H$, then the posterior distribution of v is shifted toward higher values, as compared to the prior distribution of v. If both signals (v_1, v_2) are known, then the expected value of the innovation can be written $E(v|v_1, v_2)$. This expected value is higher if the signals are $(v_1, v_2) = (H, H)$ than if they are (L, H) or (H, L) or (L, L). Suppose a single firm would be willing to invest if $E(v|v_1, v_2) \geq c$, and a rival would join the race if $1/2\ E(v|v_1, v_2) \geq c$.

Suppose that the distributions are such that a firm with signal H is always willing to invest, even if it knows the other firm has signal L, and even if it only wins the patent race with probability one-half. Suppose that a firm with signal L is also willing to invest, even if it has a rival, except in the case that the signals are (L, L). Suppose that the signals (L, L) are such bad news that even a single firm would not invest. Then we claim that the equilibrium strategies are for each firm to invest if it has signal H or if it sees the other firm investing. If neither of these conditions holds, it should not invest.

The pathology that arises is when the signals turn out to be (L, L). In that case there are two equilibrium outcomes. In one of these outcomes both firms invest, each because the other is investing. In the other outcome neither firm invests, each because the other is not investing. In the case where both invest, each reasons that the other could be either H or L, and is thus willing to invest. In the case where neither invests, each infers that the other is L, and that is why they do not invest. The equilibrium with mutually reinforcing investment decisions is inefficient. If the firms knew each other's signals, instead of making inferences about them, they would not invest.

This is a case where a patent system performs badly at eliciting the firms' private information on value, but it can easily be overcome by a clever mechanism designer. It is a general principle (Maskin and Riley 1980; Cremer and McLean 1988) that correlated information can be elicited costlessly, even if firms have incentives to misrepresent it. Suppose the invention authority asks each firm to report its signal of value, rewarding the firms if they report similar values and punishing them with a fine if they report dissimilar values. The invention authority pays the firms for agreeing and fines them for disagreeing. Even if the firms do not share their private information with each other directly, telling the truth to the invention authority increases the chance of being in agreement, since their private information is positively correlated. The invention authority can thus get the firms to reveal their private information and then employ a procurement mechanism similar to the second-price auction to achieve the innovation at minimum cost. This scheme will solve the problem of asymmetric information posed by Wright (1983), where the firms, but not the invention authority, observe the value v.

References and Further Reading

Aoki, R., and S. Nagaoka. 2002. "The Utility Standard the Patentability of Basic Research." Report CIRJE-F-160. Tokyo: Center for International Research on the Japanese Economy, University of Tokyo.

Aeppel, T. 2004, April 19. "Brothers of Inventions 'Design-Arounds' Surge as More Companies Imitate Rivals' Patented Products." *Wall Street Journal* B1.

Arrow, K. 1962. "Economic Welfare and the Allocation of Resources for Invention." In R. Nelson, ed., *The Rate and Direction of Economic Activities: Economic and Social Factors*, 609–626. National Bureau of Economic Research Conference Series. Princeton, NJ: Princeton University Press.

Ayres, I., and P. Klemperer. 1999. "Limiting patentees' Market Power without Reducing Innovation Incentives: The Perverse Benefits of Uncertainty and Non-injunctive Remedies." *Michigan Law Review* 97:985–1033.

Blair, R. D., and D. L. Kaserman. 1985. *Antitrust Economics*. Homewood, IL: Irwin.

Choi, J. 1991. "Dynamic R&D Competition under 'Hazard Rate' Uncertainty." *RAND Journal of Economics* 22:596–610.

Cornelli, F., and M. Schankerman. 1999. "Patent Renewals and R&D Incentives." *RAND Journal of Economics* 30:197–213.

Cremer, J., and R. P. McLean. 1988. "Full Extraction of the Surplus in Bayesian and Dominant Strategy Auctions." *Econometrica* 56:1247–1257.

Dasgupta, P., and E. Maskin. 1987. "The Simple Economics of Research Portfolios." *Economic Journal* 97:581–595.

Dasgupta, P., and J. Stiglitz. 1980a. "Industrial Structure and the Nature of Innovative Activity." *Economic Journal* 90:266–293.

Dasgupta, P., and J. Stiglitz. 1980b. "Uncertainty, Market Structure and the Speed of Research." *Bell Journal of Economics* 11:1–28.

Denicolò, V. 1996. "Patent Races and Optimal Patent Breadth and Length." *Journal of Industrial Economics* 44:249–265.

Eisenberg, R. S. 1989. "Patents and the Progress of Science: Exclusive Rights and Experimental Use." *University of Chicago Law Review* 56:1017–1086.

Fudenberg, D., R. Gilbert, J. Stiglitz, and J. Tirole. 1983. "Preemption, Leapfrogging and Competition in Patent Races." *European Economic Review* 22:3–31.

Fullerton, R., and P. McAfee. 1999. "Auctioning Entry into Tournaments." *Journal of Political Economy* 107:573–605.

Gallini, N. T. 1992. "Patent Length and Breadth with Costly Imitation," *RAND Journal of Economics* 44:52–63.

Gilbert, R., and C. Shapiro. 1990. "Optimal Patent Length and Breadth," *RAND Journal of Economics* 21:106–112.

Gordon, W. 1982. "Fair Use as Market Failure: A Structural and Economic Analysis of the Betamax Case and its Predecessors." *Columbia Law Review* 82:1600–1655.

Harris, C., and J. Vickers. 1985a. "Patent Races and the Persistence of Monopoly." *Journal of Industrial Economics* 33:461–481.

Harris, C., and J. Vickers. 1985b. "Perfect Equilibrium in a Model of a Race." *Review of Economic Studies* 52:193–209.

Harris, C., and J. Vickers. 1987. "Racing with Uncertainty." *Review of Economic Studies* 54:1–21.

Judd, K. L. 1985. "On the Performance of Patents." *Econometrica* 53:567–586.

Kamien, M. I., and N. L. Schwartz. 1974. "Patent Life and R&D Rivalry." *American Economic Review.* 64:183–187.

Kalow, L. 1984. "The Patent-Antitrust Intersection: A Reappraisal." *Harvard Law Review* 97:1813–1892.

Klemperer, P. 1990. "How Broad Should the Scope of Patent Protection Be?" *RAND Journal of Economics* 21:113–130.

Kremer, M. 1998. "Patent Buyouts: A Mechanism for Encouraging Innovation." *Quarterly Journal of Economics* 113:1137–1167.

Lanjouw, J. O. 1998. "The Introduction of Pharmaceutical Product Patents in India: 'Heartless Exploitation of the Poor and Suffering?'" Working Paper 6366. Cambridge, MA: National Bureau of Economic Research.

Lee, T., and L. Wilde. 1980. "Market Structure and Innovation: A Reformulation." *Quarterly Journal of Economics* 94:429–436.

Llobet, G., H. Hopenhayn, and M. Mitchell 2000. "Rewarding Sequential Innovators: Prizes, Patents and Buyouts." Staff Report 273. Minneapolis, MN: Federal Reserve Bank of Minneapolis.

Loury, G. 1979. "Market Structure and Innovation." *The Quarterly Journal of Economics* 93:395–410.

Maskin, E., and J. Riley. 1980. "Auction Design with Correlated Reservation Values." Mimeograph. Princeton, NJ: Department of Economics, Princeton University.

Maurer, S., and S. Scotchmer. 2002. "The Independent Invention Defense in Intellectual Property." *Economica* 69:535–547.

Menell, P. 2002. "Can Our Current Conception of Copyright Law Survive in the Internet Age? Envisioning Copyright Law's Digital Future." *New York Law Review* 46:63–193.

Merges, R. P., and R. Nelson. 1990. "On the Complex Economics of Patent Scope." *Columbia Law Review* 90:839–916.

Minehart, D., and S. Scotchmer. 1999. "Ex Post Regret and the Decentralized Sharing of Information." *Games and Economic Behavior* 27:114–131.

Moschini, G. 2003. "Intellectual Property Rights and the World Trade Organization: Retrospect and Prospects." Staff General Research Paper 10442. Ames: Department Agricultural Economics, Iowa State University.

Nordhaus, W. 1969. *Invention, Growth, and Welfare.* Cambridge, MA: MIT Press.

Ottoz, E., and F. Cugno. 2004. "The Independent Invention Defence in a Cournot-Duopoly Model." *Economics Bulletin* 12:1–7.

PhRMA. 2003. "Industry Profile." Available at www.phrma.org/publications/publications/profile02/index.cfm.

Reinganum, J. 1981. "Dynamic Games of Innovation." *Journal of Economic Theory* 25:21–41.

Reinganum, J. 1982. "A Dynamic Game of R&D: Patent Protection and Competitive Behaviour." *Econometrica* 50:671–688.

Reinganum, J. 1989. "The Timing of Innovation: Research, Development and Diffusion." In R. Schmalensee and R. D. Willig, eds., *Handbook of Industrial Organization*, 849–908. Amsterdam: Elsevier.

Samuelson, P., and S. Scotchmer. 2002. "The Law and Economics of Reverse Engineering." *Yale Law Journal* 111:1575–1663.

Schankerman, M. 1998. "How Valuable Is Patent Protection? Estimates by Technology Field." *RAND Journal of Economics* 29:77–107.

Schumpeter, J. A. 1942. *Capitalism, Socialism and Democracy.* New York: Harper & Row.

Scotchmer, S. 1999. "On the Optimality of the Patent System." *RAND Journal of Economics* 30:181–196.

Sobel, D. 1995. *Longitude: The True Story of a Lone Genius Who Solved the Greatest Scientific Problem of His Time.* New York: Walker.

Strandh, S. 1970. *A History of the Machine*. New York: A&W Publishers.

Tandon, P. 1982. "Optimal Patents with Compulsory Licensing." *Journal of Political Economy* 90:470–486.

Tandon, P. 1983. "Rivalry and the Excessive Allocation of Resources to Research." *Bell Journal of Economics* 14:152–165.

Taylor, C. 1995. "Digging for Golden Carrots: An Analysis of Research Tournaments." *American Economic Review* 85:872–889.

Von Hippel, E. 1988. *The Sources of Innovation*. Oxford: Oxford University Press.

Wright, B. 1983. "The Economics of Invention Incentives: Patents, Prizes and Research Contracts." *American Economic Review* 73:691–707.

5 Standing on the Shoulders of Giants: Protecting Cumulative Innovators

The discussion of intellectual property in the previous chapter assumed that innovations are isolated discoveries with no bearing on future innovations. That view limits how well the theory can be applied to modern controversies, especially those involving biotechnology, computer software, and computer hardware. These technologies have a high degree of "cumulativeness," in the sense that each innovator builds on prior developments and discoveries.

When innovation is cumulative, the most important benefit of the innovation may be the boost it gives to later innovators. The boost can take at least three forms. If the next innovation could not be invented without the first, then the social value of the first innovation includes at least part of the incremental social value provided by the second. If the first innovation merely reduces the cost of achieving the second, then the cost reduction is part of the social value provided by the first. And if the first innovation accelerates development of the second, then the social value includes the value of getting the second innovation sooner. The problem introduced for incentive mechanisms is how to make sure that earlier innovators are compensated for their contributions, while ensuring that later innovators also have an incentive to invest.

The problems that may arise are illustrated by one of the most important discoveries of the twentieth century, the laser, which was invented by Charles Townes and his colleagues in the 1950s (also see the discussion in chapter 3). As related in Townes's 1999 memoir, the inventors were inspired by a scientific theory put forward by Einstein forty years earlier, as well as by the radar research that had gone on during World War II. They understood that it should be possible to create coherent electromagnetic waves by hitting an "excited" atom with photons. The atom would then emit an additional photon, in the same direction and with the same wavelength as the incident ones. Those two properties are called coherence. Given enough excited atoms, a small number of incident photons can be amplified to high energy.

The first development of that idea, called the maser, was for microwaves instead of light. The maser then inspired development of the laser. The laser presented different technical difficulties than the maser, in particular because it required a different medium for exciting atoms. The improvements and implementations used different materials, some gaseous and then a ruby crystal.

The laser, and especially its predecessor, the maser, was initially an invention in search of a use. Although the inventors did not anticipate the specific uses that would later materialize, they were confident that there would be some. New uses are still proliferating. At least 224 laser-related patents were issued by the PTO in 2002, almost forty years later.[1] Many patents are industrial and involve using lasers for cutting and welding. Others are medical, such as surgery. Finally, many are computer related. Using lasers to read and burn CDs was already patented in 1965 (Dyson 2001).

As with many important and profitable inventions, the tale of the laser is ridden with conflict.[2] We have already described an early conflict between the Research Corporation, to which Townes assigned the 1957 maser patent, and Bell Labs, to which the 1960 Townes-Schawlow laser patent was assigned. This dispute was eventually settled amicably. The first working laser, using the ruby crystal, was patented by Theodore Maiman at the Hughes Corporation in 1960. Another laser patent—the one that led to prolonged litigation—was filed by a former graduate student named Gordon Gould in 1959, with whom Townes had discussed early stage work and ideas. Initially the Gould patent was denied due to conflict with the Townes-Schawlow disclosure. After decades of legal wrangling, this was reversed. The court eventually held that the Townes-Schawlow patent did not cover the high-output laser technology described in the 1959 Gould application. The first Gould patent issued in 1977, after two decades of delay and hundreds of thousands of dollars in legal fees. By then, new uses of the laser were growing explosively, so the delay created a windfall in licensing revenues. The Gould patent

1.   See www.patentweb.de/laser/patents.htm, a website maintained for the purpose of searching laser patents.
2.   Thomas Edison, who had about 1,000 patents, is famously said to have remarked that a patent is simply an invitation to a lawsuit (Friedel 1996, 25).

earned vast sums, while the Townes patents earned only modest sums. Einstein, the founder, earned nothing at all.

What do we learn from this tangled tale? First, and most important, innovators learn from their predecessors. Each step in the development of the laser used knowledge contributed by the earlier inventor and may not have been possible without it. Second, it is not easy to compensate the developers of basic technologies. Commercial value generally resides in products that are developed later. If the founders earn some profit, it is only because they can demand licensing fees from later developers. But this requires that later products infringe their patents. Basic scientific knowledge, such as the knowledge contributed by Einstein, is generally not patentable, in recognition of the fact that the benefits would be hard to appropriate.

As argued in this chapter, the main features of intellectual property that determine how profit is divided between successive inventors are breadth and the required inventive step. If a second-generation product both infringes an earlier patent and receives its own patent, then each inventor has blocking rights on the second product. They both have a claim on its value. For example, the courts and the PTO could have held that Gould's version of the laser infringed the Townes-Schawlow patent and was at the same time patentable. This might have been a fairer resolution. The question of blocking never came up because the Townes-Schawlow patent expired the year that the Gould patent issued.

Computer systems are another twentieth-century technology where the cumulative nature of research has caused friction among innovators, as well as market turnover. Like Gould in the laser wars, Microsoft was a second comer, but it has ended up with a dominant market position in the most popular desktop software (although we caution that history is not yet over). An informative history of desktop computing software from the 1970s to 1997 can be found in Evans, Nichols, and Reddy 1999, partly summarized in table 5.1, showing how market dominance in three software markets has shifted. The first text editor to emerge from the pack with a dominant position was WordStar. It was supplanted after seven years by Corel's Word Perfect, which was supplanted six years later by Microsoft Word, still the market leader.

The spreadsheet market had a similar history of shifting dominance, with later spreadsheets adding capabilities but clearly building on the ideas embodied in earlier ones. In the early 1990s, a bitter copyright dispute erupted between the then dominant firm Lotus 1-2-3 and a rival,

Table 5.1
Summary of category leaders for microcomputer software through 1997

	Introduction date	Leadership start date	Years to leadership	Years as leader	Approximate Shares[a] (%)		
					Leader	Second	Third
Word processors 1979–1997							
Word Star	1979	1980	1	5			
Word Perfect[b]	1980	1987	7	6	41	21	10
MS Word	1983	1993	10	5+	62	26	9
Spreadsheets 1979–1997							
VisiCalc	1979	1979	0	5			
Lotus 1-2-3	1983	1984	1	9	51	20	12
MS Excel[c]	1985	1993	8	5+	69	26	5
Operating systems 1977–1997							
CP/M[d]	1974	1977		7			
(MS or PC)-DOS	1981	1984	3	9			
Windows (16-bit)	1985	1993	8	3			
Windows 95	1995	1996	1	2+			

Source of data: International Data Corporation.
Origin of table: Evans, Nichols, and Reddy 1999.
[a] Median share for first-, second-, and third-placed competitors over the tenure of the leader.
[b] WordPerfect was released first for the Data General in 1980 and for DOS in late 1982.
[c] Excel was released for the Macintosh in 1985 and for Windows in 1987.
[d] CP/M was developed about 1974, but its first major OEM deals were in 1977.

Borland Quattro, over the extent to which the new entrant Borland could make its product compatible with the market incumbent. They fought valiantly all the way to the Supreme Court, thinking that one of them would prevail. In fact, both soon lost out in the market to Microsoft Excel, which added superior graphing capabilities.

And, of course, there is the market for desktop operating systems themselves, where market dominance moved from CP/M to MS-DOS/PC-DOS, and then to Windows, which has been its own successor, with Microsoft introducing compatible, improved updates. The open-source operating system, Linux, has not yet become user-friendly enough, and does not yet have enough applications software, to be a contender for market dominance.

Software markets illustrate the conundrums that arise from cumulative research and also call attention to an important difference between copyright and patents. Until the mid-1990s, computer programs were copyrighted but not patented. In general, there are no such things as "blocking copyrights" (Lemley 1997). Thus, the device that patent law uses to let sequential innovators share the value of improvements was generally not available under copyright law. When a new product entered the market, previous products had no claim on it.

The problem addressed in this chapter is how intellectual property organizes the division of profit among sequential innovators. To get the incentives right, not only must the innovators collectively earn enough profit to cover their joint costs, but the profit must also be divided so that it creates the right incentives at each stage of innovation. Most importantly, each innovator in the sequence must cover his or her own costs. As we will see, intellectual property is a blunt instrument for that delicate problem.

The analysis of cumulative innovation in this chapter is largely rooted in the ideas model discussed in chapter 2 and, in particular, in the notion that ideas are scarce. This is why successive innovations will be made by different innovators. When an investment is made, ideas for future progress are unknown, although the investor must have a subjective notion of their prospective worth. If all ideas for cumulative advance were available to all firms, including market incumbents, then the problem of dividing profit among successive innovators might be less acute. As we will see, different models of the creative environment present different incentive problems.

In chapter 8 we will point out that publicly funded research, especially in universities, is skewed towards basic research. One rationale is that the benefits of basic research are hard to appropriate by private parties. This chapter will equip us to evaluate that point of view as well as other rationales for publicly funding basic research.

5.1   Three Types of Cumulativeness

Three types of cumulativeness are illustrated in figures 5.1–5.3. Figure 5.1 shows that a single innovation, such as the laser, may lead to many second-generation innovations, such as surgical applications, spectroscopy, and so on. Alternatively, a first-generation tool like a gene target may lead to a single second-generation innovation, such as a new drug.

Figure 5.2 shows the case where a second-generation product requires the input of many different first-generation products, often called research tools. Some of these tools may end up embodied in the product, and some not. For example, bioengineered crop seed may require genes that code for traits such as sweetness or durability, genes that code for pest resistance such as Bt for corn borers, genes that cause the inserted genes to express, and research tools that facilitate insertion of the genes into the germplasm. The trait and expression genes end up embodied in the modified germplasm, but the research tools do not. Despite this difference, all of these prior inventions may be essential for developing the seed.

Figure 5.3 shows a quality ladder in which firms create successively better products, each improving on the previous one. Here the focus is on successive improvement, where no innovator is secure in thinking that

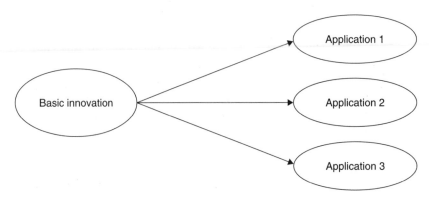

Figure 5.1
Basic research and applications

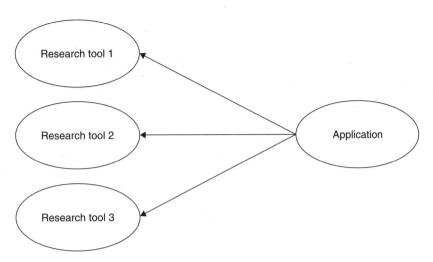

Figure 5.2
The problem of licensing many research inputs

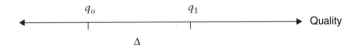

Figure 5.3
Quality ladder: competition between successive innovators

his or her innovation will be the last. The problem that arises is that competition between successive innovators may be so severe that firms are reluctant to undertake any but the most lucrative improvements. Suppose, for example, that q_o is the quality of the most recent product in the product line. If a new improved version of the product is too similar to the old one, say, q_1 in figure 5.3, then there will be two goods in the market with a quality difference Δ. The fierceness of competition between the two goods depends on this quality difference. If the quality difference is small, even the most recent innovator cannot set a very high price.

Figures 5.1 and 5.2 differ importantly in the licensing relationships that they require. The situation described by figure 5.2 requires that a second-generation inventor receive a license on each underlying research tool or other input. Biomedical researchers have expressed fear that a proliferation of such licenses could be so onerous that it would stifle research instead of promoting it. While transaction costs may justify such a view, it is also important to realize that once the research tools exist, it is in the interest of all parties to resolve conflicts in property rights in order to ensure that pharmaceuticals and other second-generation products materialize. The sole source of profit on research tools is the second-generation products that they enable. To stifle such products would be economic suicide.

The cumulativeness of research introduces two new worries in designing intellectual property rights. The main worry in a market with two stages of innovation is how to compensate the first innovator for the foundation laid for later innovators. In general, as we will see, the initial innovator cannot collect all the profit from the second-generation products, and a fortiori cannot collect all the social value. If the anticipated profit seems inadequate to cover cost, the first innovator will not invest and the whole research line will be stymied. The second worry is that profit between successive innovators will be eroded by competition between them. The price in each generation of the product may be so low, due to competition with the previous innovator, that the innovator cannot cover cost. This is the analog for sequential innovations of the problem of narrow patents, discussed in chapter 4. When patents are narrow, they are not very profitable due to competition among close substitutes.

It is hard to think of examples that fit the quality-ladder model in its stark form, but if one takes a more metaphorical view, it fits almost every important technology, including the laser and desktop software. The early history of the computer is itself a story of sequential improvers building on known inventions (McCartney 1999). Pascal initiated this effort as early as the seventeenth century, when he created a rotation device to routinize addition. Notches on a rotating drum signified digits, and after ten were reached, there was a transfer to another drum, signifying the next decimal place. After explicitly studying Pascal's work a few years later, Leibniz expanded this system so that it could do multiplication, the latter being repeated addition. The Leibniz design became the basis for the mechanical desk calculator in the nineteenth century. In that century, Babbage produced two improvements on the mechanical calculator, the Difference Engine which was more or less built, and the Analytical Engine, which was not. Babbage's second machine lays the foundation for all modern computers by making three important conceptual breakthroughs. It could (theoretically) concatenate arithmetic operations and use subroutines, it had the notion of storing numbers for later use, and it had the notion of "if/then/else" statements for branching logic. These ideas were finally brought to fruition in the twentieth century with the development of the vacuum-tube computer and electronic calculation. The final breakthroughs were the transistor and integrated circuit.

In other areas of electronics, technologies have evolved more quickly. As recounted by Dyson (2001), the idea of creating incandescent light with an electrical current was first demonstrated in 1801 by an English chemist, Humphry Davy. Although the incandescent filament burned in air and did not last long enough to be practical, the experiment inspired another English chemist, Joseph Swan, to work further on the problem. In 1860 he patented a carbon filament encased in an evacuated tube, predecessor to the modern tungsten-filament lightbulb. Development continued by Swan and then by the great American inventor Thomas Edison, who vowed to make the electric lightbulb a household item. Both Swan and Edison made workable lightbulbs about 1870 and ended up in a patent battle. The patent fight was settled by merger, much in the style of the model in section 5.4, with the two inventors each promoting the lightbulb on opposite sides of the ocean.

The important feature of these examples is that early innovations laid a foundation for later ones. Early progress on the computer was leisurely, but quality improvements to twentieth-century technologies such as desktop computer applications have been rapid. In such an environment, innovators are likely to be knocked out of the market. How can the incentives of each improver be preserved without stifling rapid progress? That is the subject of what follows.

5.2   Basic and Applied Research

We first consider basic and applied research, as described in figure 5.1. Our objective is to understand the efficacy of intellectual property rights in supporting incentives to innovate. Not only must the innovators collectively cover their costs, but each innovator must cover his or her cost individually. If most of the profit is due to the application and not to the basic research, much of the profit must be passed back to the first innovator. The instrument for doing that is licensing. Our task is to understand what the terms of license depend on, and in particular, whether the division of profit will reflect the respective costs of the two innovators. If the division of profit is insensitive to the division of costs, the incentive system will not work very well.

The strategic environment of licensing is described in figure 5.4, adapted from Green and Scotchmer 1995. Suppose the first invention costs c_1, and that x measures its per-period value to end users (as opposed to later innovators). If the innovation is patented for (discounted) length T, the social value is $x((1/r) - \ell T)$, where r is the discount rate and ℓ is the fraction of the value lost as deadweight loss during the patent life. The rightholder's profit is $x\pi T$, where π is a fraction. If the first innovation is basic research in the sense of pure science, or if it is a research tool that enables the development of the application, such as a drug target, then it has no commercial value aside from licensing, and $x = 0$.

Suppose that a second firm has an idea (y, c_2) for a second-generation product, where y is the per-period increment to market value, and c_2 is its development cost. For simplicity, suppose that the idea emerges with no delay, inspired by the first innovation. If the second product is consolidated with the first—for example, by licensing to the prior inventor—then the total profit is $(x + y)\pi T$, and it has social value $(x + y)((1/r) - \ell T)$.

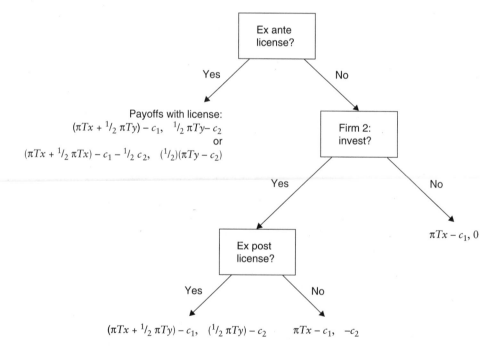

Figure 5.4
Threat points and equilibrium terms of license

Since the second-generation innovation is facilitated by the first, the social value of the first innovation should reflect the option on the second. That is, the social value of the first innovation is

$$x((1/r) - \ell T) - c_1 + \max\{0, y((1/r) - \ell T) - c_2\}$$

plus the social value of options on any other second-generation products that it enables.

With this model, we can refine the objectives we expect of the patent system. It should have the following two goals: (1) to ensure investment in the second product whenever $y((1/r) - \ell T) \geq c_2$; and (2) to transfer enough of the surplus $y((1/r) - \ell T) \geq c_2$ to the first innovator to ensure that he or she invests.

With respect to (2), it is illuminating to look at the case $x = 0$ where the first innovation has no value as a stand-alone product. Then no one would make the first innovation without profiting from second-generation products as well. Investment in the basic innovation may be socially efficient due to a high value y of the second-generation product even if $x = 0$.

Figure 5.4 describes the licensing options of the two firms, assuming that they have blocking patents on the second innovation. By blocking patents we mean that the second innovation is patentable but infringes the first patent. In this situation, either innovator can keep the second innovation from coming to market.

In figure 5.4 it is assumed that the two patent holders will resolve their blocking patents by licensing, but on what terms? The terms of license will be the outcome of bargaining, which depends on two ingredients. These two ingredients are used in many bargaining contexts. First are the *threat points*. For each firm, the threat point is the expected profit it can guarantee itself if it leaves the bargaining table. Second is the *bargaining surplus*. This is the amount by which the two firms will be richer in total if they actually make the bargain. Each firm can guarantee itself at least the amount of the threat point (that is why it is called the threat point), but there is a question as to how to divide the bargaining surplus. We will assume that they divide it equally, although the conclusions hold more generally.

The two firms can either sign a license agreement ex ante, before the second innovator invests c_2 (but after the first innovation has been made), or ex post, after the second innovator invests c_2. To figure out what terms will emerge in an ex ante license, we must therefore understand what would happen if either of them refused the ex ante agreement and forced the bargaining to take place ex post. That is what establishes the threat points for the ex ante agreement. Of course, the agreement that would be made ex post has its own threat points. In addition, it is worth noting that due to the absence of a research exemption (see chapter 3) it may be an infringement to develop the second innovation, even without marketing it, without the first patent holder's permission. In that case ex ante licensing is the only option. We return later to the implications of this restriction.

If the two firms license ex post, their threat points are $x\pi T - c_1$ and $-c_2$, respectively. Without any license at all, the second product could not come to market, because it is blocked by the patent on the first innovation. On the other hand, if they license so that the second product comes to market, they can add $y\pi T$ to their joint profit. That is the bargaining surplus. If they split this increment equally, their profits will be $(x\pi T + (1/2)y\pi T) - c_1$ and $(1/2)y\pi T - c_2$. These payoffs are shown at the bottom of figure 5.4.

If $(1/2)y\pi T - c_2 > 0$, then $(x\pi T + (1/2)y\pi T) - c_1$ and $(1/2)y\pi T - c_2$ are the payoffs in the ex ante licensing agreement as well, reflecting the fact that there is nothing further to be achieved by bargaining ex ante. These payoffs appear in the first numerical line in the upper-left branch of figure 5.4.

On the other hand, the costs c_2 of firm 2 could be so high that $(1/2)y\pi T - c_2 < 0$. Firm 2 anticipates that it will be held up for such high licensing fees ex post that it cannot cover costs. In that case, there is a bargaining surplus to be achieved by making an ex ante agreement. The licensor can ensure that the second investment goes forward by binding itself to a lower fee than it would demand ex post when the second innovator's costs are already sunk. The firms' threat points are now $x\pi T - c_1$ and 0, and the terms of license for the ex ante agreement appear in the second numerical line of the upper-left-hand branch of figure 5.4.

Three important conclusions emerge from this model. First, being constrained to resolve the blocking patents ex post might put the second generation of products in jeopardy. The second innovator knows that it may be held up for high licensing fees, and will not invest unless the difference between the value of the innovation and its cost are relatively high. Resolving the blocking patents ex ante can expand the circumstances in which the second product is developed, namely, whenever $y\pi T - c_2 \geq 0$.

Second, to ensure that the costs of both innovators are covered, the patent life might have to be longer than if the same innovator developed both generations. If the two innovations are developed by a single firm, both innovations will go forward whenever $(x + y)\pi T - c_1 - c_2 \geq 0$ and $y\pi T - c_2 \geq 0$.[3] However, in the ideas model, different firms will typically have the ideas for the successive innovations. In that case, both firms typically get a positive share of any bargaining surplus, and the second innovator will generally make strictly positive profit. If the combined profit $(x + y)\pi T - c_1 - c_2$ is close to zero, this implies that the first innovator will make negative profit. That is, it will not cover costs, and in anticipation of that outcome, might not invest. To overcome this problem, the total profit available must be larger, which can be achieved by lengthening the patent life T.

Third, society's interest may in this instance be aligned with the first innovator's interests. Since the second innovation is never in jeopardy provided ex ante licenses can be made and provided $y\pi T - c_2 \geq 0$, the harder problem is to ensure that the first innovator covers costs. In this regard, the best outcome for society as a whole would be if the first innovator could make a take-it-or-leave-it offer and collect all the net profit on the second innovation. The first investment is more crucial than the second, because without it, the second is impossible. However, the take-it-or-leave-it offer is unreasonable, since the two firms are in symmetric bargaining positions.

Perhaps counterintuitively, a research exemption on the first innovation works to the benefit of its owner.[4] The payoffs in figure 5.4 reflect an assumption that the second innovator can develop the second product without a license, but cannot commercialize it. This might be interpreted to mean that there is a research exemption. The research exemption improves the first innovator's bargaining position because it allows the bargaining to occur ex post. Absent the research exemption, the first innovator would always have to bargain ex ante, before the second innovator's costs are sunk, and that is a worse bargaining position.

---

3.   If only one innovator is involved, the problems of dividing profit vanish. However, it is unreasonable to think that Charles Townes could have thought of and developed all the applications and uses of the laser. If ideas are scarce, it is more likely that rivals will think of follow-on products than that the first patent holder will, since there are many more rivals to whom ideas could occur.

4.   As we pointed out in chapter 3, patent law does not provide for a research exemption. Developing the second product may be an infringement even without commercializing it. Whether this distinction has consequences depends on the penalty. The analysis here assumes that the remedy is an injunction against selling the second product. But if the remedy would be to nullify the second patent, as might occur without a research exemption, there would be no unlicensed entry.

Finally, the division of profit is not very sensitive to the innovators' relative costs. If c_2 becomes high enough, the first patent holder will have to offer more generous licensing terms, but there is no reason that the first patent holder should earn more profit when its own costs are higher. The division of profit does not depend on its costs because they are sunk before licensing occurs. A lengthening of the protection will help to mitigate that problem, since both firms would then earn more revenue. But of course that imposes additional deadweight loss.

A market circumstance that should improve the first innovator's share of the profit is competition among potential second innovators. But even with competition, the first innovator might not get all the net profit.

Suppose, for example, that a genomics firm has the patent on a drug target but does not have the capacity to discover the drug and bring it to market. There may be several pharmaceutical firms eager to make the investment, and the target owner may contemplate auctioning an exclusive license. Surprisingly, however, an auction will not generally garner all the profit. This is because a losing bidder may nevertheless compete for the lucrative drug patent in hope of an ex post license. If so, the threat points of the bidders are not reduced to zero. We can see this by calculating the equilibrium bid price in the auction and showing that it is less than the value of the second innovation.

The equilibrium bid price in the auction is the difference in the bidder's profit between winning and losing the bid. If the bidder must pay more than this difference, it is better to lose the bid. To figure out the equilibrium bid price, we must therefore figure out the bidder's prospects if the bidder is, respectively, the winner and loser.

If a losing bidder invests in the drug he will be racing against the winning bidder but may nevertheless succeed. Then the losing bidder and the first patent holder (or the licensee) will have blocking patents on the drug. For either to profit, they must resolve the conflict, bargaining as above. Ex post they will split the bargaining surplus, and each will receive $(1/2)y\pi T$. If there are two firms in the race for the second product, a winning bidder and a losing bidder, each wins with probability one-half. Hence, the losing bidder's expected profit is

$$\left(\frac{1}{2}\right)\left(\frac{1}{2}\right)y\pi T - c_2 \qquad (5.1)$$

The expected profit of the winning bidder can be calculated as follows. With probability one-half he wins the race and earns $y\pi T$. With probability one-half he loses the race and splits the value of the patent with the other firm, earning $(1/2)y\pi T$. Thus, if each wins with probability one-half, the expected profit of the winning bidder is

$$\frac{1}{2}y\pi T + \left(\frac{1}{2}\right)\left(\frac{1}{2}\right)y\pi T - c_2$$

The difference in profit between winning and losing the bid is therefore $(1/2)y\pi T$, which is the equilibrium bid price for the exclusive license, hence the profit of the first patent holder. The winning bid $(1/2)y\pi T$ is less than the incremental value of the second product, $y\pi T - c_2$, if (5.1) is positive (so that the losing bidder would have incentive to invest). In that case, the first patent holder cannot collect all the profit by auctioning an exclusive license.[5]

Returning to our motivating question, what is required to ensure that both generations of innovators are rewarded for their contributions? First, because of the problem of dividing profit, and because the division of profit will be mostly insensitive to the innovators' relative costs, intellectual property rights should last longer than if the same innovator undertakes both basic research and its applications. Second, the more flexibility there is in licensing, the better the incentives will work. If, for example, licenses cannot be made ex ante, protection will have to last even longer. Protection must be long enough so that $(1/2)y\pi T - c_2 > 0$. Otherwise, the second generation may be stymied for fear of such high licensing fees that the second innovator cannot cover costs.

The foregoing discussion shows that licensing is absolutely central to how the incentive system works in the case of cumulative innovation. It is thus worth reflecting on obstacles to licensing. Probably the most important obstacle is asymmetric information as to the value of the innovations.[6] The second innovator has an incentive to overstate his costs to the first patent holder, in order to convince the patent holder that, absent an ex ante license, he would not invest. Of course the first patent holder will not necessarily believe this representation. But when all is said and

---

5.   The auction is a logical way to think about contracting, but it might not be the most profitable contract. The licensor might be able to hold the bidders to less than their "apparent" reservation payoffs by setting up a "prisoner's dilemma." This depends on whether firms can commit not to renegotiate contracts, and on whether the terms of contract with a single licensee can affect the nonlicensee's reservation payoff. See Scotchmer 1996.

6.   See Gallini and Wright 1990 for a discussion of licensing in the presence of asymmetric information.

done, the fact that the patent holder is relatively uninformed, and cannot rely on the second firm for accurate information, may inhibit ex ante licensing. The value of the second innovation may also be unverifiable to the patent holder ex ante, but this problem can be mitigated by licensing with royalties. The royalty payments will automatically be linked to the true value of the innovation.

Finally, this simple model does not recognize that patent races can accelerate progress, as discussed in chapter 4. Patent races are less focal in the ideas model than in models where there is a production function for knowledge. For discussion of cumulativeness in a context where patent races occur at each stage, see Denicolò 2000.

5.3   Research Tools

Figure 5.2 illustrates the important case in which each second-generation product depends on several prior discoveries, such as research tools. Many research tools are licensed or sold anonymously at a single price, rather than in negotiation as above. Prominent examples in biomedicine include PCR and (until the patent expired) the Cohen-Boyer patent on the basic technology of bioengineering. Materials such as cell lines are often licensed in this way.

When research inputs are sold anonymously to many users at a fixed market price, the incentives can be understood much as discussed in chapter 4. The proprietary price for each tool will depend on the closeness and prices of substitutes. Of course, the problems explored in chapter 4 are still present. The patent on a tool may be too broad, extending to substitutes even though the broad patent is not required to cover the development costs of the tool. As with ordinary consumer goods, the high price of the tool will discourage use. The social loss may be compounded because the tool would presumably have been used to develop other products.

The special feature introduced by research tools is that they are typically stacked on top of each other, as shown in figure 5.2. When sold anonymously in a market, their combined price can be so high that a second-generation user is excluded. Thus, the optimistic view presented in the last section must be revised. There we argued that, since the earlier innovator can always profit by getting a later innovator to license his patent, we can be confident that there will be investment in the second-generaton product whenever the incremental contribution to profit outweighs the cost. That is not true when the research tools are licensed anonymously at nonnegotiable prices. The situation may be even worse when licenses are negotiated. If several patent holders are vying for the value of the second-generation product, and all the technologies are essential to its development, there is no natural benchmark to establish how the profit on the second-generation product should be divided. Even if the commercial value of the second-generation product outweighs its cost, bargaining may break down. These problems have been named the "anticommons" by Heller and Eisenberg (1998).[7]

One solution to the anticommons is joint ownership of the tools. In the biotechnology revolution of 1980s and 1990s, traditional hybridization methods for developing crop seeds were largely displaced by bioengineering. Seed companies wanting to modify germplasms needed to buy multiple licenses. The market response was consolidation. Seed companies either bought, or were bought by, companies that owned patents on research tools.

Another type of consolidation would be a holding company for the tools themselves, to facilitate one-stop shopping. That is, the tools could be put into a patent pool and priced jointly rather than individually. Such consolidations often raise antitrust concerns, since the arrangement looks on the surface like collusion. However, when the constituent technologies are complements, as research tools might be, these concerns are not well founded.

---

7.   However, the best theoretical reason for an anticommons that has been advanced is transaction costs. There is evidence in Walsh, Arora, and Cohen 2003 that the anticommons does not exist. Certainly, the profit motive remains a powerful reason to overcome bargaining problems. IBM's experiences with memory-technology patents during the 1950s provide mixed evidence. Bashe et al. (1986) report an August 1955 meeting with key engineers in which IBM president Thomas J. Watson, Jr. "chided them for hestitating to use ferrite cores in commercial products because of Wang's patent. He quoted his father as saying, 'That's the most ridiculous reason for not moving into a new area that I've ever heard of because, one way or another, we can negotiate with Wang.'" Watson was vindicated when IBM obtained a license. However, Watson's "confidence was deeply shaken" later in the decade when he tried to license a second memory patent from the Research Corporation. The corporation demanded a royalty of 2¢ per bit. Since twelve patents were required to use the technology, IBM argued charging 2¢ per patent per bit would force the total cost ten to twenty times above market. Instead of negotiating, the Research Corporation sued for infringement. Bashe et al. remark that "the trauma . . . is legend" within IBM (pp. 267–271).

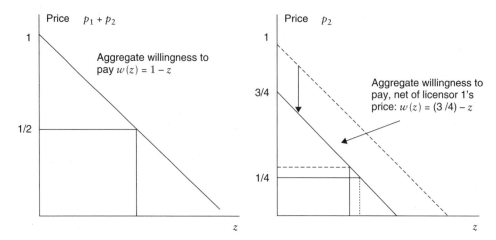

Figure 5.5
Complementary tools: the incentive to raise price

Two goods are complements if "the whole is more than the sum of the parts." Complementarity means that a user's willingness to pay for each of the goods is higher when using the others. Or to put it more conventionally, the demand for each of the goods increases if the price of the other decreases. (For substitutes, it is the other way around.) Research tools are complements if all are required for the research. In the extreme case, a tool has no value to the user at all unless the user also has access to its complements.

A surprising conclusion about licensing complementary tools (or selling complementary products) is that the joint price will be lower if they are sold as a unit by a single proprietor, as in a patent pool, than when sold separately by different proprietors.[8] Not only does "collusion" among the sellers of the complementary tools increase their profit, but it does so by lowering prices, which helps users rather than hurting them. Since this is possibly counterintuitive, and since patent pools are considered further in chapter 6, we consider the result more fully.

Figure 5.5 shows the aggregate willingness-to-pay curve (demand curve) for joint access to two complementary pieces of a technology, which must be used together to develop the user's innovation. The users

---

8.   This idea originates with Cournot ([1838] 1897) and has been discussed in many economic contexts by others—for example, Lichtman (2000) and Lerner and Tirole (2002) in the context of patent pools.

are indexed by z, and $w(z)$ represents the willingness to pay of user z for both pieces together. (Assume for expository purposes that both licenses are required for each use, but the analysis holds more generally.) In figure 5.5, the willingness-to-pay curve $w(\cdot)$ is defined by $w(z) = 1 - z$, and the combined monopoly price for using both tools together is 1/2.

Suppose that the monopoly price is divided evenly between the two tool proprietors. Each receives half—that is, $p_1 = p_2 = 1/4$. Figure 5.5 illustrates that this is not an equilibrium as long as either is allowed to raise the price. The right panel of figure 5.5 shows that licensor 2 (symmetrically, licensor 1) has an incentive to raise its fee. The demand curve faced by licensor 2 is derived by subtracting licensor 1's price $p_1 = 1/4$ from the original willingness-to-pay curve. The resulting demand curve shows how many customers will buy from both firms for each price charged by licensor 2, assuming that licensor 1's price is fixed at $p_1 = 1/4$. As shown in figure 5.5, licensor 2 can increase profit by charging something higher than $p_2 = 1/4$.[9] This illustrates a general result: separate licensors, each charging an anonymous price, will overprice their technologies relative to the case that they can collude.

An intuitive rather than graphical explanation is the following. If licensor 2 raises its price, it imposes a negative externality on licensor 1. Customers are lost to the market as a whole, reducing the profit of both licensors. For licensor 2 this loss is compensated by the increased revenue from its higher price. Licensor 2 is the sole beneficiary of the higher price, but the other licensor also loses customers. Since licensor 2 does not account for the negative externality on the other licensor, it is too willing to raise its license price, relative to the price that would maximize their joint profit.

Figure 5.6 shows graphically that, in fact, the equilibrium prices of the two tool owners are $p_1 = p_2 = 1/3$ when they price separately, so that the total price $p_1 + p_2$ is larger than the profit-maximizing price of 1/2. The left panel of figure 5.6 shows the residual willingness to pay for the purchasers of tool 1, given that they must pay $p_2 = 1/3$ for tool 2. As can

---

9.   The optimal number of users is $z^* = 1/2$, which provides profit $z^*w(z^*) = 1/4$. If licensor 1 charges half of this price, $p_1 = 1/4$, then the willingness-to-pay curve faced by licensor 2 is $(1 - z) - p_1 = 3/4 - z$. But then tool proprietor 2 wants to charge a price that will reduce z. If, for example, tool owner 2 charges $p_2 = 3/8$ instead of $p_2 = 1/4$, the number of customers is $z = 1 - (p_1 + p_2) = 1 - (1/4 + 3/8)$ instead of $z^* = 1 - (1/4 + 1/4) = 1/2$. Licensor 2 then earns $(3/8)(3/8)$, which is larger than $(1/4)(1/2)$.

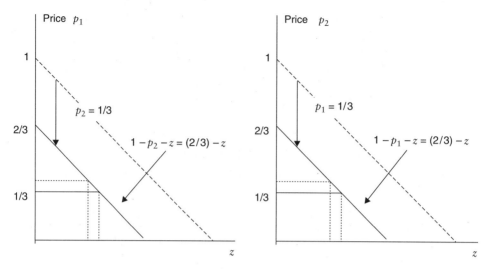

Figure 5.6
Complementary tools: equilibrium prices

be seen by inspection, the owner of tool 1 cannot increase profit by either increasing or decreasing price, and similarly for the proprietor of tool 2.[10]

5.4   Quality Ladders

On a quality ladder, there is no longer a distinction between "basic" innovators (licensors) and "applications" (licensees). There is only a sequence of products that keep getting better. Every improver will initially be in the position of market incumbent, and will then be superseded. The problem is to ensure a large enough flow of profit to cover costs, without discouraging rapid turnover in the market, and hence progress.

The quality ladder is described in figures 5.3 and 5.7. In the "ideas" model of the creative process, it is more likely that a rival thinks of the next improvement than that the incumbent thinks of it. This may be true even if ideas are more likely to occur to the incumbent, since there are

---

10.   The residual demand of tool owner 1 is $w(z) = 2/3 - z$. The profit $zw(z)$ is maximized at $\hat{z} = 1/3$, $p_1 = w(\hat{z}) = 1/3$. Since the same is true for tool owner 2, the equilibrium is $p_1 = p_2 = 1/3$, and the total profit of the tool owners is less than if they colluded on the combined monopoly price 1/2, with each charging 1/4.

many rivals and only one incumbent. Further, if ideas are scarce, disclosure of the current state of knowledge takes on a new importance. Since ideas build on the current state of knowledge, disclosure increases the probability in each period that there will be an idea for further advance, usually by a rival.

In this environment, what will create the incentive for firms to invest in improvements? The faster the improvements come, the shorter is the market incumbency of each innovator. Each innovator will lose its market dominance as soon as a replacement appears. That is, the *effective* patent life is likely to be much shorter than the statutory life. The innovation might survive, but only by selling at a price established in competition with its successor. Such a prospect might easily discourage investment. There seems to be an inevitable conflict between the rapid turnover that promotes rapid progress, and allowing each innovator a long enough incumbency to recover costs.

We will use the model of O'Donoghue, Scotchmer, and Thisse (1998) to see why the benefits of innovations are hard to appropriate in this environment of rapid turnover. Referring to figures 5.3 and 5.7, suppose that improvement takes place at the rate Δ per year. At each point in time, the profit stream will be related to Δ, the quality difference. Assume for simplicity that the price for the highest-quality product is $p = \Delta$, and that only the highest-quality product is sold. This assumption is justified, for example, if the marginal cost of producing the good (as distinct from the cost of developing it) is zero, and if consumers buy the good that provides the highest surplus $q - p$ where q is the quality. If the price were higher than Δ, the previous incumbent could also enter the market and make positive profit. By selling at a price slightly lower than $p - \Delta$, it could, in fact, have the whole market, and this will keep the price of the current incumbent at $p = \Delta$. Although the incumbent's price is determined by its quality advantage over the previous product, the price does not depend on the quality level itself.

What is the social value of an improvement of size Δ, and how much does the improver appropriate? The value of each incremental innovation lasts forever, since each subsequent innovation builds on it. Thus an increment to quality, Δ, has social value Δ/r, where r is the discount rate. However, the improver will only be the market incumbent for one period, selling at price $p = \Delta$. Thus, he only earns Δ, which is considerably smaller than the social value Δ/r, especially when r is small. Thus the profit may be inadequate to cover cost ($c > \Delta$) for many ideas that would be efficient to invest in—that is, those for which $\Delta/r > c$.

The implicit assumption here is that the incremental improvement Δ is patentable, since otherwise imitators would enter and dissipate the profit flow. Patent breadth can be used to increase the flow of profit, even keeping the rate of innovation, Δ per period, fixed and assuming that all improvements are patentable.

Suppose, for example, that each new product, with a quality improvement of size Δ (or more), infringes the previous patent. Then, to enter the market, the innovator must license from the previous patent holder. Both parties will prefer an exclusive license in order to avoid competition. The innovator selling in the market will end up with a quality advantage of 2Δ over the next best product that can be marketed. The profit flow is then 2Δ in each time period, which will be divided between the licensor and licensee. See figure 5.7, which shows the sequence of competitive situations in the market.

When an innovator's product is itself supplanted, that innovator will become a licensor. Because each innovator will eventually be in both positions, licensor and licensee, we can assess the impact on each innovator's profit without knowing how the profit is shared between licensors and licensees, provided that license terms are the same in each generation. Each innovator earns an equal share of the total profit generated. Since the flow of profit is doubled, each innovator's profit is also doubled. Each innovator earns 2Δ rather than Δ.

More generally, breadth can ensure that k sequential improvements are consolidated under the marketing authority of a single firm, so that the profit flow is $k\Delta$, and each innovator earns $k\Delta$. Meanwhile the cost of achieving the increment Δ remains c. For large enough k, it holds that $k\Delta \geq c$. In this simple environment, intellectual property should be structured to ensure the consolidation of enough improvements so that costs are covered. More consolidation than that would lead to unnecessarily high prices.

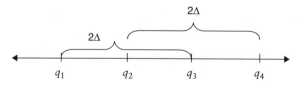

Figure 5.7
Leading breadth and consolidation of property rights

There are two ways to organize intellectual property so that ownership of sequential improvements will be consolidated (O'Donoghue, Scotchmer, and Thisse 1998). Both schemes operate by creating blocking rights on improvements, thus allowing firms to consolidate their interests through licensing without violating antitrust laws. In both of these schemes, only a limited sequence of improvements will be consolidated. However, one scheme operates by creating a limited number of infringements, so that the effective patent life ends when some improver goes beyond that limited number. The other scheme operates by making every future improvement infringe every previous patent, but only during a limited patent life. In the simple model presented here, the two are equivalent for appropriate choices of parameters, but this is not generally the case.

In figure 5.7, the "leading breadth" covers a single increment of progress, Δ. For example, the product with quality q_2 infringes the product with quality q_1, and the product with quality q_3 infringes q_2, but not q_1. If the leading breadth is $k - 1$ increments, then each innovator must license that many products, and k steps will be consolidated instead of 2, generating a profit flow of Δk. The same consolidation can be achieved by stipulating that every improvement infringes every prior patent, but the patent life is only k years. That too will generate a consolidation of k steps in the market, and will generate a profit flow of $k\Delta$.

5.5   Breadth and Inventive Step on a Quality Ladder

It is natural to think that each increment to progress on the quality ladder is patentable, since a product of that quality did not exist before. The discussion in the previous section assumes that all steps of progress are patentable, and investigates which ones should be infringing. However, the logic behind breadth is less compelling than the logic behind patentability. The previous discussion considers a notion of "leading breadth," which means that to escape infringement, an improvement must exceed the quality of a prior invention by a specified distance.

One logical problem with leading breadth is that the inventor did not invent the higher-quality products that are said to be infringing. The legal basis for infringement is therefore unclear. For purposes of this book, where our objective is to consider the best way to design incentives rather than to illuminate existing legal doctrine, this is not fatal. However, it raises the question of whether the objectives can be achieved by careful choice of the required inventive step rather than breadth. The answer is no.

Suppose that the objective is to ensure a profit flow of 2Δ in the market, as in figure 5.7. This is accomplished in the preceding discussion with blocking patents. Breadth is chosen so that each innovation infringes the preceding patent. Suppose instead that the minimal patentable inventive step is two steps, but that improved products do not infringe. An improver has two options when he receives an idea for an improvement. The first option is to invest and try to market the good, knowing that it will not be patentable. The second is to cache the improvement until the same innovator gets a second improvement and qualifies for a patent. Marketing the unpatentable improvement is clearly not sensible, since an entrant will imitate the good and erode the improver's profit. Caching the first step until the second is achieved may allow the innovator to cover costs but is not desirable from a social point of view. Secrecy will retard progress by depriving rivals of access to knowledge on which they could otherwise build.[11] In contrast, solving the problem with blocking patents encourages disclosure and allows rivals at every stage to build on the current state of knowledge.[12]

Something that cannot be stressed too much is that the optimal choice of incentives depends on the creative environment. In the ideas model, the inventive step is a less important policy lever than breadth. However, in an R&D model with a production function for knowledge, a minimum required inventive step can have the virtue of encouraging firms to be more ambitious than they otherwise would be (O'Donoghue 1998).

A production function maps R&D spending into knowledge outputs. Although the production-function model is not stressed in this book, we discuss it briefly here because it creates a role for the required inventive step as a policy lever.[13]

---

11.   This solution was explored by Scotchmer and Green (1990), comparing the situations where one inventive step versus two inventive steps are required for a patent.

12.   For a proof that disclosure accelerates progress in the ideas model, see the technical note at the end of chapter 8. With two inventors each trying to make progress, we show that if the first idea that occurs to either of them is disclosed to both of them, then the expected time to completion of two steps is shorter than if the first idea is not disclosed.

13.   The production-function model is mostly not used in this book because it carries the implication that there is no exogenous constraint on progress. All

So far we have answered a very simple question: Assuming that innovators have the opportunity to make improvements at rate Δ and cost c per innovation, how should intellectual property be organized to ensure that all innovators will cover their costs? In the more elaborated ideas model of O'Donoghue, Scotchmer, and Thisse (1998), the ideas occur at an exogenous rate and the size of the step Δ is random. But in the production-function model of O'Donoghue (1998), any desired improvement Δ can be achieved at an R&D cost given by the production function. The innovator does not need to wait for an idea.

In the production-function model, there is some notion of what rate of progress innovators should aspire to. Suppose that the production cost c is a function with values $c(\Delta)$; any improvement is possible at any time, provided enough resources are devoted to it. Then each step of progress Δ again confers a benefit that lasts forever, building a foundation for future innovators, and has social value Δ/r. Since there will be an increment to progress in each period, the discounted value of all progress is $(\Delta/r)/r$. Hence, not accounting for any deadweight loss that may arise from intellectual property rights, the social value of an annual rate of progress of size Δ is $(1/r)[(\Delta/r) - c(\Delta)]$, and (assuming that c is convex) there is some optimal rate of progress Δ^* that maximizes this value. (The maximand is slightly smaller if there is deadweight loss as well as resource costs.)

Notice that if c is a linear function, the optimal rate of progress Δ^* is either zero, when the cost per increment is higher than $1/r$, or infinite, when the cost per increment is lower than $1/r$. In general, though, the marginal cost per increment of progress will be increasing ($c'(\Delta) > 0$ and $c''(\Delta) > 0$), and the best policy will be to choose some some finite rate of progress Δ^*.

Intellectual property should then be designed for two objectives: to ensure that innovators achieve the optimal rate of progress Δ^*, and to make sure that they cover their costs, hopefully without too much profit surplus. (Profit surplus will generally imply that prices are higher than necessary, contributing to deadweight loss.) These two goals can be achieved using the two instruments, leading breadth and required

---

progress would be available instantly if society devoted enough resources to it. In contrast, the rate of progress in the ideas model is constrained by the exogenous pace at which ideas occur, which depends on the number of rivals with access to the current state of knowledge. In the ideas model, there is such a thing as "imagination."

inventive step. In particular, choose the inventive step such that improvements less than Δ^* are not protected so that firms do not invest in them. Then choose the leading breadth large enough so that costs are covered. If k is the number of prior patent holders who must be infringed, and innovators remain the market incumbent for a single period, the leading breadth k would satisfy $k\Delta^* = c(\Delta^*)$.

The economics literature has produced many other interesting approaches to the problem of protecting sequential innovators. Bessen and Maskin (2000) consider the problem of protecting innovators when there is learning from one generation to the next as on the quality ladder, but no competition between one generation and the next. Hunt (forthcoming) considers what can be done when every sequential innovation is either patentable and noninfringing or unpatentable and infringing.

5.6   Prospecting

If an innovator has blocking rights over the innovations she enables, she can share in their profit. As already stressed, this is an important reason to give such rights. For many basic innovations, it is the only way to create rewards without resorting to some form of sponsorship.

Kitch (1977) has advanced another reason to give strong rights to basic innovators, or "pioneers" as he calls them, namely, to induce "prospecting." Prospecting means that the pioneer will organize the market to develop follow-on products efficiently. (The analogy is with giving property rights to miners, who might not invest resources in finding mineral deposits if their claim to the value is uncertain.) The prospecting view recognizes, as we saw earlier, that basic innovators will profit from the second-generation innovations that they enable, especially if they can make ex ante contracts. However, the prospecting view is a bit too optimistic in asserting efficiency. What is efficient for the innovator is not necessarily efficient for society as a whole. The purpose of this section is to illuminate when private incentives work toward the public interest, and when not.

Important areas where the prospector's interests are aligned with the interests of society at large are in choosing the best follow-on ideas and in finding the most efficient firms. However, the interests may be misaligned in choosing the number of firms, which affects the probability of success and time to completion, and in ensuring competition among follow-on users of the innovation.

Looking first at the number of firms, figure 5.8 is similar to figure 4.2 but also has a curve defined by $(1/2)P(n)\Pi$. There are three numbers of interest shown on the axis, n^ℓ, n^e and n^p.

The number n^ℓ is of interest because it is the number of firms that would enter in a race if the successful firm would have to negotiate a license ex post. We will assume as before that the two firms with blocking patents will split the bargaining surplus evenly, so that each gets $(1/2)\Pi$. Firms will enter until expected profit is dissipated: $(1/2)P(n^\ell)\Pi = cn^\ell$. With ex post licensing, the pioneer earns $(1/2)P(n^\ell)\Pi$ in expectation. The number n^ℓ is smaller than n^e, which is the number of firms that will enter if the basic innovation is in the public domain and there is no obligation to license.

The number n^p, which may be larger or smaller than n^ℓ, maximizes total net profit. It is where the distance between $P(n)\Pi$ and cn is largest. The number n^p is of interest because it is how many licenses the patent holder will offer ex ante if there is no threat of unlicensed entry. The patent holder will collect the (maximal) profit $P(n^p)\Pi - cn^p$ in license fees by auctioning the licenses. (However, as explained in section 5.2, the patent holder may not succeed in collecting the maximal net profit, in this case $P(n^p)\Pi - cn^p$, if potential licensees realize that unlicensed entrants will nevertheless invest.)

Whether the patent holder licenses ex ante or ex post, the number of firms n^p or n^ℓ will be smaller than the number of firms n^e that would enter in the absence of licensing obligations. As compared to putting the basic research in the public domain, prospecting retards progress.

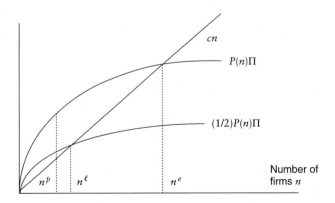

Figure 5.8
Organizing follow-on research

Intuitively, this is because some of the profit will be collected by the first patent holder, which reduces the attractiveness of entry, whether the licenses are ex ante or ex post. For example, Merges and Nelson (1990) argue that development of the gas-powered automobile was thwarted rather than accelerated due to the broad pioneer patent that issued to George Selden in 1895. (See the further discussion of the Selden patent in chapter 6.) They also suggest that development of the incandescent lightbulb was retarded by strong blocking rights after the settlement between Swan and Edison mentioned earlier in the chapter. This reduction in the research effort directed at follow-on products can be seen as a problem for competition policy.

In addition to the problem of reducing investment in R&D, a second potential problem for competition policy is that the patent holder will find it profitable to restrict competition between follow-on users. Suppose, for example, that the pioneer patent holder owns a target gene sequence that can be used to develop various drugs that would be different enough to be noninfringing. If the drug developers must all pay royalties to the owner of the gene sequence, the drug market will be cartelized, much as if the drug firms merged (see the argument in section 6.1 and technical note 6.7.1).

An example that illustrates this potential was the discovery of the technology for producing monoclonal antibodies, for which George Koehler and Cesar Milstein in Cambridge, England, won a Nobel Prize in 1984. Although they did not assert patent rights on this pioneering innovation (see the discussion in chapter 8), subsequent developments in how the technology was commercialized tell us how such rights would have affected competition. The first firm to create successful applications was Hybritech, which received a broad patent on diagnostic tests, using monoclonal antibodies. A second firm, which applied the pioneering technology in a slightly different way, was Monoclonal Antibodies, which was sued by Hybritech for infringement. The lower court held that there was no infringement, since both firms were applying a technology in the public domain. This decision, if it had held, would have led to considerable competition in the market to supply diagnostic kits and was thought by many, including Merges and Nelson (1994), to have been the right one. Unfortunately, it was overturned on appeal. As a consequence, Hybritech ended up with something like the broad pioneering rights that had been renounced by the inventors themselves and their sponsors. This can only have led to a lessening of competition in the market, as compared to the case that there was no patent on the pioneering technology.

An important type of prospecting in the early 1990s concerned the patenting of fragments of DNA sequences called express sequence tags (ESTs). A few such patents were issued, on applications where some function could be identified (Holman and Munzer 2000). The patent applications were controversial because it was unclear what had been invented. However, according to prospecting theory, EST patents should not give us pause—they will have the beneficial effect of encouraging their owners to go out and find uses. Holman and Munzer take the opposite view. Since a use may be blocked by a whole collection of prior patents, the proliferation of patents is likely to discourage the search for uses rather than encourage it. They therefore suggest that the ESTs should simply be registered and made freely available in return for a pre-specified fee. Prospecting is then not necessary.

Thus the licensing platform created by a pioneer patent can undermine competition of two types: competition in the "innovation market" (see chapter 6) and competition among users of the patented knowledge. It might be better not to give such patents. One alternative is public funding, and another is to let a later innovator who needs the pioneer innovation redevelop it. This leads to cost redundancy, but unless the tool is very expensive, such redundancy may be a lesser evil than retarding the development of later products through restrictive joint ventures or raising their price by facilitating collusion.

The discussion here previews the discussion of competition policy in chapter 6. Giving a blocking right to the basic innovator authorizes the innovator to coordinate the second-generation "innovation market" in a way that would otherwise come under the scrutiny of the antitrust authorities. Of course sometimes there is no conflict. Coordinating the market sometimes means creating efficiencies that would pass muster with the antitrust authorities under "rule of reason," discussed in chapter 6. However, as we have seen, the patent holder may alternatively coordinate the market in ways that retard progress or avoid competition among users but increase the patent holder's profit. This would not pass muster. If the second-generation innovators tried to self-organize for the objective of restricting entry in the absence of a blocking patent— for example, by forming a research joint venture—the attempt would likely be disallowed. Or if the developers of noninfringing follow-on products wanted to merge, they would be stopped. In these senses, the blocking right of the first-generation patent holder has the effect of preempting competition policy with respect to second-generation innovations.

5.7 Summary

When innovation is cumulative, an important incentive problem is to ensure that each innovator is rewarded enough to take account of the benefits conferred on future innovators. The future innovators may, in fact, be the original innovator's rivals. In addition to ensuring that there is enough profit in total to reward all the innovators, there is the problem of dividing it. Each innovator must receive enough of the total profit to cover its own costs. Some of its profit comes from selling products at proprietary prices, but the profit will often come from licensing fees paid by future innovators who use the innovation.

Intellectual property law has a rich set of policy levers, both for providing profit and for governing the division of it. Follow-on products can be patentable and noninfringing, patentable and infringing, unpatentable and noninfringing, or unpatentable and infringing. To enhance (or create) incentives for a prior innovation, follow-on innovations should be infringing, which will allow the prior innovator to share the profit through licensing, and may also avoid competition. If the follow-on product infringes the prior patent, then the incentives to develop it can be protected with an exclusive license on the prior patent, even if the follow-on product is not itself patentable. However, this strategy will not work if the time between inventions is too long or if licenses cannot be made ex ante before costs are sunk.

The policy levers of intellectual property operate differently in the cumulative context than with stand-alone innovations. Some important features are:

·   Breadth can be an important determinant of the life of the right, or at least the effective life.
·   Breadth and patentability can lead to blocking rights, which creates a vehicle for dividing profit among sequential innovators.
·   Disclosure plays the particularly important role of accelerating progress, especially by giving a boost to rivals.
·   If there is a production function for knowledge, there is a role for inventive step in encouraging innovators to be more ambitious.

One reason that basic research should be supported by public sponsors rather than private investors is that the benefits are hard to appropriate. Even if later users must license, the researcher cannot generally negotiate licenses before sinking his costs, and this weakens his bargaining position.

Quality ladders present a different incentive problem than the problem of basic and applied research. On a quality ladder, there is no clear distinction between a first-generation and second-generation innovator; all innovators will eventually be in both positions. The main question is how to ensure that there is enough profit in total, given that competition between sequential improvers will tend to erode it. Infringement (breadth) can force the consolidation of a limited number of sequential innovations in order to reduce competition and increase the flow of profit.

References and Further Reading

Bashe, C. J., L. R. Johnson, J. H. Palmer, and E. W. Pugh. 1986. *IBM's Early Computers*. Cambridge, MA: MIT Press.

Bessen, J., and E. Maskin. 2000. "Sequential Innovation, Patents and Imitation." Working Paper 00–01. Cambridge, MA: Department of Economics, MIT.

Cournot, A. [1838] 1897. *Researches into the Mathematical Principles of the Theory of Wealth*. Trans. N. Bacon. Oxford: Oxford University Press.

Denicolò, V. 1996. "Patent Races and Optimal Patent Breadth and Length." *Journal of Industrial Economics* 44:249–265.

Denicolò, V. 2000. "Two-Stage Patent Races and Patent Policy." *RAND Journal of Economics* 31:488–501.

Denicolò, V., and P. Zanchettin. 2002. "How Should Forward Patent Protection Be Provided?" *International Journal of Industrial Organization* 20:801–827.

Dyson, J. 2001. *A History of Great Inventions*. New York: Carroll & Graf.

Evans, D., A. Nichols, and B. Reddy. 1999. "The Rise and Fall of Leaders in Personal Computer Software." Cambridge, MA: National Economic Research Associates. Available at www.nera.com.

Evans. D., and R. Schmalensee. 2001. "Some Economic Aspects of Antitrust Analysis in Dynamically Competitive Industries." *Innovation Policy and the Economy* 2:1–49.

Feist Publications, Inc. v. Rural Telephone Service Co., Inc., 499 U.S. 340 (1991).

Friedel, R. 1996. *Zipper: An Exploration in Novelty*. New York: Norton.

Gilbert, R., and C. Shapiro. 1990. "Optimal Patent Length and Breadth." *RAND Journal of Economics* 21:106–112.

Gallini, N., and B. Wright. 1990. "Technology Transfer under Asymmetric Information." *RAND Journal of Economics* 21:147–160.

Gandal, N., and S. Scotchmer. 1993. "Coordinating Research through Research Joint Ventures." *Journal of Public Economics* 51:173–193.

Green, J., and S. Scotchmer. 1995. "On the Division of Profit in Sequential Innovation." *RAND Journal of Economics* 26:20–33.

Heller, M. A., and R. S. Eisenberg. 1998. "Can Patents Deter Innovation? The Anticommons in Biomedical Research." *Science* 280:698–701.

Holman, M. A., and S. R. Munzer. 2000. "Intellectual Property Rights in Genes and Gene Fragments: A Registration Solution for Express Sequence Tags." *Iowa Law Review* 85:735–748.

Hopenhayn, H., and M. Mitchell. 2001. "Innovation Variety and Patent Design." *RAND Journal of Economics* 32:152–166.

Hunt, R. Forthcoming. "Patentability, Industry Structure, and Innovation." *Journal of Industrial Economics*.

Kitch, E. W. 1977. "The Nature and Function of the Patent System." *Journal of Law and Economics* 20:265–290.

Lemley, M. 1997. "The Economics of Improvement in Intellectual Property Law." *Texas Law Review* 75:989–1083.

Lerner, J. 1995. "Patenting in the Shadow of Competitors." *Journal of Law and Economics* 38:463–495.

Lerner, J., and J. Tirole. 2002. "Efficient Patent Pools." Working Paper 9175. Cambridge, MA: National Bureau of Economic Research.

Lichtman, D. 2000. "Property Rights in Emerging Platform Technologies." *Journal of Legal Studies* 29:615–648.

Liebowitz, S. J., and S. E. Margolis. 1999. *Winners, Losers & Microsoft.* Oakland, CA: Independent Institute.

Loury, G. C. 1979. "Market Structure and Innovation." *Quarterly Journal of Economics* 93:395–410.

McCartney, S. 1999. *ENIAC: The Triumphs and Tragedies of the World's First Computer.* New York: Walker and Company.

Merges, R. P., and R. Nelson. 1994. "On Limiting or Encouraging Rivalry in Technical Progress: The Effect of Patent Scope Decisions." *Journal of Economic Behavior and Organization* 25:1–24.

Merges, R. P., and R. Nelson. 1990. "On the Complex Economics of Patent Scope." *Columbia Law Review* 90:839–916.

O'Donoghue, T. 1998. "A Patentability Requirement for Sequential Innovation." *RAND Journal of Economics* 29:654–679.

O'Donoghue, T., S. Scotchmer, and J.-F. Thisse. 1998. "Patent Breadth, Patent Life and the Pace of Technological Progress." *Journal of Economics and Management Strategy* 7:1–32.

Regibeau, P., and K. Rockett. 1996. "Optimal Patent Design and the Diffusion of Innovations." *RAND Journal of Economics* 27:60–83.

Reichman, J. H., and P. Samuelson. 1997. "Intellectual Property Rights in Data?" *Vanderbilt Law Review* 50:51–163.

Scotchmer, S. 1991. "Standing on the Shoulders of Giants: Cumulative Research and the Patent Law." *Journal of Economic Perspectives* 5:29–41.

Scotchmer, S. 1996. "Protecting Early Innovators: Should Second-Generation Products be Patentable?" *RAND Journal of Economics* 27:322–331.

Scotchmer, S., and J. Green. 1990. "Novelty and Disclosure in Patent Law." *RAND Journal of Economics* 21:131–146.

Standage, T. 1998. *The Victorian Internet.* New York: Berkley Books.

Townes, C. H. 1999. *How the Laser Happened: Adventures of a Scientist.* Oxford: Oxford University Press.

U.S. Department of Justice and Federal Trade Commission. 1995. *Antitrust Guidelines for Licensing of Intellectual Property.* Washington, DC: U.S. Government Printing Office.

Walsh, J. P., A. Arora, and W. M. Cohen. 2003. "Research Tool Patenting and Licensing and Biomedical Innovation." Paper presented at the conference "European Policy for Intellectual Property." Maastricht, the Netherlands: Maastricht Economic Research Institute on Information and Technology. Available at www.merit.unimaas.nl/epip/papers/walsh_paper.pdf.

Wright, B., 1983. "The Economics of Invention Incentives: Patents, Prizes and Research Contracts." *American Economic Review* 73:691–707.

Wright, B., and B. Koo. 1997. "Alternative Intellectual Property Protection Systems for Trade in International Agricultural Genetic Resources." Paper presented at a conference of the National Bureau of Economic Research, Cambridge, MA.

Wright, B. 200. "International Crop Breeding in a World of Proprietary Technology." In V. Santaniello, R. E. Evenson, D. Zilberman and G. A. Carlson, eds., *Agriculture and Intellectual Property Rights. Economic, Institutional and Implementation Issues in Agricultural Biotechnology,* 127–138. Wallingford, UK: CABI Publishing.

6 Licensing, Joint Ventures, and Competition Policy

A license is an agreement whereby the owner of intellectual property authorizes another party to use it. Licenses are extremely common. Based on a survey for the Intellectual Property Owners Association, Cockburn and Henderson (2003) report that 17.6 percent of patents in the respondents' patent portfolios were licensed out. An eighth of the respondents reported that they sometimes initiate technology development in the expectation that returns will be realized solely through licensing rather than through product sales. Virtually any kind of intellectual property can be licensed, including copyrights and trade secrets. In fact, a quarter of the respondents' licensing agreements do not concern patents.

Licensing is generally good for both users and innovators, since it increases the use of knowledge. At the same time it creates alliances between firms that affect production and pricing decisions. Since competition in the relevant market is already muted by intellectual property rights, it is no surprise that licensing raises antitrust issues. This chapter considers the nature of licensing, its pro-competitive uses, and some issues it raises for competition policy.

Competition policy and intellectual property policy are often seen as being in tension. Intellectual property law grants market power, and competition law reins it in. This is more a short-run tension than a long run tension, since in the long run intellectual property law leads to innovation, which improves the welfare of consumers. Since consumer welfare is the concern of competition law, there is no fundamental inconsistency. However, that is a rather lofty perspective that does not help very much in the practical question of how to achieve the right balance between encouraging innovation and protecting consumers from high prices. In this chapter we consider that balance, as well as the role of competition law in protecting the market structures that encourage innovation. Ex post, the concern of competition policy is to ensure that rightholders do not exercise more market power than Congress intended to grant them. Ex ante, the concern is that competition policy should not erode the incentive to create intellectual property in the first place.

6.1   Licensing for Productive Efficiency

Chapter 4 considered how much profit innovators should be allowed to earn, and then considered how to structure the profit, using the various policy levers of intellectual property such as length, breadth, and exemptions. Licensing is another tool that creates rewards for innovation. Ex post reasons to license include

· To produce proprietary products efficiently
· To let others use the intellectual property as inputs to innovations (research tools)
· To resolve blocking rights or to enable development of complementary inventions

These reasons for licensing are considered procompetitive, since they lead to efficient use of intellectual property in circumstances where the owner could otherwise exclude users. They improve the welfare of consumers as well as enriching the rightholder.

A license to use intellectual property in production usually includes both fixed payments and royalties. Royalties are based on units of a proprietary good sold or some other measure of use, and fixed fees are paid per unit time rather than being linked to sales. We will refer to these two instruments as (ρ, F). As we will see, the royalty helps the licensor to control the market price, since it adds to the licensee's marginal cost of production, while the fixed fee gives flexibility in sharing the profit. Royalties may also allow the parties to share risk—if the licensee cannot make any sales, there is no obligation to pay. Whether royalties "harm competition" depends on what the benchmark is. As compared to licensing without royalties, royalties usually support a higher price in the market than would occur without them. However, licensing with royalties is deemed an appropriate use of the intellectual property right.

Of the three pro-competitive reasons to license listed above, the last two were investigated in chapter 5. Here we consider the first one, that licensing can increase the efficiency of production. We first consider the introduction and production of new products, and then cost-reducing innovations. We will try to understand the terms of license that the proprietor will choose, how much she can profit from licensing, and whether she is overrewarded or underrewarded. We caution, however, that this is an imprecise question—compared to what?

A firm that introduces a new product is not necessarily the most efficient firm to produce it. In fact, if the production technology has increasing marginal cost, the average cost of supply can be lowered by producing in several firms. Licensing can achieve this. It could also be achieved by building several plants, and that would avoid licensing. One of our questions is whether these are equivalent. Can the proprietor receive as much profit by licensing as by building production plants? If not, the rewards to innovation depend on how production of the new good is organized. It is hard to see a justification for that.

Figure 6.1 shows the market demand for a proprietary good. The marginal cost for producing the good in a single production facility is represented by the function $\gamma(\cdot)$, which represents increasing marginal cost. If there are two firms using the same production technology, the marginal-cost curve of both firms together is $\tilde{\gamma}(\cdot)$, which is flattened out relative to $\gamma(\cdot)$. With two firms supplying the market, twice as many units can be produced at each marginal cost, and thus the marginal cost of the qth unit is $\tilde{\gamma}(q) = \gamma(q/2)$. With two firms, the profit-maximizing quantity and price are q^* and $p(q^*)$, as shown, where $p(q^*)$ is lower than the monopoly price with a single production facility.

If there are even more production facilities, the profit-maximizing price is even lower, because the aggregate marginal-cost curve is lower.

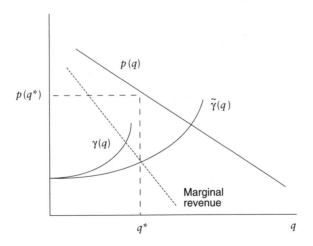

Figure 6.1
Profit-maximizing production with two firms

As the number of suppliers becomes very large, the aggregate supply curve flattens out so that the marginal cost of each unit is the same as the marginal cost of the first units produced with the single-plant supply curve $\gamma(\cdot)$. If licensees have fixed setup costs as well as marginal costs of production, it is not efficient to license so many firms that the aggregate marginal-cost curve becomes flat. By tolerating higher marginal costs, the fixed costs of setting up production facilities can be avoided.

The efficient number of production facilities depends on the setup costs. In figure 6.1 it is assumed that the efficient number is two. Then it will be efficient to divide production equally between the two firms, or at least between two production facilities. The proprietor will want to sustain the price $p(q^*)$, while collecting the profit in royalties and fixed fees.

To keep the price up, and also to collect profit, the licensor can charge a royalty. We will first suppose that she licenses two firms, and will then compare the outcome to what happens if she produces herself and licenses to a single additional firm. A guess for the best royalty would be the difference between the desired price $p(q^*)$ and the marginal cost of production in each firm $\gamma(q^*/2)$—that is, $\rho = p(q^*) - \gamma(q^*/2)$. However, this will not have the intended effect of supporting the profit-maximizing price and quantity, because each firm will want to supply some quantity less than $q^*/2$. The firms will not find it optimal to produce the supply q such that the price is equal to the effective marginal cost, $\gamma(q) + \rho$, of the qth unit. If the firm's supply q satisfies $p = \gamma(q) + \rho$, the firm will want to reduce the quantity supplied. The qth unit provides zero profit to the licensee. By cutting back, the licensee loses no profit on the last unit, but increases the market-clearing price on all the inframarginal units, thus increasing profit overall.[1]

There is a royalty rate lower than $p(q^*) - \gamma(q^*/2)$ that supports the per-licensee supply $q^*/2$ and profit-maximizing price, $p(q^*)$. This is shown in technical note 6.7.1 but can be understood intuitively. The effective marginal cost of the qth unit supplied by a licensee is $\gamma(q) + \rho$, which is the marginal resource cost plus the royalty. Just as firms will reduce supply if their marginal resource costs become higher, they will

---

1.   This argument implicitly assumes, as is more explicit in technical note 6.7.1, that the firms compete on quantity. That means that, in equilibrium, each firm chooses the most profitable supply conditional on how many units are supplied by the other firm. This is a different type of competition than, for example, price competition, where the firm that cuts back assumes that the other firm will maintain a fixed price instead of a fixed quantity.

reduce supply if the royalty becomes higher. It is therefore no surprise that with a suitably chosen royalty, the proprietor can ensure the profit-maximizing price $p(q^*)$ in the market. However, the royalty will be lower than $p(q^*) - \gamma(q^*/2)$.

As a reasonable policy objective, the licensor should be able to earn as much profit by licensing as by producing the product herself in two production facilities. There is no reason to impinge on the incentives to innovate just because the licensor cannot muster the funds to build production plants, or does not view that as her comparative advantage. The terms allowed in a license should be rich enough to ensure profit neutrality with respect to how production is organized. In this case, since the licensor cannot get all the profit with the royalty that sustains profit-maximizing price, she will have to charge fixed fees as well. The role of royalties is to govern the market price, and the role of fixed fees is to distribute any remaining profit.

However, royalties and fixed fees are not always sufficient to achieve the three policy objectives of organizing production efficiently, sustaining the most profitable price, and transferring all the profit to the licensor.

Suppose that the patent holder licenses a single licensee to use her technology and serves some of the market herself. After the license is in place, the licensee and licensor will compete in the market. However, the effective marginal cost faced by the licensee for the qth unit is the resource cost plus royalty, $\gamma(q) + \rho$, and the effective marginal cost faced by the licensor is only $\gamma(q)$. As a consequence, the licensor and licensee will not supply the same quantities in equilibrium, and production will not be efficient. (See technical note 6.7.1 for an elaboration of this argument.) Other license terms can remedy this inefficiency, such as capping the licensor's output at $q^*/2$. Although royalties and fixed fees are generally uncontroversial in license agreements, clauses that fix supply may call forth an antitrust inquiry. Nevertheless, if the innovator is not allowed to write such terms, she will be penalized in terms of profit and efficiency, as compared to the benchmark case that she serves the whole market, using two production facilities, or licenses to two firms and stays out of the market. Consumers are also penalized if the inefficiency leads to higher prices.

The type of innovation described in figure 6.1 is a new product. Other inventions that may call for licensing are cost-reducing technologies. Figure 6.2 shows a competitive market where the firms initially have constant marginal cost c, so that the market price is $p = c$. Suppose that

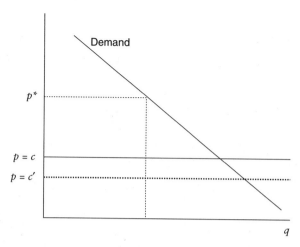

Figure 6.2
Cost-reducing innovation

a firm achieves a proprietary cost-reducing innovation so that its marginal cost is c'. If the cost c' is much lower than c, then the monopoly price with cost c' may also be lower than c, in which case the innovator will act as a monopolist with no threat of entry. There is no need for licensing.

However, if the cost reduction is relatively small, as shown in figure 6.2, then even with the new, lower marginal cost c', the profit-maximizing price p^* is above c. But the innovator cannot sustain a price higher than the old marginal cost c because entrants using the original technology will compete the price down to c.

Of course it is inefficient to allow entry using the old technologies. If rivals are supplying part of the market, the more efficient arrangement would be to license the new technology at royalty $\rho = c - c'$, which is the highest price rivals would pay. Indeed, the innovator will find it profitable to do this. A royalty smaller than the cost reduction would lead to a market price less than c. The innovator would prefer a price higher than c, but cannot arrange it, since rivals would rather use the old technology than pay a royalty higher than $\rho = c - c'$. If that is the royalty, all the profit is transferred to the innovator.[2]

---

2.   For a synthesis of economics literature on the best way to license cost-reducing innovations, see Kamien 1992, which makes this point using a model of Cournot competition. Kamien refers to an extensive literature based on different assumptions about whether, for example, the proprietor auctions the

The market outcome with royalty $\rho = c - c'$ creates sensible incentives. If the innovator could support the monopoly price, the reward would come from a more lucrative source than the value of the innovation, namely, from cartelizing the market. The social value of the innovation is not measured by the monopoly profit in the market (the innovation did not open a new market), but rather by the cost reduction made available in the existing market. (See Maurer and Scotchmer 2004.)

Licensing for productive efficiency is generally considered pro-competitive, since it allows the efficient use and sharing of intellectual property. In addition, such licensing does not seem to restrict competition beyond the rights embedded in intellectual property. We caution, however, that this type of statement is circular if the restrictions on licensing are considered part of the design of intellectual property rights in the first place.

Based on the discussion so far, one would conclude that licensing is not a threat to competition. That is because we have considered the circumstances most favorable to pro-competitive outcomes. The remainder of this section gives a flavor for how licensing can also be anticompetitive. The question then arises of what restrictions should be placed on licensing, and in what circumstances.

Suppose that prior to the innovation, there are two firms in the market, both using the old technology with marginal cost c. For simplicity, assume that firms compete on price. Each sets a price that is profit maximizing conditional on the other firm's price.[3] With price competition, the firm with lower cost will supply the whole market, but at a price equal to the higher marginal cost. A higher price cannot be an equilibrium because one of the firms would have an incentive to undercut the other firm and attract the whole market. On the other hand, the lower-cost firm has no reason to price significantly under the rival firm's higher cost, since the lower-cost firm can attract the whole market with only a trivial price advantage.

---

licenses or simply states the terms and accepts all comers. See Kamien and Tauman 1984, 1986; Katz and Shapiro 1985; Kamien, Tauman, and Zang 1988; Kamien, Oren, and Tauman 1988.

3.   Much of the literature on efficient licensing, such as that summarized by Kamien 1992, assumes that firms compete on quantity—that is, each firm's quantity supplied is optimal given the quantities supplied by the other firms. The arguments are more complicated in that case, and slightly different, but the insights about the anticompetitive uses of licensing are similar. Our argument concerning product innovations assumed that the firms compete on quantity.

If firm 1 is the innovator and firm 2 is an unlicensed rival, then the two firms' marginal costs are c' and c, respectively. The market price is $p = c$. Firm 1 supplies the whole market and earns profit $c - c'$ on each unit sold. If, instead, firm 1 licenses to firm 2 at royalty $\rho = c - c'$, then firm 2's effective marginal cost, the resource cost plus royalty, is $c' + \rho = c$, which results in the same market price. Indeed, it results in the same market price as when there are an unlimited number of potential entrants.

But when there is a single potential licensee, will a royalty $\rho = c - c'$ be the best the innovator can do? Let p^* be the profit-maximizing price using the lower-cost technology, and suppose that firm 2 takes a license with royalty $\rho = p^* - c'$. (Under our assumptions, firm 2 makes zero profit whether or not it takes this license.) Then the market price will be the monopoly price p^*, and the innovator collects all the profit. Of course this will only work if there are no additional firms that can enter with the old technology. Such firms would compete the price down. And it will only work if the licensee agrees to pay the royalty regardless of which technology is used. Otherwise, having signed the license, the licensee will nevertheless revert to the old technology, since it is better to use the old technology with marginal cost c than to use the new technology with an effective marginal cost $\rho + c' > c$.

It is obvious in these circumstances how the firms can write an agreement to support the monopoly price, but it is also clear how to guard against it. The licensee must be allowed to avoid royalties by reverting to the old technology. Of course, an even more reliable antidote is competition. If firms other than the licensee can enter the market with the old technology, the restrictive license will be irrelevant. In fact, this can be understood as a general principle. Entry by unlicensed firms using public-domain technologies goes a long distance toward relieving the harm that would otherwise arise from restrictive licensing practices. This explains why much of the case law in this area concerns oligopolistic markets where all the potential entrants are parties to the restrictive license.

Rules about licensing have evolved in the twentieth century as a back-and-forth between firms finding inventive ways to use licensing for collusion, and the courts responding with rules against those practices. However, this is not an easy task. Without a clear articulation from Congress of the proper bounds on intellectual property rights and licensing, the courts are making policy. For example, one could imagine an alternative design of intellectual property rights in which the collusive arrangement described earlier is permitted, but the property right only lasts a short period. Should it be the courts or Congress that decides on such policy?

6.2   Competition Policy in the Innovation Context

Competition policy is mainly concerned with horizontal competition, as addressed by the Sherman Act and Clayton Act, especially section 7 on mergers. Section 1 of the Sherman Act prohibits combinations in restraint of trade and section 2 prohibits monopolization. The Sherman Act is the basis for stopping collusive licensing among firms in circumstances where it is not justified by sharing intellectual property, and where the firms have market power.

The enforcers of antitrust policy are ultimately the courts. Cases may be brought by one of the two federal agencies that oversee competition policy, the Department of Justice Antitrust Division and the Federal Trade Commission, referred to here as "the agencies." To notify firms of what actions will attract their scrutiny, the agencies have published their interpretation of what is permissible and impermissible in the 1992 *Merger Guidelines* and the 1995 *Antitrust Guidelines for Licensing Intellectual Property*. The latter are particularly relevant here.

Private parties as well as the government can bring antitrust actions. However, it would not suffice to depend on private firms to bring antitrust actions, because the main harm is usually to consumers, not firms. In fact, rivals can be among the beneficiaries of collusion. If firms in the market are colluding to keep prices high, the high prices soften competition for other firms. The two antitrust agencies are a voice for consumers in the antitrust process.

As discussed earlier, if the only goal of competition policy were to keep prices low, then competition policy and intellectual property would be in tension. However, the 1995 *Guidelines* recognize that competition serves consumers, not only by keeping prices low, but also by ensuring a healthy degree of competition in providing them with new products and cheaper production techniques. Thus, the *Guidelines* take the view that intellectual property is not intrinsically anticompetitive. The *Guidelines* begin by saying that

- for the purpose of antitrust analysis, the agencies regard intellectual property as being essentially comparable to any other form of property;

• the agencies do not presume that intellectual property creates market power in the antitrust context; and

• the agencies recognize that intellectual property licensing allows firms to combine complementary factors of production and is generally procompetitive. (1995 *Guidelines*, §2.0)

These principles implicitly refer to legal concepts as much as to economic concepts. The first makes it clear that intellectual property cannot be used to justify tortious or criminal acts any more than physical property can, and that intellectual property law grants a right to exclude, just as the owner of real property can exclude trespassers. The second seems to contradict the fact that intellectual property rights are an explicit grant of exclusive rights in a market. However, the term "market power" is used here as a legal term more than an economic term. Together with the qualifier "in the antitrust context," the principle can be interpreted to mean that the market power conferred by intellectual property is legitimate, and not per se in conflict with other principles of competition policy. The third principle explicitly recognizes the pro-competitive reasons to license discussed here and in chapter 5.

Aside from a few practices that are per se antitrust violations and do not require an inquiry, courts do not generally find harm to competition unless a firm has "market power" in a well-defined "market." Most antitrust disputes are about the extent of the market. If the market can be defined to be large, the firm can be deemed to have a small market share and little market power. That may exempt a firm's licensing tactics from antitrust scrutiny, or make it less likely that a court will enjoin them.

The 1995 *Guidelines* extended the concept of "market" beyond production and sales of goods to "technology markets" and "innovation markets." Technology markets are markets for licensing intellectual property rights, much as discussed in sections 6.1, 6.4, and 6.5. An innovation market consists of "the research and development directed to particular new or improved goods and processes . . . and close substitutes" (1995 *Guidelines*, §3.2.3). By defining the notion of an innovation market, the agencies formalized the notion that competition to innovate can increase consumer welfare. They put firms on notice that they may oppose mergers and other alliances that reduce competition in developing new technologies.

The general principles of the 1995 *Guidelines* superseded a previous set of guidelines promulgated by the agencies in the 1970s, which were directed at specific licensing practices. These had been known as "the nine no-no's of licensing." These practices are no longer automatic triggers for antitrust scrutiny, but they alert us to some important ways that licensing can restrict competition in technology markets, and are thus worth listing.

1. Royalties not reasonably related to sales of the patented products
2. Restraints on licensees' commerce outside the scope of the patent (i.e., tie-outs)
3. Requiring the licensee to purchase unpatented materials from the licensor (i.e., tie-ins)
4. Mandatory package licensing
5. Requiring the licensee to assign the patentee patents that may be issued to the licensee after the licensing arrangement is executed (i.e., exclusive grantbacks)
6. Licensee veto power over grants of further licenses
7. Restraints on sales of unpatented products made with a patented process
8. Postsale restraints on resale
9. Setting minimum resale prices on resale of the patented products

There is a body of case law on each of the nine practices, reflecting the fact that their economic consequences can be either pro- or anticompetitive. An excellent postmortem of the nine no-no's has been written by former Deputy Assistant Attorneys General for Antitrust, Richard Gilbert and Carl Shapiro (1997). They divide the practices into four groups. The first three might be attempts to restrain trade beyond the rights embodied in the intellectual property. The fourth practice might be an attempt to elevate the value of some constituent patents even though they have substitutes. An important concern with the fifth practice, grantbacks, is that if a licensee promises to give the licensor exclusive rights to any follow-on innovation created, he may have implicitly promised not to invest in such follow-ons. This may leave the licensor as the sole potential innovator, thus depriving the innovation market of competition. That is the same concern that is now central in protecting innovation markets. The sixth practice—giving veto power over further licenses to a previous licensee—is similar to granting an exclusive license, which is generally thought to be a legitimate exercise of intellectual property rights. The last two practices, which seem on the surface to be anticompetitive, can achieve efficiencies such as causing licensees to compete on quality and service rather than price.

In general, the antitrust agencies and courts do not oppose exclusive licenses. Exclusivity is a right given to the patent holder, and it is hard to see why the economic consequences are different if exclusivity is transferred to a licensee. However, another type of exclusivity is exclusive dealing, generally treated as less benign. Exclusive dealing arises when the licensor constrains the licensee from dealing with other suppliers. An interesting example was a 1994 Department of Justice case against Microsoft (following an earlier investigation by the FTC), in which the Department of Justice challenged licensing contracts between Microsoft and computer manufacturers. The license required royalties on every processing unit sold, whether or not the processing unit embodied the Microsoft operating system. Such contracts gave the equipment manufacturers a strong incentive to use the Microsoft operating system instead of a competitive operating system such as (at the time) IBM's OS/2, and thus put other operating systems at a market disadvantage vis-à-vis Microsoft.

6.3   Ex Ante Mergers and R&D Joint Ventures

When firms announce that they want to merge their assets into a new firm, or to merge a research effort in a joint venture, the antitrust agencies may oppose it. In ordinary markets for goods and services, their inquiry will be whether the market is competitive and whether the merger lessens competition and raises prices. If so, the firms must have a good reason to merge. They will typically argue that the merger will lead to cost efficiencies, for example, in marketing. The court will assess the efficiency arguments and balance them against any perceived harms to competition. This balancing is called *rule of reason*.

The type of mergers and other alliances that concern us here are those that harm competition in innovation markets. The 1995 *Guidelines* implicitly identify two types of harm that may arise from research joint ventures, mergers, or other alliances between innovative firms.

- Alliances may reduce competition to innovate and retard progress.
- Alliances may reduce the number of substitute innovations and undermine competition ex post in a product market.

The first type of harm occurs under the economic hypothesis that competition leads to more R&D than cooperation. One justification for this hypothesis, given in sections 4.4 and 5.6, is that competitive entry into the innovation market can increase the probability of success or decrease the time to completion, even though it dissipates profit. See also example 1 in technical note 6.7.2. Consumers benefit from competition because they get innovations sooner or with higher probability. If the firms cooperate in a research joint venture, they may cut back on R&D spending to avoid dissipation of profit. But cutting back can reverse the benefits of competition. Cutting back may retard progress or reduce the probability of success.

The motivating hypothesis of the 1995 *Guidelines* is that the benefits that accrue to consumers from competition in an innovation market outweigh any loss to firms. However, this premise remains controversial. Whether competition promotes innovation better than, for example, a market with concentrated market power depends, among other things, on the nature of the innovative process and the innovative environment. Lurking behind the disagreement is Schumpeter's classic 1942 book, arguing that market concentration encourages innovation. The *Guidelines* largely reflect the opposite view, that concentration inhibits innovation. This point of view was originally argued by Arrow (1962) (see section 4.6) and is reflected in the model discussed in sections 4.1 and 5.6, and in technical note 6.7.2. Other recent inquiries deliver mixed messages. Gilbert and Sunshine (1995b) summarize arguments on both sides, despite being framers of the *Guidelines*.

In current U.S. policy, most antitrust analysis relies on rule of reason. Rule of reason balances cost efficiencies that may arise from merger or other alliances against harm to consumers. In the context of innovation, cost efficiencies may include avoiding duplication of effort (see example 2 in technical note 6.7.2), delegating effort to the more efficient firms (Gandal and Scotchmer 1993), sharing technical information that might be hidden if firms compete (see Bhattacharya, Glazer, and Sappington 1990; Brocas 2004), and sharing spillovers of the knowledge created (see Katz and Shapiro 1987; d'Aspremont and Jacquemin 1988; Kamien, Muller, and Zang 1992; Suzumura 1992; Aoki and Tauman 2001). These effects can benefit both firms and consumers, but they must be balanced against any perceived harms from lessened competition. See the appendix to Hoerner 1995 for a compendium of early cases in which courts and the agencies have made judgments about the relative merits of various arguments, and also Gilbert and Sunshine 1995a, 1995b, for an authoritative account of the agencies' reasoning.

Turning to the second bullet point, mergers or other alliances can lessen competition in the ex post product market if the merging firms develop a single product to serve the market when otherwise they would have developed competing products. Suppose, for example, that the firms would be in the business of developing drugs. If the drugs would be non-infringing, then it would be a mistake to allow an ex ante merger between the drug companies, resulting in a single product, since that would deprive the market of substitutes and low prices.

This puts courts in the awkward position of having to anticipate what types of intellectual property the members of a proposed alliance would develop, absent the merger. The firms that propose to merge will presumably not announce that they would otherwise develop noninfringing substitute products. Instead they will argue that competition will be wasteful and duplicative, and that only one firm will, in the end, have a viable product. Given this incentive to dissemble, the agencies and the court might rightfully be skeptical. Making wise judgments in these circumstances is a daunting task.

As pointed out in section 5.6, when mutually noninfringing follow-on products infringe a common prior patent, courts and the antitrust authorities lose their ability to intervene in the coordination of research efforts, and cannot even restore competition ex post in the market for follow-on products. If the patent holder licenses the underlying patent ex ante, she may give an exclusive license to a single developer. If the licensing occurs ex post, she may give licenses to both developers but will sustain the monopoly price with high royalties, as discussed in section 6.1. Both strategies lead to monopoly pricing, even though, absent the underlying patent, the market would be served by noninfringing substitutes. Nothing in antitrust law makes these strategies illegal, and both result in market power that would have been avoided, absent the underlying patent.[4]

Thus, a concern to promote competition among developers of follow-on products might be a reason not to grant basic or pioneer patents. Especially if the cost of developing the basic innovation is relatively low, it might be better to insist that each innovator develop it separately, in order to preserve competition at the next stage of research. Alternatively, this may be another argument for why basic research should be publicly sponsored and put in the public domain.

As pointed out in section 6.1, a licensor's inability to license every potential entrant goes a long distance toward mitigating any potential harm from collusive licensing practices. The same thing is true with respect to mergers in innovation markets. If a joint venture cannot

---

4.   See Denicolò 2002 for a related discussion.

include every potential entrant, it cannot avoid profit-eroding competition. The *Antitrust Guidelines* acknowledge that potential competition can be as effective as actual competition in disciplining the market. Of course, the power of entry is double-edged. Entry can protect consumers from competitive harm, but it can also restore the inefficiencies that alliances would usefully eliminate—for example, inefficient duplication of efforts, or investments by less efficient firms. Whether the effects of a research alliance are beneficial or deleterious, entry can nullify them.[5]

6.4   Ex Post Mergers and Patent Pools

In this section we return to how intellectual property rights are used ex post, rather than how the innovation market is organized ex ante. Section 6.1 discussed licensing by a single rightholder, assuming that she holds the only intellectual property rights in a given product or technology. However, it often emerges that there are several patent holders with rights on different aspects of a given product or process. Some kind of joint licensing arrangement is required to bring such products or processes to market.

A patent pool is an agreement under which the owners of several proprietary technologies license them as a bundle. There is no single protocol for how members of patent pools share profit, and there is also considerable variance in the subsidiary rules about such matters as whether patents can also be licensed individually, and whether nonmembers can be licensees as well as members, and on what terms (Merges 1996, 1999; Gilbert 2002; Lerner and Tirole 2002).

Two large and famous patent pools of the early twentieth century were the aircraft pool (the Manufacturer's Aircraft Association, formed in 1914), and radio broadcast pool (undertaken by RCA in 1920, which was formed for that purpose). Both industries were plagued by blocking patents. The aircraft pool was encouraged by the Secretary of the Navy during World War I, when it became necessary to overcome blocking patents in order to produce airplanes. The main constituents of the pool were the two major patents held by Glenn Curtis and the Wright

---

5.   Many of the publications in the reference section at the end of this chapter investigate contexts where entry is limited—for example, the deterrence to innovation discussed by Gallini (1984), and Gallini and Winter (1985), and the argument of Katz and Shapiro (1987) are subject to this qualification. However, see Kamien 1992 for a discussion of licensing models where the threat of entry is the primary focus; see also Maurer and Scotchmer 2002.

brothers. In litigation, the improved airplane design of Glenn Curtis had been held to infringe the Wright patent, but the Wright brothers would not license. By the end of World War I there were also many subsidiary patents. All the contributors to the patent pool were allowed to use the patents royalty-free, but nonmembers had to pay a license fee. The pool was essentially a cross-licensing arrangement aimed at avoiding litigation. Although the contract provided that other patent holders could petition an arbitration panel for royalty standing, it was mainly Curtis and the Wright brothers who received royalties, and the other pool members only received the right to manufacturer airplanes without threat of litigation and without license fees.[6]

The RCA Corporation was formed in the 1920s to consolidate broad, blocking patents on radio technologies, in particular, those owned by the Marconi Wireless and Telegraph Company (including Marconi's patent on the diode vacuum tube), AT&T (the assignee for deForest's patent on the triode vacuum tube, which infringed Marconi's patent on the diode vacuum tube), and various other radio technologies owned by other companies, including General Electric and Westinghouse. Like the Manufacturer's Aircraft Association, RCA consolidated these blocking-patent rights with the blessing of the U.S. Navy, which needed to get radios into production. Potential manufacturers had been stymied by the fear of litigation. RCA's monopoly position vis-à-vis radio technologies was challenged on antitrust grounds in 1958, long after the original patents had expired.

Joint licensing has many advantages for both the rightholders and licensees. If the proprietary technologies are complements, in the sense that effective use of one technology requires the simultaneous use of another, or if the value of using one technology increases with use of another, then licensees would ordinarily want to use all the complementary pieces. Although licensing from a pool saves transaction costs, its main advantage may be in allowing the joint pricing of complementary pieces of intellectual property (Shapiro 2001; Gilbert 2002). Recall the discussion in chapter 5 of how joint pricing of complements leads to lower prices than individual licensing does.

In contrast, there is a danger for competition if the pool includes noninfringing substitutes rather than complements. In that case, the pool becomes a cartel in the technology market, avoiding the competition that the proprietors of rival technologies would otherwise face. Users could

---

6.   For more discussion, see Bittlingmayer 1988.

end up paying higher fees than if the intellectual property is licensed separately.

Three modern examples of patent pools with complementary pieces are the MPEG-2 video compression technology, which combines patents of eight major electronics firms and one university, and two pools that combine technologies for the DVD standard, one for DVD-video and another for DVD-ROM (Merges 1999; Shapiro 2001). The latter combine patents of both electronics firms and content providers, such as Time Warner. Users of the DVD patents must license from both pools, so that the complements problem is not entirely eliminated. In approving all three patent pools, the Department of Justice required certification by an independent expert to make sure that the pool only includes patents that are "essential," and not patents that would be substitutes for others in the pool.

A 1998 example of a patent pool that was judged by the agencies to serve cartelization purposes rather than resolving blocking patents was a patent pool for laser eye surgery attempted by Summit Technology, Inc., and VisX, Inc. The agencies argued that the patents placed in the patent pool were, in fact, substitute technologies. But the companies argued that since the patents were mutually blocking, their pool was pro-competitive instead of anti-competitive. The case was eventually dismissed by a settlement in which the pool was dissolved. However, in discussing this case, Shapiro (2001, 139) points out:

The Summit and VisX case raises a number of very interesting and tricky issues regarding patent pools and joint licensing programs. First, if Summit and VisX reasonably believed that their patents blocked each other at the time they formed the pool, was that sufficient to justify the formation of a pool? How hard were they required to look into the validity of each other's claims before agreeing to form Pillar Point Partners? Second, if each believed it could, at considerable expense, delay, and risk, invent around each other's patents, should the two firms be prohibited from forming a pool and rather forced to attempt to invent around each other's patents, under the view that consumers *might* thereby enjoy the benefits of direct competition (although the product may be delayed, or never introduced, if the blocking positions are not later cleared)? Third, is there competitive harm in placing some potentially rival patents into the pool, assuming that each party in fact controls valid blocking patents, making *some* type of pool pro-competitive? Fourth, can the pool be attacked on antitrust grounds based on the argument that a less restrictive alternative, namely a cross-license, would have achieved the same legitimate purposes and created additional competition? If so, does it matter in this assessment that Summit and VisX agreed that the pool would license their patents to third parties, something that a cross-license would not permit, unless it contained rather unusual sublicensing rights?

For the most part, these questions have not yet been answered.

So far we have discussed patent pools from an ex post point of view, focusing on pricing in the market for licenses, and on issues of competition. However, patent pools also have implications for incentives to innovate. Incentives are determined by how the pool distributes profit, by whether nonmember innovators can join the pool, and on what terms, and how new technologies are received into the pool. Prospective inventors face different rewards if their intellectual property goes into a patent pool than if they license individually. Barton (2002) points out that cross-licensing can stifle the incentive to innovate. If the pool provides for royalty-free cross-licensing within the pool but royalties must be paid by nonmembers, then all pool members benefit equally from a member's innovation. The incentive of a pool member to bear the cost of innovation can thus be diluted. The dilution of incentives was partly muted in the case of the aircraft pool by an innovator's right to petition a board for compensation. However, the right was seldom exercised.

As for nonmembers of the pool, the pool can act as a barrier to entry. Even in the case of complements, where pools seem pro-competitive, a nonmember with a new technology that improves on a technology in the pool faces the difficulty of getting the pool members to restructure, using the new technology instead of the old one. Would the previous property owner have to be compensated for eviction from the pool? Such compensation would reduce the incentive for the other pool members to embrace a new technology, and thus reduce the incentive for the nonmember to invest. Graham (1986, 41) suggests that such a dynamic was at work in the radio broadcasting industry after the formation of RCA: "Perhaps the most important enduring consequence of the policy was that it made it uneconomic for most other companies to do radio-related research, because they could not recoup their investment." However, the net effect is ambiguous. The bulk of Graham's account supports the view that, under the management of commercial radio pioneer David Sarnoff, the central mission of RCA itself was to improve their technologies.

As to distribution of royalties within the pool itself, the share of profit that a rightholder can demand depends mainly on his options if he drops out. In the case of complements, a patentholder that drops out can exploit the low prices charged by the pool, raising his own price at their expense. To overcome this temptation, he must believe that his own departure will undermine the rest of the patent pool and cast all of them back to a situation of autarky. If autarky is the pool member's next best option, each rightholder must receive at least as much in the patent pool as with the profit-dissipating high prices that would prevail in autarky. This consideration may not give much guidance about how profit must be divided in the pool.

We close this section with a comment on patent pools as a solution to litigation and infringement. A patent pool or some other ex post consolidation of intellectual property rights is a common way to settle a dispute as to infringement or validity. Instead of fighting it out in court as to whether patent A infringes patent B, and whether patent B should have issued in the first place, the owners of patents A and B may decide to merge their interests into a single firm and jointly exploit the technology. If it is already established that the patents are blocking, there is little competitive harm to such a settlement. The problem arises when the pool forms before infringement or validity is established. The pool can then prevent competition in a market where Congress intended that firms would compete. (For more complete and nuanced discussions, see Hovenkamp, Janis, and Lemley 2003; Shapiro 2003.)

A well-known example of a patent pool based on a shaky patent was the Association of Licensed Automobile Manufacturers (ALAM), a group of car manufacturers that consolidated in 1903 to recognize the validity of the Selden patent. The latter was a broad patent issued in 1895 to George B. Selden on "the basic elements necessary for the construction of a motor vehicle propelled by a petroleum product" (Flink 1970, 17). Many commentators believe that the broad patent was an error, since much of the invention was already known, due to a decade of experimentation with gasoline-powered vehicles in Germany and Belgium. In 1899, Selden had assigned the patent to the Electric Vehicle Company. Electric cars were then a contender in the market, and historian Flink speculates that the motive of the Electric Vehicle Company was to hedge their bets with respect to the two technologies. (In fact, there were three technologies; steam-powered cars were another option that died out.)

The Selden patent was first litigated in 1900, but the suit settled, with the alleged infringer recognizing validity. At that point "several other prominent manufacturers of gasoline automobiles who had initially viewed the patent as a threat began to realize that it might provide a means to regulate competition and prevent disruptive practices in the industry" (Flink 1970, 317). The ALAM was formed, charging royalties to its members and hoping to embrace within its fold all the manufacturers in the industry. However, important members of the industry still believed that the patent should be invalid and refused to be cartelized. Greenleaf (1961) describes the patent wrangling that ensued. Henry Ford was sued for infringement and lost in District Court in 1909. The ALAM's victory persuaded many of the previously recalcitrant independents to join, but not Henry Ford. He won on appeal in 1911, in the sense that the broad claims of the Selden patent were very much narrowed, and Ford was declared not to infringe. However, that was only one year before expiration of the patent.

There are at least three lessons to be learned from the Selden patent. First, there is competitive harm in issuing shaky patents. A patent justifies licensing with royalties or other market alliances, which typically have the effect of keeping prices high. Second, settlements of infringement suits can be anticompetitive. The ALAM came into existence on the strength of an early settlement in which an alleged infringer was induced to recognize the validity of a patent that eventually fell, due to the obstinacy of Henry Ford. However, Ford might have improved his market position by "admitting" the legitimacy of the Selden patent and settling with the ALAM on terms that muted the competition between them while giving Ford a share in the ill-gotten gains. Third, the possibility of entry undermines a cartel. There was always a large reserve of independent manufacturers refusing to join the ALAM. The manufacturing techniques of the time were such that entry was relatively easy. Even if Ford had joined, the ALAM's market power could have been undermined by other independents. The ALAM was not very successful in maintaining market power, largely because entry was easy.

6.5   Collective Rights Management Organizations and Compulsory Licencing

Collective rights management organizations are a type of pool, although generally for copyrighted content rather than for patents. For example, Broadcast Music, Inc. (BMI) and American Society of Composers, Authors and Publishers (ASCAP) are organizations that license performance rights to radio and television stations, bars, restaurants, and other public users of music, on behalf of their pooled members. The works in these pools are, in some sense, both complements and substitutes. Listeners obviously value a radio station that plays several artists more than a radio station with only one artist, and in this sense, the components of the licensed package are complements. On the other hand, artists vie for the public's ear.

Following Besen, Kirby, and Salop 1992, figure 6.3 shows a much oversimplified model of the collective rights organization, which gives some idea of why collective licensing might affect competition. On the horizontal axis, the variable n represents the number of artists. The function $w(\cdot)$ represents broadcasters' willingness to pay per unit time for a license to play these artists' works. It is drawn as concave because if only few compositions are available, each has high marginal value, but if many are available, the additional ones do not add very much. We will see from this diagram that the incentive to become an artist depends on the licensing arrangements, and if licensing is organized in a collective, it depends on who controls membership in the collective.

Let c be the opportunity cost of each artist for being an artist. The membership n^* that maximizes total surplus satisfies

$$w(n^*) - w(n^* - 1) > c \geq w(n^* + 1) - w(n^*)$$

or $w'(n^*) = c$ if we pretend that the number of artists is a continuous variable. At the optimal number of artists, if each artist licenses separately to the broadcasters, the maximum an artist can charge for a license is $w(n^*) - w(n^* - 1)$, since that is the marginal value contributed. For $n > n^*$, $w(n) - w(n - 1) < c$, which means that, with individual licensing, there would not be more than the optimal number of artists.

Assume, for illustrative purposes, that a collective rights organization can collect the whole social value $w(n)$ if there are n members. Since each artist receives $w(n)/n$ and pays cost c, then more artists will want

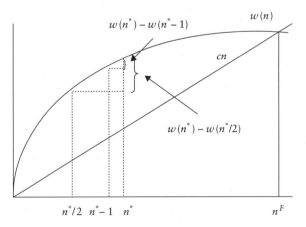

Figure 6.3
Collective licensing

to create works and join whenever $w(n)/n - c > 0$. Entry will stop at n^F in figure 6.3, where $w(n^F)/n^F - c = 0$. Thus, an open membership policy may inspire more creation than is socially optimal. Of course, there are reasons that the collective cannot collect all of $w(n^F)$, such as that the broadcasters may exercise some bargaining power, and that the copyrights do not last forever.

Suppose, though, that the previous members can restrict membership. Then even if the collective can collect the whole social value, they have an incentive to reduce membership below n^F, and even below n^*. For all n, $w(n)/n - c$ is decreasing with n. Whatever the number of members, the profit of each member is increased if membership is reduced.[7] However, if they downsize too much, then there will be an incentive for a parallel organization to emerge. Fragmentation will again reduce their profit. If, for example, there are two organizations, each with half the optimal number of members, the most that each half can collect (conditional on the other organization being present) is $w(n^*) - w(n^*/2)$. Each artist earns a smaller amount, namely, $\{w(n^*) - w(n^*/2)\}/(n^*/2)$, instead of $w(n^*)/n^*$.

Thus, depending on how much of the social value the collective rights organization can collect, and depending on who controls membership, it may give too much incentive to invest in creative works and will leave less surplus for the licensees. For licensees like restaurants and bars, which are very competitive, the higher fees will lead to higher prices and less benefit to consumers. In contrast to restaurants and bars, radio and TV broadcasters are generally immune to entry, due to the fixed supply of spectrum, so the higher fees might simply be a transfer from shareholders to artists.

We now give a short history of how collective rights organizations have developed for music, and then turn to modern developments.

Before collective rights organizations could start collecting money from broadcasters, the public-performance right had to be created. Prior to the twentieth century, there were no collective rights organizations in the United States, although France had collective rights organizations

---

7.   This assumes $w(\cdot)$ is concave as shown. However, the shape of w for low n will not really be as shown. The function $w(\cdot)$ will be more "S-shaped," so that $w(n)$ is close to zero for low n (that is, broadcasters do not get much benefit until the number of artists in their repertoire becomes reasonably large), and then starts to rise and becomes concave. In that case, the membership that maximizes per-member surplus will be greater than 0 but still less than the membership that maximizes total surplus.

since 1829 for large-scale "dramatic performances" and since 1851 for "small" performances (Besen and Kirby 1989). Performance rights became protected in the United States under the Copyright Act of 1909. That act also provided many exemptions, such as for educational and religious uses, but performance rights were again strengthened in the Copyright Act of 1976. ASCAP came into existence as a nonprofit organization in 1914. A much smaller cooperative, SESAC (which originally stood for Society of European Stage Authors and Composers) came into existence in 1931, mainly to represent European copyright holders in the United States. During World War II it transformed itself into an organization that largely represented two particularly American musical expressions, gospel and country.

In the United States and many other places in the world, music is commercially distributed under two copyrights. The composer/author has a copyright in the composition, usually assigned to a publisher, and the performer/recording company has a copyright in the recording, usually owned by the recording company. The recording companies earn revenues from sales of recordings, and the composer/publisher earns royalties from recording companies and through the collective rights organizations for public performances. When all is said and done, the total revenue comes from sales of recordings and royalties paid through collective rights organizations. The revenue is distributed according to contracts among composers, publishers, performers, and recording studios (Craft 2001). Until recently there has not been an obligation for radio broadcasters and others who create public performances to pay royalties to the recording companies. The royalties are paid instead to the composers and their publishers; it is they who are members of the collective rights organizations.

The royalties themselves are collected and distributed differently in different collective rights organizations. ASCAP divides the revenues among its members according to a sampling procedure designed to reward artists according to the popularity of their music, and to impose costs on the broadcasters and other public performers related to the revenue potential of the listening audience. Subject to a rather low barrier as to legitimacy, ASCAP accepts all artists. SESAC has a less nuanced compensation scheme, because it is too small to absorb the cost of sampling for differentiated rewards. It is selective in its membership. BMI was founded in 1939 in opposition to ASCAP, which had been raising its license fees. It is owned by the broadcasters rather than the artists, but exists for the same purpose, namely, to avoid the transaction costs of licensing between artists and broadcasters. Its artists are called "affiliates" rather than "members."

Collective licensing through performing rights organizations raises the same issues for competition policy as patent pools raise. The essential message of figure 6.3 is that per-artist license fees may be higher under the management of a collective rights organization than with individual licenses. In 1941, the Department of Justice responded to complaints from the National Association of Broadcasters about the fees being charged, and filed suit against both ASCAP and BMI. Eventually both suits were settled with consent decrees, in which ASCAP and BMI agreed to modify their fee-setting practices and agreed to open membership, subject to minimal showings of something to contribute. These consent decrees grant regulatory oversight to a federal district court, in both their original form and subsequent modifications. For example, the court can set prices whenever the organization and the licensee disagree, an option not invoked until 1988. Nevertheless, the threat of judicial intervention has likely had a moderating influence on prices.[8] The licensing schedules are complicated, but ASCAP charges 1.615 percent of gross revenue for broadcasters with revenues below $150,000, and 1 percent for broadcasters with higher revenues. BMI charges 1.75 percent of gross revenue. ASCAP claims to return 84 percent of its revenue to members, while BMI returns 82 percent to the affiliates.

The remuneration of composers and musicians was changed by the Digital Performance Rights in Sound Recordings Act of 1995, extended by the Digital Millennium Copyright Act of 1998. Both pieces of legislation apply to performances distributed and transmitted in digital form, such as webcasting. They depart from the institutional arrangements described above in that they create compulsory licenses for the copyrights in the sound recordings. The collective rights organizations already collect royalties for the copyrights in the compositions, but there had not previously been an obligation to pay the recording companies. The introduction of new digital modes of delivering music, such as subscription webcasting (as opposed to traditional radio broadcasts), has given the recording industry an opportunity to reopen the question of who gets paid for public performances. The required royalties are determined by a Copyright Arbitration Royalty Panel (CARP), which takes testimony from all the concerned parties, in setting the rates.

8.   For further discussion of the legal wrangling, see Besen and Kirby 1989.

The economic consequences of these new compulsory licensing laws are still unclear. In a fundamental economic sense, it may not matter whether the payments by broadcasters and webcasters are destined for composers, recording companies, or performers, since that triumvirate can redistribute the money by revising their contracts with each other. If license fees must be paid directly to recording companies by webcasters, the recording industry becomes even more lucrative. If the recording industry is at all competitive (a hypothesis doubted by many commentators), we would expect some of that lucre to find its way to composers and performers, as recording companies bid for their services. In that scenario, the most important question is how much money in total is being transferred from broadcasters and webcasters to the music industry triumvirate as a whole, since the distribution of funds among composers, publishers, performers, and recording studios can be renegotiated.

Ultimately, the new obligation for compulsory licensing will increase the flow of money to the music industry, and when all is said and done, that should give it a boost, attracting more musicians and performers.

An orphan in this new legislation is peer-to-peer file sharing, which is not in the category of either public performance or webcasting. This raises the question of whether there could be a similar compulsory license system for peer-to-peer file sharing. One of the problems is that, with peer-to-peer sharing rather than broadcasting or webcasting, it is much harder to sample how much a piece of music is used, and therefore it would be difficult to link remuneration to usage. Another problem is in where to collect the money. Unlike webcasters and broadcasters, which are firms, most file sharing is done by individuals using personal computers.

6.6   Licensing versus Sale of Protected Works

Digital products are increasingly distributed under license instead of sale. This is mainly true of computer software, which is typically licensed to the user, even if distributed in hard form, as on a CD. There is no reason that entertainment products such as movies, music, and books cannot also be distributed under license. The licensing of copyrighted works represented a stark departure from the practice of distributing copyrighted works by selling copies. When copies of works such as CDs and books are sold, certain rights inhere in the sold copies under copyright law. Under a legal notion that the rightholder exhausts his rights when the item is sold, the buyer can do with the copy what he wishes, including resale or lending. There is no restriction on how many times he can read the book or listen to the CD, or how many times this can be done by a person to whom he subsequently sells it. Under fair-use provisions, he can parody or quote the work and use the information learned from it for his own innovative activities. If using the product causes him harm, he can sue for damages in state court. Pretty much the only thing he cannot do is copy it.

When the user clicks "I agree" in downloading software purchased on the Internet, he is sometimes agreeing to license terms that prevent uses of the legitimately acquired copy that would have been legal if the copy had been purchased instead of licensed (Radin 2003). Among the license terms that have caused concern are provisions that prevent the user from reviewing the product in a trade publication, restrictions on where a lawsuit can be filed in case of damages, and restrictions on damages—for example, to the price paid for the software. In thoughtlessly agreeing to such terms, users give up rights that would be automatic under copyright law if they bought copies instead of licensing them. The license terms could even give pass-through rights, such as grantback provisions for any creative works that the licensed work inspires. Of course these terms may not stick, since they require a certain inattention on the part of the buyer. A legal basis for challenging such license terms is that they are not truly negotiated; buyers click "I agree" without truly considering the implications. This is an area of the law that is still evolving.

State laws governing commercial transactions in the United States mostly conform to the Uniform Commercial Code (U.C.C.), which is a harmonized set of laws suggested by a national committee of scholars and policymakers called the National Conference of Commissioners on Uniform State Laws. States must individually adopt or reject their recommendations. In the late 1990s, this body suggested an amendment to the U.C.C., first known as Article 2B and later known as UCITA (Uniform Computer Information Transaction Act), which would, loosely speaking, legitimate click-wrap or shrink-wrap licenses. The suggestion has proved very controversial and has only been adopted in a couple of states. For an overview of the issues, see Samuelson 1999 and the articles cited there.

6.7   Technical Notes

6.7.1   Royalties and Profits

We will now see that if a patent holder has two licensees and does not produce herself, fixed fees and royalties linear on units supplied are sufficient to support the profit maximum. This is not true if the patent holder competes with a licensee using the same technology. To support the profit maximum in that case, additional licensing terms are required.

Suppose that the inverse demand curve (the willingness to pay of the marginal consumer at quantity q) is defined by $p(q) = 1 - q$, where q is the total supply of all firms. When there are two firms supplying the market with quantities q_1, q_2, the market price will therefore be $p(q_1 + q_2) = 1 - (q_1 + q_2)$. Suppose the firms are Cournot competitors: each firm chooses its supply optimally, taking the other firm's supply as given. At an equilibrium $(\hat{q}_1, \hat{q}_2)$, neither firm has an incentive to change its quantity. We will see that the royalty rate

$$\rho = \frac{1}{2} q^* \tag{6.1}$$

supports the profit-maximizing price where q^* is the total quantity that maximizes total profit Π, defined as

$$\Pi(q) = p(q)q - 2\int_0^{q/2} \gamma(\hat{q})d\hat{q} - C_1 - C_2$$

where C_1, C_2 are the fixed costs. The profit Π will be divided between the licensor and licensees according to the licensing agreement. The q^* that maximizes their summed profit satisfies the condition that marginal revenue equals marginal cost

$$1 - 2q^* = \gamma\left(\frac{q^*}{2}\right) \tag{6.2}$$

and the profit-maximizing price is

$$p(q^*) = 1 - q^* = \frac{1}{2}\left(1 + \gamma\left(\frac{q^*}{2}\right)\right)$$

Conditional on a royalty ρ that the licensees must pay, write their profit functions as $\pi^1(q_1, q_2)$ and $\pi^2(q_1, q_2)$. Both quantities appear in each profit function, because the price in the market depends on both licensees' supplies.

Licensee 1's profit function is

$$\pi^1(q_1, q_2) = (p(q_1 + q_2) - \rho)\ q_1 - \int_0^{q_1} \gamma(\hat{q})d\hat{q} - C_1$$

The optimum for licensee 1, conditional on the royalty rate and on the supply q_2 of licensee 2, satisfies

$$\frac{\partial \pi^1(q_1, q_2)}{\partial q_1} = 0 = 1 - q_2 - 2q_1 - \gamma(q_1) - \rho$$

and symmetrically for licensee 2. If these conditions are satisfied at $(\hat{q}_1, \hat{q}_2)$, then $(\hat{q}_1, \hat{q}_2)$ is an equilibrium.

Then if licensee 2 chooses $q_2 = q^*/2$, and (6.1) holds, it is optimal for licensee 1 to choose $q_1 = q^*/2$:

$$\left. \frac{\partial \pi^1(q_1, q_2)}{\partial q_1} \right|_{q_1 = q_2 = \frac{q^*}{2}} = \left. [1 - 2q_1 - q_2 - \gamma(q_1) - \rho] \right|_{q_1 = q_2 = \frac{q^*}{2}}$$

$$= 1 - \frac{3}{2}q^* - \gamma\left(\frac{q^*}{2}\right) - \frac{1}{2}q^* = 0$$

Since licensee 1's profit function is strictly concave, this is the optimum, and symmetrically for licensee 2. Hence, the two licensees are at an equilibrium with each supplying half of the profit-maximizing quantity.

In this outcome, the licensee earns a higher price on each unit sold than the royalty paid plus the marginal cost of the unit. Nevertheless, it is possible that the fixed costs are so high that the licensees end up with negative profit. In that case, unless the patentholder can make fixed rebates, she cannot sustain the profit maximum. Assuming, however, that the licensees have profit left over, the licensor can collect the excess by charging positive fixed fees. In this way, the licensor can sustain the most profitable outcome and collect all the profit.

However, the licensor cannot sustain the optimum if she has a single licensee and also produces herself. This is because, for any positive, constant royalty rate, the licensor will have an incentive to produce more than the licensee, and this will lead to inefficient production.

With a single licensee and a royalty rate ρ, the profit functions of the licensor (firm 1) and licensee (firm 2) are

$$\pi^1(q_1, q_2) = p(q_1 + q_2)q_1 + \rho q_2 - \int_0^{q_1} \gamma(\hat{q})d\hat{q} - C_1$$

$$\pi^2(q_1, q_2) = (p(q_1 + q_2) - \rho)q_2 - \int_0^{q_2} \gamma(\hat{q})d\hat{q} - C_2$$

(6.3)

The optima for firms 1 and 2, each conditional on the supply of the other, satisfy

$$\frac{\partial \pi^1(q_1, q_2)}{\partial q_1} = 0 = 1 - q_2 - 2q_1 - \gamma(q_1) \tag{6.4}$$

$$\frac{\partial \pi^2(q_1, q_2)}{\partial q_2} = 0 = 1 - q_1 - 2q_2 - \gamma(q_2) - \rho \tag{6.5}$$

Thus, in equilibrium,

$$q_1 + \gamma(q_1) = q_2 + \rho + \gamma(q_2) \tag{6.6}$$

This proves that if the licensor charges a royalty, the licensee will produce less than the licensor, and production will not be efficient. On the other hand, with no royalty the firms will not price at the profit-maximizing price. Maurer and Scotchmer (2004) propose several solutions to this problem—for example, that the licensor can cap her output at no more than $q*/2$ units. Another solution is to make the royalty rate a decreasing function of the licensor's output. Then the licensor will be punished for increasing production beyond $q*/2$ by losing royalties.

6.7.2   Mergers in Innovation Markets: Two Models

Example 1 illustrates that competition among firms in an innovation market can promote consumer welfare by causing each innovator to invest more than if the two firms agreed to maximize joint profit. This example is a variant on the analysis in section 4.4, which showed how entry dissipates profit, even though it increases the overall probability of success. As shown in section 5.6, coordinating investments for maximum profit will generally reduce the number of participants and reduce the overall probability of success.

Example 2 reiterates that patent races can be duplicative. If the innovation effort has high fixed costs, patent races can have the deleterious effect of increasing social costs without accelerating innovation. In that instance, it is hard to see how a patent race can increase consumer welfare. The patent race involves costs without benefits.

Example 1   Suppose that firms 1 and 2 can invest at rates x_1, x_2, respectively, and that their individual probabilities of success, $p(x_1)$, $p(x_2)$, depend on how much they invest. If each firm gets the patent with probability one-half if both succeed, firm 1's probability of receiving the patent is

$$p(x_1)\left[1 - p(x_2) + \frac{1}{2}p(x_2)\right]$$

If the value of the intellectual property is one, firm 1's expected profit is therefore $p(x_1)[1 - p(x_2) + (1/2)p(x_2)] - x_1$, and analogously for firm 2. In a patent race, firm 1 and firm 2 will invest at the rates x_1^R, x_2^R that solve

$$p'(x_1^R)\left[1 - \frac{1}{2}p(x_2^R)\right] = 1$$

$$p'(x_2^R)\left[1 - \frac{1}{2}p(x_1^R)\right] = 1$$

(6.7)

If the two firms join their efforts and choose their rates of investment jointly, say x_1^J, x_2^J, they will maximize their joint profit

$$1 - [1 - p(x_1)][1 - p(x_2)] - x_1 - x_2$$

The optimal joint rates of investment satisfy

$$p'(x_1^J)[1 - p(x_2^J)] = 1$$

$$p'(x_2^J)[1 - p(x_1^J)] = 1$$

(6.8)

Consider the symmetric situations where $x_1^J = x_2^J = x^J$ and $x_1^R = x_2^R = x^R$. Since $p'(x^J)[1 - (1/2)p(x^J)] > p'(x^J)[1 - p(x^J)] = 1$, the investments that maximize joint profit are not the equilibrium of a race. Each firm can increase expected profit by increasing investment.

The rates of investment in the patent race are generally higher than the rates of investment that maximize the firms' joint profit, and may even be higher than the socially optimal rates of investment. The private value that a firm, say firm 1, perceives when it increases investment includes a crowding-out effect: if firm 1 wins the race with higher probability, then firm 2 wins with lower probability. The crowding-out creates a benefit for firm 1, but a loss for firm 2. There is a social benefit, namely, the increase in overall probability of success, but the social benefit is muted by the negative externality on firm 2. Because of the crowding-out effect, there may be more investment in equilibrium than maximizes joint profits, and possibly more than maximizes social welfare.

Example 2   Suppose that in order to participate in the patent race, each firm must spend K to build a laboratory and set up experiments. Afterward the variable costs of R&D are negligible, and the firm has probability $1/n$ of achieving the result before the other firm, when n firms participate. Suppose the resulting intellectual property is worth $5K$. Then five firms will participate in the race, and each one's expected profit will be zero. The total social cost of achieving the innovation is $5K$. In contrast, if the five firms receive approval to merge their efforts, they only need to invest K and will split the proceeds. Thus each one makes $4K/5$. Consumers get the same product with or without the merger, while the firms save costs. In this case, the merger should pass the rule-of-reason test, because the efficiency gains available to the firms do not obstruct any other purpose of competition policy.

Example 2 has high fixed costs of R&D efforts, and these can be saved by merger or joint venture. Duplicated costs have no offsetting social virtue such as accelerating progress or increasing the probability of success. In contrast, example 1 shows that the competitors' desire to beat out the competition can increase the probability of success. Merger will be efficient for the firms in the sense of reducing their joint costs and increasing their expected joint profit, but inefficient for consumers, since the joint venture will reduce the aggregate probability of success (or delay the discovery).

References and Further Reading

Aghion, P., and P. Bolton. 1987. "Contracts as a Barrier to Entry." *American Economic Review* 77:388–401.

Aitken, H. G. H. 1985. *The Continuous Wave: Technology and American Radio, 1900–1932.* Princeton, NJ: Princeton University Press.

Anderson, R., and N. Gallini, eds. 1998. *Competition Policy and Intellectual Property Rights in the Knowledge-Based Economy.* Industry Canada Series. Calgary, Alberta: University of Calgary Press.

Anton, J. J., and D. A. Yao. 1994. "Expropriation and Inventions: Appropriable Rents in the Absence of Property Rights." *American Economic Review* 84: 190–209.

Aoki, R., and J.-L. Hu. 1999. "Licensing vs. Litigation: Effect of the Legal System on Incentives to Innovate." *Journal of Economics and Management Strategy* 8:133–160.

Aoki, R., and T. J. Prusa. 1993. "International Standards for Intellectual Property Rights and R&D Incentives." *Journal of International Economics* 35:251–273.

Aoki, R., and R. Tauman. 2001. "Patent Licensing with Spillovers." *Economics Letters* 73:125–130.

Areeda, P. 1974. *Antitrust Analysis: Problems, Text, Cases.* Boston: Little, Brown.

Arrow, K. 1962. "Economic Welfare and the Allocation of Resources for Invention." In R. Nelson, ed., *The Rate and Direction of Inventive Activity.* Princeton, NJ: Princeton University Press (for the National Bureau of Economic Research).

Barton, J. 2002. "Antitrust Treatment of Oligopolies with Mutually Blocking Patent Portfolios." *Antitrust Law Journal* 69:851–882.

Besen, S. M., and S. N. Kirby. 1989. *Compensating Creators of Intellectual Property.* Report R-3751-MF. Santa Monica, CA: RAND Corporation.

Besen, S. M., S. N. Kirby, and S. C. Salop. 1992. "An Economic Analysis of Copyright Collectives." *Virginia Law Review* 78:383–411.

Bhattacharya, S., C. d'Aspremont, and J.-L. Gerard-Varet. 2000. "Bargaining and Sharing Innovative Knowledge." *Review of Economic Studies* 67:255–271.

Bhattacharya, S., J. Glazer, and D. E. M. Sappington. 1990. "Sharing Productive Knowledge in Internally Financed R&D Contests." *Journal of Industrial Economics* 39:187–208.

Bhattacharya, S., J. Glazer, and D. E. M. Sappington. 1992. "Licensing and the Sharing of Knowledge in Research Joint Ventures." *Journal of Economic Theory* 56:43–69.

Bhattacharya, S., and D. Mookherjee. 1986. "Portfolio Choice in Research and Development." *RAND Journal of Economics* 17:594–605.

Bittlingmayer, G. 1988. "Property Rights, Progress, and the Aircraft Patent Agreement." *Journal of Law and Economics* 227:31–54.

Brocas, I. 2003. "Vertical Integration and Incentives to Innovate." *International Journal of Industrial Organization* 21:457–488.

Brocas, I. 2004. "Optimal Regulation of Cooperative R&D under Incomplete Information." *Journal of Industrial Organization* 52:81–120.

Cockburn, I., and R. Henderson. 2003. "Survey Results from the 2003 Intellectual Property Owners Association Survey on Strategic Management of Intellectual Property." Mimeograph. Boston: School of Management, Boston University, and Cambridge, MA: Sloan School of Management, Massachusetts Institute of Technology.

Craft, K. 2001. "The Webcasting Music Revolution Is Ready to Begin, as Soon as We Figure out the Copyright Law." *Hastings Communications and Entertainment Law Journal* 24:1–42.

d'Aspremont, C., and A. Jacquemin. 1988. "Cooperative and Noncooperative R&D in Duopoly with Spillovers." *American Economic Review* 5:1133–1137.

Denicolò, V. 2002. "Sequential Innovation and the Patent-Antitrust Conflict." *Oxford Economic Papers* 54:649–668.

Flink, J. J. 1970. *America Adopts the Automobile: 1895–1910*. Cambridge, MA: MIT Press.

Gallini, N. 1984. "Deterrence by Market Sharing: A Strategic Incentive for Licensing." *American Economic Review* 74:931–941.

Gallini, N., and R. Winter. 1985. "Licensing in the Theory of Innovation." *RAND Journal of Economics* 16:237–252.

Gallini, N., and B. Wright. 1990. "Technology Transfer under Asymmetric Information." *RAND Journal of Economics* 21:147–160.

Gandal, N., and S. Scotchmer. 1993. "Coordinating Research through Research Joint Ventures." *Journal of Public Economics* 51:173–193.

Gilbert, R. 2002. "Patent Pools: 100 Years of Law and Economic Solitude." Paper presented at the conference "Competing Monopolies: Challenges at the Intersection of Competition and Intellectual Property Laws." Toronto, ON: Center for Innovation Law and Policy, University of Toronto. Available at www.innovationlaw.org/pages/patent_pools.doc.

Gilbert, R., and C. Shapiro. 1997. "Antitrust Issues in the Licensing of Intellectual Property: The Nine No-No's Meet the Nineties." In C. Winston, ed., *Brookings Papers on Microeconomic Activity*, 283–349. Washington, DC: The Brookings Institution.

Gilbert, R., and G. C. Sunshine. 1995a. "Incorporating Dynamic Efficiency Concerns in Merger Analysis: The Use of Innovation Markets." *Antitrust Law Journal* 63:569–602.

Gilbert, R., and G. C. Sunshine. 1995b. "The Use of Innovation Markets: A Reply to Hay, Rapp and Hoerner." *Antitrust Law Journal* 64:75–82.

Gilbert, R., and W. K. Tom. 2001. "Is Innovation King at the Antitrust agencies?: The Intellectual Property Guidelines Five Years Later." *Antitrust Law Journal* 69:43–86.

Graham, M. 1986. *RCA and the VideoDisc: The Business of Research*. New York: Cambridge University Press.

Greenleaf, W. 1961. *Monopoly on Wheels: Henry Ford and the Selden Patent Suit*. Detroit: Wayne State University Press.

Hoerner, R. J. 1995. "Innovation Markets: New Wine in Old Bottles?" *Antitrust Law Journal* 64:49–73.

Hovenkamp, H. 1985. *Economics and Federal Antitrust Law*. St. Paul, MN: West.

Hovenkamp, H., M. Janis, and M. A. Lemley. 2003. "Anticompetitive Settlement of Intellectual Property Disputes." *Minnesota Law Review* 87:1719–1766.

Jorde, T., and D. Teece. 1989. "Innovation, Cooperation and Antitrust." *High Technology Law Journal* 4:1–113.

Jorde, T., and D. Teece. 1990. "Innovation and Cooperation: Implications for Competition and Antitrust." *Journal of Economic Perspectives* 4:75–96.

Kamien, M. I. 1992. "Patent Licensing." In R. Aumann and S. Hart, eds., *Handbook of Game Theory*, 331–354. Amsterdam: North-Holland/Elsevier Science.

Kamien, M. I., E. Muller, and I. Zang. 1992. "Research Joint Ventures and R&D Cartels." *American Economic Review* 82:1293–1306.

Kamien, M. I., S. Oren, and Y. Tauman. 1988. "Optimal Licensing of Cost Reducing Innovation." *Journal of Mathematical Economics* 21:483–508.

Kamien, M. I., and Y. Tauman. 1984. "The Private Value of a Patent: A Game Theoretic Analysis." *Journal of Economics (Supplement)* 4:93–118.

Kamien, M. I., and Y. Tauman. 1986. "Fees versus Royalties and the Private Value of a Patent." *Quarterly Journal of Economics* 101:471–491.

Kamien, M. I., Y. Tauman, and I. Zang. 1988. "Optimal Licensing Fees for a New Product." *Mathematical Social Sciences* 16:77–106.

Kaplow, L. 1984. "The Patent-Antitrust Intersection: A Reappraisal." *Harvard Law Review* 97:1813–1892.

Katz, M. 1986. "An Analysis of Cooperative Research and Development." *RAND Journal of Economics* 17:527–543.

Katz, M., and J. Ordover. 1989. "R&D Co-operation and Competition." In M. N. Bailey and C. Winston, eds., *Brookings Papers on Economic Activity*. Washington, DC: Brookings Institution.

Katz, M., and C. Shapiro. 1985. "On the Licensing of Innovations." *RAND Journal of Economics.* 16:504–520.

Katz, M., and C. Shapiro. 1986. "How to License Intangible Property." *Quarterly Journal of Economics* 101:567–590.

Katz, M., and C. Shapiro. 1987. "R&D Rivalry with Licensing or Imitation." *American Economic Review* 77:402–420.

Lerner, J., and J. Tirole. 2002. "Efficient Patent Pools." Working Paper 9175. Cambridge, MA: National Bureau of Economic Research.

Mathewson, F. G., and R. A. Winter. 1987. "The Competitive Effects of Vertical Agreements: Comment." *American Economic Review* 77:1057–1062.

Maurer, S. M., and S. Scotchmer. 2002. "The Independent Invention Defence in Intellectual Property." *Economica* 69:535–547.

Maurer, S. M., and S. Scotchmer. 2004. "Profit Neutrality in Licensing: The Boundary between Antitrust Law and Patent Law." Working Paper CPC04-43. Berkeley, CA: Department of Economics, University of California.

Merges, R. P. 1992. "Patent Law and Policy: Cases and Materials." Charlottesville, VA: Michie.

Merges, R. P. 1996. "Contracting into Liability Rules: Intellectual Property Rights and Collective Rights Organizations." *California Law Review* 84: 1293–1349.

Merges, R. P. 1999. "Institutions for Intellectual Property Transactions: The Case of Patent Pools." In R. Dreyfuss, ed., *Intellectual Products: Novel Claims to Protection and their Boundaries*. Oxford: Oxford University Press.

O'Hare, M. 1985. "Copyright: When is Monopoly Efficient?" *Journal of Policy Analysis and Management* 4:407–418.

Ordover, J. A., and R. D. Willig. 1985. "Antitrust for High-Technology Industries: Assessing Research Joint Ventures and Mergers." *Journal of Law and Economics* 28:312–333.

Radin, M. J. 2003. "Regulation by Contract, Regulation by Machine." Mimeograph. Stanford, CA: Law School, Stanford University. Available at siepr.stanford.edu/programs/SST_Seminars/Reg_K,_Reg_Mach.pdf.

Rasmusen, E. B., J. M. Ramseyer, and J. S. Wiley, Jr. 1991. "Naked Exclusion." *American Economic Review* 81:1137–1145.

Rockett, K. E. 1990. "Choosing the Competition and Patent Licensing." *RAND Journal of Economics* 21:161–171.

Samuelson, P. 1999. "Intellectual Property and Contract Law for the Digital Age: Forward to a Symposium." *Stanford Law Review* 87:1–16.

Schumpeter, J. A. 1942. *Capitalism, Socialism and Democracy*. New York: Harper & Row.

Scotchmer, S. 1998. "R&D Joint Ventures and Other Cooperative Arrangements." In R. Anderson and N. Gallini, eds., *Competition Policy and Intellectual Property Rights in the Knowledge-Based Economy*, 203–222. Industry Canada Series. Calgary, Alberta: University of Calgary Press.

Shapiro, C. 1985. "Patent Licensing and R&D Rivalry." *American Economic Review* 75:25–30.

Shapiro, C. 2001. "Navigating the Patent Thicket: Cross Licenses, Patent Pools, and Standard-Setting." *Innovation Policy and the Economy* 1:119–150.

Shapiro, C. 2003. "Antitrust Limits to Patent Settlements." *RAND Journal of Economics* 34:391–411.

Spier, K. E., and M. C. Whinston. 1995. "On the Efficiency of Private Stipulated Damages for Breach of Contract: Entry Barriers, Reliance, and Renegotiation." *RAND Journal of Economics* 26:180–202.

Suzumura, K. 1992. "Cooperative and Noncooperative R&D in an Oligopoly with Spillovers." *American Economic Review* 5:1307–1320.

U.S. Department of Justice and Federal Trade Commission. 1995. *Antitrust Guidelines for the Licensing of Intellectual Property*. Washington, DC: Department of Justice and Federal Trade Commission.

U.S. v. Microsoft Corp. Civ. No. 94-1564LO (D.D.C. 1994).

Whinston, M. D. 1990. "Tying, Foreclosure, and Exclusion." *American Economic Review* 80:837–859.

7 Litigation and Enforcement

A message of chapter 2 was that intellectual property does its work by creating exclusion rights to knowledge or information. The problem of enforcement lies at the very heart of this attempt and is anything but trivial. If the innovator chooses intellectual property over trade secrecy, the technical details are generally disclosed. This is a legal requirement for patents. For copyrighted works, the intellectual property is generally visible on the surface, hence vulnerable to being copied. This is especially true of movies, music, software, and books distributed in digital form, although some of those are amenable to technical protections, as discussed in this chapter.

If a protected work is used without authorization of the rightholder, then the rightholder is entitled to remedies. The first step is to prove that the rights have, in fact, been infringed. In legal jargon, the plaintiff must prove "liability," a nontrivial step. For patents, where the protected subject matter is divided into claims, infringement entails that every element of at least one claim is embodied in the offending product. Although this sounds stringent, we must bear in mind that the claims were chosen by the patent applicant, and approved by the patent examiner, as the minimum combination of elements that constitute an invention. Nevertheless, there is plenty of scope for legal argument regarding what it takes to infringe a claim.

A dispute over intellectual property usually begins as a claim of infringement. In the case of patents, the alleged infringer often counterclaims for patent invalidity—the best defense is a good offense. The counterclaim can be, for example, that the invention was obvious to someone skilled in the art, and therefore did not embody a sufficient inventive step to warrant a patent.

In 1994, the University of California applied for a patent on a technology developed by its researchers for making web-browsing capabilities interactive with websites. The technology allows small inter-active programs, so-called plug-ins, applets, and scriptlets, to be embedded into web documents. In 1998, UC was awarded U.S. patent 5,838,906. In the meantime, it licensed this technology to a start-up firm, Eolas, founded by its inventor. While the patent application was pending, Microsoft Cor-poration, having previously turned down the opportunity to license the technology, embedded such a technology into Internet Explorer, the web browser that is integrated into the Windows operating system. UC sued for infringement. Microsoft defended itself by claiming that the technology had previously been invented by someone else, and therefore the UC patent should be invalidated. The court rejected this defense, affirmed the valid-ity of the patent, and awarded damages of $520.6 million. Microsoft promised to appeal. Meanwhile, Tim Berners-Lee, director of the World Wide Web Consortium, weighed in with the opinion that the technology was anticipated in prior art, and, bypassing the court system, convinced the PTO to reexamine the patent. This led to a (contestable) decision of the USPTO to nullify the patent (Stevenson 2004).

Most intellectual property disputes do not involve sums of that mag-nitude and do not result in reexaminations of patents. However, a coun-terclaim of invalidity following a complaint of infringement is typical.

For copyrights, the defense is often fair use instead of invalidity. There is a presumption of validity unless the author copied the work from someone else. In theory, infringement of a copyrighted work should be a straightforward matter of checking the offending document against the original, to see if they are "substantially similar." However, the defen-dant may argue that she had never even seen the original, and although her work looks similar, it was independently achieved, hence not an infringement. Depending on the circumstances, this defense can obvi-ously strain credulity. If the defendant claims a fair-use exception, as dis-cussed in chapters 3 and 4, the court must adjudicate whether, as a matter of law, the alleged offense is a fair use.

In the 1990s, when the hottest sitcom on television was Jerry Seinfeld and his three disaffected friends, the Carol Publishing Group published a trivia book, the *Seinfeld Aptitude Test* (SAT), in which readers were invited to test their knowledge of "the trifling, picayune and petty annoyances encountered by the show's characters on a daily basis."[1]

---

1.   As quoted from the author, Beth Golub, by the court of appeals. An example of the SAT cited by the court of appeals is: Who said, "I don't go for those nonrefundable deals . . . I can't commit to a woman . . . I'm not com-mitting to an airline." Multiple-choice answers: (a) Jerry, (b) George, (c) Kramer.

However, the publisher did not have a license to use the Seinfeld characters or to quote from the episodes. The Seinfeld publisher sued. Carol Publishing argued that they only copied minimal parts of the episodes, and even if not minimal, using the material was a fair use. The court rejected both arguments. It held that the SAT passes the test of being substantially similar to the original work, even if there was no literal copying, and also held that the work was not "transformative" in a way that would entitle it to a defense of fair use. The court awarded damages of $403,000.

Whether or not the alleged infringer prevails in court, a good-faith belief in fair use or patent invalidity can avoid the conclusion that infringement was willful. Willfulness is relevant to the penalties that can be invoked. The Copyright Act goes so far as to impose criminal penalties (jail time) if copying is willful and for commercial purposes, although criminal penalties are seldom invoked. Patent law provides for treble damages in cases of willful infringement.

Plaintiffs can also be opportunistic and can try the patience of courts, just as willful infringers can. As we will see in the next section, a nontrivial percentage of patents are litigated, and most litigation involves high-value intellectual property, which can be a tempting target.

After J. K. Rowling achieved success in the late 1990s with her Harry Potter books for children, a writer named N. K. Stouffer in Pennsylvania filed an infringement suit, claiming she had previously circulated works with a certain Larry Potter, also skinny, bespectacled, and preadolescent (Kirkpatrick 2001). Like Harry Potter, Larry Potter consorted with characters called "muggles." The characters are similar enough to suggest copying, but also different. Harry has magical powers, but Larry does not. Rowling's muggles are ordinary folk, whereas Stouffer's muggles are short, hairless, quasi-human mutants.

Part of Rowling's defense was that she had never laid eyes on Stouffer's work, and therefore could not have copied it. However, that would seem extraordinary, given the similarities. The simple explanation believed by the court was that Stouffer had made fraudulent claims and cooked the evidence. The case was dismissed on that basis, with Stouffer forced to pay some of Rowling's legal fees (Italie 2002).

Like other legal disputes, intellectual property disputes often settle out of court.[2] In a settlement, the litigants agree to withdraw their

---

2.   For more on patent settlements, see Shapiro 2003; Hovenkamp, Janis, and Lemley 2003.

complaints in return for certain payments and/or licensing provisions. Often a settlement will involve the type of license or joint venture that would occur if the case was litigated and a court found infringement and validity. For example, the alleged infringer may abandon his counter-claim of invalidity and assign his own rights to the patent holder, in return for money. Or the patent holder may abandon her claim of infringement and grant a license on reasonable terms. In some cases, the litigants merge, or one firm buys the rights of the other.

One thing the litigants are likely to agree on is that the settlement should maximize their joint profit—for example, by imposing high royalties. The settlement gives the two rivals an opportunity to write a contract that joins their interests. As we saw in chapter 6, licensing with royalties can keep prices high. The profit can then be divided by other terms of license such as fixed fees. However, this raises an issue for competition policy. If the court would have found invalidity or infringement, and the disputants would then have been competitors, the settlement is anticompetitive. For this reason, settlement of a lawsuit can come under antitrust scrutiny, just as ordinary licensing contracts can. Sometimes the litigants ask the court to issue an order called a *consent decree*, containing the terms of settlement. This makes the settlement easier to enforce, which may be beneficial to the parties, but also gives the court an opportunity to exercise oversight as to the settlement's appropriateness.[3]

There is a strong incentive to settle even if the parties disagree on their prospects and the dispute is legitimate. Litigation is very costly. A patent litigation can cost each litigant between $1 million and $3 million per suit (Graham et al. 2003; American Intellectual Property Law Association, 1999) or about $500,000 per patent claim (Barton 2000). As we will see in chapter 9, the value of most patents is considerably less than these litigation costs. Although national litigations in Europe are less costly, between €50,000 and €500,000 (Graham et al. 2002), they might have to be repeated in different countries. Almost 2 percent of patents are litigated. It is difficult to calculate the same statistic for copyrights, because there is no requirement that copyrights be registered, so it is difficult to identify the population that generates litigation.

---

3.   The court does not always issue the consent decree proposed by the parties, even when the plaintiff is the U.S. government. For example, the court rejected the first consent decree proposed by the parties in the 1994 Department of Justice antitrust case against Microsoft on grounds that it was not in the public interest. See the appendix to Hoerner 1995 for references.

The next section summarizes some evidence on litigation. Following that is a discussion of remedies for infringement, and how they affect equilibrium profits, a discussion of technical protection measures as a solution to the enforcement problem, and an evaluation of the threat that arises from unauthorized sharing of copyrighted works.

7.1   Evidence on Litigation

One of the things that economists have difficulty explaining is why disputes ever reach the courts. Firms can avoid litigation costs by settling. One of the most expensive parts of litigation is "discovery," the process by which the litigants are allowed to find things out about each other's cases—for example, by deposing the involved parties or exchanging the views of their experts who would testify at trial on technical matters. Through the discovery process, the firms refine their beliefs about the likely outcome of litigation. Indeed, settlements often occur during this process. However, it is not because the litigants are certain of the outcome that they have an incentive to settle, but only because they are in close agreement on the prospects. If they agree that the outcomes are equally likely, for example, then they should settle on terms that "split the difference" and save the remaining litigation costs.

There is also a question as to why infringement would ever occur in equilibrium. If infringement is tempting due to weak remedies or because an infringer is unlikely to be held liable, that should be known to both parties. They can save money and trouble by licensing to avoid the infringement. If infringement nevertheless occurs, the parties can still do better by settling instead of litigating. In fact, settlement may be even more attractive for infringement disputes than for other kinds of disputes, since it may allow the firms to license in a way that increases their joint profit, as compared to the likely outcome of litigation.

Nevertheless, the sparse evidence on litigation suggests that it is prevalent, at least for some types of patents. The author knows of no systematic evidence about the prevalence and cost of litigating copyrights.

The prospect of wasting resources in litigation makes intellectual property a less effective incentive mechanism, just as losing profit to infringers does. Further, if the profit dissipation falls disproportionately on large and small firms, market structure becomes an important determinant of the incentives to innovate. We would therefore like to know how much profit is dissipated through litigation, and which innovators bear the cost. Of course we would also like to know how much profit is dissipated through unremedied infringement, but that is more difficult. We can at most observe litigation, not infringement.

The most comprehensive evidence on patent litigation is due to Lanjouw and Schankerman (2001, 2004) who make inferences germane to the questions just raised from a data set they constructed on litigated and unlitigated patents. This data set includes information about the characteristics of the patent owners, the firms' patent portfolios, and characteristics of individual patents. Much of the data comes originally from the database of issued patents made available by the USPTO. The PTO assigns Patent Classification numbers to every patent, which designate the technological areas. The number of claims, characteristics of the patent owner such as foreign or domestic, the year of application, and backward citations (the prior patents that are cited) can be read directly from the patent document. The PTO's data also include identifier numbers assigned to patent applicants, so that the database can be used to link all the patents owned by a particular company—that is, the company's portfolio of patents. The authors then processed the PTO data into a data set that includes forward citations (the patents that come afterward that cite a given patent), self-citations, and portfolio measures (how many patents are held by a given company in a given technology class).

Litigation data are also included in the PTO's database. When a patent suit is filed in a district court, the clerk of the court is obligated to report it to the PTO. Although such reporting is unreliable, by comparing the PTO data to data collected by the Federal Judicial Center, Lanjouw and Schankerman reject the hypothesis that cases are underreported in any systematic way. They use that comparison to adjust for the underreporting. The Federal Judicial Center also gives information on the disposition of cases, such as whether they settle and when. A third data source used by Lanjouw and Schankerman is Standard and Poor's database on companies that are publicly traded, which allows them to know characteristics of the company such as size. By using this data, they can tell whether litigation risks are higher or lower for patents owned by individuals rather than, for example, publicly traded firms.

It turns out that patent litigation varies widely by industry and size of firm, but is frequent and costly for high-value patents, especially in emerging technologies. The overall litigation rate is about 2 cases per

100 patents, concentrated on high-value patents. This litigation rate seems high enough to dissipate a substantial fraction of the reward for innovating. An earlier study by Lerner 1994 was even more pessimistic. Lerner estimated that 6 in 100 biotechnology patents were litigated.

However, even though the number of patent litigations rose in the 1978–1999 period of Lanjouw's and Schankerman's study, the underlying propensity to litigate did not increase. The increased litigation is attributable to the changing composition of patents, and to the overall increase in patenting. There was a 71 percent increase in patent grants from 1978 to 1995. Most of the increase in patent suits has been in drugs, biotechnology, and computers and other electronics, which have always been highly litigated and have been increasing as a percentage of total patent grants.

The work also paints a rather bleak picture for small innovators. All else equal, a patent held by a large firm is less likely to be litigated than a patent held by a small firm. Previous studies have turned up other disadvantages to small firms. Lerner (1995) concluded that small firms avoid technology areas where litigation is prevalent, and Lanjouw and Lerner (2001) showed that, in the litigation process itself, preliminary injunctions are used strategically by large firms against small firms.

The result that goes most directly to the question of market structure is that patents held by firms in concentrated markets (where patenting is dominated by only a few companies) are less likely to be litigated. A large patent portfolio reduces the probability that any constituent patent is litigated, other things equal. This effect is even more important for small firms, but one suspects that small firms are less likely to have large patent portfolios.

Other specific findings of Lanjouw and Schankerman include the following:

• The overall rate of litigation is about 19 filed suits per 1,000 filed patents. The lowest rates are in chemicals (about 12), electronics (about 15), and mechanical (about 17). Pharmaceuticals are only a little higher than average, but computers and biotechnology are much higher.
• Corporate owners of patents are less likely to be involved in patent suits than individual owners.
• Litigated patents have more claims than average, more forward citations, and fewer backward citations. An interpretation is that the more valuable patents in the newer technologies are most likely to be litigated.

- Ninety-five percent of filed patent suits are settled before trial.
- Firms with the largest portfolios of patents also have the most highly cited (interpreted as most valuable) patents, but nevertheless, the lowest litigation rates.
- The heterogeneity in litigation burden shows up mainly in the propensity to file suits, but not in the subsequent rates of settlement, or disposition at trial.
- Broader patents (those with more PTO technology classifications) are litigated less than narrower patents.

Given the cost and prevalence of litigation, we can conclude that it constitutes an important modification to the profitability of intellectual property rights, and one that differs across different types of firms and technologies.

As shown by the examples at the beginning of the chapter, litigation also gives courts an opportunity to modify the design of intellectual property law itself. This has been of particular interest after 1982, when the Court of Appeals for the Federal Circuit was instituted to hear appeals on patent-infringement cases. The court was established partly because of dissatisfaction among patent litigants over what they perceived as a lack of technical expertise and consistency on the part of federal judges. Patent disputes are still litigated in federal district courts, but most appeals go to the Federal Circuit.

There is at least some evidence that the Federal Circuit has been more "pro-patent" than appellate courts previously handling patent matters. This is a difficult thing to measure, due to the selection of what cases are litigated, and then what cases are appealed. One should be skeptical of attempts to characterize judges' proclivities by counting outcomes of litigated cases. Nevertheless, scholars have done so, and the data are of some interest.

Harmon ([1991] 1998) summarizes data about three types of patent appeals. In one group, defendants in infringement suits are still pressing their claims of patent invalidity, trying to reverse the decisions of district courts against them. The appellate court thus has opportunity to invalidate a patent. Not doing so might be interpreted as "pro-patent." In the second group, defendants are trying to reverse a district court's finding of infringement. The appellate court has an opportunity to exonerate them. Not doing so might again be interpreted as "pro-patent." In the third group, plaintiffs who lost their suits in district court are asking the appellate court to reverse a finding of invalidity or to overturn a finding of noninfringement. Doing so might be interpreted as "pro-patent."

In the first two categories, Harmon ([1991] 1998) reports that the Federal Circuit has affirmed about 85 percent of district courts' findings for plaintiffs that patents were valid and infringed, and in the third category, that the Federal Circuit has reversed about 25 percent of decisions against the patent holder. Thus, the patent holder has a higher chance of being successful on appeal at the Federal Circuit than the accused infringer does. The accused infringer only has a one-in-seven chance of being successful, while the patent holder has a one-in-four chance of being successful.

In the 1991 version of his work, Harmon reported the same data for a sample from appellate courts prior to Federal Circuit and found they were less favorable to the patent holder. However, in comparing Federal Circuit decisions to a sample of decisions of prior appellate courts, Lunney (2004) finds the opposite. He aggregates the three types of appeals and considers whether the patent holder "succeeded," which means that the patent holder obtained, at least in part, the remedy sought, such as injunction or damages. He finds that patent holders succeeded in 33.5 percent of appellate cases prior to establishment of the Federal Circuit, but in only 28.3 percent of cases afterward. There was a spike of patentee successes just after the court was established, which may account for the widespread perception that the court is "pro-patent," but the success rate then tapered off.

What is perhaps of even more interest is that patentees succeed (or avoid failing) in the Federal Circuit for different reasons than they succeeded previously in other appellate courts. Prior to establishment of the Federal Circuit, three-fourths of patentee failures were because some claim of the patent was invalidated. That rate has dropped to about a third during the Federal Circuit period; the Federal Circuit is invalidating fewer patents. Prior to establishment of the Federal Circuit, only about a quarter of patentee failures were because the allegedly infringing device or process was found to be outside the scope of the patent. In the era of the Federal Circuit, this fraction has risen to about two-thirds; the Federal Circuit is narrowing the breadth of patents. Lunney (2004) concludes that these data "leave the indelible impression that the Federal Circuit is deliberately and systematically changing the nature of patent law. . . . By eviscerating the nonobviousness requirement, the Federal Circuit has substantially reduced the level of creativity required to establish a valid patent," and "the

Federal Circuit has also limited patents to a correspondingly narrow scope."

7.2   Remedies for Infringement and How They Matter

There are two kinds of remedies that courts can mete out, injunctive relief and damages. An injunction is a court order to the infringer to stop using or selling the infringing product. Once the court order is in place, the resumption of sales becomes a criminal act, with the possibility of jail time, rather than the mere payment of money to the rightholder. Intellectual property disputes seldom come to this. However, as already mentioned, the battle over liability and damages can be fierce and expensive. It typically involves the testimony of both percipient witnesses and expert witnesses on both the technical merits and the damages.

Damages serve two purposes: they compensate an infringed rightholder for the loss suffered, thus making sure that the rightholder's ex ante incentive to invest in R&D is intact despite the possibility of infringement, and they can deter the infringement in the first place. We will say that infringement is deterred if the profit available from infringement is less than the prospective damages that the infringer must pay. The two purposes of compensation and deterrence are alternatives: there is no need for compensation if the prospect of damages serves its purpose of deterring infringement.

There have been two theories of damages in the common law: the infringer must pay the rightholder his *lost profit*, or the infringer must disgorge his *unjust enrichment*. The measure now used in the United States is lost profit, which is aimed at replacing the infringed rightholder's losses. Unjust enrichment would be aimed at making sure the infringer does not profit from his misdeeds. Oddly enough, neither doctrine seems explicitly aimed at deterring infringement, although either may do so, as we will see.[4] The court also has the option to impose additional punitive damages if the patent infringement is deemed willful, and criminal penalties are available under copyright law.

---

4.   The discussion here is based mostly on Schankerman and Scotchmer 2001, especially in its emphasis on equilibrium profits, as determined by the threat of infringement and damages. See Calabresi and Melamed 1972 for the key treatment distinguishing property and liability rules, and Conley 1987 for a good description of how the judicial treatment of remedies has evolved. See Heath, Henkel, and Reitzig 2002 for a discussion of how these rules have been developed in different countries.

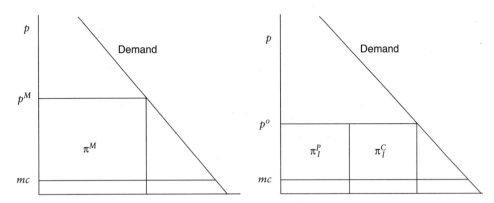

Figure 7.1
Equilibrium and infringement

7.2.1   Remedies: Product Patents

Figure 7.1 shows the difference between lost profit and unjust enrichment when a product patent is infringed. The left diagram shows the rightholder's per-period monopoly profit, absent the infringement. The right diagram shows the rightholder's oligopoly profit when competing with the infringer, and when the two firms share the market as shown. Let π_I^P and π_I^C represent their respective profits if they compete, where the subscript on π denotes (I)nfringement and the superscripts denote (P)atentholder and (C)ompetitor (infringer). Competition lowers the market price, and, in addition, the rightholder loses market share. The patent holder's lost profit would be $\pi^M - \pi_I^P$, and the infringer's unjust enrichment would be π_I^C. Since the monopoly profit π^M is always larger than the sum of the two firms' oligopoly profits $\pi_I^P + \pi_I^C$ (else the monopolist would have chosen a lower price), it follows that $\pi^M - \pi_I^P > \pi_I^C$. Thus, due to price erosion, the lost-profit rule yields larger damages for the rightholder than the unjust-enrichment rule does.[5]

Suppose now that the purpose of the damages rule is to deter infringement. The lost-profit rule will do so, since $\pi^M - \pi_I^P > \pi_I^C$. But the

5.   Commentators sometimes claim that the unjust-enrichment measure is larger than the lost-profit measure whenever the infringer is more efficient at working the patent than the patent holder. That view does not take account of licensing. If the infringer is more efficient, the likely (efficient) equilibrium outcome would be licensing by the patent holder, not production by the patent holder. See the next subsection, which discusses how to measure lost profit when licensing would alternatively be the equilibrium outcome.

unjust-enrichment rule might also deter infringement. Since the infringer is made to disgorge the entire ill-gotten gain, he is indifferent between infringing and not, and it is reasonable to assume that he will be deterred, especially if there is any chance that punitive damages will be imposed.

In the case depicted here, the lost-profit rule is better for the infringed rightholder when deterrence fails, since he is "made whole." This is not true under the unjust-enrichment rule. However, if infringement is deterred in equilibrium, this argument may not matter. It does not matter what would happen in the out-of-equilibrium event of infringement, since an out-of-equilibrium event is not expected to occur. Nevertheless, if both rules deter infringement, there is no harm in choosing the one that makes the rightholder whole in the event of infringement.

Even so, there is a problem knowing how to calculate lost profit. In the circumstance depicted by figure 7.1, experts would have to estimate the demand curve and then use it to predict the price that would have prevailed, absent the infringement. The court would have to make a judgment as to the equilibrium in the left-hand diagram and calculate the lost profit $\pi^M - \pi_f^p$. Naturally courts are reluctant to do this. It is tempting to use a more limited notion of lost profit, which assumes that the prevailing price with infringement, p^o in figure 7.1, would prevail even absent the infringement. Lost profit is then calculated as lost sales at that price. In figure 7.1, this calculation would lead to a damage estimate of π_f^G. This method avoids the problem of predicting the price that would have prevailed, absent the infringement, but can significantly underestimate the loss. Another alternative is simply to take account of price erosion but not the loss in sales. This method also underestimates the true loss. The estimate would be π_f^p times the price erosion, $(p^M - p^o)/p^o$. The underestimation matters for both compensation and deterrence. The infringed is not compensated, and the infringer may not be deterred.

Licensing changes this story in its details but does not change the conclusions, provided the true lost profit can be imposed as damages. Suppose that the rightholder is infringed but that marginal cost is increasing instead of constant, as in the model of section 6.1. There are four possible counterfactuals to infringement in that situation. One possibility is that the rightholder would have supplied the whole market inefficiently, using a single production facility. Another possibility is that the rightholder would have built a second plant and supplied the whole market efficiently. A third possibility is that the rightholder would not have produced at all, licensing two firms instead. A fourth possibility is that, absent the infringement, the rightholder would have supplied part of the market and would also have licensed the infringer.

With all these counterfactuals, which should the court use? And how should it be applied? With constant marginal cost, it was natural to assume that the rightholder would have supplied the market in a single production facility. The only problem was to estimate demand and find the profit-maximizing price. Here, the task is first to figure out the right counterfactual, and then to calculate the lost profit. Some of the counterfactuals involve licensing and some do not. Some involve efficient production and some do not. The counterfactual lost profit may include both lost sales revenue and lost licensing revenue.

The view taken by Schankerman and Scotchmer (2001), followed here, is that lost profit should be calculated by reference to an equilibrium that "should have occurred." This perspective goes a long distance toward cutting through the complexities of the competing counterfactuals. At a minimum, an equilibrium should be efficient. We can eliminate the counterfactual with inefficient production in a single facility, because that will not be profit maximizing for the rightholder. The rightholder will either build a second plant or license. Among the other three options, we saw in section 6.1 that if the licensor can use royalties and fixed fees, she can make the same profit by licensing two firms as by supplying the market herself, producing in two production plants. With enough permissible terms of license, she can also do as well by licensing a single firm and supplying part of the market herself. We can therefore take this maximum profit as the reference point, without specifying which of those three efficient options she would use. Of course, in one of those outcomes the profit would be earned entirely through licensing fees, in another it would be earned entirely through sales revenues, net of costs, and in the third, it would be earned through both sales and license fees. But all would give the same profit to the rightholder.

Suppose, then, that absent the infringement, the patent holder would have earned profit π^J. In the notation of section 6.1, $\pi^J = q^* p(q^*) - 2\int_0^{q^*/2} \gamma(\hat{q})d\hat{q}$ and π^J is larger than the profit that the rightholder would have earned as a monopolist with a single production facility. As before, we can let π_I^P and π_I^C represent the patent holder's and competitor's (infringer's) profits with infringement. Since $\pi^J > \pi_I^P + \pi_I^C$, it remains true that the patent holder's lost profit $\pi^J - \pi_I^P$ is larger than the infringer's gain π_I^C. Thus, the lost-profit rule will deter infringement.

For this argument, we have not had to disaggregate the lost profit into lost sales net of costs and lost licensing revenue. However, that is where it gets difficult from a practical point of view. Although it is firmly established in legal doctrine that lost profit can be lost royalty ("reasonable royalty"), there are no clear guidelines for calculating it. Since the putative equilibrium never happened, the court cannot refer to the licensing arrangements or sales revenue that underlie π^j, and in any case, there are various licensing arrangements that could do so, including no licensing at all. To reduce the degree of speculativeness, courts may feel constrained to choose between a measure of damages based solely on lost sales and a measure of damages based solely on lost royalties.

Thus, although the lost-profit doctrine grants enough penalties to deter infringement even without punitive damages, it is difficult to calculate the benchmark level of profit. Fortunately, infringement may be deterred even if lost profits are underestimated. That is because, in the case of product patents, infringement dissipates profit in total, as well as the rightholder's profit. The profit dissipation is itself punitive, so that the minimum damages required to deter infringement are less than the lost profits. If lost profits are measured accurately, infringement is "overdeterred."

That simple story changes when licensors and their licensees are not competitors in the market, such as in the licensing of research tools.

7.2.2   Remedies: Licensed Research Tools

As stressed earlier, the difficulty in calculating lost profit is that it can only be calculated with reference to some hypothetical equilibrium that should have occurred but did not occur. Since profit is an equilibrium concept, "lost profit" is also an equilibrium concept. But the problem of calculating the equilibrium that should have occurred is compounded when licensing is at stake, because the license fees at which the infringer "should have licensed" are also part of the equilibrium that did not occur. This problem was avoided in the case of patented products by referring to a benchmark level of profit that could be achieved in various ways, with or without licensing. That dodge will not be possible in what follows.

The focus here is mainly on research tools. Tools have become particularly important in biotechnology, where the process of developing new drugs or other products requires (1) a suitable host, like bacteria, tobacco plants, or (for agricultural products) a germplasm, (2) techniques for inserting foreign genes into the host, (3) genetic sequences that code for the desired trait or protein, (4) genetic sequences that code instructions to the host, such as suppression of other genes, or expression, and (5) techniques to extract the product without killing the host. The developer of a bioengineered product will not typically own the intellectual property that gives access to all five pieces, and must therefore license.

In this circumstance, the lost-profit doctrine leads to an indeterminacy in licensing fees that may undermine the incentive to invest in research tools. This is due to a circularity in the definition of lost royalty.

Suppose that the license fee is some number of dollars, L, and the damages for infringement under the lost-profit doctrine would be some number d. Looking at the court's calculation of damages under the lost-profit doctrine, damages should satisfy $d = L$. The maximum that a potential licensee would pay for a license is the damage he would otherwise have to pay, d. Further, the minimum that a licensor would charge is also d, since she could get d in a court award afterward. Thus, it must hold that $L = d$. But what determines the mutual values of d and L? There is nothing to nail it down, except that the mutual value must be less than the licensee's willingness to pay. By definition, a licensee would not pay more than his willingness to pay, and such a fee could therefore not be lost profit.

In short, the whole line of reasoning is circular, and hence not very satisfying. It means that the profitability of the licensed innovation is indeterminate, and the possibility of low rewards may discourage innovation.

To elaborate this argument, suppose that the market for the research tool is anonymous, in the sense that the licensor cannot price discriminate according to the user's willingness to pay. The market demand for such licenses is shown in figure 7.2. Figure 7.2 might depict, for example, the market for PCR licenses. PCR is a chemical procedure, extremely useful in biomedical research, that allows DNA to be replicated easily for experimental use. For such tools, each user's willingness to pay is either determined by the convenience of not using the next best alternative, or by the value of the research program it enables.

At the original demand curve, or willingness-to-pay curve (the solid line), the licensor's best option is to charge the monopoly price, L^M. That price should be self-sustaining. An infringer would have to pay damages $d = L^M$, since that is the prevailing price, and is thus the lost profit when an infringement occurs.

Suppose, though, that demand shifts to the dotted line in figure 7.2. The monopoly price that the licensor would then like to charge is $\hat{L}^M$. Can the price be raised?

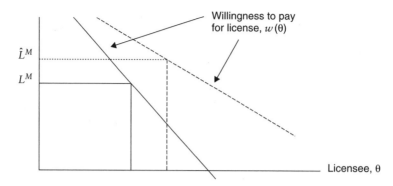

Figure 7.2
A market for licenses

Due to the self-reinforcing nature of damages and license fees, increasing the price will be difficult once it is established, with the consequence that the prevailing price can be somewhat arbitrary. If the licensor suddenly tries to charge the price $\hat{L}^M$ to a new licensee, the licensee may well reason that infringement is a better option. The court will charge damages of $d = L^M$, which is the observable prevailing price and hence the court's assessment of lost profit. Unless the licensor can find a way to change the price for all licensees simultaneously, it will be difficult to adjust the price.

The same argument can be made without reference to a shift in demand. If, for any unspecified reason, the licensor finds herself charging a price that is lower than the most profitable one, she will have trouble adjusting it, due to the self-reinforcing nature of the damage measure and license fees. Thus, there is nothing to pin down the equilibrium license fee and damages, and they may be somewhat arbitrary. A licensor can get locked into an equilibrium with price lower than the most profitable price.

7.3   Enforcement of Copyrights by Technical Protection Measures

Intellectual property rights are inherently difficult to enforce, since they are exclusive rights to "information," and information has the character of a public good. It can be copied or used freely once it exists. For manufactured objects, the threat of infringement is kept under control because infringement does not take place at the level of individuals, but rather at the level of firms. It requires a production and distribution facility, which are public enough to be detected.

Intellectual property law provides a legal means by which inventors can exclude unauthorized users from using their creations. There are also technical means, such as encryption and copy controls. The technical means may obviate the need for legal means, but they are not equivalent.

Technical protection measures will be particularly important if the legal means of exclusion fail—that is, if copyrights or other intellectual property rights are not enforceable. Technical protections have been more widely deployed in the copyright realm than the patent realm, but even in the patent realm, there is at least one important example, the so-called terminator gene. This is a gene developed by Monsanto that, if inserted into genetically modified crop seeds, will prevent a second generation of seeds from germinating. As a consequence, the farmer cannot save seed for planting the next crop. Saving seed would generally be prohibited by license for patented genetically modified crops in any case, but such a prohibition is hard to enforce. The terminator gene solves the enforcement problem but is controversial for other reasons, such as its potential for finding its way into other seeds.

Technical protections have been more widely introduced for so-called digital content such as movies, music, computer software, and computer games (see Samuelson and Scotchmer 2002). If these products are distributed on CDs, they are easy to copy without detection. Of course, print books and music distributed on audiotapes have long been vulnerable to copying. Such copying has not undermined their market in the past, because the inconvenience of copying has been more costly for most consumers than the price of a legitimate copy.

The threat to copyright holders has evolved as technology has evolved.[6] In the 1970s, when videocassette recorders were introduced, movie producers and other vendors of broadcast and cable content feared that home videotaping would undermine their ability to collect box-office fares or rent videos. Did the viewer have a right to tape movies for personal use? This issue went back and forth in the courts in the 1970s and 1980s.

To some extent analog tapes have self-limiting copy potential, in that the quality of each successive copy degrades. Thus it is difficult to

---

6.   See Goldstein 1994 for an interpretive history and Litman 2001, Samuelson 2002, and Menell 2002 for subsequent developments in software and digital products.

make unlimited copies of copies, which to some degree limits the threat of copying. In contrast, digital content can be copied faithfully. When digital audiotapes (DATs) were introduced in the mid-1980s, content providers feared that the ability to make faithful copies of copies would lead to widespread infringement. By 1992 they had persuaded Congress to adopt a copy-management solution in the Audio Home Recording Act. This act mandated that DATs and DAT players must contain a Serial Copy Management System, a technological modification that limits the making of copies.

The 1980s saw technical protections fail in the market. In the late 1980s, software for personal computers was sold with a one-installation feature. Users (hence vendors) found this annoying, because any glitch in installation would render the software unusable. Further, users could not make backup copies of the software, or install it on both their home and office computers, as they might think "fair."

Ultimately the one-installation feature disappeared from the market. In any case, today's computers could copy one-installation disks before installation, thus undermining the system. The modern incarnation of the one-installation feature is to download software directly from the Internet to the user's computer. Downloading is a double-edged sword. For computer software, it is a convenient and controlled way to sell a single installation without circulating a disk. But for content such as music, it can facilitate the distribution of illicit copies, as in the Napster case discussed later.

Other solutions to the copying of digital content are encryption and watermarks. These are attempts to make the digital content uninterpretable or inaccessible without use of a code key. Access to the key must be authorized by license or sale, often with the sale of the content itself. Of course, one might ask what is different about selling access to a key rather than access to the content. If the content can be copied, so can the key. Further, the key is typically a password, and if the user really wants to overcome it, he can use the computer to try passwords seriatum. A more reliable version of the key system is call-home authorization, a version of the direct download. Instead of downloading and installing the software from the CD alone, the user logs on to a website in order to pay the vendor and receives an authorization code for the software he has received on CD.

A watermark, by analogy with watermarks on paper stationery, is a piece of software code embedded in a program. It may have two purposes. First, if illicit copies of the software circulate, the watermark can identify the original buyer or licensee of the copy that is circulating. This may or may not be useful, depending on whether the original buyer or licensee can be held liable. The second purpose works in conjunction with code embedded in an authorized platform required to use the digital content. For example, the movie industry has developed digital versatile disks (DVDs), which are protected by a technology called the Content Scrambling System (CSS). CSS authorizes access by matching a code embedded in disks to a code embedded in DVD players. Manufacturers of DVD players must license the CSS system, which must itself be protected for the system to work. The sound-recording industry tried to implement a similar system, called Secure Digital Music Initiative (SDMI), by which digital sound recordings would embody special authorization signals to be detected by authorized players. For various reasons, that system has not succeeded.

These systems shift the enforcement problem from protecting the content to protecting the players. In their most extreme implementation, the content would not be protected at all. The entire enforcement burden would be moved to players. Protecting players is not a perfect substitute for protecting content, however, since it is difficult to distribute the revenue from players in a way that rewards content according to its popularity. Another problem with this solution (a problem for antitrust authorities, but not necessarily for content providers) is that the joint ownership of the players' authorization technology might allow an implicit collusion among content providers that would be avoided by protecting content directly (Scotchmer and Park 2004). And at the technical level, the system might not work because the technical protection system might be reverse engineered, thus opening the player market to unlicensed entry.

The message in the preceding account is that technical protections are so far limited in their ability to protect content. There is probably no perfect way to exclude unauthorized users from access. At best, technical protection measures can make it costly to get at the content—for example, by having to circumvent a password, encryption system, or watermark. But even encrypted digital content is vulnerable to copying. To use the content, it must at some point live unencrypted in a computer's memory. At that point, even if no other, it is vulnerable. In short, according to what the market has produced so far, getting around technical protection systems is simply a matter of being willing to bear the cost.

In response to the perceived inadequacies of technical protections, Congress enacted the Digital Millennium Copyright Act (DMCA) in 1998. Among other provisions, and with some exceptions, the DMCA prohibits circumventions of technical protection systems.[7] That is, it creates legal protections for technical protections.

A logical question is why legal protections for technical protections are likely to work, given that legal protections for digital content are assumed not to. One obvious answer is that, in addition to creating rules to protect the protections, the DMCA imposes ferocious penalties for violating the rules. Under the DMCA, it is a criminal act to circumvent a technical protection measure for a commercial purpose. That is, the guilty citizen can expect jail time rather than the financial penalties discussed earlier. Under the No Electronic Theft Act of 1997, it is also possible to incur criminal liability for direct copyright infringement, even without a circumvention, and for copyright infringements with no commercial value. Both of these acts have exceptions that may exempt the inadvertent infringer.

Even if not entirely effective, technical protections can have important economic consequences. These include:

1. All technical protection measures involve wasted costs, at least as compared to an idealized world in which users automatically respect intellectual property rights. The waste is compounded if users and providers get caught in a measures-on-countermeasures war with every attempt at technical protection defeated with a countermeasure, leading to escalation on both sides.

2. If technical protection measures become truly effective, they will likely undermine fair uses of digital content, since fair users are excluded from access, just as infringers are. As mentioned in chapter 4, there are solid policy reasons to grant fair use of copyrighted content. These may be sacrificed if technical protection measures become truly effective.

3. If technical protection measures are truly effective, there is no reason to think that the duration of protection will accord with the provisions of intellectual property law. If an inventor can protect his invention for twenty years using a technical protection measure, then why not thirty? That is, he can protect it as a trade secret much longer than it would be protected with the legal protection of a patent.

---

7.   For a discussion of the limitations on this threat, and how they had been applied by 2002, see Samuelson and Scotchmer 2002.

4.   Technical protections can avoid the disclosure requirement that would be required in the case of patents. To assess the economic consequences, one must have a theory for why disclosure is required; see chapter 5. To the extent that disclosure aids rivals, technical protection aids the rightholder, but it may inhibit innovation in aggregate.

Thus, limitations on intellectual property rights may vanish if the rights are protected technologically rather than legally. This observation should give pause to the enthusiast who thinks that legal protection should give way to technological protection. To the extent that technical protection systems are truly effective, the issues of designing intellectual property discussed elsewhere in this book may become moot.

However, because technical protections are expensive to implement, and because some users have the ability to circumvent them for personal use without detection, it is not obvious that technical protections will lead to higher prices for users. Even though Congress has legislated severe penalties for individual acts of circumvention as well as for commercializing circumvention tools or commercializing pirated works, individual acts of circumvention are hard to detect. If users will circumvent the protection system when the cost of circumvention is lower than the price, the threat of circumvention will have a moderating effect on the pricing strategy of vendors, as follows.

Index the strength of protection by e, and for simplicity, assume that e also represents the cost of circumvention. The vendor cannot sell units at a price higher than e. By choosing the strength of protection, e, the inventor thus chooses the maximum feasible price.

Suppose that the demand at price p is $q(p)$, and that the marginal cost of supplying units of the content is zero. Then the monopoly price with perfect legal enforcement would be the p^* that maximizes $pq(p)$.

The profit available in the market with protection e, as depicted in figure 7.3, can be written

$$\Pi(e) = \begin{cases} p^* q(p^*) & \text{if } e \geq p^* \\ eq(e) & \text{if } e < p^* \end{cases}$$

The vendor will not raise price higher than p^*, even if the protection system is strong enough to permit it. Doing so will not increase profit. Thus, the profit function $\Pi(e)$ flattens out for $e \geq p^*$, as shown. If the protection system will not sustain a price as high as p^* due to the threat of circumvention (i.e., if $e < p^*$) then the vendor will price as high as possible while avoiding circumvention.

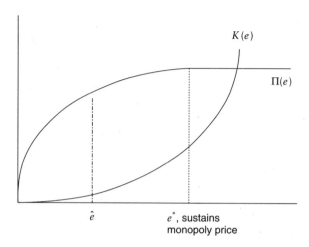

Figure 7.3
Optimal technical protections

Let $K(e)$ represent the cost of implementing a protection system of strength e. The cost of protection may account for the cost of updating an encryption or watermark system to stay ahead of the hackers, or it may simply be an upfront cost. The cost curve K, assumed to be increasing, is also drawn in figure 7.3. The optimal level of protection is where the distance $\Pi(e) - K(e)$ is greatest, which is $\hat{e}$. The optimal level of protection is less than the level of protection that would support the monopoly price, e^*. By reducing protection marginally from $e^* = p^*$, the vendor reduces the costs of implementing the system, but there is very little impact on profit.

Thus, a reliance on technical protection has a moderating influence on price, which reduces per-period deadweight loss. Weighed against this reduction in per-period deadweight loss, however, is that the protection system is costly, and it can continue indefinitely, rather than terminating at a stipulated time, as intellectual property protection does. When we take account of these offsetting effects, it is not obvious whether the threat of circumvention reduces social welfare.

Surprisingly, it is possible that a reliance on technical protections can benefit both consumers and vendors. This follows from the arguments in chapter 4, which showed that consumers may be better off if the intellectual property right is longer, provided the price in each period is lowered enough so that discounted profit stays the constant. The same reasoning carries over to technical protections. The technical protection regime may prolong protection, but also leads to a lower price.

Internet service providers (ISPs) are also important actors in the enforcement environment, possibly as contributors to infringement, and possibly as allies in the enforcement wars. In copyright law, contributory infringement is a willful attempt to encourage or facilitate infringement by someone else, and the facilitator becomes liable. ISPs bear such a risk if the websites they host contain pirated content. As a consequence, they persuaded Congress to write a provision in the DMCA that gives them a safe harbor unless informed of the violation.

A general economic principle is that monitoring for enforcement should be done by the actor who can do it at least cost. This may be either the content providers or the ISPs. Content providers have a clearer sense of what constitutes a violation and have an incentive to inform ISPs. However, they will likely be aggressive in claiming infringement, and thus put pressure on ISPs to evict sites that might be legitimate fair users. The ISPs will be under the burden of making legal judgments as to potential liability, whether they themselves are the monitors, or simply assume liability when informed.

7.4   Limited Sharing of Copyrighted Works

The ease and accuracy of copying digital content have made providers fearful of large-scale piracy. These fears have been fueled by episodes of widespread copying in Asia, as well as well-publicized technologies for unauthorized sharing that have invaded the American market, such as the now defunct Napster. Napster was a database that allowed users of music to find other users in possession of music they wanted. After the two users found each other, one user could download music from the other user's computer. Napster was shut down after a lawsuit by music producers, on grounds of contributory infringement. Similar websites are now operating, and several charge fees that can be passed back to content providers.

In the "old" economy, wide-scale infringement was detectable because it typically required a production facility. A production facility is hard to obscure. In contrast, digital content can be copied by anyone with the capacity to burn a CD or download from the Internet.

But exactly what threat does this pose? Perhaps the most important lesson of Napster is not that copying is easy, but that the music

industry succeeded in shutting it down. This is again because the infringement was taking place on a scale that was hard to miss.

Under the first-sale principle of copyright law, buyers can dispose
of their lawfully acquired copies in any way they want to, including
resale or lending. This right extends to digital content such as CDs, provided the CD is borrowed as a physical object and not copied. The threat
perceived by content providers is that the CD is likely to be copied
instead of borrowed. Most of us know people who have engaged in some
form of illicit sharing through copying. However, if such sharing is hard
to detect, it is presumably because the sharing circle is small. The kind
of sharing that takes place at the level of friends is limited in scope.

Bakos, Brynjolfsson, and Lichtman (1999) argued that, if sharing
is limited in scope, content providers might actually make even more
profit if they anticipate sharing than if not. They will price in a way that
anticipates the sharing. To see why this might be true, suppose there are
six customers, with willingnesses to pay (1,1,4,5,6,7). If the content is
sold at a monopoly price, the most profitable price is 4, yielding profit
16. There are four buyers with willingness to pay greater than 4.

Suppose instead that these buyers coalesce into sharing groups of
size two. In that case, the willingness to pay of each group can be treated
as a single number, the assumption being that there will be some sort of
side payment between the friends that resolves their disagreements about
what to buy. The following are two ways that the same aggregate willingness to pay can be distributed in groups of size two:

$(5, 6, 13)$ $(6, 7, 11)$

These divisions into sharing groups yield different market demand
and call for different profit-maximizing prices. The profit-maximizing
prices are, respectively, 5 and 6. In both cases, all three groups will buy
the content, yielding profits 15 and 18. The total profit is lower than 16
in the first division of consumers and greater in the second. Thus, sharing
can either increase or decrease profit, depending on the groups that form.

However, an important criticism of this line of reasoning is that it
takes group formation to be exogenous. Of course it is true that much
sharing takes place informally in groups that are thrown together for
other reasons, such as living on the same floor of a dormitory. Nevertheless, such groups are not random. In fact, the members are likely to
have a lot in common. This is reinforced by unspoken protocols of
sharing, such as that each member must occasionally subscribe to a magazine that everyone likes or buy a piece of software that they all want.

A member who contributes nothing that the others want would soon be evicted from the group. Thus, although sharing groups probably do not form strategically for the sole purpose of sharing intellectual property, they are also not random.

Suppose, then, that we study the opposite extreme, that groups form for the dedicated purpose of sharing software or content, and that there are informal side payments within the group to share the costs. Some of these side payments may take the form that different members buy different contributions. It is shown by Scotchmer (2005) that, in this situation, there is neither a profit advantage nor a profit disadvantage to sharing, provided the maximum size of the sharing group that can escape detection is fixed.

To see this, suppose that each consumer has willingness to pay either a or x for each CD, $a > 2x$. An agent of type-v_1 has high willingness to pay for jazz and low willingness to pay for classical, and for type-v_2, it is the other way around. The two types are equally represented in the population. That is, their willingnesses to pay are

type of person	v_1	v_2
WTP classical	x	a
WTP jazz	a	x

Suppose first that the monopolist sellers of the classical CD and jazz CD sell separately to single buyers. Since the problem is symmetric for the two sellers, consider the profit of the classical monopolist only. There is no point charging any price between a and x. At price $p = a$, half the consumers buy, so profit per capita is $a/2$. If the monopolist sells at price $p = x$, then everyone buys, so the expected profit per capita is x, but that is less profit than selling to half the buyers at the higher price, since $a/2 > x$.

Now suppose that the monopolist sells to pairs of buyers who share the CD—everybody has a friend. At given prices, the pair will buy the CD if their combined willingness to pay exceeds the price. If one of them values it more than the other, they will find some way to compensate within the sharing groups, so it evens out.

There are three types of groups: two people with tastes v_1, two people with tastes v_2, and mixed groups with one person of each type. In a group with one person of each type, the joint willingness to pay is $a + x$ for each type of CD. At prices for classical and jazz $(p_c, p_j) = (a + x, a + x)$, they will buy both CDs. If all the consumers are matched in that way, then the total profit per capita is $(a + x)/2$, which is larger than the profit when selling to single buyers at either $p = a$ or $p = x$. This is the type of phenomenon pointed to by Bakos, Brynjolfsson, and Lichtman (1999), who point out that if the willingnesses to pay for each CD are negatively correlated within the group, then the proprietors can actually make more money, not less, when consumers share. The buyers with low willingness to pay are not left out of the market, because they are paired with high willingness to pay, and the combined willingness to pay may be enough to induce a sale.

Matching the consumers in mixed groups maximizes the profit for the proprietors. However, there is no reason to think that groups will form in this way. Suppose instead that they form randomly, such as according to who happens to be neighbors. Then the distribution of willingnesses to pay of the groups is given by:

Probability	1/4	1/2	1/4
Group type	both v_1	one v_1, one v_2	both v_2
WTP classical	$2x$	$a + x$	$2a$
WTP jazz	$2a$	$a + x$	$2x$

The most profitable prices are still $(p_c, p_j) = (a + x, a + x)$.

However, it is rather odd to assume that the pairs will be assembled in any way that is not rational for the buyers, conditional on the prices. Certainly if the prices are $(p_c, p_j) = (a + x, a + x)$, it is best for consumers to assemble according to shared tastes. Suppose that v_1 consumers pair up with other v_1 consumers, and the same for v_2. Then at prices $(p_c, p_j) = (a + x, a + x)$, the pair of type-$v_1$ consumers will not buy the classical CD but will buy the jazz CD. Instead of getting zero surplus from their purchases, as the mixed groups do, they get a positive surplus: $2a - p_j = a - x > 0$.

In fact, whatever prices are offered by the proprietors, the consumers will pair up optimally, which means in this simple example that they always pair up with someone who shares their taste vector, v_1 or v_2. (In a more general model, where all the consumers can have different tastes, the optimal way of forming groups will depend on the prices (Scotchmer 2005).) Further, if they always pair up optimally conditional on the prices, the proprietors end up with exactly as much profit as if they sold to individual consumers. The proprietors will sell at higher prices, but only high enough to account for the fact that they are selling to groups of consumers rather than to individuals.

To see this neutrality result in the example, let the prices (p_c, p_j) be arbitrary, and consider four agents, two of each type. The total consumers' surplus in two mixed groups is smaller than the total consumers' surplus available if the same consumers split into two homogeneous groups, one of which has two v_1 consumers and the other of which has two v_2 consumers.

Consider the classical CD. (The argument for jazz is the same.) If $p_c < 2x$, then all the consumers will buy the CD regardless of how they are grouped. If $2x < p_c < a + x < 2a$, then the mixed groups will buy the CD, with total consumers' surplus $2(a + x) - 2p_c$. The v_2 groups will buy the CD but not the v_1 groups. The total consumers' surplus with homogeneous groups is $2a - p_c$, which is larger than with mixed groups. If $a + x < p_c < 2a$, then the mixed groups do not purchase the CD and receive no consumers' surplus from classical CDs. However, the homogeneous v_2 groups will buy it and receive positive consumers' surplus $2a - p_c$. This shows that grouping the consumers according to taste cannot reduce the consumers' surplus, and may well increase it. With homogeneous groups, the proprietors make the same profit as by selling to individuals.

References and Further Reading

Allison, J. R., and M. A. Lemley. 1998. "Empirical Evidence on the Validity of Litigated Patents." *AIPLA Quarterly Journal* 26:185–275.

American Intellectual Property Law Association. 1999. *Report of Economic Survey*. Washington, DC: American Intellectual Property Law Association.

Bakos, Y., and E. Brynjolfsson. 1999. "Bundling Information Goods: Prices, Profits and Efficiency." *Management Science* 45:1613–1630.

Bakos, Y., E. Brynjolfsson, and D. Lichtman. 1999. "Shared Information Goods." *Journal of Law and Economics* 42:117–155.

Barton, J. H. 2000. "Reforming the Patent System." *Science* 287:1933–1934.

Besen, S., and S. Kirby. 1989. "Private Copying, Appropriability and Optimal Copyright Royalties." *Journal of Law and Economics* 32:255–275.

Blair, R. D., and T. F. Cotter. 1998. "An Economic Analysis of Damages Rules in Intellectual Property Law." *William and Mary Law Review* 39:1585–1694.

Calabresi, G., and A. D. Melamed. 1972. "Property Rules, Liability Rules, and Inalienability: One View of the Cathedral." *Harvard Law Review* 85:1089–1126.

Castle Rock Entertainment v. Carol Publishing Group. 150 F.3d 132 (2nd Cir. 1998).

Computer Science and Telecommunications Board, Committee on Intellectual Property Rights and the Emerging Information Infrastructure. 2000. *The Digital*

Dilemma: Intellectual Property in the Information Age. Washington, DC: National Academy Press.

Conley, D. 1987. "Economic Approach to Patent Damages." *AIPLA (American Intellectual Property Law Association) Quarterly Journal* 15:354–380.

Eisenberg, R. 1989. "Patents and the Progress of Science: Exclusive Rights and Experimental Use." *University of Chicago Law Review* 56:1017–1055.

Eolas Technologies v. Microsoft Corp. N.D. Ill., No. 99 C 626, 8/11/03.

Gilbert, R., and M. L. Katz. 2001. "When Good Value Chains Go Bad: The Economics of Indirect Liability for Copyright Infringement." *Hastings Law Journal* 52:961–982.

Goldstein, P. 1994. *Copyright's Highway: The Law and Lore of Copyright from Gutenberg to the Celestial Jukebox.* New York: Hill and Wang.

Graham, S., B. H. Hall, D. Harhoff, and D. Mowery. 2003. "Patent Quality Control: A Comparison of U. S. Patent Re-examinations and European Patent Oppositions." In W. Cohen and S. A. Merrill, eds., *Patents in the Knowledge-Based Economy*, 74–119. Washington, DC: National Academies Press.

Hall, B. H., and R.-M. Ziedonis. 2001. "The Patent Paradox Revisited: An Empirical Study of Patenting in the U.S. Semiconductor Industry, 1979–1995." *RAND Journal of Economics* 32:101–128.

Harhoff, D., and M. Reitzig. "Determinants of Opposition Against EPO Patent Grants—The Case of Biotechnology and Pharmaceuticals." Discussion Paper 3645. London: Center for Economic Policy Research.

Harmon, R. L. [1991] 1998. *Patents and the Federal Circuit.* Rev. ed. Washington, DC: Bureau of National Affairs.

Heath, C., J. Henkel, and M. Reitzig. 2002. "Who Really Profits from Patent Infringements? Innovation Incentives and Disincentives from Patent Indemnification Rules." Working Paper 2002-18. Copenhagen: Center for Law, Economics and Financial Institutions, Copenhagen Business School.

Hoerner, R. J. 1995. "Innovation Markets: New Wine in Old Bottles?" *Antitrust Law Journal* 64:49–73.

Hovenkamp, H., M. Janis, and M. A. Lemley. 2003. "Anticompetitive Settlement of Intellectual Property Disputes." *Minnesota Law Review* 87:1719–1766.

Italie, H. 2002, September 20. "Harry Potter Prevails in Court." New York: CBS News. Available at www.cbsnews.com/stories/2002/09/19/print/main522563.shtml.

"Jury Awards $520.6 Million against Microsoft for Infringement of Web Browser Patent." 2003. *Patent, Trademark and Copyright Journal* 66:1634–1635. Available at ipcenter.bna.com/pic2/ip.nsf/id/BNAP-5QFQ8J?OpenDocument&PrintVersion=Yes.

Kaplow, L., and S. Shavell. 1996. "Property Rules versus Liability Rules: An Economic Analysis." *Harvard Law Review* 109:715–789.

Kirkpatrick, D. D. 2001, April 1. "Harry Potter and the Court Battle over Creativity." *New York Times* (section: National Desk).

Lanjouw, J. O., and J. Lerner. 2001. "Tilting the Table? The Predatory Use of Preliminary Injunctions." *Journal of Law and Economics* 44:573–603.

Lanjouw, J. O., and M. Schankerman. 2001. "Characteristics of Patent Litigation: A Window on Competition." *RAND Journal of Economics* 32:129–151.

Lanjouw, J. O., and M. Schankerman. 2004. "Protecting Intellectual Property Rights: Are Small Firms Handicapped?" Forthcoming in *Journal of Law and Economics* 47.

Lerner, J. 1994. "The Importance of Patent Scope: An Empirical Analysis." *RAND Journal of Economics* 25:319–333.

Lerner, J. 1995. "Patenting in the Shadow of Competitors." *Journal of Law and Economics* 38:463–496.

Litman, J. 2001. *Digital Copyright*. New York: Prometheus Books.

Lunney, G. S., Jr. 2004. "Patent Law, the Federal Circuit and the Supreme Court: A Quiet Revolution." Forthcoming in *Supreme Court Economic Review*.

Menell, P. 2002. "Envisioning Copyright Law's Digital Future." *New York Law Review* 46:63–199.

Merges, R. P. 1996. "Contracting into Liability Rules: Intellectual Property Rights and Collective Rights Organizations." *UCLA Law Review* 84:1293–1393.

Merges, R. P. 1999. "As Many as Six Impossible Patents Before Breakfast: Property Rights for Business Concepts and Patent System Reform." *Berkeley High Technology Law Journal* 14:588–615.

Office of the President, University of California. 2003. "Questions and Answers about UC/Eolas patent infringement suit against Microsoft." Available at www.ucop.edu/news/archives/2003/aug11art1qanda.htm.

Priest, G., and B. Klein. 1994. "The Selection of Disputes for Litigation." *Journal of Legal Studies* 13:1–55.

Rohde, L. 2003, November 12. "Microsoft Gets W3C Allies in Eolas suit that prompted IE changes." *PCWorld* using IDG News Service. Available at www.pcworld.com/news/article/0,aid,113393,00.asp.

Samuelson, P. 2002. "Toward a 'New Deal' for Copyright for an Information Age." *Michigan Law Review* 100:1483–1505.

Samuelson, P., and S. Scotchmer 2002. "The Law and Economics of Reverse Engineering." *Yale Law Journal* 111:1575–1663.

Schankerman, M., and S. Scotchmer. 2001. "Damages and Injunctions in Protecting Intellectual Property." *RAND Journal of Economics* 32:199–220.

Scotchmer, S. 2005. "Consumption Externalities, Rental Markets and Purchase Clubs." *Economic Theory* 25:235–253.

Scotchmer, S., and Y. Park. 2004. "Technical Protection Measures and the Pricing of Digital Content." Mimeograph. Berkeley, CA: Department of Economics, UC Berkeley.

Shapiro, C. 2003. "Antitrust Limits to Patent Settlements." *RAND Journal of Economics* 34:391–411.

Somaya, D. 2003. "Strategic Decisions not to Settle Patent Litigation." *Strategic Management Journal* 24:17–38.

Spier, K. 1992. "The Dynamics of Pretrial Negotiation." *Review of Economic Studies* 59:93–108.

Stevenson, R. 2004, March 5. "Patent Central to Microsoft Case Invalidated." London: Reuters News Service. Available at www.reuters.com/newsArticle. jhtml?type=internetNews&storyID=4509756&section=news.

Trajtenberg, M. 1990. "A Penny for Your Quotes: Patent Citations and the Value of Innovation." *RAND Journal of Economics* 21:172–187.

United States Code Annotated, Title 35: Patents. 1984; updated 1998. St. Paul, MN: West.

Varian, H. 2000. "Buying, Renting, Sharing Information Goods." Mimeograph. Berkeley, CA: School of Information and Management Systems, UC Berkeley.

8 Innovation Today: A Private-Public Partnership

with Stephen M. Maurer

The chief protagonist in the mythology of invention is a creative genius toiling alone in his garage, scorned by his peers for his outlandish ideas and waste of money but ultimately victorious.

As noted in chapter 1, the mythology is outdated. There are, of course, some famous discoveries by single-minded geniuses—John Harrison with his nautical clocks; Tycho Brahe making celestial observations year after year on his island in the Øresund between Sweden and Denmark; the Wright brothers with their homemade wind tunnel in North Carolina; Charles Babbage with his Analytical Engine; deForest and Marconi competing on opposite sides of the Atlantic for the foundational technologies of broadcast radio. Some of these were truly independent pioneers, working on ideas that they alone conceived, but others were working in response to external incentives funded by someone else. John Harrison was trying to win a substantial prize, and Tycho Brahe was in the employ of the Danish king. Even the famous story of Archimedes is misleading in this regard. When he sat up in the bath and shrieked "Eureka!" he had simply found what he was being paid to look for.

Research today is largely done in organized teams looking for solutions to well-understood problems. Although much of it is done by industry, it would be a mistake to say that the private sector is the only, or even the main, engine of technological growth. The recent history of innovation is awash in public funds. The packet-switching technology of the Internet was funded by the U.S. Department of Defense. The protocols of the worldwide web were conceptualized and developed by researchers who were on the payroll at CERN, the Swiss physics laboratory that is jointly funded and operated by European states (Berners-Lee 2000). The technology for inserting foreign genetic material into bacteria, which underlies all of biotechnology, was developed jointly by researchers at the University of California, San Francisco, and Stanford University. The first bioengineered human proteins, human insulin and human growth hormone, grew out of technologies discovered by researchers at UC Berkeley, and UC San Francisco. The digital computer was developed mainly at the University of Pennsylvania. The laser was invented at Columbia University. How can we possibly believe that the private sector is the main driver of technological growth?

R&D is a cooperative undertaking of industry, universities, and public agencies. Sections 8.1 through 8.3 document the spending patterns and institutions that support public R&D, and how they have changed. We then turn to the question of why or whether these institutions make sense.

Chapter 2 discussed several ways that R&D could be funded, emphasizing that intellectual property is only one incentive mechanism among many. The discussion was rather binary—the incentive system could either rely on the private sector investing in response to intellectual property incentives, or it could rely on some form of public sponsorship funded out of general revenue. In this chapter we will see that the options are much broader than that, both in theory and in practice. In section 8.4 we consider the evolving system by which private sponsors match public funds in return for intellectual property rights. Much of public science is performed with additional funding from private firms, and the private firms often receive intellectual property rights in return. Does that make sense? What is the rationale?

One of the things emphasized in chapter 2 was that prizes and other rewards for innovating must be linked to the value of the innovation; otherwise the system would be exploited and ultimately collapse. Despite this logic, science in universities is largely funded by grants given in advance to cover costs, rather than being given as rewards ex post. In section 8.5 we ask why such a system could possibly work.

Section 8.6 investigates whether public science has an advantage over private science in encouraging scientists to share their research outputs.

8.1   The Tangled Web of Funding Relationships

Figures 8.1 and 8.2 give an aggregate view of the R&D landscape in the United States in the year 2000. The two pie charts show R&D performance and R&D funding, respectively. The government pays for much more research than it actually performs; conversely, firms and

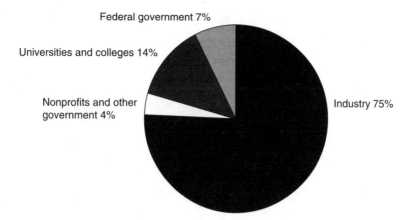

Figure 8.1
U.S. R&D performance sectors, 2000. R&D performed by FFRDCs is included
where the FFRDC is located, either industry or universities
Source: National Science Board, 2002, appendix table 4-3.

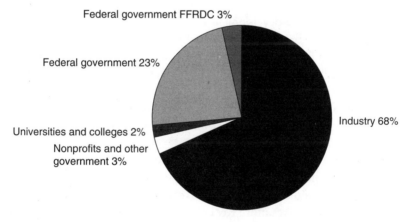

Figure 8.2
U.S. R&D funding sources, 2000
Source: National Science Board, 2002, appendix table 4-5.

universities perform much of their research under federal grants and contracts.

The percentage of total R&D paid for by the federal government was about two-thirds after World War II and has fallen steadily to the present, now being less than one-third. However, it is still much larger than the percentage in the 1930s, which was between 12 and 20 percent (Mowery and Rosenberg 1998, 27).

Figure 8.1 shows that R&D performed by industry now comprises a hefty three-fourths of the total. Nevertheless, the R&D performed by universities and the federal government is also substantial. Something not shown in the figures is that most industrial R&D is applied, while most R&D in universities is basic research. Even though universities only perform 14 percent of R&D, they perform about half of total basic research. Since applied research and development depend heavily on basic underlying knowledge, these aggregate spending statistics may understate the importance of universities.

Figure 8.2 shows that the federal government funds 26 percent of total R&D, including grants to universities, firms, and federally funded research and development centers (FFRDCs), which are run by universities and firms but not owned by them.[1] The most noteworthy thing to be seen by comparing figures 8.1 and 8.2 is that only about a quarter of federally funded research takes place intramurally in government laboratories. Even though the federal government funds 26 percent of total R&D, its own employees perform only 7 percent of total R&D. The difference accounts for why industry and universities perform much more R&D than they fund.

For most of the twentieth century, the federal government funded R&D more heavily in industry than in universities, as shown in figure 8.3. Although the gap has narrowed dramatically in recent years, industry still receives more R&D funds from the federal government than universities and colleges receive. But since industry also invests more on its own, the federal R&D dollars are less central to industry budgets. Industry only receives about 10 percent of its R&D budget from the federal government (down from much higher percentages earlier in the twentieth century), while universities and colleges receive about 60 percent. Still, 10 percent of industry's R&D budget is a lot of funding from the

---

1.   Federal government and state governments also subsidize by educating scientists and other workers. Except for graduate student research funds, this huge subsidy is not included in the federal R&D figures.

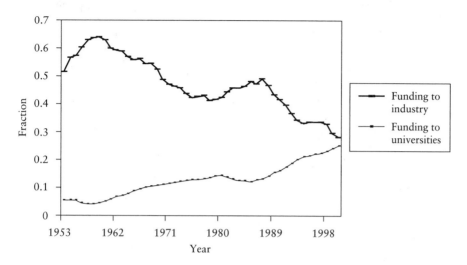

Figure 8.3
Federal R&D funding to industry and universities
Source: National Science Board, 2002, appendix table 4-5.

federal government, and it comprises a huge percentage of funding in some industries, such as aerospace.

As reported by the National Science Foundation (2004), federal R&D is heavily concentrated on national defense (50%), health (23%), space technology and aeronautics (10%), and general science and basic research (6%).[2] Each subject tends to have its own separate bureaucracy as shown in table 8.1. The Department of Defense (DOD) and the National Aeronautics and Space Administration (NASA) dominate space technology and aeronautical research, and the country's $5.5 billion general science budget is divided between the National Science Foundation (NSF, 58%) and Department of Energy (DOE, 42%).[3] The National Institutes of Health (NIH) administer 94 percent of the federal government's health care R&D budget. Other agencies also have

---

2.   Smaller, but still substantial, programs are devoted to pollution control (2%), conservation, resource mapping, oceanography, and weather (2%), agriculture (2%), and energy (1%).
3.   The largest items on NSF's budget are mathematics and physical sciences (28%), earth sciences (18%), biology (15%), engineering (14%), and computer science (14%). The biggest items on DOE's budget are nuclear and high-energy physics (37%), fusion and energy research (36%), advanced scientific computing (5%), human genome research (4%), and other types of biological and environmental research (15%).

Table 8.1
2001 R&D budgets of U.S. agencies, and how they were spent

Total R&D Budget (millions)		Federal intramural (%)	Industrial firms (%)	Total FFRDC (%)	Universities and colleges (%)	Other nonprofit (%)	State/local government (%)	Foreign (%)
$83,609		23.67	40.17	8.88	21.43	5.01	0.49	0.34
$36,462	Defense	23.66	69.43	2.06	4.21	0.42	0.03	0.18
$19,463	HHS	19.90	5.92	1.32	56.47	15.40	0.68	0.31
$9,966	NASA	25.16	48.67	13.19	7.90	3.86	0.11	1.11
$7,656	Energy	11.38	15.32	63.05	9.43	0.78	0.04	0.01
$3,431	NSF	1.78	3.91	6.73	81.26	5.63	0.20	0.50
$1,892	Agriculture	72.09	0.58	0.00	26.48	0.48	0.16	0.21
$1,163	Commerce	69.82	16.08	0.00	10.92	2.06	1.03	0.00
$882	Interior	88.06	3.06	0.00	7.74	0.16	0.81	0.32
$672	DOT	32.77	36.96	0.68	6.92	2.04	20.52	0.11
$620	EPA	18.60	47.62	0.00	22.62	9.38	1.64	0.30
$1,401	Others	51.25	7.07	2.50	14.78	20.41	2.50	1.57

Source: National Science Board, 2002, appendix table 4-25.
Notes: First column: agency spending on R&D, totaling $83,609; first row of numbers: how the federal R&D budget is spent, according to column headings, totaling 100%; other rows: How the agency's R&D budget is spent, according to column headings, totaling 100%.

mission-specific labs, notably the National Oceanographic and Atmospheric Administration (NOAA) and National Institute of Standards and Technology, both in the Department of Commerce.

In the Departments of Agriculture, Commerce, and Interior, research is mostly done intramurally. However, these are not the agencies with the really large research budgets. In the agencies with large research budgets, the R&D dollars are primarily given out as contracts or grants.

The largest flows from the federal government to the private sector are from the DOD and NASA. The largest flows from the federal government to universities are from NSF and Health and Human Services (HHS), which includes NIH. In the past, DOD and NASA have also given large amounts of funding to universities, sometimes up to 50 percent of universities' R&D funding. In the current era, their contribution is smaller in both dollars and percentage terms.

The NSF and NIH fund research in a very different manner than DOD and NASA. Whereas the DOD and NASA target their contracts to specific objectives, the NSF and NIH mostly fund research ideas that originate with the grantees themselves. The NSF gives away about 99 percent of its research budget in grants, more than 80 percent to universities. The NIH disperses an even larger budget than the NSF, giving away about four-fifths in grants and using the remainder to support its own in-house laboratories. Its mission is focused on biomedical research. NSF funds a much broader group of researchers, including engineers, physicists, geologists, economists, legal scholars, psychologists, and political scientists.

In the 1990s, funding priorities at the NSF and NIH moved away from the physical sciences to the life sciences, and to some extent to engineering (Board on Science Technology and Economic Policy, 2001). More than half of university R&D (57%) is in the life sciences and medicine. The rest is mostly in engineering (16%), physics (4%), chemistry (3%), computer science (3%), and mathematics (1%).

Finally, 8.8 percent of U.S. R&D is conducted by the 700 FFRDCs, usually called national laboratories. These laboratories are owned by the federal government and most of their funding comes from the DOE, but they are managed under contract by universities and large corporations. They are research organizations that apply for funding much like universities and work under contracts, mostly from the DOE. Most of the DOE's research budget goes to support them.

Most national labs were created during and after World War II to address special national needs such as learning about nuclear weapons and electronics.[4] There have been important civilian spin-offs, such as nuclear energy and radar, and the laboratories now have other research agendas as well, such as advanced materials, batteries and fuel cells, insulation, and energy conservation. Some famous institutions that survive from the World War II era and shortly thereafter are the Lawrence Berkeley National Laboratory, Lawrence Livermore National Laboratory, and Los Alamos National Laboratory, which have historically been administered by the University of California. These labs still receive most of their funding from DOE but also get paid by industry for providing access to large, unique facilities such as wind tunnels and the Advanced Light Source at Berkeley. Scientists in many of these institutions have close working relationships with the scientists in the universities that manage them as well as with scientists in industry, and their success is evident, inter alia, in the Nobel Prizes they have won, especially in particle physics. At Lawrence Berkeley Laboratory, Nobel Prize winners include Glenn Seaborg, Edwin McMillan, Luis Alvarez, and Owen Chamberlain, and at Stanford Linear Accelerator Center, Burton Richter.

Thus, industrial laboratories, university laboratories, and the national laboratories are all infused with both public and private money. The boundaries between public and profit-motivated science are correspondingly fuzzy.

When we spoke of public sponsorship in chapter 2, we had in mind a free-access model in which publicly sponsored innovations were made available for unrestricted use. For such a model, it does not matter who performs the research, as long as neither the funding agency nor its contractee asserts intellectual property rights. However, for the most part, that is not the prevailing model, as we will see.

Oddly, if public-domain science has been eroded, it is probably due more to the assertion of intellectual property rights by universities and national labs than to the tight relationships between federal sponsors and industry. The 1980 Bayh-Dole and Stevenson-Wydler acts authorized the patenting of federally sponsored innovations in universities and national labs, and patenting in those institutions has increased several fold (Maurer 2002). The acts grew out of a fear that potential users of university inventions were either unaware of what was available, or were dissuaded from commercializing the technologies by a fear of competi-

---

4.   For an interesting interpretive history see Mowery and Rosenberg 1998. See also Jaffe and Lerner 2001.

tion. The rationale thus rests on the paradoxical idea that the way to put knowledge into use is to put restrictions on using it. We will say more about this.

8.2   University Innovation

In principle, university scientists are primarily motivated by the pursuit of knowledge for its own sake. However, they must also be concerned with publication and recognition by other scientists to achieve tenure and further advancement. The virtue of this system is that it encourages openness in science. The main way to achieve reputation and acclaim is to publish results. Although it may be possible to publish results without making the underlying data and research useful to rivals, the necessity of publishing may still have advantages over a commercial model where there are financial rewards to secrecy.

However, the profit motive has infiltrated the university. Sixty percent of university research is funded by the federal government.[5] In 1980, the Bayh-Dole Act authorized universities and faculty to patent federally funded research outputs.[6] The act has induced universities to open licensing offices and seek licensees. By the end of the twentieth century, the licensing offices had more than tripled the rate at which universities patented discoveries. Oddly, however, this had little effect on overall financing. For example, the University of California earned only $13.0 million from patent licenses in 1999, net of costs, which is less than 1 percent of the $1.5 billion that UC researchers received from the federal government (University of California, Technology Transfer Office, 2000).

The average university licensing office receives sixty-nine invention disclosures per year and applies for patents on about half of them. But universities apply for four times as many patents per R&D dollar as private industry (Abramson et al. 1997). On average, licensing offices negotiate twenty-three new licenses or options agreements with private

5.   Unless otherwise noted, the data cited in this chapter came from National Science Board 2002.

6.   So far, American universities have resisted proposals to make patents a factor in tenure or advancement. However, a Japanese committee of politicians and experts has called on funding agencies and ministries to give patents and intellectual property equal importance with publications when evaluating researchers ("Japanese Push," 2003).

partners each year. Licensing offices earned an average of $6.6 million in the year 2000 (Association of University Technology Managers, 2002). This average is probably misleading because it includes a handful of highly successful offices like Stanford and Berkeley. More typical are university licensing offices that do not yet cover their own costs. Until they do, university administrators may well impose pressure to pay more attention to profit than to dissemination of research.

Although most university licensing offices do not explicitly seek to maximize profits, they frequently measure success by close proxies, such as the number of patents issued or licenses executed (Maurer 2002, 24). They also have a penchant for giving exclusive licenses (Mowery et al. 2001). An exclusive license insulates the licensee from competition, and the resulting monopoly profit can be shared with the university through the fees. Nonexclusive licenses are usually reserved for situations where the university perceives it has no other choice—for example, where industrial users threaten to challenge or design around the university's patents (Colyvas et al. 2002). According to Jensen and Thursby (2001), 74 percent of university licensing offices "almost always" grant sponsors the right to negotiate exclusive licenses.[7]

Government agencies rarely try to regulate their grantees' licensing practices but have made an exception for research tools. Grantees of the NIH have repeatedly complained of lengthy licensing negotiations, complicated user restrictions, and high royalty rates. Licensing fees are often paid by one grantee to another. Such fees are at best transfers among NIH grantees, and at worst a drain on their grantees' research funds, since the fees may leak out of laboratory budgets to the general accounts of the grantees' licensing offices. The National Institutes of Health (1999) issued an explicit warning against indiscriminate patenting, and pointed out that exclusive licenses are "not the only, nor in some cases the most appropriate, means of implementing" the dissemination of information between universities.

---

7.   The distinction between exclusive and nonexclusive licensing is a bit artificial, since the profit advantage of exclusive licensing can often be achieved with nonexclusive licenses and high royalties. High royalties can sustain high prices even when there are many licensees. For research tools, the same conclusion holds, but the mechanism is slightly different. Royalties would be pass-through royalties from the product developed with the tool. Nonexclusive licenses for competing uses would lead to patent races instead of competition in a market, but entry into the patent race would be restricted because the pass-through royalties reduce the profitability of winning. See chapter 5.

Universities increasingly rely on funds from corporations. Bekelman, Li, and Gross (2003, 456) report on studies that suggest "23% to 28% of academic investigators in biomedical research receive research funding from industry . . . 43% receive research-related gifts. . . . And approximately one third . . . have personal financial ties with industry sponsors." Older studies showed that about 37 percent of investigators in the National Academy of Sciences had dual affiliations with universities and firms, and a 1992 analysis of articles in medical journals found that the lead authors of one-third of them had relevant financial interests in their work, such as patents, equity, or positions on boards of directors. Moreover, roughly one-half of all engineering and biotechnology faculty have substantial consulting practices or serve on company advisory boards (Abramson et al. 1997). In the 1980s, a whopping 46 percent of biotechnology firms supported university research (Blumenthal et al. 1986). Virtually all intellectual property that arises from consulting contracts is assigned to the private sponsor.

The Bayh-Dole Act led to the creation of research units within universities designed to attract and accept commercial funds, often by promising to transfer intellectual property rights on resulting discoveries especially in new technologies like biotechnology, microelectronics, manufacturing, materials science, and artificial intelligence.[8] Universities took advantage of the biotechnology boom by signing massive research contracts, such as the $70 million deal between Hoechst and Harvard in 1984. In most of these deals, industry received generous promises of intellectual property that was at least partly funded by federal sponsors. Observers have blamed these trends for making academic biology more secretive and patent conscious.

Although norms vary from discipline to discipline, private firms usually impose more restrictions on how the research outputs are used than government agencies do. Openness in science is largely contrary to their objectives. The objective of industry is generally to leverage the expertise of university scientists for profit, tying funds to prespecified problems. In return for funding, private sponsors typically receive exclusive licenses on a fixed fraction of the resulting patents, together with access to research results, seminars, faculty, and student researchers. This is especially true in biology.

---

8.   The total number of organized research units (ORUs) grew 30 percent between 1980 and 1985. By 1990, most academic researchers worked for ORUs. One-fourth of them were supported by soft money. See Geiger 1993, chap. 10.

At a minimum, private sponsors usually receive the right to delay or censor publications until intellectual property rights are secure. They may also restrict the grantee's ability to communicate with colleagues and prevent him or her from consulting with other companies (Thursby and Thursby 2002). Some sponsors such as tobacco companies may pressure scientists to slant or suppress opinions that conflict with sponsors' economic interests. The worry is that these effects may influence the results reported and may compromise science. Bekelman, Li, and Gross (2003) summarize evidence that sponsored studies are likely to have conclusions in line with their sponsors' interests.

Private funds and public funds are often blended in the same university laboratory, so that intellectual property transferred to the private firm is partly paid for with public funds. This is especially controversial when the public money is "ours," and the private sponsor is foreign. In 1992, the Swiss pharmaceutical maker Sandoz offered $300 million to the Scripps Research Institute in San Diego in return for 100 percent of the resulting intellectual property rights. Scripps is a private, nonprofit research organization largely funded by NIH. Congress and NIH eventually forced them to scale back both the level of funding and the percentage of intellectual property rights, a policy that was then institutionalized in nonbinding guidelines of the NIH.[9] However, it is not clear that this is a solution. As we will see in chapter 9, the distribution of patent values is highly skewed. If the private sponsor can cherry-pick the most valuable patents, then 50 percent of the patent rights may be effectively the same as all of them.

Perhaps the most dramatic means of technology transfer from universities to the private sector is the formation of start-up companies. Famous examples include the companies that founded the biotechnology revolution such as Genentech and Chiron, begun by faculty members of the University of California. In return for assigning intellectual property rights to the start-ups, licensing offices receive equity. This is in contrast to the deals they typically make with more established firms, which pay cash royalties. Critics complain that the university gets very little in return for signing over the patents. The start-up typically has no other assets, and no funds to pump back into university labs. Further, a large financial stake in a new venture can shift the proprietor's loyalty even if

---

9.   See National Institutes of Health, 1994. This document urges institutions to limit the fraction of intellectual property rights that a sponsor can receive.

she retains a faculty position, thereby undermining open science.[10] Licensing offices take equity stakes in about half of start-ups but only earn about 15 percent of their income by cashing in equity (Association of University Technology Managers, 2002).

Compared to the straightforward links between the federal government and universities, the links between industry and universities are complex and create obscure incentives. Even though industry only contributes 7 percent of university R&D funding,[11] those funds may have a big impact on the conduct of science.

Based on how university-industry relations have developed in recent decades, we might conclude that profiting from public science is a new idea. This is not so. The prospect of turning academic science to profit has been with us for nearly a century, beginning with the Research Corporation in 1914, discussed in chapter 1, which still exists and has been extremely aggressive in its exploitation of patents. But, although research budgets have been replenished throughout the past century with patent rights on some of their discoveries, the tight relationships between industrial sponsors and university laboratories, where industrial sponsors sit alongside faculty members and deans on advisory boards, and where intellectual property rights are assigned before the research agenda is set, is relatively new.

The links between universities and industry leave many open questions about both the direction of research and its dissemination. Currently and in the past, almost 70 percent of research in universities has been categorized by the NSF as basic, while this is more or less reversed in industry. Does the lure of profit shift the university's mission away from basic research? Does industry's desire to leverage faculty expertise and exploit intellectual property rights interfere with communication

---

10. This has become enough of a concern that *Nature* was persuaded to publish a letter from a professor at a respected research university, contrasting the mutually beneficial relationships between universities and established firms with the one-sided relationships between universities and faculty start-ups. With respect to the latter, the correspondent claims that "the driving principle is not to benefit university research, but to benefit the faculty member financially." He refers to biased publications, undeclared conflicts of interest, unregistered transfers of university intellectual property, and other unsavory practices. He says that the only "resolution" is "for universities to ban their academic staff from simultaneously holding equity in a company" (Koehn 2001).

11. This fraction has been rising from a low of less than 3 percent in the 1960s, when public funding was at its peak.

within and between universities? Does industrial support crowd out public support, to the detriment of open science? Is there any justification for the hybrid system in which public support is mixed with industrial support, and industry then asserts intellectual property rights on the resulting innovations? We turn to these questions after discussing the national laboratories.

8.3   Government Innovation

The nature and extent of federal funding have changed substantially over the past century. Before World War II, R&D funding by the federal government was a small percentage of total R&D, and what existed was mostly intramural. During and after the war, the federal government became a primary source of R&D funds, and there was a transition toward a grant process rather than intramural funding. At the same time, many of the national labs were established.

Innovations that originate with government funding are made available to users under two sets of rules, which operate rather differently. We will call the two sets of rules the *commercialization model* and the *free-access model*. The commercialization model is used extensively in university labs and in the FFRDCs (national labs), under various legislative authorities we have already mentioned. The free-access model mostly applies to government intramural research and data collection.

In the commercial model, innovations are transferred from federally funded research labs to commercial firms in two ways: by licensing intellectual property, as authorized by the 1980 Stevenson-Wydler Act, and by establishing Cooperative Research and Development Agreements (CRADAs) with private firms, as authorized by the 1986 Technology Transfer Act. Congress has also passed legislation requiring each national laboratory to establish an Office of Research and Technology Applications for promoting technology transfer. These are analogous to the Technology Licensing Offices in universities. In addition, Congress passed subsidies for "precompetitive technologies" and small businesses that use laboratory technologies.[12]

---

12.   The American Technology Preeminence Act (1991) provides for subsidies for "precompetitive" technologies, and the Small Business Technology Transfer programs subsidize cooperative R&D between small firms and universities, labs, and nonprofit organizations.

Subsequent to this legislation, laboratories have expanded licensing. By the early 1990s, federal laboratories went from licensing about 4 percent of their patents to the private sector to 50 percent. Despite this, royalties contribute less than 1 percent to most laboratories' budgets, although they can be a powerful incentive for individual researchers (Rood 2000). We caution that the expansion in licensing should not necessarily be interpreted as "success." Users might have taken up these technologies in any case.

The main way that technologies are transferred from the national labs to industry are through CRADAs, which are a type of research joint venture. In a typical CRADA, the industrial partner agrees to fund a joint R&D program in return for intellectual property rights. Both parties contribute expertise, staff, and equipment. By the mid-1990s, national laboratories were signing about 1,000 CRADAs every year.

National labs also transfer technology through spin-off companies. Several dozen are formed each year. Sandia National Laboratory even offers entrepreneurial leave to researchers who want to start businesses without losing employee benefits. Similarly, NASA tries to encourage start-ups by operating business incubators that provide below-cost advice and services. Finally, some laboratories are associated with nonprofit venture capital funds. Examples include ARCH (University of Chicago/Argonne National Laboratories) and Technology Ventures (Lockheed Martin/Sandia).

Some observers claim that CRADAs and licensing have shifted programs away from basic research. By using exclusive licenses and high royalties, they may also inhibit the dissemination of research. Rood (2000) suggests on the basis of case studies that individual scientists in national labs are less interested in broad-based research, university collaborations, and academic publishing than they were during the 1980s. Instead, they have shifted their focus toward industry, patents, and promoting their CRADA partners' technologies.

The federal government also operates intramural labs such as those at the National Institute of Standards and Technology (NIST). In contrast to the national labs, they mostly distribute their innovative output under the free-access model, in which the government does not claim patents or copyrights, and distributes information at or below the marginal cost of reproduction rather than charging proprietary prices.

From an economic standpoint, the free-access model is what we meant in chapter 2 when we assumed that publicly sponsored research would be put in the public domain for unrestricted use. The federal government has various legal bases for this model, including Executive Order A-130, which requires that government data and other information be distributed at the cost of dissemination.

The free-access model has generated huge economic spin-offs and has tangibly served the objective of disseminating knowledge. During the 1990s, for example, private-sector entrepreneurs turned NOAA's public-domain weather data into a $500 million per year industry (Weiss 2003). Value-added products and services currently include the Weather Channel, weather-based financial instruments, and weather data tailored to the needs of aviation and other specialized users.

In some cases, government providers have taken on private partners to share the costs, blurring the line between the free-access model and the commercialization model. An interesting example involves NASA's SeaWIFS ocean surveillance satellite. Industrial partners agreed to contribute between 60 and 70 percent of the project's life-cycle cost. In return, they receive exclusive real-time data that is useful to commercial fisheries and others. NASA embargoes the information for fourteen days. After that, the data are released to academic scientists (Maurer 2002).

There is so far no clear articulation of how public sponsors should choose their research agendas. In practice, commerce tends to trump public sponsorship—if private firms are willing to undertake a research or development effort, public agencies generally step aside. An exception may be when the private sector enters areas of research that agencies are already funding, such as the genome project. In the late 1980s, NIH launched a project to sequence the human genome. The outputs of the project were to be disseminated to all users at the cost of making them available. But then, during the late 1990s, private investors launched massive parallel efforts to sequence various types of human, mouse, and rice DNA, hoping that the sequences would be patentable and useful for drug discoveries or other commercially valuable applications. Instead of withdrawing, the NIH stepped up its effort to get sequences in the public domain before they could be tied up with intellectual property. Sequences with unknown functions were eventually found by the PTO to be unpatentable, but many single-nucleotide polymorphisms (SNPs), which can be tied to biologically useful functions, are thought to be patentable. The legal status of these patents is still unresolved.

8.4   Mixed Private-Public Incentives

A message of the last two sections is that a single innovation may be funded in two ways: by the public sector out of general revenue, and through proprietary prices under an intellectual property regime. The blending of intellectual property incentives with other funding incentives extends even beyond universities and national labs. For example, DARPA has offered a $1 million Grand Challenge prize for winning a race among robotic ground vehicles (Defense Advanced Research Projects Agency, 2003). Entrants not only compete for this rather substantial prize, but will own any intellectual property that results.

The Bayh-Dole Act has defenders and detractors. The main problem is that intellectual property subverts the rationale for public sponsorship that was given in chapter 2, namely, that public sponsorship and open access can avoid exclusions on use. Taxpayers voice their objection somewhat differently: Why should they pay for the innovations twice?

But defenders argue that Bayh-Dole achieves its stated purpose, namely, "to promote utilization of inventions arising from federally supported research or development . . . without unduly encumbering future research and discovery" (§200). By reading only this statement of the objective, one might guess that the rest of the act prohibits patenting, since patenting gives the right to restrict use. To the contrary, the rest of the Bayh-Dole Act authorizes patenting; that is the purpose of the act.

Two possibilities have been suggested for how to reconcile the apparent contradiction between disseminating knowledge and patenting it. One is that patenting gives the university an incentive to find licensees, and the other is that patenting gives users an incentive to make collateral investments to commercialize inventions. Neither rationale is entirely convincing. It is odd to assume that potential users of new knowledge, or any other economic good, cannot be trusted to find the good when given free access. University research should be especially easy to find, since scientists usually publish it. In fact, the prospect of intellectual property works in the wrong direction here, since it often causes sponsors to bar publication until their intellectual property rights are secure.

As to the problem of collateral investments, we have discussed at length in chapter 5 that investors who build on earlier innovations are typically protected by separate patents. Suppose, for example, that the university's discovery is a research tool. The drugs or other inventions that the research tool enables should receive their own intellectual property, and if the patent system is correctly designed, that should be sufficient. It should not matter for patentability of the drug whether the underlying research tool was patented or put in the public domain. Of course the drug manufacturer or other follow-on innovator would prefer to have an exclusive license on the underlying innovation in order to avoid competition, but there is a whole body of antitrust law designed to keep that impulse in check.

Recall the case of monoclonal antibodies, mentioned in chapter 5. Amidst philosophical disputes about open science versus patents, and pragmatic concerns that the technology might not be patentable, the British funding agencies decided against patenting Milstein's and Kohler's discovery. The decision in favor of open science led to 3,600 derivative products patented in the USPTO by 2002, and more than 14,000 citations in scholarly journals (Oliver and Liebeskin 2003). Would patenting have encouraged broader or faster dissemination? Some British policymakers now see the failure to patent monoclonal antibody technology as a mistake, but this might be due to international transfers (see chapter 11). Many of the users were not British.

It remains possible that patents are badly designed, so that the collateral investments of commercial users are not protected for some types of follow-on products. If that is the case, the simplest solution would be to fix the thing that's broken, namely, the design of patent law, rather than amending an otherwise well-functioning system of open science.

Many public-private ventures involve "big science" projects that neither the private sector nor the public sector alone can "afford" to fund. Frequently cited examples include fusion-energy research and low-cost access to space. However, the cost argument is not very convincing, since large benefits should attract large investments, even if the funds have to be borrowed. There has been at least some private investment in low-cost access to space since the 1980s. In any case, no organization has greater ability to raise money than the federal government.

The argument we now give for the dual system of funding is not the rationale contained in the Bayh-Dole Act. It does not focus on the difficulty of raising money, or on ex post dissemination, but addresses other problems that afflict the sponsors. For big science, industry has the problem that, although an innovation may have some commercial value, the commercial value under existing intellectual property laws may not be sufficient to cover costs. This is especially true for investments that have unappropriable social benefits, or where intellectual property rights are so narrow that the benefits will be eroded by competitors. The public sector could simply fund such projects, but then it faces the problem of choosing the ones likely to be fruitful, or making sure the funds are used as intended, especially when the expertise resides mostly in the private sector.

In the next section we show how a grantor can overcome these problems for small, frequent innovations, simply by threatening to cut the innovator out of the grant process if he or she does not deliver enough innovations, or innovations of high enough value. But big science does not deliver small, frequent innovations, regardless of how meritorious it is. In fact, for many big science projects such as energy through nuclear fusion, the real quality indicator is the likelihood of success, and even the best project may fail. The public sponsor therefore needs some mechanism to screen for the right investments, and to make sure that the researchers invest as directed.

A system of matching funds can mitigate the dual problems of ensuring that industry covers its cost, and avoiding wrong investments by the public sector.

We will use the "ideas" model presented in chapter 2. An idea is a pair (v, c), which represents per-period social value and cost. The variable v represents the per-period consumers' surplus with competitive supply. If the social value lasts forever, then if the invention is in the public domain, the discounted social value is $(1/r)v$. If the invention is marketed by a proprietary firm, we will assume that the per-period profit is πv, where π is a fraction less than one. Then the proprietary profit available under a patent that lasts for discounted length T is $\pi v T$.

Each point in figure 8.4 represents an idea (v, c). We will suppose that industry is the repository of the best information about investments, so that the value and cost (v, c) are known to the industrial sponsor but

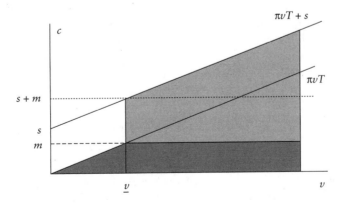

Figure 8.4
Hybrid funding: subsidies with industry matching and IP

not to a government sponsor. The objective of the government sponsor is to invest in those ideas for which $(1/r)v - c > 0$, but it cannot identify which ideas they are. The value of the intellectual property available to a private firm if it invests on its own is $\pi v T$, and without a government subsidy, it will invest if $\pi v T - c > 0$. In figure 8.4, the area under the lower diagonal line, labeled $\pi v T$, represents the ideas for which the private incentives in intellectual property would be sufficient.

Suppose, however, that there are high-value ideas that are more costly than the value of the intellectual property right (above the line $\pi v T$), but still worth doing $((1/r)v > c > \pi v T)$. The government might like to sponsor these.

Suppose that the government simply offers a subsidy s. Then all the ideas (v, c) under the higher diagonal line $\pi v T + s$ will be undertaken. The subsidy will increase research, but indiscriminately. In particular, there are likely to be many low-v ideas, toward the origin in figure 8.4, for which the subsidy of s is a waste of money. It is easy to imagine an endless series of subsidy claims for worthless innovations.

The government can solve this problem by insisting that the claimant make a matching commitment of funds in some amount, say m. Then to claim the subsidy, the sponsor and the claimant will contribute s and m respectively to the research budget, and invest in ideas suggested by the claimant. If the claimant suggests an idea (v, c) such that $c > s + m$, then he or she must provide the required supplement. In that case, the industrial partner pays $c - s$ rather than m. If the claimant suggests an idea (v, c) such that $c < s + m$, then the surplus goes to supporting graduate students or other research enterprises. For simplicity, we assume in figure 8.4 that the claimant receives intellectual property in amount $\pi v T$ on the subsidized innovations, although in practice, the sponsor may require a reduction in intellectual property rights for some broader social purpose. For example, the NIH imposes guidelines under which research tools must be made freely available to other academic researchers, with an intent to protect other grantees of the NIH.

We can now see what happens under this incentive mechanism.

First, ideas (v, c) that satisfy $c < m$ will not be subsidized. The industrial partner can get the intellectual property rights even if not subsidized, and it is more profitable to get these property rights for the lower cost c rather than m. Thus, the dark shaded area that is below both the diagonal line $\pi v T$ and below the horizontal line m represents ideas that industry will invest in without claiming any subsidy.

· It is only in ideas (v, c) that satisfy $\pi v T > m$ that the industrial partner would claim a subsidy. These ideas are all to the right of $\underline{v}$ in figure 8.4. This is what solves the "moral hazard" problem. Partners will not try to collect subsidies on worthless innovations because that would obligate them to commit funds in amount m.

We can further refine the ideas for which the industrial partner would be willing to accept a subsidy, namely, the higher shaded area in figure 8.4. These are the ideas to the right of $\underline{v}$, above the horizontal line m, and below the line $\pi v T + s$. Ideas such that $c > \pi v T + s$ will not be attractive to an industrial partner because the partner must pay the surfeit $c - s$.

We thus see that the partnership with mandatory matching funds will allow the public sector to subsidize ideas that would otherwise not elicit investment (those between the lines $\pi v T + s$ and $\pi v T$, to the right of $\underline{v}$), without causing the sponsor to hemorrhage money in subsidies to worthless innovations.

8.5   The Government Grant Process

As we have discussed, the U.S. federal government funds research in three ways: intramural research, contracts or other procurement, and grants. The three forms of funding have always been in use, but a development of the twentieth century was to institutionalize the grant process.

A rationale often invoked for intellectual property is that diligence on the part of researchers is self-enforcing. If they do not devote their energy to useful objectives, they will not be rewarded. Prizes have the same property. Grants, on the other hand, have the opposite property. Since the whole point is to reimburse costs before they are incurred, the grant is given up front. It is not a reward for a success, at least in a prima facie sense. Nevertheless, almost all of the NSF budget and about half of the NIH budget is given out as grants, with very little direct oversight.

The grant system is relatively new. As we have explored in chapter 1, in-house funding was the norm for most of history. European monarchs supported research by attaching gifted individuals, like the mathematicians Leonhard Euler and Joseph-Louis Lagrange, to their courts. Before that, the Library of Alexandria in Egypt supported in-house scholars such as Archimedes. Universities have long supported in-house research—for example, by Galileo and Isaac Newton.

When technological development became more expensive in the nineteenth century, a grant process evolved in which inventors would propose research or development on a sui generis basis, often retaining rights to it. Sui generis grants still exist, especially for big science, and are still funded by finding a friendly sponsor in government. However, the modern U.S. grant process is much more routine.[13] Congress authorizes a total budget for the NSF and NIH, and they then accept proposals generated by researchers for how to spend it. Curiosity-driven research is solicited, although the proposer must convince a panel of peers that something interesting or useful will emerge. If it does not, the grantee will probably not be successful in future grant competitions.

Chapter 2 emphasized that when ideas are scarce, targeted research is not the right concept; a sponsor cannot offer targeted prizes for discoveries it has not conceived of. The NSF and NIH grant systems operate very much like blue-sky prize systems, except that the funding is given in advance instead of afterward. The purpose is to cover the researcher's costs after certifying that the idea is worth implementing. But then two problems arise: researchers may misrepresent whether they can really implement the proposed idea, and they may simply abscond with the funds instead of investing as promised. Our purpose in this section is to show how the grant system avoids these problems. Even though the grant giver cannot monitor the grantee or withdraw payment in case of failure, and has limited ability to monitor the past record, the system can do a very good job of selecting the best researchers and making sure that they perform. However, as we will see, the system ends up being more costly than if these problems were not present.

The grant agency's main instrument of coercion is that it can cut off funding. This is what makes the grant system different from a system of employing researchers directly. It is much harder to fire an employee than to turn down a grant proposal.

The funding agency evaluates ideas (proposals), but will only fund an idea, even if good, if the researcher has delivered in the past. To stay in the system, researchers will have to be honest about their ideas for grants—or they will not succeed—and must actually incur the costs of implementing their ideas. The funding agency presumably wants to reward the researchers with the most fertile minds, by which we mean those with the most frequent or most valuable ideas. We show that this

13. The focus here is on United States institutions, since grant systems differ more internationally than other aspects of the incentive system, such as intellectual property laws. For example, French institutions rely more on public employees than on the grant-supported style of research described here.

can be accomplished even if the granting agency cannot actually observe the fertility of a researcher's mind or keep track of how many innovations the researcher has made.

Instead the system works by self-selection. Only researchers with less fertile minds have an incentive to propose ideas they cannot implement or to run off with the money, and they can only do it once.

We will assume for simplicity that all ideas have the same value and cost, (v, c), but that researchers receive ideas at different rates $\lambda \geq 0$ per year, where λ represents the fertility of the researcher's mind. The objective of the grant agency is to reward high-λ researchers.

When the researcher thinks of an idea, she can file a grant proposal with the sponsor, and the sponsor will decide whether to fund her. For a researcher with creativity λ, the expected present discounted value of investing in all the ideas conceived in a given period at date t is the following, when r is the discount rate and the size of the grant per idea is ρ:

$$\frac{\lambda}{(1+r)^t}(\rho - c)$$

Suppose now that the researcher has received a grant of size ρ. She must decide whether to perform the research or go to the beach. The researcher's net gain if she fails to perform is the saved cost c. The researcher's net loss from lost future grants is

$$\sum_{t=1}^{\infty}\frac{\lambda}{(1+r)^t}(\rho - c) = \lambda(\rho - c)\sum_{t=1}^{\infty}\frac{1}{(1+r)^t} = \frac{\lambda}{r}(\rho - c)$$

Thus, the researcher will perform instead of pocketing the money if

$$c \leq \frac{\lambda}{r}(\rho - c)$$

or

$$c \leq \frac{\lambda}{\lambda + r}\rho \qquad (8.1)$$

We can see that, for fixed awards ρ, only researchers who expect to have lots of ideas (high λ) will perform in return for future options on grants. If the inequality (8.1) holds for any λ, it also holds for any researcher with a higher value of λ. We can also see that, for a fixed rate of idea formation λ, researchers will only perform if the rewards ρ are high enough. And, of course, they will never perform if the award ρ is smaller than the cost c.

Let H be the cumulative distribution of λ in the population of researchers, so that $1 - H(\lambda)$ is the fraction of researchers with parameter greater than λ. For a fixed award size ρ, let $\hat{\lambda}(\rho)$ be the minimum λ for which (8.1) holds—that is, the value for which (8.1) holds with equality. The function $\hat{\lambda}$ is decreasing in ρ: for higher prospective awards, even less creative researchers are willing to perform in return for future options on grants. Then the number of funded researchers $1 - H(\hat{\lambda}(\rho))$ increases with the size of the award, ρ. The total budget of the sponsor per unit time is

$$B(\rho) = \rho \int_{\hat{\lambda}(\rho)}^{\infty} \lambda \, dH(\lambda)$$

The only researchers who continue to apply for grants are those with creativity parameters larger than $\hat{\lambda}(\rho)$, and all of them are funded. The only way to increase the amount of research (number of researchers) is to increase ρ for all researchers, which means that the budget increases by more than the payments made to new researchers.

We have so far assumed that the sponsor cannot condition the size of the award on the past success rate. However, doing so could reduce the total budget required to support a given amount of innovation.

Suppose the sponsor could observe the fertility λ of the researcher's mind. Then it could make different payments for different researchers; the grant per idea, ρ, would be a function of λ. For each λ, it would choose a prize $\rho(\lambda)$ for which (8.1) holds as an equality. The function ρ would then be a decreasing function of λ; more productive researchers would receive less money per funded idea. Despite this, one can also see from (8.1) that, since $c(\lambda + r) = \rho(\lambda)\lambda$, the more creative researchers (those with higher λ) would receive more grant funding per unit time, $\lambda\rho(\lambda)$.

However, given that the grantor cannot observe λ, the grantor is probably well advised not to estimate it. If it estimates λ by using the researcher's past rate of success, then a researcher will have an incentive to suppress ideas rather than risk a lower grant per idea. This would undermine the objective.

Thus, the grant process serves the dual purposes of making sure that researchers invest as intended, and selecting the most productive researchers. It is only the more productive researchers who will stay in the system, and to stay in the system, they must perform. Intramural research could provide the same incentives for the in-house researchers, but it is harder to cut them out if they do not perform. In most employment contracts, a researcher can be fired for obvious fraud but cannot usually be fired for lack of creativity.

We close this section with a comment on serendipity in science. It is remarkable how often discoveries are made without the researcher intending them. If a discovery is made without the researcher having anticipated in advance that such a discovery was possible, or having set upon the task of looking for it, then it is hard to say that incentives played any role, or indeed, that incentives *could* play any role. In this book, we have formalized the concept of serendipity and reconciled it with an incentive system. The ideas model recognizes up front that there is an exogenous process by which ideas occur—that is serendipity. Whether a researcher has an incentive to invest in them depends on the market value and cost—that is where incentives play a role.

Perhaps the most famous example of serendipity is penicillin, which was accidentally discovered in the course of culturing bacteria in an influenza investigation (Roberts 1989). Alexander Fleming had noticed the absence of bacterial growth where a bit of mold had fallen, a mold that creates penicillin. There are two aspects of this event that we wish to emphasize. First, it would not have happened if Fleming had not been engaged in research that involved growing bacteria in petri dishes. Second, the idea would not have come to fruition without considerable additional time and funds; there was a clear distinction between the idea and the innovation.

A second famous example of serendipity was Antoine-Henri Becquerel's discovery of radioactivity (Pais 1986). Becquerel had observed that what he thought were phosphorescent materials acted like X-rays on photographic plates. Since phosphorescence is powered by sunlight, he could not experiment on cloudy days. Waiting out the Paris weather, he stored the plate in a closet, in proximity to the supposedly phosphorescent material, which happened to be a uranium salt. He later developed the plate for no particular purpose, and found, to his great surprise, that it showed an exposure. Since phosphorescence depends on sunlight, the exposure must have come from something else. Becquerel had discovered radioactivity.

The same two comments apply about the discovery of radioactivity as about the discovery of penicillin: the idea of radioactivity would not have occurred to Becquerel if he had not been engaged in related research, but development of the idea also required additional effort.

The grant model goes some distance toward recognizing that, although ideas are exogenous, they can be stimulated by related research. Even though the grant process is focused on specific proposals, there is an unspoken recognition that fertile minds will generate ideas in the ordinary course of science, and that this is part of the process. The rate λ at which a researcher has ideas is the thing that is exogenous and is also what is selected in the grant process. That said, mistakes may be made in getting the idea process flowing. If researchers with potentially high rates of idea formation are never given an initial chance or have initial bad luck, fertile minds might never be tapped. This initial selection process is not solved very well by either the grant process or our model of it.

8.6   The Virtues of Open Science

"Open science" usually means that scientists must publish, hence disclose, their discoveries (David 2003). Open science is generally contrasted with commercial science, where researchers have an incentive to withhold results until intellectual property rights are secure.

In this section we turn to the question of how or whether the rate of idea formation can be influenced by rules of disclosure imposed by the grant agency. In the model of the previous section, we assumed that the rate of idea formation was fixed for each researcher. But if research proceeds cumulatively, as discussed in chapter 5, then the rate of progress depends on the norms of openness in which the scientists operate. Scientists cannot have ideas for further advance if they do not know what has already been discovered.

Suppose that two researchers receive ideas at the same rate, λ, per time period, and suppose that the ideas are distributed as a Poisson distribution. This assumption is described more fully in the technical note at the end of the chapter, but the idea is straightforward. The Poisson distribution implies that, regardless of when the researcher had her last idea, the probability of an idea at each point in time starting from the present is the same, and the time, say x, until the researcher receives the next idea is a random variable with exponential distribution with parameter λ (also described in the technical note). The time until the next idea has expected value $1/\lambda$.

Suppose now that two researchers are pursuing the next step of progress. Then ideas are arriving at twice the rate in aggregate as with one researcher—that is, 2λ ideas per unit time—and the average time until an idea arrives from one of the two researchers is $1/2\lambda$. Thus, provided the researchers share their ideas, so that each researcher's next idea builds from the highest level of progress that either has achieved, aggregate progress occurs at the rate 2λ steps in each unit of time.

This scheme is better than letting only a single researcher invest because progress toward the goal is twice as fast, and the total costs per idea are the same, even though they are brought forward in time.

We can now see how sharing accelerates progress. To achieve the rate of progress 2λ steps per unit time on average, the researchers must share their ideas. One means is to publish them. Suppose instead that the researchers do not do this, perhaps because it is not required by the grantor. More specifically, suppose that the grantor funds ideas in increments of two steps instead of one step to save administrative costs, and does not require publication at the intermediate stage. If the researchers do not disseminate their results until they are two steps beyond the public state of knowledge, then there will be times when one researcher has made an (unpublished) advance and the other is behind. A researcher who believes that he or she is behind may simply drop out, which clearly retards progress, or may duplicate an advance that has already been made but not disclosed. In both outcomes, the researchers are working inefficiently. We show in the technical note that without disclosure, the average length of time between steps of progress is then $5/8\lambda$ instead of the smaller $1/2\lambda$.

In the model we have been considering, it is known that ideas arrive at some rate, but the ideas themselves are unknown in advance. Ideas are scarce in the sense that they occur to one researcher at a time. This is a realistic description of many research environments, possibly including the Fabrique Lyonnaise discussed in chapter 2, where inventors were given prizes or rewards for presenting technological advances in weaving on condition of making sufficient efforts to disseminate the knowledge.

There are similar virtues to openness in almost any other context where knowledge is cumulative. Another model of cumulative effort is where it is known in advance what steps of progress are required, but the time required to accomplish them is random (e.g., Scotchmer and Green 1990). An example might be the search for a drug, which involves the successive elimination of candidate chemicals. Then clearly each researcher would benefit from knowing what candidates the other researchers have eliminated, since that will prevent the duplication of effort.

We should not mistake the virtues of open science for an argument that publicly funded researchers will be more generous in sharing their intermediate results than private firms will be. Both may have incentives to withhold intermediate progress if there is a bigger reward for the final step than for intermediate steps. In a commercial environment, the reward for the final step may be intellectual property rights. In an academic environment, it may be tenure and acclaim, or even a Nobel Prize. Oddly, though, commerce has a tool for encouraging openness that is not available in the context of open, public-domain science. If the intermediate steps of progress are patentable, firms have an incentive to patent and disclose them. The analogous thing for academic researchers might be publication, but publication does not give the researcher exclusive rights in the same way as patenting.

It turns out that the incentives for academics to be secretive have been documented. A group of researchers associated with Massachusetts General Hospital surveyed geneticists on the question of hoarding data. Their findings include the following:

Forty-seven percent of geneticists who asked other faculty for additional information . . . reported that at least one of their requests had been denied in the preceding 3 years. Ten percent of all post-publication requests . . . were denied. Twelve percent said that in the previous 3 years, they had denied another academician's request. . . . Among geneticists who said they had intentionally withheld data . . . , 80% reported that it required too much effort . . . ; 64%, that they were protecting the ability of a graduate student, postdoctoral fellow or junior faculty member to publish; and 53%, that they were protecting their own ability to publish. (Campbell et al. 2002, 473)

Thus the motive to publish, like the profit motive, can be an impediment to sharing. One solution is for granting agencies and journals to give money and publication only on condition of openness. The celebrated Bermuda Protocols do this for basic gene sequencing research.

8.7   Technical Note: Disclosure and Expected Time to Discovery

If ideas arrive at rate λ, then the time x between ideas has a probability distribution with an exponential density function $\lambda e^{-x\lambda}$, and the expected time per idea is

$$\frac{1}{\lambda} = \int_0^\infty \lambda x e^{-x\lambda} dx$$

Similarly, if the ideas arrive at twice the rate, 2λ, with each idea shared between the people receiving them, the expected time between ideas is $1/2\lambda$.

Now let x represent the time until two ideas occur instead of one. Then x has a gamma distribution with density function

$\lambda^2 x e^{-\lambda x}$

and the cumulative distribution, which we will denote by the function F, satisfies

$$F(x) = \int_0^x \lambda^2 \hat{x} e^{-\lambda \hat{x}} d\hat{x} = \int_0^{\lambda x} \hat{x} e^{-\hat{x}} d\hat{x} = (1 - (1 + \lambda x) e^{-\lambda x})$$

We now let x_1, x_2 be the random lengths of time until researcher 1 and researcher 2, respectively, achieve two ideas. We assume here that the first idea is not shared with the other researcher. Our objective is to show that the expected time until two ideas are achieved by a single researcher is longer than $1/\lambda$, which is the expected length of time if they share the first idea that arrives to either.

The minimum length of time until one of the researchers has received a sequence of two ideas is $x = \min\{x_1, x_2\}$.

The density of the minimum is

$$2\lambda^2 x e^{-\lambda x}(1 - F(x)) = 2\lambda^2 x e^{-\lambda x}(1 + \lambda x) e^{-\lambda x} = 2\lambda^2 x e^{-2\lambda x} + 2\lambda^3 x^2 e^{-2\lambda x}$$

and the expected value of x is

$$2\int_0^\infty \lambda^2 x^2 e^{-2\lambda x} dx + 2\int_0^\infty \lambda^3 x^3 e^{-2\lambda x} dx = \frac{1}{2\lambda} + \frac{3}{4\lambda} = \frac{5}{4\lambda} > \frac{1}{\lambda}$$

References and Further Reading

Abramson, H. N., J. Encarnacao, P. P. Reid, and U. Schmoch, eds. 1997. *Technology Transfer Systems in the United States and Germany: Lessons and Perspectives*. Washington, DC: National Academy of Engineering, National Academies Press.

Association of University Technology Managers. 2002. "AUTM Licensing Survey: FY 2000." Available at www.autm.net/surveys/2000/summarynoe.pdf.

Bekelman, J. E., Y. Li, and G. P. Gross. 2003. "Scope and Impact of Financial Conflicts of Interest in Biomedical Research: A Systematic Review."*Journal of the American Medical Association*, 289:454–464.

Berners-Lee, T. 2000. *Weaving the Web*. New York: Harpers Business.

Blumenthal, D., M. Gluck, K. S. Louis, and D. Wise. 1986. "Industrial Support of University Research in Biotechnology." *Science* 231:242–246.

Board on Science Technology and Economic Policy. 2001. "Trends in Federal Support of Research and Graduate Education." Washington, DC: National Research Council, The National Academies. Available at www.nap.edu/catalog/10162.html.

Campbell, E., B. Clarridge, M. Gokhale, L. Birenbaum, S. Hilgartner, N. Holtzman, and D. Blumenthal. 2002. "Data Withholding in Academic Genetics: Evidence from a National Survey."*Journal of the American Medical Association* 287:473.

Cohen, W., R. Nelson, and J. Walsh. 2000. "Protecting Their Intellectual Assets: Appropriability Conditions and Why U.S. Manufacturing Firms Patent (Or Not)." Working Paper 7552. Cambridge, MA: National Bureau of Economic Research.

Colyvas, J., M. Crow, A. Gelijins, R. Mazzoleni, R. Nelson, N. Rosenberg, and B. Sampat. 2002. "How Do University Inventions Get into Practice?" *Management Science* 48:61–72.

Dasgupta, P., and P. David, 1994. "Toward a New Economics of Science." *Research Policy* 23:487–521.

David, P. 2003. "The Economic Logic of 'Open Science' and the Balance between Private Property Rights and the Public Domain in Scientific Data and Information: A Primer." In National Research Council, *The Role of the Public Domain in Scientific and Technical Data and Information*, 19–34. Washington, DC: National Academies Press.

Defense Advanced Research Projects Agency. 2003. *DARPA Grand Challenge.* Available at www.darpa.mil/grandchallenge/.

Geiger, R. L. 1993. *Research and Relevant Knowledge: American Research Universities Since World War II.* New York: Oxford University Press.

Jaffe, A., and J. Lerner. 2001. "Reinventing Public R&D: Patent Policy and the Commercialization of National Laboratory Technologies." *RAND Journal of Economics* 32:167–198.

"Japanese Push for Patents 'Sidelines Basic Research.'" 2003, July 17. *Nature* (News in Brief) 424:244.

Jensen, R., and M. Thu..by, M. 2001. "Proofs and Prototypes for Sale: The Licensing of University Inventions." *American Economic Review* 91:240–259.

Kenney, M. 1986. *Biotechnology: The University-Industrial Complex.* New Haven, CT: Yale University Press.

Koehn, R. 2001, March 20. "Faculty Start-Ups Offer Temptation to Breach Academic Rules . . ." *Nature* (correspondence) 410:513.

Mansfield, E. 1986. "Patents and Innovation: An Empirical Study." *Management Science* 32:173–181.

Marshall, E. 1997. "A Bitter Battle over Insulin Gene." *Science* 277:1028–1030.

Maurer, S. 2002. "Promoting and Disseminating Knowledge: The Public/Private Interface." Washington, DC: National Academies of Science. Available at www7.national academies.org/biso/Maurer background paper.html.

Maurer, S. 2003, November 24–25. "New Institutions for Doing Science: From Databases to Open Source Biology." Paper presented at the conference "Copyright and Database Protection, Patents and Research Tools, and Other Challenges to the Intellectual Property System," organized by the Network on European Policy for Intellectual Property at Maastricht Economic Research Institute on Innovation and Technology. Available at www.merit.unimaas.nl/epip/programme.htm.

Morgan, R., C. Kruybosch, and C. Kannankutty. 2001. "Patenting and Invention Activity of U.S. Scientists and Engineers in the Academic Sector: Comparisons with Industry." *Journal of Technology Transfer* 26:173–183.

Mowery, D., and N. Rosenberg. 1998. *Paths of Innovation.* New York: Cambridge University Press.

Mowery, D., R. Nelson, B. N. Sampat, and A. A. Ziedonis. 2001. "The Growth of Patenting and Licensing by U.S. Universities: An assessment of the Effects of the Bayh-Dole Act of 1980." *Research Policy* 30:99–119.

National Institutes of Health. 1994, November 8. "Developing Sponsored Research Agreements: Considerations for Recipients of NIH Research Grants and Contracts." *Federal Register* 59:55673.

National Institutes of Health. 1999. "Principles and Guidelines for Recipients of NIH Research Grants and Contracts on Obtaining and Disseminating Biomedical Research Resources." *Federal Register* 64:72090.

National Science Board. 2002. *Science and Engineering Indicators—2002.* Arlington, VA: National Science Foundation (NSB 02-1). Available at www.nsf.gov/sbe/srs/seind02/start.htm.

National Science Foundation, Division of Science Resources Studies. 2004. *Federal Funds for Research and Development: Fiscal Years 2001, 2002, and 2003* (NSF 04-310). Available at www.nsf.gov/sbe/srs/nsf04310/.

Nelson, R. 1993. *National Innovation Systems: A Comparative Analysis.* New York: Oxford University Press.

Oliver, A. L., and J. P. Liebeskin. 2003. "Public Research and Intellectual Property Rights: A Tale of Two Inventions." Mimeograph. Los Angeles: Marshall School of Business, University of Southern California.

Pais, A. 1986. *Inward Bound: Of Matter and Forces in the Physical World.* Oxford: Oxford University Press.

Roberts, R. M. 1989. *Serendipity: Accidental Discoveries in Science.* New York: Wiley.

Rood, S. A. 2000. *Government Laboratory Technology Transfer: Process and Impact.* Burlington, VT: Ashgate.

Ruttan, V. W. 2001. *Technology, Growth and Development: An Induced Innovation Perspective.* Oxford: Oxford University Press.

Scotchmer, S., and J. Green. 1990. "Novelty and Disclosure in Patent Law." *RAND Journal of Economics* 21:131–146.

Stephan, S. 2001. "Educational Implications of University-Industry Technology Transfer." *Journal of Technology Transfer* 26:199–205.

Taylor, M., E. W. Rubin, and D. A. Hounshell. 2003. "Effect of Government Actions on Technological Innovation for SO_2 Control." *Environmental Science & Technology* 37: 4527–4534.

Thursby, J., and M. Thursby. 2002. "Who Is Selling the Ivory Tower? Sources of Growth in University Licensing." *Management Science* 48:90–104.

University of California, Technology Transfer Office. 2000. *Annual Report.* Available at www.ucop.edu/ott/ars/ann00/ar00.pdf.

Weiss, P. 2003. "Conflicting International Public Sector Information Policies and Their Effects on the Public Domain and the Economy." In J. Esanu and P. Uhlir, eds., *The Role of Scientific and Technical Data and Information in the Public Domain*, 129–132. Washington, DC: National Academies Press. Available at www7.nationalacademies.org/biso/.

9   The Value of R&D and Patents

Previous chapters have been concerned with how to design incentives, and not with evidence about whether they work. We have taken on faith that incentives will lead to R&D, that R&D will lead to innovations, and that innovations will lead to improvements in consumer welfare or economic growth. This chapter turns to the difficult question of whether any of that can be measured. Given that 2.6 percent of GDP was devoted to R&D in the year 2000 (and comparable percentages in other years), we would like to know if the funds are well spent. Does R&D drive economic growth?

Since this book is about incentives, we would actually like to know more than that. Which incentive systems work? Even members of the Intellectual Property Owners Association depend on a larger toolkit than only patents and copyrights. In the survey of their members undertaken by Cockburn and Henderson (2003), only two-thirds of the members said that their competitive advantage would quickly erode without patents. That fraction is much lower for copyrights (one-third), and considerably higher for trade secrets (four-fifths).

One would guess that a more representative sample of firms would turn up even less dependence on intellectual property rights. Cohen, Nelson, and Walsh (2000) surveyed a more random sample of large firms and asked each one to state, for each type of protection, the percentage of their innovations for which that protection is effective. The five types of protection they included are listed at the top of table 9.1. What is remarkable about the responses is the relative unimportance of patents. In almost no industry do the respondents report that patents are effective for a higher percentage of their innovations than secrecy and lead time are. In the bottom row, where all the respondents are aggregated, patents rank lower than any other category except the residual category "other legal." The most important types of protection are informal: the time-honored business strategies of trying to secure lead time and secrecy.

Table 9.1
Effectiveness of appropriability mechanisms for product innovations

Selected industries	Sample size	Secrecy	Patents	Other legal	Lead time	Complementary sales service	Complementary manufacturing
Food	89	58.54	18.26	21.18	53.37	39.83	51.18
Petroleum	15	62.00	33.33	6.33	48.67	40.33	35.67
Basic Chemicals	35	48.00	38.86	11.57	38.29	45.86	44.71
Drugs	49	53.57	50.20	20.82	50.10	33.37	49.39
Machine Tools	10	61.50	36.00	9.00	61.00	43.00	34.50
Computers	25	44.20	41.00	27.20	61.40	40.20	38.00
Electrical equipment	22	39.09	34.55	15.00	33.41	32.27	31.82
Semiconductors and related	18	60.00	26.67	22.50	53.33	42.22	47.50
Medical equipment	67	50.97	54.70	29.03	58.06	52.31	49.25
Autoparts	30	50.83	44.35	15.65	64.35	44.84	53.06
All	1118	51.00	34.83	20.71	52.76	42.74	45.61

Source: Cohen, Nelson, and Walsh 2000, table 1.
Note: Each number is a mean response, representing the percentage of product innovations in the row category for which the type of protection in the column is deemed "effective." The response categories are <10%, 10%–40%, 41%–60%, 61%–90%, >90%.

Thus, there is a sense in which we misled you in chapter 3, where we claimed that patents were the gold standard of intellectual property protection. That may be true if patents are compared to other formal legal protections, but there are many instances where informal business strategies like secrecy and lead time may protect more strongly.

Some of the "ineffectiveness" of formal intellectual property protection is by design. As chapters 4 and 5 stressed, it is not always true that stronger intellectual property rights are better. Intellectual property should be designed to achieve the right balance of protection for innovators, protection for consumers, and opportunity for rivals to make improvements. Protection through secrecy can obstruct these objectives.

There will be more about the value of patents and patent protection later in this chapter. The first task is to investigate whether the effect of aggregate R&D spending on economic growth can be measured. The aggregate approach captures the effects of the incentive system as a whole, instead of single instruments such as patents or copyrights.

Figure 9.1 shows how total R&D grew over the last half of the twentieth century, in real dollars (billions of dollars, at the 1996 price

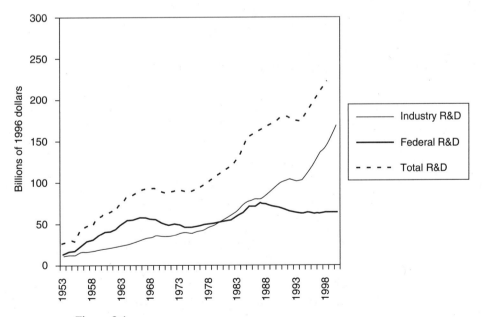

Figure 9.1
Who funds U.S. R&D: 1953–2000
Source: National Science Board, 2002, appendix table 4-19.

level). Even in real terms, R&D spending grew substantially. The most striking thing about figure 9.1, however, is the transformation in who pays for it. Prior to 1980, the federal government funded more research than private industry, and for much of that period, almost twice as much. By the year 2000, this was reversed. The private sector was funding twice as much as the public sector. This may reflect the complex changes in the relationship between the public and private R&D sectors that are discussed in chapters 1 and 8.

While R&D has been growing substantially in real terms, it has only kept pace with gross domestic product (GDP). Figure 9.2 shows that R&D spending has not changed much in recent decades as a percentage of GDP. The percentage of GDP devoted to R&D is between about 1 and 3 percent in all seven countries. If one includes defense spending, the percentages are still less than 3 percent About a sixth of U.S. R&D spending is related to defense.

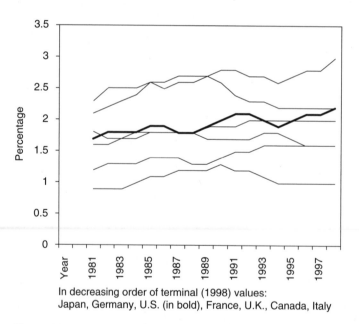

In decreasing order of terminal (1998) values:
Japan, Germany, U.S. (in bold), France, U.K., Canada, Italy

Figure 9.2
Nondefense R&D spending as a percentage of GDP
Source: National Science Board, 2002, appendix table 4-41.

9.1   R&D and Productivity Growth

Growth in GDP is the most common measure of the success of R&D spending. However, as a measure of consumer welfare, GDP is a seriously flawed proxy. The main reason to use it is that economists, like other empiricists, are stuck "looking under the lamp post." We study GDP because someone (the Department of Commerce) measures it.

If all markets are competitive and firms earn zero profit, then GDP measures the value of inputs. Since every dollar earned is also spent, GDP also measures revenues earned in final goods markets. In this sense, GDP is a useful indicator of economic activity, and, to the extent that costs are related to consumers' surplus, GDP gives some indication of total consumers' surplus.

If industries are not perfectly competitive, firms may earn economic and accounting profits. Then GDP includes profits as well as input costs. This has the odd implication that if a competitive market becomes cartelized, GDP goes up even though consumers' surplus goes down. Of course, in the innovation context, cartelization is not typically how firms gain market power. Firms gain market power by introducing new goods that are protected by intellectual property.

But then another problem arises: the ratio of consumers' surplus to what is measured in GDP, namely, the value of inputs plus profit, is different for proprietary goods than for those that are competitively supplied. For this reason, the interpretation of GDP growth is ambiguous if the mix of proprietary goods and competitively supplied goods changes over time.

Public spending also confounds how R&D is reflected in GDP. If the inventions that result from public spending are put in the public domain to be used by many competitive users, then the benefits accrue mainly to consumers—for example, through low prices—rather than to firms. What is reflected in GDP is the value of the R&D input, like scientists' salaries, and not the value of the R&D output. Indeed, if a public research agenda lowers the costs of producing goods and services, it can actually *reduce* GDP. The expected effect of R&D spending on GDP should depend both on the proportion of R&D that is publicly sponsored, which has been declining, and the arrangements under which publicly sponsored research is distributed. As discussed in chapter 8, an increasing proportion of these arrangements lead to intellectual property.

As it turns out, the papers referenced at the end of this chapter (and others discussed by Hall [1996]) show that the measured impact of public R&D spending on private indicators of value is, as expected, smaller than that of private R&D spending. In fact, many studies find no measurable effect at all. A single exception is Hall and Mairesse (1995), who show that in France, public R&D subsidies of at least 20 percent of a firm's R&D spending may increase its market value. This effect may be due to the fact that the outputs of the subsidized research are then sold back to the public sector at negotiated prices.

Despite the flaws in GDP as a measure of national welfare, it is the most visible thing under the lamp post, and the economics literature therefore investigates the sources of growth as if GDP were the object of interest.[1] Most studies have focused on the relationship between R&D spending and GDP in a single country, usually the United States. Except as modified later, the implicit assumption is that R&D spending does not change relative prices, as might be true if the benefits were spread evenly across industries. If relative prices do not change, the main problem is to convert nominal GDP into constant-dollar GDP by deflating the price level to a chosen year. For example, if the year 1990 is chosen, then the nominal GDP of the year 2000 would have to be multiplied to 80 percent (deflated), since the price level in the year 1990 was only about 80 percent of its level in year 2000.[2]

The "productivity" of the economy is often defined as total output divided by total labor, Q/L, where Q is measured as GDP in constant dollars, and L is person-hours of labor. A slightly more general approach to productivity is the "total factor productivity" (TFP) model, as follows.

The TFP model conceives of aggregate output Q as depending on capital stock C, labor L, knowledge K, and "disembodied technical change" T. If we know the aggregate production function F, the output Q can be written as $Q = F(C, L, K, T)$. Each of the inputs to production is growing over time. The labor supply grows as population grows

---

1.   Mostly this line of inquiry has been undertaken by the Productivity Group of the National Bureau of Economic Research, under the leadership of Zvi Griliches. The ideas and facts discussed here come largely from that body of work, cited in the references. The citations here are a little sketchy to avoid being distracting.

2.   Price deflators can be found on the Department of Commerce, Bureau of Economic Analysis, website at www.bea.doc.gov/bea/dn/nipaweb/index.asp.

and capital grows when investment exceeds depreciation. Knowledge grows because there is continual investment in R&D. Although knowledge occasionally becomes obsolete, that is usually because it is replaced with knowledge or technology that is more advanced. Knowledge can be measured by some aggregation of past R&D investments, perhaps with a depreciation factor.

For each of these variables we can define a growth rate from year $t - 1$ to year t. The growth rates $\Delta C_t/C_t$, $\Delta L_t/L_t$, and $\Delta K_t/K_t$ can all be defined analogously to the following, for capital stock:

$$\frac{\Delta C_t}{C_t} = \frac{C_t - C_{t-1}}{C_t}$$

If we are not too fussy about precision, these growth rates can all be measured.

The difficult part is to estimate the production function F. If we knew F, then we could calculate how output changes over time as the inputs change over time. However, we do not know F. What we can observe is how the output Q and the inputs C, L, and possibly K have grown over time. The whole point of the exercise is to figure out something about F so that we know what caused the growth in Q. We would like to know, for example, whether output would have grown at the same rate if knowledge had stayed fixed while capital and labor grew. If that were so, we would conclude that R&D spending has rather little impact on economic growth.

The clever trick that has been used to attack this problem is to use something else we know about the economy, namely, that it is in equilibrium (Solow 1957). We may not know the function F, but we know that the marginal productivity of each factor of production should equal the input price. More specifically, in equilibrium, the wage rate equals the marginal productivity of labor, and the rate of return to capital equals the marginal productivity of capital. We will write F_C and F_L for the marginal productivities of capital and labor, and assume that they are respectively equal to the rate of return on capital and the wage rage. Similarly, we can write F_K and F_T for the marginal productivities of knowledge accumulation and other technical change.

The following relationship holds at each point in time, essentially by definition:[3]

$$\Delta Q = F_C \Delta C + F_L \Delta L + F_K \Delta K + F_T \Delta T$$

That is, the increase in output, $\Delta Q = Q_t - Q_{t-1}$, can be attributed to increases in the inputs. The effect of each input depends, by definition, on its marginal productivity. This relationship can be rearranged as

$$\frac{\Delta Q}{Q} = \frac{CF_C}{Q}\frac{\Delta C}{C} + \frac{LF_L}{Q}\frac{\Delta L}{L} + F_K\frac{\Delta K}{Q} + F_T\frac{\Delta T}{Q}$$

But now we can use what we know about equilibrium. The total wage bill in the economy is the total labor times the wage, namely, LF_L. Hence the labor share of GDP is LF_L/Q, which we will denote by $\beta < 1$. Using the same relationship for capital, and denoting the capital share of GDP as $\alpha < 1$, we can write

$$\frac{\Delta Q}{Q} - \alpha\frac{\Delta C}{C} - \beta\frac{\Delta L}{L} = F_K\frac{\Delta K}{Q} + F_T\frac{\Delta T}{Q}$$

The rates of growth $\Delta Q/Q$, $\Delta C/C$, $\Delta L/L$, and possibly $\Delta K/K$, as well as the capital and labor shares of GDP, α and β, are observable from accounting data. Thus, accounting data give us enough information to calculate the right-hand side, which expresses the "net" growth, once labor and capital are accounted for, namely,

$$\frac{\Delta Q}{Q} - \alpha\frac{\Delta C}{C} - \beta\frac{\Delta L}{L} \tag{9.1}$$

This quantity can be calculated for each year.[4] The resulting list of values is a time series. The elements of the time series are "unexplained" residuals in growth, or more precisely, residuals that are not explained by labor or capital growth. If the residuals have small values, then we would conclude that most growth is accounted for by growth in capital and

---

3.   This is even clearer using the calculus. Write the inputs as functions of time and the aggregate production function as $Q(t) = F(C(t), L(t), K(t), T(t))$. Taking a total derivative of the production function F, and using a "dot" to represent the derivative with respect to time (e.g., $\dot{Q} \equiv dQ(t)/dt$),

$$\dot{Q} = F_c(\cdot)\dot{C} + F_L(\cdot)\dot{L} + F_K(\cdot)\dot{K} + F_T(\cdot)\dot{T}$$

$$\frac{\dot{Q}}{Q} = \frac{CF_c(\cdot)}{Q}\frac{\dot{C}}{C} + \frac{LF_L(\cdot)}{Q}\frac{\dot{L}}{L} + F_K(\cdot)\frac{\dot{K}}{Q} + F_T(\cdot)\frac{\dot{T}}{Q}$$

4.   This is one example of a general method originating with Solow (1956, 1957). For an elaboration of the discussion here and its underpinnings, see Griliches 1988 and the papers referenced there.

labor, and, in particular, that R&D spending is unimportant. If the residuals are large and variable, there is an unexplained cause of growth, which may be linked to R&D spending.

The first half of the twentieth century was a period of remarkable growth when output per unit of labor almost doubled. Over that period the rate of change of output, the first term in (9.1), was about 2.75 percent, a rate at which per capita output will double in twenty-five years. Growth was even higher between 1950 and 1970, after which the rate of productivity growth slackened considerably, sometimes referred to as the "productivity slowdown." Only about half of the growth residual in the first half of the century can be explained by growth of capital and labor.[5] The capital and labor shares of GDP were about 35 percent and 65 percent respectively, and the rates of growth of capital and labor were about 1.0 percent and 1.75 percent. Putting this together, the value of the residual (9.1) is about 1.49 percent per year. Thus, the proportion of growth that is not accounted for by labor and capital in the first half of the century is 1.49/1.75, or slightly more than half. This should serve to convince us that better explanations for growth are in order. The growth in GDP in the twentieth century cannot be explained solely by the growth in capital stock and labor. However, there is a line of work that applies a similar methodology at the sectoral level, and concludes that most growth in the postwar period can be explained by growth of capital and labor (Jorgenson 1995a,b; Jorgenson, Gollop, and Fraumeni 1987), but realizing that technological improvement is built into the qualities of these other variables.

Motivated partly by the productivity slowdown in the 1970s, economists have investigated whether the growth residual is linked to R&D spending. There are no systematic data on R&D spending prior to about 1950, when output per capita was growing rapidly. However, as can be seen in figure 9.1, R&D expenditures were growing quite fast from 1953 to 1968, about 8 percent per year, and then declined by about 2 percent per year until 1975. After 1975 they turned up again. As already mentioned, productivity grew rapidly up to about 1970, and again in the 1990s, but with a slowdown in the 1970s and 1980s. Since growth seems to track R&D spending, it is natural to ask whether the decline in R&D spending can be blamed for the slowed productivity growth in that period.

---

5.   Following Solow, the details of this calculation can be found in Nicholson 1995, 336.

R&D spending is not the same as the knowledge variable K, since R&D is a flow variable, and knowledge is a stock variable. It is not only the current R&D spending that affects productivity, but the whole history of R&D spending that the current spending adds to. Thus, for empirical purposes, the knowledge variable K is typically constructed as a weighted sum of past R&D spending, depreciated for obsolescence. This constructed variable is then used as an explanatory variable for the time-series residual (9.1). Intuitively, the question is whether the residual (9.1) is large mainly when R&D spending $\Delta K/Q$ is large. The coefficient that links them can be estimated using regression analysis, regressing the times series (9.1) on $\Delta K/Q$. The resulting coefficient estimates the marginal contribution of knowledge to growth, F_K. This coefficient is probably the main variable of interest, because it tells us to what extent our innovation policy is effective at stimulating growth in output.

Griliches (1988) concludes that, although there is a measurable effect of R&D spending on growth, the slowdown in R&D spending does not account for very much of the slowdown in growth of output in the 1970s. Nevertheless, the estimates of the R&D impact are of interest: how much bang for the buck? Griliches (1988) summarizes a large body of work to conclude that the marginal contribution to GDP of an additional dollar invested in the accumulated stock of R&D capital is between 20 and 50 percent. Hall (2000, 1999) summarizes other work estimating private rates of return in various contexts of between 7 and 43 percent, with social rates of return well over 100 percent. Each estimate depends on whether output is measured as an aggregate, GDP, at the level of industries, or at the level of firms. It also depends on which R&D is included. As mentioned earlier, private R&D spending has a larger impact on GDP than public spending does.

These estimates of the marginal productivity of "knowledge" are a little higher than the marginal productivity of other capital investments, but not radically so. Real stock market returns have seldom been as high as 10 percent when averaged over several years. However, we must be a bit careful in how we interpret this coincidence. Suppose that the private rate of return on R&D spending was exactly the same as for other investments. The most immediate thing that would tell us, and perhaps the only thing, is that firms behave rationally. If the rates of return were different for the two kinds of investment, then profit-maximizing firms would shift investments toward the higher rate of return.

As to efficiency, there is an important difference in how we should interpret the two rates of return. For ordinary capital investments, such as machinery, investment is efficient (assuming markets are competitive) if the rate of return at the margin is equal to the rate of discount. But for investments in R&D, unlike ordinary capital, the social value of a marginal investment is not equal to the private value. Suppose, for example, that the reward for winning a patent race is a very lucrative patent. Shifting investments toward R&D might mean entering a dissipative patent race. Even if this is the right business decision from the point of view of the firm, the duplication of costs in the patent race might be wasteful from a social point of view. In that case, R&D spending is inefficiently high, even though privately optimal.

Alternatively, R&D investments might be too low. Due to the non-rival nature of knowledge, a firm might not be able to appropriate the value of its investments. The knowledge could spill over to competitors. With spillovers, the investing firm does not appropriate all the benefits, and may not invest. This phenomenon has been investigated, for example, by Jaffe (1986) and Jaffe, Trajtenberg, and Henderson (1993).

Probably the most important defect of using GDP to estimate the value of technical change is that R&D causes relative prices to change. There are very few innovations that stimulate economic activity evenly across all industries. Instead, some innovations open new markets, and others reduce prices of selected consumer products by making them cheaper to produce.

If relative prices are changing in addition to the overall price level, there is no easy fix that permits us to study productivity changes by considering aggregates such as GDP. If the effect of R&D is to change the price as well as the quantity supplied, but we only observe the change in revenue pq, then we know very little about the social value that has been generated. Sales can stay more or less the same whether price falls and output rises, or output falls and price rises. In the first case, R&D has a beneficial impact on both productivity (growth in output) and consumers (fall in price). But in the second case, there is neither benefit. By just observing sales, we cannot distinguish these two cases.

Data compiled by the U.S. Department of Commerce (2000) show that price effects have been striking in the computer industry. The price of a megabyte of memory was only 1/500 in 1999 of its level in 1988, a period in which the overall price level rose. Similarly, the price of a quality-adjusted computer was less than 1/10 of its 1987 price. Quality-adjusted output of computers grew about 12 percent per year in the early

1990s and about 40 percent per year subsequently. If sales of computers are included in GDP as if their price tracked the consumer price index, then the growth in computer output is hugely underrepresented and the estimated impact of R&D on growth in computer output is too low.

Griliches (1994), Hall and Mairesse (1995), and Hall (1996) have gotten around these price changes by focusing on the output of particular industries or firms as the quantity affected by R&D. They apply different price deflators to different industries or firms, to make sure that the change in output is measured rather than the change in revenue. Disaggregating the data at the level of industries, Griliches (1994) estimated the rate of return in units of output at 30 percent when the computer industry is included, but at only about 12 percent if the computer industry is excluded. Similarly, using data at the firm level rather than industry level, Hall and Mairesse (1995) and Hall (2000) estimate the rate of return in units of output to be about 10 percent when computer firms are included, but only about 1 percent without them. Thus, R&D in the computer industry has had a large effect that could be missed if the changes in relative price were not accounted for. Without using a computer-specific price deflator, the rate of return to R&D in terms of revenue or sales appears to be only about 2.5 percent. In contrast, the rate of return in terms of output is 11 percent.

These papers point to a subtle shift away from the macroeconomic perspective, with its focus on aggregates, to a microeconomic perspective, with a focus on demand analysis and consumers' surplus in particular industries. If data on price are available, and if something is known about the demand curve, then we can measure benefits to R&D as a change in consumers' surplus plus a change in firms' profits, as is done in cost-benefit analysis. This is particularly important when R&D opens a new market. "Growth in output" makes little sense if the output was previously zero, as is true of new products. Trajtenberg (1990a, 1993) introduces a technique of valuing new products by their attributes, using a logit model, and applies it to CT scanners. Bresnahan (1986) estimates the value of the computer revolution by using the derived demand for computer services in the financial sector.

9.2 Patent Data and the Private Value of R&D Spending

Since R&D spending leads to intellectual property, R&D spending and intellectual property should, to some extent, measure the same thing. On the other hand, R&D spending is a measure of inventive *inputs*, while patents and other intellectual property are measures of inventive *outputs*. It is easy to waste money in a futile R&D venture but hard to convince the PTO that a worthless invention should be patented.[6] For this reason, we might expect patents to explain a larger portion of productivity growth than R&D spending.

Ideally, the output measure should include all intellectual property. However, we only have systematic data for patents. This is because of the administrative procedures of examining and publishing them. There are no comparable requirements for copyrights. Like GDP, patents are something we find under the lamp post. Patent counts can be observed at the level of firms and industries, and a patent document itself contains indicators of the invention's worth, such as the number of technology classes it pertains to and its citations.

Economists have a long history of trying to study innovation by studying patenting behavior. This goes back at least to Jacob Schmookler in the 1950s and 1960s, and continues with the work of F. Michael Scherer, Edwin Mansfield, Zvi Griliches, and the NBER Productivity Group. The enterprise has been reinvigorated by easy electronic access to patents, which makes it easier to cull the detailed information they contain, such as citations (see Hall, Jaffe, and Trajtenberg 2002, 2004; Jaffe and Trajtenberg 2002).

The question that "hovers" over this work, as Griliches (1990) puts it, is, What can one use patent statistics for?[7] There is a strong intuition that, being so visible, patent data must be good for something. The inquiry that is consistent with this chapter is whether patent data can help us to evaluate the effects of R&D spending on growth and consumer welfare.

A crude investigation of the correlation between R&D spending and patent grants can be made by looking at figure 9.3, and remembering that R&D spending and GDP are fairly well correlated in the last half of the twentieth century (this is implied by figure 9.2). Figure 9.3 graphs domestic R&D and domestic patent grants. It is worth noting,

---

6.   This can be disputed. The PTO is frequently criticized for approving patents that violate known laws of physics. Robert Park of the American Physical Society routinely publicizes these; see www.aps.org/WN/. See also Ord-Hume 1977. Merges 1999 and Allison and Lemley 2002 provide discussions based more on the legal institutions.

7.   This short discussion does not improve on the longer discussion and surveys of Griliches (1989, 1990), except to add a discussion of more recent citation-based approaches.

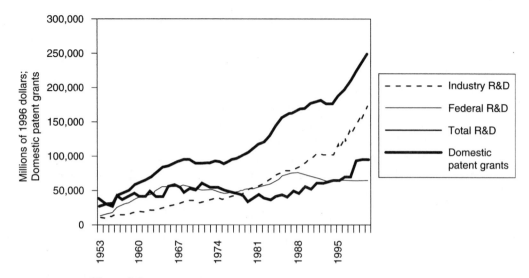

Figure 9.3
R&D spending and domestic patent grants
Sources: USPTO Technology Assessment and Forecasting Reports. National
Science Board, 2002.

however, that the percentage of foreign patents granted by the PTO rose
from 18 percent in 1963 to 48 percent in 2002.

Domestic patent grants have fallen as a percentage of both
R&D and GDP over most of the century, with an upturn in the 1990s
(Kortum and Lerner 1999). There was a downturn in patenting in the
1970s, corresponding to a downturn in total R&D expenditures, but
patenting did not pick up in the 1980s commensurately with R&D
spending.

Before turning to the formal investigations of how R&D affects
patenting, we pause to ask what can be inferred about the cost of patents,
by comparing patent grants to R&D expenditures. Figure 9.3 suggests
that in the past few decades, industry spent between $1 million and $2
million per patent.[8] Of course this is a very imprecise method of accounting. For example, there are lags between R&D expenditures and patent
grants, and also between the date of application and date of grant. In
the 1960s more than 40 percent of applications were delayed more than

8.   In figure 9.3, the foreign patent grants are subtracted out. The data series
prior to 1963 did not separate foreign and domestic patents, so 18 percent
foreign grants are assumed, which is the same as in 1963.

three years. The lag fell in the 1970s (about 20% had a lag in excess of three years), increased in the 1980s, decreased in the early 1990s, and has recently increased again. Another problem is that it is hard to associate patents with industries, due to how patents are classified into technology groups, and an even more basic issue is whether public spending should be included.

The cost of patents varies widely by industry, as shown by Griliches (1989) using industry-level data from 1957, 1976, and 1985. Drug patents are relatively costly, and aircraft patents even more so. On the other hand, there is quite a lot of patenting per dollar in the chemical and communication equipment industries, so that the cost of patents is relatively low. Across the board, there were about 1.4 patents per million private R&D dollars (1976 dollars), which works out to about $700,000 per patent, or about $1.6 million in 1996 dollars. This is consistent with figure 9.3. However, in a later and larger sample studied by Hall, Jaffe, and Trajtenberg (2000), the R&D cost per patent is somewhat higher, about $1.6 million in 1980 dollars, or about $2.8 million in 1996 dollars. Echoing the Griliches study, Lanjouw and Schankerman (2004) show the variation in average patent cost in the 1980–1993 period, with the cost per drug patent being (in 1998 dollars) almost $4 million, the costs of health, chemical, and mechanical patents being less than $2 million, and patents in electronics a bit more than $2 million. The point of their paper is to address the apparent decline in "patent productivity," or inversely, the increase in R&D dollars spent per patent. They show that, in some industries, this change over time can be accounted for by an increase in what they call patent quality, as measured by the number of claims, the number of times the patent is cited, the number of other patents it cites, and the number of patent jurisdictions in which it issued.

Economists have also tried to uncover the true relationship between R&D spending and patenting by studying industries and firms. If we think of the number of patents, P, as a (nonnegative) function of R&D spending r, written as $P(r)$, then we can define the elasticity of patent grants with respect to R&D spending as

$$\frac{\Delta P(r)}{\Delta r} \frac{r}{P}$$

A natural question is whether the effectiveness of R&D spending in producing patented innovations declines as R&D increases—that is, is the function $P(\cdot)$ concave? If it is strictly concave, then $P(r)/r$ is declining.

Further, strict concavity implies that $dP(r)/dr < P/r$, so the elasticity is less than one. Thus, the empirical inquiry is whether the elasticity is less than one.

One might think that this inquiry would be a straightforward investigation of the function $P(\cdot)$. In fact, the inquiry is far from straightforward. The following are among the problems that have been addressed empirically: Are we concerned with comparing high-R&D firms with low-R&D firms in the same time period, or do we want to know the prospects for patenting if a low-R&D firm increases its expenditures? How do we disaggregate the data, as to types of inventions or types of firms? What is the right lag structure between R&D spending and patents?

These issues and others have been addressed, for example, by Bound et al. (1984), who studied a cross-section (different firms in the same time period), and Hausman, Hall, and Griliches (1984), who studied a time series (following the same firms across time). In the cross-section, among firms that report positive R&D expenditures, firms with R&D spending less than $2 million in 1976 dollars receive more patents per R&D dollar than those with higher R&D spending. However, for those firms with higher R&D spending, patents grow more or less proportionately to R&D spending. This suggests that returns to scale in the patents-to-R&D relationship are more or less constant for larger firms.

The constant returns in the patents-to-R&D relationship in the cross-section are inconsistent with the estimates for the time series. The best estimates of the elasticity in a times series seem to be around 0.5 instead of 1, which suggests that an expansion in firms' R&D spending would lead to diminishing returns. See, in particular, Hausman, Hall, and Griliches (1984), who report elasticities less than 1. These estimates should be interpreted with caution, due to the noisiness of the data. It is not clear that the estimated coefficients address the experiment of increasing the R&D spending in firms, since other circumstances of the invention environment change. This point of view is central to the work of Nagaoka (2003), who views both patents and R&D as endogenous to other underlying variables.

Here we should stop and remind ourselves of the question that hovers over us: What are patent data good for? Surely it is not the relationship between R&D spending and patents that is ultimately of interest. Our ultimate question is how to measure the consumer value created by R&D spending, and patents are mainly of interest if they help us to do that. By investigating the relationship between R&D and patents, we may uncover something about the cost side of patents, but we are still uninformed about their value. The next section turns to valuation.

9.3   The Skewed Distribution of Patent Values

The objective of this section is to uncover something about the private value of patent rights. However, we begin with two caveats. The first is the same as for GDP: private value captures profit, but does not measure the additional social value that arises from consumers' surplus or other spillovers.

The second is that the private value of a patent right is not the same as the private value of the invention. Recall our data at the beginning of the chapter, suggesting that other forms of protection such as trade secrecy can protect innovations as much as, or more than, patents. The private value of receiving a patent depends on the counterfactual, which tells us what the owner loses if there is no patent right. The counterfactual may be that (1) the invention is not made at all, (2) the invention is made, but a rival owns the patent, (3) the invention is made and put in the public domain, or (4) the inventor remains the proprietor but keeps the technology secret instead of patenting it. The different methods of valuing patent rights implicitly refer to different counterfactuals, so that the estimates are somewhat noncomparable. For a more precise discussion see Harhoff et al. 1999.

Despite these differences, the methodologies all turn up the following general themes: (1) the values of patent rights are very dispersed, (2) the distribution of values is very skewed, with most of the value provided by a few high-earning patents, and (3) the average value of patent rights is much lower than the average R&D cost of innovation.

For example, table 9.2 from Scherer and Harhoff 2000 reports on the results of several investigations into patent value, based on different methodologies.[9] Instead of reporting patent values, the authors report the percent of value accounted for by the 10 percent of highest-earning patents. All the methodologies lead to the conclusion that most of the value is concentrated in the top-earning patents. The first two rows are based on a survey of patents that were granted in 1977 by the German

---

9.   See also Scherer 1998, which describes some of these studies in more detail. Scherer's most provocative argument is that the distribution of values might be so skewed that the mean of the distribution is not even finite. This implies that, whatever the mean of the sample already drawn, there is a nontrivial chance that any additional data will make the mean noticeably larger.

Table 9.2
Proportion of innovation samples' total value realized by the most valuable 10% of innovations

Data set	Number of observations	Percent of value in top 10%
German patents	772	84
U.S. patents	222	81–85
Harvard patents	118	84
Patents in six universities		
1991 royalties	350	93
1992 royalties	408	92
1993 royalties	466	91.5
1994 royalties	411	92
Venture economics start-ups	383	62
Horseley-Keogh start-ups	670	59
Initial public stock offerings (IPOs)—1995 stock value	110	62
Grabowski-Vernon		
1970s drugs	98	55
1980s drugs	66	48

Source: Scherer and Harhoff 2000, table 1.

patent office, with the 222 grants to Americans studied separately. Each respondent was asked retrospectively to estimate the asset value of the patent, namely, the minimum price he would have sold it for shortly after it issued, if he had known at that time the profit flow that would ensue.

The next several rows, reporting the value of university patents, are based on royalty data. After that are three rows on the value of start-up firms, based on asset appreciation or stock values. The last two rows, on the profitability of drug patents, rely on sales data.[10]

10. Given the skewness, one might ask how many patents are used at all, and how much the average value of patents in a given industry or technology diverges from the median. This question was addressed much earlier by Rossman and Sanders (1957) and Sanders, Rossman, and Harris (1958), who surveyed 2 percent of patent grantees from the years 1938, 1948, and 1952. Over 55 percent of those responding said their patents were in use. Among the patents in use, the mean value was about half a million dollars, but the median was only about $25,000. If one includes all the patents, the mean is about $112,000, equivalent to about $473,000 in 1988 dollars. For more discussion see Griliches 1990, 1679.

Besides using surveys, economists have tried to estimate the value of patents by using patent-renewal data. Unlike other intellectual property rights, patent rights have to be renewed, or the invention lapses into the public domain. Although the renewal fees are not very substantial, European data show that they are nevertheless high enough so that only about 50 percent of patents are renewed after ten years. Except for "small entities," U.S. patent fees in 2003 were $1,300, $890, $2,050, and $3,150 at, respectively, issuance, then three and a half, seven and a half, and eleven and a half years. European fees are similar in magnitude.[11]

Since the U.S. renewal system has only been in effect since the early 1980s, most renewal studies have used European data. The first such study, by Pakes and Schankerman (1984), used a combined sample of German, French, and British data. More recent studies (Schankerman and Pakes 1986; Lanjouw 1998; Schankerman 1998) have used other European data.

The inquiry is premised on the assumption that intellectual property rights decay over time. This implies that, if per-period fees are nondecreasing, a patentee will stop renewing the patent when the fee at the next renewal exceeds the incremental profit available by keeping the patent in effect. This is shown in figure 9.4, where $C(t)$ represents renewal fees at time t and $R(t)$ represent the revenues generated by the patent at time t. The figure is drawn as if renewal fees are continuous, so that the patent holder will stop renewing at the date when the two curves cross. Patentees whose inventions are represented by higher revenue curves will stop renewing at a later date. In reality, the renewal fees occur at intervals, which makes the renewal behavior a little harder to describe.

The objective is to estimate the distribution of patent values, using renewal data. The estimation technique can be understood by reference to figure 9.4. Three patents are represented. For each patent, the data tell us how long it is renewed, shown by the intersection with $C(\cdot)$, represented by a large black dot. However, the renewal data alone do not

---

11.   Of course, the most important cost of patenting does not consist of the fees. Most of the cost is an up-front cost consisting of the attorneys' fees required to prepare the application and see it through to issuance. The total costs of applying for a U.S. patent can be anywhere between $5,000 and $100,000, although most are probably at the low end. Applying to the European Patent Office can add another $30,000. See Graham et al. 2003, citing other authors. This cost should have an impact on what gets patented in the first place.

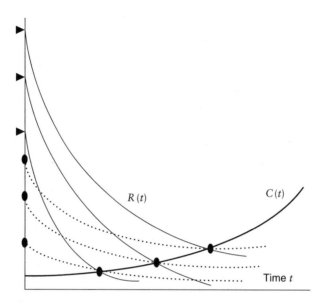

Figure 9.4
Two profiles of patent revenue over time, for three patents

tell us whether the profit is initially high ($R(0)$ is high) and decays rapidly (represented by the three solid curves), or whether profit starts out low and decays slowly (represented by the three dotted curves).[12]

Notice that both families of curves predict the same renewal dates, since the curves intersect $C(\cdot)$ at the same places. However, the patents' decay rates and initial values are different for the two families of curves. Using the fact that there is a figure like 9.4 for every cohort (application date) of patents and every industry, and that the function $C(\cdot)$ has changed in the time periods they studied, the authors find the family of curves that fits the data best.

The data show that, in the four technology classes considered—pharmaceuticals, chemicals, mechanical inventions, and electronic inventions—only about half of patents are renewed after ten years.

12. The term *decay* suggests that the value decreases over time, perhaps as described in chapter 5, where rivals supplant the patent technology with better technologies. Another interpretation of the renewal system is that it is a selection mechanism that rewards innovations with different value differently; see Scotchmer 1999 and Cornelli and Schankerman 1999. See also Crampes and Langinier 1998 for how renewals may be governed by strategies about disclosing information.

Schankerman (1998) estimates decay rates of between 5 and 15 percent per year. Pharmaceuticals and chemicals have lower rates of decay and lower initial values, while mechanical and electronic inventions have higher decay rates and higher initial values.

The authors estimate the distribution of patent values as well as decay rates. To do that, they assume a functional form for the distribution of initial values $R(0)$ (in fact, the data also give guidance as to the functional form), and then find the "best fit" for decay rates and initial values. Finding this best fit entails an estimate of the mean and variance of initial values, from which the whole distribution of patent values can be understood, including the value of innovations in the tail of the distribution.[13]

This technique yields remarkably low estimated values for patent rights, at least on average. The highest is for electronic inventions, with a mean value in 1980 dollars of $68,502. Notice that this is much lower than the average cost of patents discussed previously—for example, the $1.6 million per patent in 1980 dollars estimated by Hall, Jaffe, and Trajtenberg (2000), and also much lower than estimates of litigation costs cited in chapter 7. The value of the median patent is much lower than the mean, indicating that the distribution of values is very skewed. The top 5 percent of patents account for 34 percent of total value in the pharmaceutical industry, 38 percent in chemicals, 50 percent for mechanical inventions, and 55 percent for electronic inventions. Similarly, Schankerman and Pakes (1986) report that half of all the estimated value of patent rights accrues to between 5 and 10 percent of all patents. These numbers reinforce the estimates of skewness reported in table 9.2.

The estimated patent values can be combined with data on national R&D expenditures to calculate the percentages of total R&D recovered as patent revenues. The percentages recovered are remarkably low, reinforcing the lesson of table 9.1, that patent protection is not the main source of an invention's private value. For example, Schankerman (1998) calculates that patents only recover about 15 percent of R&D expenditures when public spending is included, and only about 24 percent of private spending. Lanjouw (1998) comes to an even lower estimate, 10 percent, using German data.

---

13. Pakes (1986) uses a variant of this technique in which the earning stream is uncertain, and the patent may be renewed for its option value, even if the expected return in the next renewal period is less than the renewal fee. Lanjouw (1998) augments the renewal technique to account for the possibility of having to litigate the patent to defend its value.

A final technique for finding the private value of patent rights is to look at the effect of patents on the capitalized value of the firm. Unlike using renewal and survey data, this technique will not give us a distribution of patent values. Instead it estimates the expected value of an additional patent by measuring the effect of a marginal patent on the value of a firm.

We start with the following accounting relationship that links a firm's tangible assets or capital, A, and its stock of "knowledge capital" K to its market valuation V:

$$V = q(A + gK) = qA\left(1 + \frac{gK}{A}\right)$$

The variable q is the market premium of stock value over replacement cost of capital, which would equal one in certain idealized circumstances. The variable g is the shadow price of knowledge assets, answering the question of how much capital A is equivalent in generating market value to a unit of the knowledge stock K. The shadow price g is the variable of interest. The accounting relationship can be written as follows:

$$\ln\left(\frac{V}{A}\right) = \ln q + \ln\left(1 + \frac{gK}{A}\right) \cong \ln q + g\frac{K}{A}$$

recognizing that $\ln(1 + (gK/A))$ can be approximated by gK/A if the latter is small. If we think of $\ln q$ being generated partly by a random process and partly by a systematic term, then we can write

$$\ln\left(\frac{V}{A}\right) = a + g\frac{K}{A} + u \tag{9.2}$$

where a is a constant and u is a random variable. This equation can be estimated by regressing the variable $\ln(V/A)$ on K/A, each observed for different firms in a cross-section or for the same firms in a time series.

The intuitive meaning of the market-value equation (9.2) is that the (logarithm of the) value-to-assets ratio depends on the shadow price of knowledge, g, and the knowledge-to-assets ratio, K/A. Actually, it is easier to see the meaning of (9.2) by taking its total derivative, assuming that V changes with K:

$$\frac{dV}{V} = g\frac{dK}{A}$$

or

$$\frac{dV}{dK} = g\frac{V}{A} \tag{9.3}$$

This means that the shadow price g determines how a change in knowledge stock K affects the capitalized value V. The objective is to estimate the shadow price g. The estimated shadow price must be normalized by the ratio V/A, which is observable. For example, one can use the average V of the sample divided by the average A.

If the knowledge stock K is measured as an accumulation of R&D spending over time, perhaps depreciated for obsolescence, then $g(V/A)$ tells us the boost to a firm's capitalized value that comes from a boost in its R&D spending. If the knowledge stock K is measured as a patent count, then $g(V/A)$ tells us the boost due to an additional patent.

Cockburn and Griliches (1988) estimated a regression equation like (9.2), using two knowledge variables instead of one, namely, R&D stocks and patent counts. They showed that if only the patent counts are included, then the estimated value contributed by a patent is about $500,000 in 1980 dollars. However, if R&D is added as a second knowledge variable in the equation, much of the explanatory value is transferred to R&D, and the marginal value of a patent falls to about one-quarter of its previous value. Thus, although patent counts have an impact on firm value, they are not the whole story, and not even the most important story.

More recent studies use the rich store of information contained in the patent document itself, in particular, citation counts. A patent must cite all the "prior art" that is relevant to it, and will be cited as prior art for future patents in the same technology line. These citations are respectively called backward citations and forward citations. It is not obvious in advance how citations should correlate with a patent's value. One possibility is that citations indicate there are rivals in the same technology line, which would reduce the value of the patent. Instead, Harhoff et al. (1999) show, based on their survey of German patents, that both backward and forward citations are positively correlated with patent value.

Since citations are a predictor of patent value, they might be a better predictor of how R&D affects firm value than, for example, R&D spending or patent counts. This hypothesis is investigated by Hall, Jaffe, and Trajtenberg (2004), who estimate the amount of variation in firms' value that can be accounted for by patent counts, patent citation counts, and R&D spending. They again find that R&D spending explains more of the variation in firms' values than either patent counts or citations, although citations add additional explanatory value, and are themselves a better predictor than patent counts. The importance of R&D spending, eclipsing patents or even citations, reinforces the finding in table 9.1 that firms protect the output of their R&D efforts in many ways that do not involve intellectual property.

The papers using this methodology reinforce the conclusion that firms increase R&D spending up to the point that the marginal R&D investment has more or less the same value as a capital investment.

The rich data available about patents provide many other avenues for inquiry. For example, Putnam (1996) shows that the number of jurisdictions in which the same invention is patented, called "family size," is also highly correlated with patent values.

9.4   Summary

Private spending on R&D shows up in the data as private value. Further, the marginal private return to R&D spending is comparable to the marginal return to investment in ordinary capital goods. However, this does not answer the main question of whether the amount of R&D spending is optimal from a social point of view. Private R&D spending may be either excessive, due to overly attractive R&D incentives, or deficient, due to spillovers.

In contrast, the value of public spending on R&D is hard to find in the data. Evidently, firms capture very little of this value. Following the logic of chapter 2, this is as it should be: knowledge is a public good, and if provided by the taxpayers, it should be put in the public domain for the benefit of everyone. Although this avoids deadweight loss, it also prevents the benefits from showing up as profit. This leaves us without markers to show whether public spending has taken the right path. Despite the discussion in chapter 8 of how the outputs of public spending are increasingly being privatized, privatization is still far from complete.

The evidence indicates that a remarkably small percentage of R&D expenditures are recovered as profit due to patent grants. This is partly because innovators have many other tools at their disposal. We should therefore make a clear distinction between the private value of an invention and the value of a patent. The value of an invention is usually greater than the incremental value of patenting it.

We also saw that patent values are very dispersed, with most of the total value collected by a small percentage of very successful inventions.

Skewness implies that an observed discrepancy between the profitability of high-profit patents and the costs of achieving them may be appropriate. It is the *expected* payoff of an R&D investment that matters for incentives. If the R&D investments fail with high probability, they must pay off handsomely in the case of success in order to create incentives for research.

References and Further Reading

Abramovitz, M. 1956a. "Catching Up, Forging Ahead, and Falling Behind." *Journal of Economic History* 46:385–406.

Abramovitz, M. 1956b. "Resources and Output Trends in the U.S. Since 1870." *American Economics Associations Papers and Proceedings* 46:5–23.

Adams, J. 1990. "Fundamental Stocks of Knowledge and Productivity Growth." *Journal of Political Economy* 98:673–702.

Allison, J. R., and M. A. Lemley. 2002. "The Growing Complexity of the United States Patent System." *Boston University Law Review* 82:77–145.

Bound, J., C. Cummins, Z. Griliches, B. H. Hall, and A. B. Jaffe. 1984. "Who Does R&D and Who Patents?" In Z. Griliches, ed., *R&D, Patents and Productivity*, 21–54. Chicago: University of Chicago Press.

Bresnahan, T. F. 1986. "Measuring Spillovers from Technical Advance: Mainframe Computers in Financial Services." *American Economic Review* 76:741–755.

Cockburn, I., and Z. Griliches. 1988. "Industry Effects and Appropriability Measures in the Stock Market's Valuation of R&D and Patents." *American Economic Review* 78:419–423.

Cockburn, I., and R. Henderson. 2003. "Survey Results from the 2003 Intellectual Property Owners Association Survey on Strategic Management of Intellectual Property." Mimeograph. Boston, MA: Department of Economics, Boston University, and Cambridge, MA: Department of Economics, MIT.

Cohen, W. M., R. R. Nelson, and J. P. Walsh. 2000. "Protecting Their Intellectual Assets: Appropriability Conditions and Why U.S. Manufacturing Firms Patent (or Not)." Working Paper 7552. Cambridge, MA: National Bureau of Economic Research.

Cornelli, F., and M. Schankerman. 1999. "Patent Renewals and R&D Incentives." *RAND Journal of Economics* 30:197–213.

Crampes, C., and C. Langinier. 1998. "Information Disclosure in the Renewal of Patents." *Annales d'Economie et de Statistique* 49/50:262–288.

Dernburg, T., and N. Gharrity. 1962. "A Statistical Analysis of Patent Renewal Data for Three Countries." *Patent, Trademark and Copyright Journal* 5:340–361.

Giummo, J. M. 2003. "An Empirical Examination of the Value of Patented Inventions Using German Employee Inventors' Compensation Records." Unpublished doctoral dissertation, Department of Economics, UC Berkeley.

Gollop, F. M., B. M. Fraumeni, and D. W. Jorgenson. 1999. *Productivity and U.S. Economic Growth*. Cambridge, MA: MIT Press.

Grabowski, H., and J. Vernon. 1990. "A New Look at the Returns and Risks to Pharmaceutical R&D." *Management Science* 36:804–821.

Grabowski, H., and J. Vernon. 1996. "Returns on New Drug Introductions in the 1980s." *Journal of Health Economics* 13:383–406.

Graham, S., B. H. Hall, D. Harhoff, and D. Mowery. 2003. "Patent Quality Control: A Comparison of U.S. Patent Re-examinations and European Patent Oppositions." In W. Cohen and S. A. Merrill, eds., *Patents in the Knowledge-Based Economy*, 74–119. Washington, DC: National Academies Press.

Griliches, Z. 1988. "Productivity Puzzles and R&D: Another Nonexplanation." *Journal of Economic Perspectives* 2:9–21.

Griliches, Z. 1989. "Patents: Recent Trends and Puzzles." *Brookings Papers on Economic Activity, Microeconomics*. Washington, DC: Brookings Institution.

Griliches, Z. 1990. "Patent Statistics as Economic Indicators: A Survey." *Journal of Economic Literature* 28:1661–1707.

Griliches. 1994. "Productivity, R&D, and the Data Constraint." *American Economic Review* 84:1–23.

Griliches, Z., B. H. Hall, and A. Pakes. 1987. "The Value of Patents as Indicators of Inventive Activity." In P. Dasgupta and P. Stoneman, eds., *Economic Policy and Technological Performance*, 97–124. Cambridge: Cambridge University Press.

Hall, B. H. 1986. "Fishing out or Crowding Out: An Analysis of the Recent Decline in U.S. Patenting." Mimeograph. Berkeley, CA: Department of Economics, UC, Berkeley. Available at emlab.berkeley.edu/users/bhhall/bhpapers.html#value.

Hall, B. H. 1996. "The Private and Social Returns to Research and Development: What Have We Learned?" In B. L. R. Smith and C. E. Barfield, eds., *Technology, R&D, and the Economy*, 140–183. Washington, DC: The Brookings Institution and American Enterprise Institute.

Hall, B. 1999. "Private and Social Returns to R&D." Remarks before the British Treasury. Powerpoint slides. Available at emlab.berkeley.edu/users/bhhall/bhpapers.html#value.

Hall, B. H. 2000. "Innovation and Market Value." In R. Barrell, G. Mason and M. O'Mahoney, eds., *Productivity, Innovation and Economic Performance*, 177–198. New York: Cambridge University Press.

Hall, B. H., A. B. Jaffe, and M. Trajtenberg. 2002. "The NBER Patent Citations Data File: Lessons, Insights and Methodological Tools." Cambridge, MA: MIT Press.

Hall, B. H., A. B. Jaffe, and M. Trajtenberg. 2004. "Market Value and Patent Citations." Forthcoming in *RAND Journal of Economics*.

Hall, B. H., and J. Mairesse. 1995. "Exploring the Relationship between R&D and Productivity in French Manufacturing Firms." *Journal of Econometrics* 65:263–298.

Harhoff, D., F. Narin, F. M. Scherer, and K. Vopel. 1999. "Citation frequency and value of patented inventions." *Review of Economics and Statistics* 81:511–515.

Harhoff, D., F. M. Scherer, and K. Vopel. 2003. "Citations, Family Size, Opposition and the Value of Patent Rights: Evidence from Germany." *Research Policy* 32:1343–1363.

Hausman, J., B. H. Hall, and Z. Griliches. 1984. "Econometric Models for Count Data with an Application to the Patents-R&D Relationship." *Econometrica* 52:909–938.

Jaffe, A. B. 1986. "Technological Opportunity and Spillovers of R&D." *American Economic Review* 76:984–1001.

Jaffe, A. B., and M. Trajtenberg. 2002. *Patents, Citations, and Innovations: A Window on the Knowledge Economy.* Cambridge, MA: MIT Press.

Jaffe, A. B., M. Trajtenberg, and R. Henderson. 1993. "Geographic Localization of Knowledge Spillovers as Evidenced by Patent Citations." *Quarterly Journal of Economics* 108:577–598.

Jorgenson, D. W. 1995a. *Productivity, Vol. 1: Postwar U.S. Economic Growth.* Cambridge, MA: MIT Press.

Jorgenson, D. W. 1995b. *Productivity, Vol. 2: International Comparisons of Economic Growth.* Cambridge, MA: MIT Press.

Jorgenson, D., F. Gollop, and B. Fraumeni. 1987. *Productivity and U.S. Economic Growth,* Cambridge, MA: Harvard University Press.

Kortum, S., and J. Lerner. 1999. "What Is Behind the Recent Surge in Patenting." *Research Policy* 28:1–22.

Lanjouw, J. O. 1998. "Patent Protection in the Shadow of Infringement: Simulation Estimations of Patent Value." *Review of Economic Studies* 65: 671–710.

Lanjouw, J. O., and M. Schankerman. 2004. "Patent Quality and Research Productivity: Measurement with Multiple Indicators." *Economic Journal* 114:441–465.

Lerner, J. 1994. "The Importance of Patent Scope: An Empirical Analysis." *RAND Journal of Economics* 25:319–333.

Mansfield, E., J. Rapoport, A. Romeo, S. Wagner, and G. Beardsley. 1977. "Social and Private Rates of Return from Industrial Innovations." *Quarterly Journal of Economics* 91:221–240.

Merges, R. 1999. "As Many as Six Impossible Patents Before Breakfast: Property Rights for Business Concepts and Patent System Reform." *Berkeley High Technology Law Journal* 14:577–615.

Nagaoka, S. 2003. "Determinants of R&D and Its Productivity: Identifying Demand and Supply Channels." Working Paper #03-12. Tokyo: Institute of Innovation Research, Hitotsubashi University.

Nagaoka, S. 2004a. "Evaluating the R&D Management of Firms by Patent Citation." Mimeograph (preliminary draft). Tokyo: Institute of Innovation Research, Hitotsubashi University.

Nagaoka, S. 2004b. "R&D and Market Value: Appropriability vs. Preemption." Working Paper #04-03. Tokyo: Institute of Innovation Research, Hitotsubashi University.

National Science Board. 2002. *Science and Engineering Indicators—2002.* Arlington, VA: National Science Foundation, 2002 (NSB-02-01).

Nicholson, W. 1995. *Microeconomic Theory: Basic Principles and Extensions,* 6th ed. New York: Dryden Press.

Ord-Hume, A. W. J. G. 1977. *Perpetual Motion: The History of an Obsession.* New York: St. Martin's Press.

Pakes, A. 1985. "On Patents, R&D and the Stock Market Rates of Return." *Journal of Political Economy* 93:390–409.

Pakes, A. 1986. "Patents as Options: Some Estimates of the Value of Holding European Patent Stocks." *Econometrica* 54:755–784.

Pakes, A., and M. Schankerman. 1984. "The Rate of Obsolescence of Patents, Research Gestation Lags, and the Private Rate of Return to Research Resources." In Z. Griliches, ed., *R&D, Patents, and Productivity,* 164–190. Chicago: University of Chicago Press.

Putnam, J. 1996. "The Value of International Patent Rights." Unpublished doctoral dissertation, Department of Economics, Yale University.

Rossman, J., and B. S. Sanders. 1957. "The Patent Utilization Study." *Patent, Trademark and Copyright Journal* 1:74–111.

Sanders, B. S., J. Rossman, and L. J. Harris. 1958. "The Economic Impact of Patents." *Patent, Trademark and Copyright Journal* 2:340–362.

Schankerman, M. 1998. "How Valuable Is Patent Protection? Estimates by Technology Field." *RAND Journal of Economics* 29:77–107.

Schankerman, M., and A. Pakes. 1986. "Estimates of the Value of Patent Rights in European Countries during the Post-1950 Period." *Economic Journal* 97:1052–1076.

Scherer, F. M. 1965a. "Corporate Inventive Output, Profits and Growth." *Journal of Political Economy* 73:290–297.

Scherer, F. M. 1965b. "Firm Size, Market Structure, Opportunity and the Output of Patented Inventions." *American Economic Review* 55:1097–1125.

Scherer, F. M. 1983. "The Propensity to Patent." *International Journal of Industrial Organization* 1:107–128.

Scherer, F. M. 1984a. *Innovation and Growth: Schumpeterian Perspectives.* Cambridge, MA: MIT Press.

Scherer, F. M. 1984b. "Using Linked Patent and R&D Data to Measure Interindustry Technology Flows." In Griliches, ed., *R&D, Patents and Productivity*, 417–464. Chicago: University of Chicago Press.

Scherer, F. M. 1998. "The Size Distribution of Profits from Innovation." *Annales d'Economie et de Statistique* 49/50:495–516.

Scherer, F. M., and D. Harhoff. 2000. "Technology Policy for a World of Skew-Distributed Outcomes." *Research Policy* 29:559–566.

Schmookler, J. 1966. *Invention and Economic Growth.* Cambridge, MA: Harvard University Press.

Scotchmer, S. 1999. "On the Optimality of the Patent Renewal System." *RAND Journal of Economics* 30:181–196.

Solow, R. M. 1956. "A Contribution to the Theory of Economic Growth." *Quarterly Journal of Economics* 70:65–94.

Solow, R. M. 1957. "Technical Change and the Aggregate Production Function." *Review of Economics and Statistics* 39:312–320.

Stern, S., M. E. Porter, and J. L. Furman. 2002. "The Determinants of National Innovative Capacity." Working Paper 7876. Cambridge, MA: National Bureau of Economic Research.

Stigler, G. J. 1947. *Trends in Output and Employment.* New York: National Bureau of Economic Research.

Trajtenberg, M. 1990a. *Economic Analysis of Product Innovation: The Case of CT Scanners.* Cambridge, MA: Harvard University Press.

Trajtenberg, M. 1990b. "A Penny for Your Quotes: Patent Citations and the Value of Innovations." *RAND Journal of Economics* 21:172–187.

Trajtenberg, M. 1993. "The Welfare Analysis of Product Innovations, with an Application to Computed Tomography Scanners." *Journal of Political Economy* 97:444–479.

U.S. Department of Commerce. 2000. "Digital Economy 2000." Available at www.esa.doc.gov/pdf/DIGITAL.pdf.

The World Bank Group. 2004. "Data and Statistics." Available at www.worldbank.org/data/databytopic/GDP.pdf.

10 Networks and Network Effects

In chapter 5, we discussed how technology rolls forward in a process of creative destruction governed, among other things, by intellectual property. Intellectual property affects competition between successive market incumbents, the average duration of market incumbency, and—through the incentive to make improvements—the pace of progress. The market dynamics in which one product replaces another have been particularly evident in digital technologies such as video games, text-editing software, Internet browsers, spreadsheets, and operating systems.

This chapter revisits the phenomenon of market turnover and market entrenchment in a context where proprietary products are subject to *network effects*. A network is a group of consumers who consume the same good or a compatible good. The network confers *network benefits* if the utility it provides to each individual user increases with the total number of users. An example of a good with network benefits is text-editing software. The value to each user is greater if he or she can share files with other users. For example, students can send their homework to professors by e-mail, coauthors can work alternately on the same document file, and editors can insert their changes directly into authors' documents. A network good can also be created by a common standard, such as the convention that cars have brake pedals on the left and gas pedals on the right. The standard allows drivers to share cars.

These are examples of "direct" network benefits in the sense that the number of other users affects a user's utility function directly. "Indirect" network effects arise when users care about some feature of the network good that is likely to be enhanced in a large network, such as the number of applications developed for an operating system, but do not care directly about the number of users.

The interplay among network effects, intellectual property, and innovation was central in the 1998 lawsuit, *U.S. v. Microsoft*, brought by the Department of Justice (DOJ). So far, this case and its kin brought in Europe and by individual U.S. state governments are the main cases where competition policy has met network effects. Although the 1998 case reveals that network effects have important effects on market outcomes, particularly in conjunction with intellectual property in an innovation context, the case was ultimately decided on relatively narrow factual circumstances. It therefore left unanswered many policy questions that are likely to resurface.

The DOJ charged that Microsoft illegally attempted to monopolize the market for Intel-compatible operating systems and the browser market.[1] The trial court agreed and ordered Microsoft broken up. Microsoft appealed to the D.C. Circuit.

The court begins its analysis by complaining that "there is no consensus among commentators on the question of whether, and to what extent, current monopolization doctrine should be amended to account for competition in technologically dynamic markets characterized by network effects." In this chapter we consider some of the economic complexities behind the court's remarks.

The core of the court's dilemma is that under the Sherman Act, attempts to acquire or maintain a monopoly are illegal, even though merely being a monopolist is not. This distinction is especially important in markets with intellectual property, since intellectual property already grants a "legal monopoly." As pointed out in chapter 5, well-designed intellectual property rights can create healthy competition for product improvements, and can lead to sequential market dominance. With sequential dominance, any snapshot of the market will turn up a firm with high market share, but its dominance may be short lived. This was one of Microsoft's replies to the district court's finding that it had 95 percent of the market for Intel-compatible desktop operating systems.

Microsoft's other reply was that the market for operating systems should be defined to include all operating systems that run the same "middleware," and in that market, they did not have a 95 percent share. Middleware is software such as Netscape or Java that sits between the operating system and the application, and makes the application com-

---

1.   In addition to these two charges under section 2 of the Sherman Act, the DOJ brought exclusive dealing and tying charges under section 1. These were respectively rejected by the appellate court and remanded for further consideration. For a discussion of the economics related to these claims, see Gilbert and Katz 2001.

patible with the operating system. Like Windows Internet Explorer, Netscape lets users access the web. Java was a development tool created for the express purpose of making applications cross-platform compatible. If the market is defined to include all the operating systems that run the same middleware, the Windows operating system does not have a 95 percent share.

The court rejected this argument, holding instead that middleware had not yet achieved the objective of creating a unified market that extended to all operating systems, and that, by trying to kill the cross-platform capabilities of Java and Netscape, Microsoft was trying to avoid that outcome.

In trying to kill these cross-platform capabilities, Microsoft was overzealous and committed various "bad acts" that made it liable under the antitrust laws. These bad acts included putting pressure on vendors not to ship Netscape to buyers. In addition, Microsoft created a so-called polluted Java that ran faster on Windows than the original Java, but was no longer cross-platform compatible. The court would have accepted polluted Java as a legitimate technical choice except for evidence that Microsoft deceived applications developers into thinking that polluted Java still had cross-platform capabilities.

In retrospect, it seems possible that Microsoft could have achieved the same results without resorting to the specific acts that the court relied on to make its judgment. The case therefore does not reach the deeper questions of whether any of this should be illegal as a business strategy. What is proper conduct in network markets? Where do legitimate business strategies stop and illegal attempts to monopolize begin? We will return to the Microsoft case later in this chapter.

The main objective of this chapter is to develop the ideas of direct and indirect network effects, and how they may cause the market to tip entirely to one product. The need for a common physical infrastructure additionally changes the way network effects do their work. This is illustrated using the examples of the Internet and cell phone standards.

Intellectual property is the policy lens through which we will view the problem of market power in the presence of network effects and exclusive applications. There are three parts of a system that might be protected: the operating system itself, the interface that allows applications to run on the operating system, and the applications. It is natural to assume that the operating system and applications are true "inventions" that need to be protected, but interfaces are not always in the same category.

10.1   Direct Network Benefits

In the "old" microeconomics, consumers' demands for products depend only on the relative prices of the products, and not, for example, on consumption by other consumers. Thus, each consumer's demand curve stays fixed if the other consumers make different decisions about what to consume. With fixed demand curves, consumers make their choices based on price alone. If a single price rises, each consumer reduces his or her consumption of the good, moving along the demand curve. In contrast, in a market with direct network benefits, each consumer's willingness to pay for a good depends on the number of other users. Because of this, consumer demand is described differently than in chapters 2 and 4.

Instead of writing the demand function as the quantity demanded (or number of buyers) depending on price, as in chapters 2 and 4, we will write demand as a willingness-to-pay function. To define the willingness-to-pay function, line up the consumers on the horizontal axis, each θ representing a different consumer. The height of the willingness-to-pay function at θ is the maximum amount that the consumer θ could pay for the good and still be better off than not consuming it. The consumers are ordered such that, for two consumers, θ and θ', the consumer named θ has higher willingness to pay than the consumer named θ' if $\theta < \theta'$. This is why the willingness-to-pay functions are downward sloping.

Three willingness-to-pay functions of the form $w(\cdot, n)$ are drawn in figure 10.1. The variable n is the network size. By including it as a variable in the willingness-to-pay function, we recognize that each consumer's willingness to pay depends on the network size. This captures the notion that for goods like text editors, each consumer's willingness to pay for the good depends on how many others are using it. In the figure, the network sizes are ordered $n_o < n_m < n_c$. Consider the consumer named θ_o. Looking vertically upward at the two curves above θ_o, we see that the consumer's willingness to pay in a network of size n_m is larger than his or her willingness to pay in a network of size n_o—that is, $w(\theta_o, n_o) < w(\theta_o, n_m)$. Since the willingness-to-pay curves satisfy $w(\theta, n_o) < w(\theta, n_m) < w(\theta, n_c)$ for each θ, the willingness to pay of each consumer increases with the size of the network.

In the old microeconomics, equilibrium entails that each consumer buys the good if his willingness to pay, as indicated by the demand curve, is greater than the price. With network effects the same principle applies,

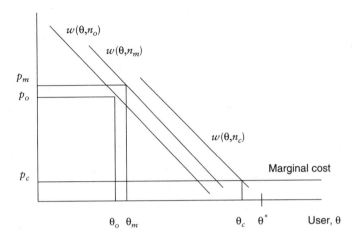

Figure 10.1
Pricing in network markets

but we must ask, which demand curve? The demand curve shifts every time the price changes, because a different price elicits a different number of users, and each user's willingness to pay depends on the number of other users.[2]

Figure 10.1 is labeled using the convention that there are n_o users with willingness to pay at least as high as the consumer labeled θ_o, n_m users with willingness to pay at least as high as the consumer labeled θ_m, and n_c users with willingness to pay at least as high as the consumer labeled θ_c. Thus, at price p_o, there are n_o users $\theta < \theta_o$ who buy the good. It would be inconsistent to read the number of users at price p_o from the demand curve $w(\cdot, n_m)$ because there are only n_o users, not n_m users, such that $\theta \leq \theta_o$.

Figure 10.1 thus shows three situations that the monopoly seller could find herself in, selling at three different prices, $p_o = w(\theta_o, n_o)$, $p_m = w(\theta_m, n_m)$, $p_c = w(\theta_c, n_c)$.

Note that neither the price nor the revenue at that price is monotonic in the size of the network. Even though $\theta_o < \theta_m < \theta_c$ so that $n_o < n_m < n_c$, it does not hold (as it would in a market without network benefits) that $p_o > p_m > p_c$. Instead, $p_m > p_o > p_c$.

---

2.   See Farrell and Klemperer 2001 for a discussion of the antecedents of this idea and others in this chapter, and for more precise discussions of how expectations about the ultimate size of the network may be formed.

The monopolist earns more profit at the combination (p_m, n_m) than at the combination (p_o, n_o), and earns zero profit at the combination (p_c, n_c), since p_c is equal to marginal cost. The small network n_o cannot sustain a high price because the network is too small to support a high willingness to pay. On the other hand, a very large network n_c might also not sustain a high price because, to expand the network that far, consumers with lower and lower willingness to pay must be included. The price is equal to the willingness to pay of the marginal consumer. As the network expands, the increasing network benefits might not outweigh the fall in willingness to pay of the marginal consumer. If so, there will be some intermediate-size network that maximizes the revenue. In figure 10.1, the most profitable size is n_m.

We can use figure 10.1 to understand three focal sizes of the network: the socially efficient size, the size that a monopolist supplier would prefer, and the size that a competitive market would support. These arguments are given formally in technical note 10.5.1. Figure 10.1 shows that the optimal-size network may be smaller than the whole potential user group, and that the networks produced by both a competitive market and a monopolist are likely to be inefficiently small. However, if the network effects are strong enough (not shown in figure 10.1), a monopolist seller and a competitive market would both include the whole potential user group, and that would be optimal.

If the standard that defines this network market is proprietary—for example, text-editing software or an operating system—the seller can choose the price. If the standard is an "open" standard not owned by anyone, firms will enter in response to positive profit and depress the price to marginal cost, p_c. The locations of the brake and gas pedals are an example of an open standard. All car manufacturers adhere to the standard, but if it were for some reason proprietary (patent law has not yet gone this far), then one could imagine that manufacturers would have to pay for locating their pedals in that way. Competing standards might develop.

In a competitive market, an open standard will lead to marginal-cost pricing—that is, p_c in figure 10.1. However, even marginal-cost pricing will lead to a network that is inefficiently small. The optimal usage may be represented by a marginal user such as θ^* in figure 10.1. This is because the network benefits are an uncompensated externality. Pushing the usage beyond n_c creates benefits for the other members of the network. Since the marginal users do not account for the external benefits, their decision whether to join the network at the marginal-cost price is socially too conservative. To put this another way, the other members of the network would pay the marginal entrant to join, but have no institutional way to do so.

A proprietor will prefer an even smaller network—for example, the combination (p_m, n_m). This is the usual problem that arises as a consequence of monopoly: in order to maximize profit, the proprietor must inefficiently restrict usage. However, in network markets, the proprietor has an additional problem. How can the price and network combination (p_m, n_m) be guaranteed? This is by no means easy, and depends on where the proprietor starts. For example, if the proprietor is an entrant trying to introduce a new standard, she will have to build the market from nothing, perhaps luring customers away from other networks.

Table 5.1 shows how software products have sequentially invaded the market, driving out previous products as innovators made improvements. That kind of tippiness—the market tipping from one product to the next—is also (perhaps especially) a feature of network markets. The inertia created by network effects can work in both directions: it can foster market conservatism or lead to avalanches of adoption.

Adoptions in network markets are likely to be driven by users' expectations about prices, other users' adoptions, and the likelihood of new products entering the market. Entrants' pricing policies must take account of this. To build a network, the proprietor needs some early adopters. Early adopters of a new network good may fear they will be left stranded if everyone else chooses a different network. This may kill the network before it gets started. To attract the initial adopters, the network owner must convince them that the network will be successful, perhaps offering additional incentives like a price break.

Referring again to figure 10.1, suppose that by random good luck or an introductory offer, the proprietor gets into the market with a small user base, such as n_o in figure 10.1. Other potential users may be using a rival product or no substitute product at all. Simply raising the price to p_m is likely to have the opposite effect of that intended: the proprietor may scare customers away instead of attracting them. To attract them, she will have to organize a concerted action so that many join her network at the same time, raising its value to each user. That is probably easiest if she lowers the price in the first instance, even though she eventually wants to raise it.

The customers that the entrant is trying to lure may be of two types: current users of a previous network and neophyte users entering the market for the first time. Even with high expectations of success, it may be difficult to lure customers of the current market incumbent. They have already paid for the previous good, and goods such as software can be used forever without paying anything further. This advantage is compounded by the fact that the user might have to bear a switching cost to learn how to use the improved product.[3] The previous incumbent is presumably aware of this advantage and may try to maximize it—for example, by ensuring that the new, improved product is incompatible with his own. For example, when Borland tried to break into the Lotus 1-2-3 market with an improved spreadsheet in the late 1980s, it tried to make its product backward compatible with Lotus 1-2-3. Lotus 1-2-3 filed a lawsuit alleging copyright infringement, presumably to preserve a switching advantage.

Thus, even where customers of the previous incumbent are willing to upgrade to an improved product, the entrant may have to offer a deal that is considerably better than the value of the improvement. These market dynamics are slightly different than the ones described in chapter 5, in the sense that switching costs and network benefits make it harder for an improved product to drive out an entrenched product. Nevertheless, a sufficient improvement may succeed. That said, the incumbent may have more incentive to create improvements than a rival has, which will entrench its market power even further.

All of this calls into question whether an incumbent's share of a network market is a good test of market power for antitrust purposes.[4] With tippy markets, any snapshot of the market will find some firm with a dominant market share. But sequential monopoly is only a problem for competition policy if the price charged by each sequential monopolist is high. As we have argued, the price is constrained at first by the proprietor's need to attract users of the previous product, and later by a fear of scaring users into embracing a successor. The same fears will cause the incumbent to keep innovating.

High prices are only one source of inefficiency in network markets. If it is difficult to start an avalanche of buying, an entrant may have trouble entering the market despite a superior product. Ease of entry depends largely on consumers' expectations about the adoptions of others. As a consequence, the market may coordinate on the wrong standard, or fail to switch to a new standard that is better.[5] This effect can

---

3.   See Farrell and Klemperer 2001 for a more complete discussion.
4.   See Evans and Schmalensee 2002 for more discussion of this point.
5.   See Farrell and Saloner 1986a, 1986b, 1987; Farrell and Klemperer 2001.

be especially large where the standard is open, since an open standard does not have a proprietor who can profit from trying to organize a switch.[6]

In network markets, there are the same trade-offs between incentives to innovate and protecting consumers from high prices as in any other innovative environment. Open, or nonproprietary, standards are better for consumers once the network good exists, since competition will drive profit to zero. This looks good for consumers, but may also undermine the incentive to improve network goods. Developers of improved products must be granted some immunity from competition in order to recover their costs of innovation. This is the same argument for intellectual property as in other contexts.

Finally, we come to the question of what keeps a network proprietary. So far we have assumed that the proprietor can prevent rivals from entering with products that take advantage of a common network. In fact, however, many network standards are open, so that network goods are competitively supplied. Examples of open standards include sports equipment, where standards for tennis balls, golf balls, and so on are set by clubs that sponsor competitions, and the standard placement of gas pedals and brake pedals in cars. Examples of proprietary network goods are text-editing software and computer games. In addition to the network goods themselves, the interfaces that make software run on certain hardware, such as games on consoles and software on operating systems, may be protected by patents, copyrights, or trade secrets. That is the topic of the next section.

Perhaps the most important example of open standards are the protocols of the Internet. TCP/IP governs data transfer among servers, and HTTP/HTML is a common standard for writing websites that are readable by all browsers. The openness of these standards creates network benefits without monopoly power. If the protocols had been proprietary, competing vendors with different standards would have wanted to gain market dominance and then charge users for access to the Internet. This

6.   See Katz and Shapiro 1994 for examples of inferior standards or products that became entrenched due to network benefits. Liebowitz and Margolis (1999) agree that this is possible in theory but marshal evidence that it has been rare in practice. They argue from contemporaneous product reviews that in many high-profile instances where one network won out over another, it was because the winning product was better. Examples include Excel spreadsheets winning out over Lotus 1-2-3 and Quattro, and VHS winning out over Beta for home video recording. See also Evans, Nichols, and Reddy 1999; David 2000.

standards war did not happen. One reason is that development of these protocols was heavily funded by the public sector. If left to the private sector, the protocols would likely have been proprietary. This would have rewarded the inventors, but might also have retarded the Internet revolution by facilitating high prices and creating compatibility problems.

We have so far not considered the possibility that incompatible proprietary goods can be made compatible by conversion (see Farrell and Saloner 1992). For example, the Microsoft Word and WordPerfect text editors started out as incompatible market rivals, but in current versions, users of either text editor can save files in formats readable by the other. Similarly, software files written for the Apple operating system can be converted so that they can be read on the Windows operating system. In both of these examples, the converted user file runs on proprietary software.

Whether conversion requires a license depends on the nature of the intellectual property. If conversion does not require a license, or can be facilitated by some type of reverse engineering, it will undermine the rightholder's ability to profit from the network, just as if the network good were not protected. If conversion requires a license, then a proprietor can maintain the network monopoly by licensing at a high royalty, so that the market price never falls to marginal cost.

10.2   Systems Competition and Proprietary Interfaces

In contrast to direct network effects, indirect network effects arise because of the feedback between applications development and demand. The stylization is that there is a "platform," such as a game console or a computer operating system, and applications, such as games or text-editing software, which can only be used on that platform. Typically, there is also an interface that makes the applications compatible with the platform (or not). An important part of market structure depends on whether applications are compatible with multiple platforms, or just one.

The indirect network effect arises because applications developers want to write for popular platforms, and consumers want to buy platforms that give access to many applications. Popularity thus feeds on itself, even if there are no direct benefits to consumers of belonging to a network with many members. As a consequence, the proprietor of a platform can try to tip the market to its platform, by creating many exclusive applications. It then becomes very difficult for a rival to enter without a menu of comparable applications.

Following is a simple economic model that shows why proprietary standards might tip a market to monopoly. Assume that platform owners sell systems with incompatible software. If there are two systems, consumers may intrinsically prefer one to the other, but their preference can be overcome by higher quality (more applications) or lower price. As a consequence one system may drive the other out of the market.

Assume there are two competing platforms, and that each consumer must choose one platform or none. Each consumer has a preference parameter θ that designates how much more (or less, if θ is negative) the consumer is willing to pay for platform 1 than for platform 2. If platform 1 has a_1 applications and is sold at price p_1, assume that the utility received by a consumer with taste parameter θ is $\theta + (a_1 - p_1)$. Similarly, the utility received by a consumer of platform 2 is $a_2 - p_2$. The consumer buys platform 1 rather than platform 2 if

$$\theta + (a_1 - p_1) \geq (a_2 - p_2)$$

This relationship makes it clear that, out of the total potential users, the number who use each platform will depend on their relative advantages, $(a_1 - p_1)$ and $(a_2 - p_2)$. If $(a_1 - p_1) > (a_2 - p_2)$, then only those users with a strong preference for platform 2 (negative θ) will buy platform 2. From this fact, and the distribution of θ, we can derive the numbers of users of the platforms, as they depend on the prices and applications. These are the demand curves shown in figure 10.2, $n_1(p_1; p_2, a_1, a_2)$ and $n_2(p_2; p_1, a_1, a_2)$. They are derived more formally in technical note 10.5.2.

Figure 10.2 shows consumer demand for the two platforms when $a_1 > a_2$. The demand for each platform depends on the price of the other, as well as on the numbers of applications. The numbers of applications (a_1, a_2) are assumed to be fixed, and the firms' demands, $n_1(p_1; \hat{p}_2, a_1, a_2)$ and $n_2(p_2; \hat{p}_1, a_1, a_2)$, are each evaluated at a fixed price for the other platform.

When the proprietor of platform 1 considers the demand response to a change in his own price or applications, he assumes that the price of platform 2 stays fixed at $\hat{p}_2$, and symmetrically for platform 2.

We now investigate the prices that platform owners will charge, and whether they have incentive to increase the number of applications in order to boost demand. That is, what determines $\hat{p}_1$ and $\hat{p}_2$? In practice, the incentives will depend on the market dynamics, as discussed earlier for direct network benefits. However, insight can be gained by

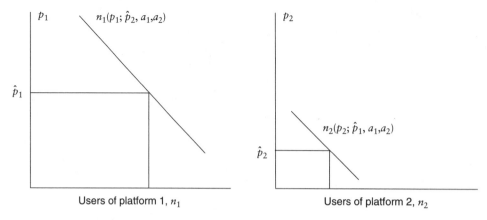

Figure 10.2
Demand for integrated systems

considering a static stylization of the problem in which the firms first commit to their applications (a_1, a_2) and then set their prices (p_1, p_2).

Figure 10.2 shows an asymmetric situation where firm 1 provides more applications than firm 2. We use this diagram to show that an initial advantage in applications can feed on itself to drive the other firm out of the market. In the two diagrams, the equilibrium prices are $(\hat{p}_1, \hat{p}_2)$. These depend on the applications (a_1, a_2) already in place. With the numbers of applications fixed at (a_1, a_2) , firm 1's equilibrium price $\hat{p}_1$ is optimal conditional on firm 2's price, and vice versa. Firm 1's optimal price $\hat{p}_1$ is the solution to

$$\max_{p_1} \; p_1 \, n_1(p_1; \hat{p}_2, a_1, a_2) \tag{10.1}$$

and symmetrically for firm 2.

In characterizing the prices, we are assuming that the costs of developing the applications and platforms are sunk, and (for simplicity) that the marginal cost of providing access to an additional consumer is zero. In deciding how high to price—in other words, in finding the solution to (10.1)—firm 1 takes account of firm 2's price $\hat{p}_2$, and of both firms' attractiveness in terms of applications, but assumes that they are fixed.

The prices $\hat{p}_1, \hat{p}_2$ shown in figure 10.2 are equilibrium prices that solve (10.1) and symmetrically for firm 2. In technical note 10.5.2, the solution is worked out algebraically. The incentives to change price can be seen intuitively by inspecting figure 10.2. In choosing its price, firm

1 (symmetrically, firm 2) takes $(\hat{p}_2, a_1, a_2)$ as fixed, so that its own demand curve is fixed. If firm 1 changes its own price, demand will shift along the demand curve. A marginal price increase will reduce revenue by reducing the number of customers. However, it will also increase revenue by collecting more profit from each customer that remains. When these two effects cancel, the firm has no incentive to either raise or lower price. The optimal price thus has a property familiar from monopoly markets: each firm sets the price where marginal revenue equals marginal cost. This implies that the firm with more applications (higher demand) will charge a higher price, as shown. These are the pricing rules that the firms anticipate when they choose their applications initially.

We can now ask what combinations of applications (a_1, a_2) will be stable in the sense that neither firm has an incentive to increase or decrease its applications, realizing that such a change will have an impact on both firms' prices. Figure 10.3 shows how applications and consumer demand feed on each other. The higher demand curve in figure 10.3 represents the increased demand for platform 1 when another application is added—that is when a_1 becomes $\hat{a}_1$. If firm 1 then raises the price just enough to keep the net attractiveness of the platform fixed (it increases price to $\tilde{p}_1$), then the number of users of each platform stays fixed, and firm 1 collects more revenue in amount equal to the horizontally striped area. Alternatively, firm 1 might keep its price fixed and thus attract customers from the other platform. This would increase its profit in amount

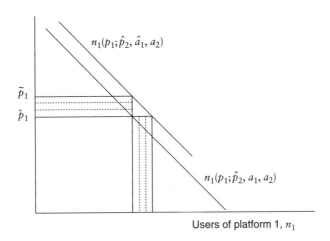

Users of platform 1, n_1

Figure 10.3
Profiting from more applications

equal to the vertically striped area. Finally, firm 1 could choose a price between these extremes, collecting more revenue from each user but also attracting some customers from the other platform.

Now compare the profit opportunities available to firm 2 (not shown), which starts with fewer applications and a lower price. If firm 2 adds another application, the profit opportunities will be described in a diagram similar to figure 10.3, but with a lower demand curve, hence lower profit opportunities. This suggests that the firm with more applications has a bigger incentive to increase them still more until the other platform finally drops out of the market.

Of course this story does not account for the fact that both firms will change their prices in response to either firm's change in applications. Nevertheless, it suggests correctly that the asymmetric situation described in figure 10.2 will not be an equilibrium. The equilibrium described here is solved in technical note 10.5.2. There are only two types of equilibria: the firms can share the market equally, or one firm can drop out entirely. However, the equal-sharing solution is dynamically unstable for the reasons shown in figure 10.3. In fact, this argument may explain why Microsoft was so keen to diminish the cross-platform capabilities of Netscape and Java. Once it was in the dominant market position, it could entrench that position by creating capabilities and applications exclusive to Microsoft.

The fact that closed standards may tip the market to a single platform, so that one proprietor ends up with an "applications barrier to entry" like that in the Microsoft case, is only the beginning of the story. There are at least three subsidiary questions to address: (1) From society's perspective, is tipping to a single standard necessarily a bad outcome? (2) From a business perspective, when do firms prefer closed interfaces, and when do they prefer open interfaces? (3) From society's perspective, what policy tools are available to achieve open interfaces when that is best?

As to the first question, a single monopoly with a proprietary standard offers significant efficiency advantages. Every application is available to every user. Further, costs are not duplicated in developing similar applications for different platforms. For both reasons, more applications will be developed, and they will be used by each user. This is shown formally in technical note 10.5.2. In contrast, competition between incompatible systems will lead to duplicated costs, and each system may have fewer applications than the monopoly. However there are also positive aspects. A duopoly may lead to lower prices, and may provide platform variety that consumers value. Other economics models that this one broadly follows (Chou and Shy 1990; Church and Gandal 1992a, 1992b; Farrell and Saloner 1986b) leave the impression that if the market outcome is not efficient, it is generally because there is not enough standardization, even taking account of users' preferences for variety. However, the market outcome depends sensitively on the model, on whether applications can be cross-platform compatible when standards are open, and on whether the platforms and applications are both proprietary.

Given these trade-offs, an open standard might be the best of all possible worlds. With open interfaces, applications need not be under the control of a platform owner. Instead, platforms and applications can be priced and sold separately. Prices for each piece of the system will be determined by the breadth of intellectual property rights rather than by the market entrenchment of a dominant standard due to network effects. Of course, this still does not make network benefits irrelevant. If there are huge network benefits to using a single application, then openness may only transfer the market power from the platform owner to the application owner. The application will be used on all platforms. The main drawback is practical: open standards can be hard to achieve if intellectual property is available for interfaces. (But in at least one case, *Lotus v. Borland* (1995), the court did not uphold copyright in an interface.)

Turning to the second question, whether standards are open or closed is generally a business decision rather than a policy choice. What is the best business strategy? Will proprietors always choose closed interfaces? Referring to the *Microsoft* case, the cross-platform capabilities created by Netscape and Java served as open standards, since they allowed the same applications to run on Windows and other operating systems. But Microsoft seems to have flip-flopped on whether cross-platform compatibility is a good idea. At some point, Microsoft must have consented to making Netscape and Java compatible with the Windows environment, since Microsoft's applications programming interfaces (APIs) are not public. On the other hand, the 1998 case is largely about Microsoft's later attempts to get rid of these capabilities. Apparently its business strategy changed, perhaps in making the transition from young upstart entrant to dominant market incumbent.

The ambiguities of the best business strategy can also be seen in the 1992 case, *Sega v. Accolade*. Sega was an integrated firm that sold game consoles and games, while Accolade was a game developer that supplied games for the IBM platform. Accolade reverse engineered the

Sega interface to make its IBM games compatible with the Sega console. One might have thought that Sega would welcome the additional games, which would make its platform more valuable to consumers. Instead, Sega sued Accolade for copyright infringement of the interface. How should we understand this apparent contradiction?

Sega did not necessarily bring the lawsuit because it thought it would be better off with fewer applications. Rather, it wanted to keep control of its interface. If Accolade needed a license to write for Sega's console, Sega could demand exclusivity. It is true that adapting the IBM games to Sega would dilute any advantage that its rival IBM might have, but making games *exclusive* to Sega would improve its market advantage even further.

The structure of the video-game market has been unstable. This may reflect the incentives to compete for the whole market. However, it also reflects the fact that, in two-sided markets (platforms and applications), there is no reason to think that the market should be driven by one side rather than the other. In the late 1980s and early 1990s, game consoles were provided by integrated vendors, so that games were seldom compatible across consoles. The demand for consoles was driven by the demand for compatible applications. More recently, games have taken center stage. Today, consoles must compete for game developers' favors. In this environment, developers may prefer to make their games compatible with all consoles and to sell them separately.

So far, we have looked at how dominant firms manipulate standards. What about entrants? Apple Computer, which was the first commercially successful desktop computer, was introduced in the early 1980s. It was an integrated system, with proprietary interfaces and proprietary applications. The IBM personal computer, based on the DOS operating system, was introduced shortly afterward. IBM faced a serious challenge in trying to penetrate the market for desktop computers. It therefore chose to make its interfaces open so that third-party vendors could provide a rich supply of applications, and thus make the IBM PC competitive with Apple. The tactic also encouraged third-party computer vendors to enter the market, thereby assuring consumers that IBM would not raise prices if the PC succeeded and leave them unsupported if it did not. IBM's strategy was successful, and in subsequent years the market shares of Apple and the PC reversed. But computer prices also plummeted, which was good for consumers but bad for IBM. Along with applications, the open standards invited entry of clones into the computer hardware market, in direct competition with IBM. Compaq and Dell are among the companies that began manufacturing IBM-compatible desktop computers.

Similar tactics were used in videocassette recorders. Here, the standard referred to certain protocols that allow a videotape to be played in certain players. There were two competing standards in the early 1980s: Sony's Betamax and JVC's VHS. VHS was a second comer and needed a strategy to gain a foothold in the market. It achieved this by making the standard open. Like IBM, its success came at the cost of enabling competition.[7]

Thus, although the best system for society as a whole may be open interfaces with appropriate intellectual property for platforms (hardware) and applications (software), the foregoing cases suggest that firms are often able to keep interfaces proprietary, either as trade secrets or with formal intellectual property protection. Furthermore, they often have an incentive to do so, especially if they can tip the market. The silver lining is that rivals may decide that open interfaces are the best strategy to get into the market. If an entrant succeeds, it will have changed the market structure from one of closed interfaces or standards to one of open interfaces or standards.

Finally, policy tools for keeping interfaces open seem sparse and unreliable. A right to reverse engineer them, such as discussed by Samuelson and Scotchmer (2002), is a partial antidote, but not reliable for complex interfaces such as the APIs in Microsoft Windows. It is also not available for patented interfaces. Courts may occasionally demand that interfaces be made public, but this can only be done if there is a serious antitrust violation. A federal district court found that the "bad acts" identified in the Microsoft case did not rise to this threshold. More generally, the dominant firms in network markets may win their market power quite legally. The best that courts may be able to do in these circumstances is to make sure that firms that promise open standards or interfaces in order to enter a market do not change their minds afterward.

10.3   Physical Networks: The Internet

Who owns the Internet? Who sets the prices for all those fiber-optic lines that send packets of information on their way? How do we pay for it? How *should* we pay for it?

---

7.   See Katz and Shapiro 1994 for more discussion.

A remarkable thing about the Internet is how invisible it is to the end user, as a physical network. In their day, railroads and long-distance telephone service were high-profile undertakings. By contrast, the Internet seems to have simply appeared. In the previous section, we stressed that the Internet is a virtual network stitched together by common protocols of data transfer called TCP/IP, topped by the worldwide web, with common protocols for reading and writing webpages embodied in HTML and related languages. Here we explore the physical side of the Internet. The Internet is mostly a collection of fiber-optic lines carrying data packets, connected by routers and other hardware. In fact, it is a collection of local networks, which can transfer data using standard protocols.

The Internet had its origin in ARPANET in the 1960s and 1970s. ARPANET was a network of computers created by the U.S. Department of Defense's Advanced Research Projects Agency, now known as the Defense Advanced Research Projects Agency or DARPA. DARPA's most enduring innovation was the TCP/IP data-transfer protocols that make the Internet possible. In the 1980s, the Internet was taken over by the National Science Foundation, which wanted to extend data-transfer capabilities to universities and other research institutions. NSF eventually divested its interest to the private sector, and the NSFNET grew into the Internet.

Why, exactly, did the data-transfer capabilities of ARPANET create a globally networked world? Partly it was just an extremely good idea whose time had come. It was embraced wholeheartedly by researchers in government laboratories and universities. In addition, when NSF lifted its restrictions against commercial use, private firms began to interconnect and extend the Internet.

The Internet has a lot in common with "natural monopolies" such as an electricity grid. However, there is an important difference. In addition to being a physical network, the Internet is a virtual network of users who use the same data-transfer protocols to transfer files. Dividing an electricity grid into two grids with different users would not impinge very much on efficiency, as long as each user was connected, and each of the parts had enough power generators and users to smooth supply and demand. But if someone divided the Internet into two networks, either physically or virtually, then the direct network benefits of sharing would be reduced. The same is true of a telephone system. If the physical network is divided, not every pair of users are connected, and the direct network benefits of a unified network are diminished. In the case of the Internet and telephone exchange, a unified network is not only efficient in terms of minimizing the cost of delivering services, like the electricity grid, but it enhances the value to users by letting all of them communicate with each other. It provides direct network benefits. These network benefits strengthen the "naturalness" of monopolies.

In this regard, it is worth pointing out something that did not happen: there was no standards war as to the protocols that would underlie the Internet. The protocols of the Internet and worldwide web were developed at public expense and put in the public domain. Given what turned out to be at stake, that is probably one of the most fortunate accidents in industrial history. Imagine if there had been competing vendors trying to lure users onto different networks with different, incompatible proprietary standards. The importance of this nonproblem will become more apparent when we discuss attempts to establish the third generation of cell phone technologies, where owners used intellectual property to make conflicting standards a reality.

We stressed in section 10.1 that open standards have the virtue in network markets that entry will depress the price to marginal cost, and that this is a better outcome for society than monopoly and also better than having multiple proprietary networks. However, when the standard can only be used in conjunction with a physical network, the prospects for marginal cost pricing might be undermined by natural monopoly. Even if an open standard avoids a standards war, regulation may still be necessary.

Of course, most people do not conceive of the Internet as a monopoly at all, natural or otherwise. Instead we conceive of it as a disorganized and decentralized collection of entrepreneurs attaching and detaching from each other at will. The information highway has different lanes owned by different companies, and there are lots of networked cul de sacs throwing out packets of information that romp merrily down the highway, changing lanes whenever convenient to get there as fast as possible. This does not sound like monopoly.

How, then, is all of this paid for? Who sets the prices, and can they be understood as competitive?

An important feature of natural monopolies is that they cease to be natural monopolies as soon as the original infrastructure reaches capacity, and must be duplicated in order to meet demand. Of course, to engender competition, the duplication must be such that each user has two or more potential suppliers, pricing independently. If each user is still hostage to a single supplier, monopoly power persists. For example, building two electricity grids and dividing the users between them would not get rid of monopoly power. Things might be different if a second firm were allowed to lay transmission lines in the first firm's conduit, so that it reaches the same users. But the first firm is likely to oppose this, forcing competitors to dig new trenches. Given this alternative, it is probably more sensible to regulate the natural monopolist.

In the case of the Internet, increasing capacity generally means laying more fiber-optic cable. Duplication may be expensive in the same way as digging trenches. However, due to the network benefits of interconnection, it seems even more difficult to engender competition on the Internet than on an electricity grid. Even with capacity owned by different firms and reaching all users, the owners of the duplicative infrastructure must interconnect. Because money will change hands when they carry each other's traffic, they may not compete vigorously for users. Competition may be dampened by the fact that the infrastructure providers may profit from carrying each other's traffic.

The problem of interconnection afflicts telecommunications more generally. In 1996, the United States passed a new Telecommunications Act, designed in part to promote competition in local telephone markets, and thus to make them self-regulating. However, the Telecommunications Act does not pretend that just because incumbents are forced to interconnect with rivals, there will be competition. Instead the act sets cost-based "guidelines" for reasonable interconnection fees. (See Benjamin, Lichtman, and Shelanski 2001 or Laffont and Tirole 2000 for more complete discussions.)

It is not our purpose here to unravel the arcane ways telecommunications services are priced and regulated, and the economic consequences, but only to point out that when a unified physical network is needed to achieve the network benefits of an open standard, it is not self-evident that we can rely on competition to avoid monopoly pricing. Nevertheless, we close this discussion with a short overview of how Internet services are priced.

The original public investments in infrastructure provided a cushion of support that launched the Internet and avoided the funding problem, at least in the beginning. After the original infrastructure was privatized, telecommunications companies like MCI and Sprint made available for Internet traffic their long-haul fiber-optic telecommunications lines. Local user networks then began to connect to this backbone infrastructure, with Internet service providers paying the backbone providers and charging their users for access. The backbone providers grant reciprocal "peering" privileges to each other, exchanging similar amounts of Internet traffic without charge.

To oversimplify, users give money to service providers, who give money to backbone providers, who trade traffic with each other. (In some cases, service providers give money to small network providers, who then pay the backbone provider.) There is certainly competition among service providers competing for customers. However, the prices they can offer are constrained by what they pay to the next level up in the hierarchy. If the top level of the hierarchy were a monopoly, competition at the bottom of the hierarchy would not help very much. At the top, the backbone providers increasingly charge traffic-based fees rather than "peering" (Telegeography, 2000). The hope is that backbone providers will compete for paying users since the Internet usually offers several different paths for going from one point to another. Nevertheless, the economic consequences of these arrangements are anything but clear. At root, this system potentially has the same problem as telecommunications more generally, which is that there must be fees for interconnection. If there is a point of stricture where potential competitors price jointly, monopoly pricing can infect the entire system. This is still in flux.

In summary, open standards will not lead to marginal cost pricing if the network is a physical as well as a virtual network. Open standards still have virtues—they can avoid standards wars or competing networks—but they will not have all the virtues pointed to in section 10.1. To emphasize the importance of avoiding standards wars, we now turn to a physical network where intellectual property in standards has defined the market.

10.4 Physical Networks: Cell Phones

An example that links direct network effects, physical networks, and intellectual property is the problem of cell phone standards.

Cell phones transmit information from the user to a cell tower, which then usually connects to the local telephone exchange. The local exchange transmits the information by landline. Information can only be transmitted between the cell phone and tower if both pieces of hardware send and receive information in the same way. They must use the same transmission standard (the same way of coding information in radio waves) and the same radio frequency. Firms can only make roaming agreements, which allow one firm's customers to use another firm's cell towers, if they share the same transmission technology and radio frequency. The second-generation standard mostly used outside of the United States is called GSM. It is widely cross-licensed among a consortium of equipment manufacturers. Since American cell phones embed many different transmission standards, they are often not compatible with each other or with GSM. Hence, U.S. companies cannot make roaming agreements with many Japanese and European companies, and even with some other American companies.

One would have hoped that the roaming problem would be solved by the new generation of improved transmission technologies currently being deployed, called 3G (third generation). The standard that is technically most efficient, in the sense of maximizing the information that can be transmitted with given bandwidth, is said to be CDMA2000, developed by the American firm Qualcomm, which holds numerous patents on it. The Europeans, who do not want to be held hostage to a proprietary American standard, have developed a slightly different version of CDMA, called W-CDMA. W-CDMA uses some Qualcomm patents under license, but adds its own patented variations. If adopted, the proprietary aspects of W-CDMA would create a counterweight against Qualcomm's strong patent position. W-CDMA does, however, have the virtue of being backward compatible with cell towers equipped with Europe's earlier, GSM standard. W-CDMA is being promoted by the European equipment manufacturers over the better transmission technology, CDMA2000. Due to the backward compatibility, the Europeans say this is efficient. The Americans say it is strategic.

At this writing the proprietors are having a full-blown standards war, battling it out at every level; see Cowhey, Aronson, and Richards, forthcoming. The players include international standards-setting bodies, high-level government representatives, and also the bodies that allocate spectrum, since compatibility requires a common transmission frequency. At the heart of the problem is big business and protectionism. Europe has large, successful equipment manufacturers that do not want to lose their market power to American patents. American equipment manufacturers want access to lucrative world markets. Second-generation providers outside the United States have an incentive to support standards compatible with their already installed GSM towers. But third-generation entrants can try to unseat the second-generation incumbents by supporting the better technology, CMDA2000. For this reason, the rivalries and conflicts spill across national boundaries.

If United States and Asian companies variously adopt CDMA2000 and W-CDMA and European companies adopt W-CDMA, and China adopts a third variant TD-SCDMA, potential network benefits outside of Europe are likely to be limited. Roaming will either be impossible or cell phones will have to embody several standards and radio bands. How the market will tip, if at all, is not yet clear. Every time a cellphone company is "signed" for one side or the other, there is a big press announcement. Sprint and Verizon have chosen CDMA2000. AT&T Wireless chose W-CDMA. Different providers in China have so far chosen different standards. In Japan, the incumbent telephone company DoCoMo chose W-CDMA, and the rival entrant is betting on CDMA2000.

Cell phones illustrate the important fact that direct network benefits can be provided by membership in a unified physical network, and that such a network requires adherence to a common standard. If the standard is open, rival firms can supply equipment compatible with the standard, and users will have the dual benefits of competitive supply and a fully integrated network that permits roaming. This is essentially what Europe achieved outside the United States with the second-generation GSM standard. In view of what has happened with the third generation, that achievement looks more and more miraculous.

Standards wars are likely to erupt when standards are proprietary. If standards were only costless, arbitrary choices, there would be no need to make them proprietary. However, CMDA2000 is a real invention, which was achieved at real cost. The absence of patent protection might have dissuaded the inventor from investing. Later on, however, proprietary standards can hinder the development of a unified network.

One added complication is that the efficient adoption path is not obvious. W-CDMA and TD-SCDMA have the advantage of using installed transmission towers, whereas CDMA2000 will require more infrastructure. On the other hand, if eventual adoption of the more efficient transmission standard CDMA2000 is inevitable, why not do it sooner rather than later? The standards war may eventually be resolved with cross-licensing in which all equipment and telephone networks are compatible for roaming just as they are how compatible for interconnection (see Gandal, Salant, and Waverman 2003). However, that result has been a long time coming.

10.5   Technical Notes

10.5.1   Direct Network Effects

Suppose that the consumers are indexed by $\theta \in [0, \infty]$, with mass one on each unit interval. Suppose that each consumer receives external benefits in amount $f(n)$ when there are n consumers in the network. The number of consumers in the network is $\int_0^n d\theta = n$. Assume that the marginal cost of serving each consumer is c, and that the willingness to pay of a consumer indexed by θ is

$$w(\theta, n) = \frac{1}{\theta} + f(n) \tag{10.2}$$

Thus, consumers are ordered by the inverse of their willingness to pay. For any given price, it is the low-θ consumers who will join the network, since they have the highest willingnesses to pay.

To ensure that the network good will be provided, assume that for some $n > 0$, $w(n, n) > c$.

The social benefits of a network of size n are

$$S(n) = \int_0^n (w(\theta, n) - c) d\theta$$

The optimum n^* either satisfies $n^* < \infty$ and

$$\frac{d^2 S(n)}{dn^2} \bigg|_{n=n^*} \leq 0$$

$$\frac{dS(n)}{dn} \bigg|_{n=n^*} = \frac{1}{n^*} + f(n^*) - c + n^* f'(n^*) = 0 \tag{10.3}$$

or it is optimal to include everyone in the network ($n^* = \infty$).

Now consider the pricing behavior of a monopolist. Since the monopolist has no direct control over the size of the network (it only controls the price), there may be multiple equilibria. This is a problem, but suppose the monopolist can engage in marketing strategies to choose the size of network, and can sustain a network of size n by charging a price

$$p(n) = w(n, n) = \frac{1}{n} + f(n)$$

That is, it charges a price equal to the lowest willingness to pay of any user on the network. Its profit for a network of size n is then

$$\Pi(n) = n[p(n) - c]$$

The monopolist's optimum is either to include everyone and charge a price equal to $\lim_{n \to \infty} f(n)$ or to choose a network $\hat{n}$ that satisfies

$$\frac{d^2\Pi(n)}{dn^2}\Big|_{n=\hat{n}} \leq 0$$

$$\frac{d\Pi(n)}{dn}\Big|_{n=\hat{n}} = \frac{1}{\hat{n}} + f(\hat{n}) - c + \hat{n}\left[\frac{-1}{\hat{n}^2} + f'(\hat{n})\right] = 0 \quad \text{if } \hat{n} < \infty \qquad (10.4)$$

Finally, consider what would happen in a competitive market with a nonproprietary standard. Zero profit implies that the price must satisfy $p = c$. If $\lim_{n \to \infty} w(n, n) > c$, we assume that everyone will be on the competitive network. Otherwise, the size of the network is n^c satisfies

$$\frac{dw(n,n)}{dn}\Big|_{n=n^c} \leq 0$$

$$w(n^c, n^c) = \frac{1}{n^c} + f(n^c) = c \qquad (10.5)$$

We can now compare the sizes of networks. For some functions w, the optimal network, the monopoly network, and the competitive network include the whole customer base—for example, if the network benefits described by $f(\cdot)$ lead to large willingness to pay for all consumers. In that case, monopoly and competition are equally efficient, even though customers pay higher prices to a proprietor than they would pay to competitive firms using an open standard.

It is more interesting to consider preferences for which, as the network expands, the willingness to pay of the marginal user eventually falls faster than the network benefits increase. In that case, there will be discrepancies between the competitive network, the optimal network, and the monopoly network.

In particular, suppose that $f(n) = 1 - 1/2n^2$. Then

$$w(n,n) = \frac{1}{n} + \left(1 - \frac{1}{2n^2}\right)$$

$$\frac{dS(n)}{dn} = \frac{1}{n} + 1 + \frac{1}{2n^2} - c = 0$$

$$\frac{d\Pi(n)}{dn} = 1 + \frac{1}{2n^2} - c = 0$$

$$\frac{dS(n)}{dn} = \frac{d\Pi(n)}{dn} + \frac{1}{n}$$

The optimal-size network n^* is larger than the monopolists' network $\hat{n}$. Further, the competitive network satisfies

$$w(n^c, n^c) = \frac{1}{n^c} + 1 - \frac{1}{2}\frac{1}{(n^c)^2} = c$$

One can see that

$$\frac{d\Pi(n)}{dn}\bigg|_{n=n^c} < 0$$

and

$$\frac{dS(n)}{dn}\bigg|_{n=n^c} > 0$$

Hence the monopolist will prefer a smaller network than the competitive network, and the socially optimal network is larger than the competitive network.

The monopolist will arrange for a smaller network by charging a price higher than the competitive price. Thus, when $w(n, n)$ is decreasing in n, $\hat{n} < n^c < n^*$.

The reason that $n^c < n^*$ is that an expansion of the network from n^c would create benefits for the inframarginal members of the network that are not captured by the competitive firms. Indeed, they will have to lower their price below c to attract new customers. From society's point of view, this is a good deal, since inframarginal members of the network benefit, while the discrepancy between the marginal consumer's willingness to pay and the cost of serving him or her is tiny. But since the firms cannot capture the benefits to inframarginal members, they will not expand the network.

10.5.2 Multiple Equilibria in Systems Competition

To derive the demand functions, assume that θ is distributed uniformly on $[-1, 1]$. Since consumers can drop out of the market and receive utility 0, impose that $(a_2 - p_2) \geq 0$. Thus, the alternative to buying platform 1 is buying platform 2, and buying platform 2 is no worse than dropping out of the market. The demands for the platforms, shown in figure 10.2, are

$$n_1(p_1; p_2, a_1, a_2) = \begin{cases} 0 & \text{if } 1 - (a_2 - p_2) + (a_1 - p_1) < 0 \\ 1 - (a_2 - p_2) & \text{if } 0 < 1 - (a_2 - p_2) + (a_1 - p_1) < 2 \\ \quad + (a_1 - p_1) & \\ 2 & \text{if } 2 < 1 - (a_2 - p_2) + (a_1 - p_1) \end{cases}$$

$$n_2(p_1; p_2, a_1, a_2) = \begin{cases} 0 & \text{if } 1 + (a_2 - p_2) - (a_1 - p_1) < 0 \\ 1 + (a_2 - p_2) & \text{if } 0 < 1 + (a_2 - p_2) - (a_1 - p_1) < 2 \\ \quad - (a_1 - p_1) & \\ 2 & \text{if } 2 < 1 + (a_2 - p_2) - (a_1 - p_1) \end{cases}$$

The equilibrium can be solved in two stages. First, conditional on (a_1, a_2), characterize the prices $\hat{p}_1(a_1, a_2)$, $\hat{p}_2(a_1, a_2)$ that arise in the subsequent Nash equilibrium where firm 1 (symmetrically, firm 2) chooses price to maximize (10.1). The Nash equilibrium prices satisfy $\hat{p}_2(a_1, a_2)$ $\leq a_2$ and $\hat{p}_1(a_1, a_2) \leq 1 + a_1 - (a_2 - \hat{p}_2(a_1, a_2))$, and the following:

$$\begin{aligned} -2\hat{p}_1(a_1, a_2) & \\ +1 + a_1 + (\hat{p}_2(a_1, a_2) - a_2) & \begin{cases} \leq 0 & \text{if } \hat{p}_1(a_1, a_2) = 0 \\ = 0 & \text{if } 0 < \hat{p}_1(a_1, a_2) \leq 1 + a_1 - (a_2 - \hat{p}_2(a_1, a_2)) \end{cases} \end{aligned}$$

$$-2\hat{p}_2(a_1, a_2) + 1 + a_2 + (\hat{p}_1(a_1, a_2) - a_1) \begin{cases} \leq 0 & \text{if } \hat{p}_2(a_1, a_2) = 0 \\ = 0 & \text{if } 0 < \hat{p}_1(a_1, a_2) \leq a_2 \end{cases}$$

Solving these two equations, we can write the equilibrium prices as a function of the prespecified numbers of applications, (a_1, a_2):

$$\hat{p}_1(a_1, a_2) = \begin{cases} (1/3)(3 + (a_1 - a_2)) & \text{if } 3 \geq (a_1 - a_2) \geq -3 \\ (1/2)(1 + a_1 - a_2) & \text{if } (a_1 - a_2) > 3 \\ 0 & \text{if } (a_1 - a_2) < -3 \end{cases}$$

$$\hat{p}_2(a_1, a_2) = \begin{cases} (1/3)(3 - (a_1 - a_2)) & \text{if } 3 \geq (a_1 - a_2) \geq -3 \\ (1/2)(1 + a_1 - a_2) & \text{if } (a_1 - a_2) < -3 \\ 0 & \text{if } (a_1 - a_2) > 3 \end{cases}$$

Thus $\hat{p}_1(a_1, a_2) - \hat{p}_2(a_1, a_2) = (2/3)(a_1 - a_2)$ if $3 \geq (a_1 - a_2) \geq -3$, and the number of customers of firm 1 is $n_1(p_1; p_2, a_1, a_2) = 1 + (a_1 - a_2)$ $-(\hat{p}_1(a_1, a_2) - \hat{p}_2(a_1, a_2)) = 1 + (1/3)(a_1 - a_2)$. If $a_1 - a_2 > 3$, the firm 1 has all the customers, namely, a mass of two.

We can now define the firms' profit functions, as a function of (a_1, a_2). Suppose that there is a pool of applications developers with different talent or efficiency, so that the marginal cost of providing applications is increasing. Assume the total cost of providing a applications is $a^2/6$, regardless of how the applications are split between the firms.

Assume in addition that each firm pays its proportional share of the total cost of applications development—for example, firm 1 pays

$$(1/6)(a_1 + a_2)^2 \frac{a_1}{a_1 + a_2} = (1/6)a_1(a_1 + a_2)$$

Then

$$\Pi^1(a_1; a_2) = \begin{cases} 2(1/2)(1 + a_1 - a_2) - (1/6)(a_1 + a_2)a_1 & \text{if } a_1 > a_2 + 3 \\ -(1/6)(a_1 + a_2)a_1 & \text{if } a_1 \leq a_2 - 3 \\ (1/9)(3 + a_1 - a_2)^2 - (1/6)(a_1 + a_2)a_1 & \text{if } a_2 + 3 \geq a_1 \geq a_2 - 3 \end{cases}$$

The profit function of firm 2 is the same, except with the subscripts reversed.

There are two Nash equilibria in the number of applications. There is a symmetric equilibrium with two firms in the market offering $a_1 = a_2 = 4/3$ applications, and there is a monopoly outcome with one firm offering $a_1 = 3$ and the other offering $a_2 = 0$ applications (or vice versa). This can be checked directly from the profit functions.

In this simple model it is almost inevitable that tipping to a single provider is efficient. That is because the single provider saves duplicated costs of applications, and, since the applications are marketed to all consumers, it provides more of them. The duopoly has the benefit of lower prices, but in this model there is no extensive margin (all consumers are in the market), so the lower prices do not avoid deadweight loss due to exclusion.

References and Further Reading

Benjamin, S. M., D. G. Lichtman, and H. A. Shelanski. 2001. *Telecommunications Law and Policy.* Durham, NC: Carolina Academic Press.

Chou, C., and O. Shy. 1990. "Network Effects without Network Externalities." *International Journal of Industrial Organization* 8:259–270.

Church, J., and N. Gandal. 1992a. "Integration, Complementary Products and Variety." *Journal of Economics and Management Strategy* 1:651–675.

Church, J., and N. Gandal. 1992b. "Network Effects, Software Provision and Standardization." *Journal of Industrial Economics* 40:85–104.

Cowhey, P. F., J. D. Aronson, and J. E. Richards. Forthcoming. "The Peculiar Evolution of 3G Wireless Networks: Institutional Logic, Politics, and Property Rights." In W. Drake and E. Wilson, eds., *Governing Global Electronic Networks.* Cambridge, MA: MIT Press.

David, P. 1985. "Clio and the Economics of QWERTY." *American Economic Review* 75:332–337.

David, P. 2000. "Path Dependence, Its Critics and the Quest for 'Historical Economics.'" In P. Garrouste and S. Ionnides, eds., *Evolution and Path Dependence in Economic Ideas: Past and Present.* Cheltenham, UK: Elgar Publishing.

Economides, N. 1988. "Desirability of Compatibility in the Absence of Network Externalities." *American Economic Review* 79:1165–1181.

Evans, D., A. Nichols, and B. Reddy. 1999. "The Rise and Fall of Leaders in Personal Computer Software." Cambridge, MA: National Economic Research Associates. Available at www.nera.com.

Evans, D., and R. Schmalensee. 2002. "Some Economic Aspects of Antitrust Analysis in Dynamically Competitive Industries." *Innovation Policy and the Economy* 2:1–50.

Farrell, J., and M. Katz. 1998. "The Effects of Antitrust and Intellectual Property Law on Compatibility and Innovation." *Antitrust Bulletin* 48:609–650.

Farrell, J., and P. Klemperer. 2001. "Coordination and Lock-in: Competition with Switching Costs and Network Effects." Oxford: Nuffield College, Oxford University. Available at www.paulklemperer.org. Forthcoming in M. Armstrong, and R. H. Porter, eds., *Handbook of Industrial Organization*, vol. 3. Amsterdam: North-Holland.

Farrell, J., and G. Saloner. 1986a. "Installed Base and Compatibility: Innovation, Product Preannouncements and Predation." *American Economic Review* 76:940–955.

Farrell, J., and G. Saloner. 1986b. "Standardization and Variety." *Economics Letters* 20:71–74.

Farrell, J., and G. Saloner. 1987. "Competition, Compatibility and Standards: The Economics of Horses, Penguins and Lemmings." In H. Gabel, ed., *Product Compatibility as a Competitive Strategy*, 1–21. Amsterdam: North-Holland.

Farrell, J., and G. Saloner. 1992. "Converters, Compatibility and the Control of Interfaces." *Journal of Industrial Economics* 40:9–36.

Gilbert, R., and M. Katz. 2001. "An Economist's Guide to *U.S. v. Microsoft.*" *Journal of Economic Perspectives* 15:25–44.

Gandal, N. 1994. "Hedonic Price Indexes for Spreadsheets and an Empirical Test for Network Externalities." *RAND Journal of Economics* 15:160–170.

Gandal, N., M. Kende, and R. Rob. 2000. "The Dynamics of Technological Adoption in Hardware/Software Systems: The Case of Compact Disc Players." *RAND Journal of Economics* 31:43–61.

Gandal, N., S. Salant, and L. Waverman. 2003. "Standards in Wireless Telephone Networks." *Telecommunications Policy* 27:325–332.

Greenstein, S. 1993. "Did Installed Base Give an Incumbent Any (Measurable) Advantages in Federal Computer Procurement." *RAND Journal of Economics* 24:19–39.

Katz, M., and C. Shapiro. 1985. "Network Externalities, Competition and Compatibility." *American Economic Review* 75:424–440.

Katz, M., and C. Shapiro. 1986a. "Product Compatibility Choice in a Market with Technological Progress." *Oxford Economic Papers* 38:146–165.

Katz, M., and C. Shapiro. 1986b. "Technology Adoption in the Presence of Network Externalities." *Journal of Political Economy* 94:822–841.

Katz, M., and C. Shapiro. 1992. "Product Introduction with Network Externalities." *Journal of Industrial Economics* 40:55–84.

Katz, M., and C. Shapiro. 1994. "Systems Competition and Network Effects." *Journal of Economic Perspectives* 8:93–115.

Kindleberger, C. 1983. "Standards as Public, Collective and Private Good." *Kyklos* 36:377–396.

Klein, B. 2001. "The Microsoft Case: What Can a Dominant Firm Do to Defend Its Market Position?" *Journal of Economic Perspectives* 15:45–62.

Klimenko, M. M. 2003. "Compatibility Standards and Trade Policies for Industries with Network Externalities." Mimeograph. San Diego, CA: Department of Economics, UC San Diego.

Laffont, J.-J., and J. Tirole. 2000. *Competition in Telecommunications.* Cambridge, MA: MIT Press.

Liebowitz, S. J., and S. E. Margolis. 1999. *Winners, Losers and Microsoft: Competition and Antitrust in High Technology.* Oakland, CA: Independent Institute.

Lotus Development Corporation v. Borland International, Inc. 49 F.3d 807 (1st Cir. 1995).

Matutes, C., and P. Regibeau. 1992. "Mix and Match: Product Compatibility without Network Externalities." *RAND Journal of Economics* 19:221–234.

Saloner, G., and A. Shepard. 1995. "Adoption of Technologies with Network Externalities: An Empirical Examination of the Adoption of Automated Teller Machines." *RAND Journal of Economics* 26:479–501.

Samuelson, P., and S. Scotchmer. 2002. "The Law and Economics of Reverse Engineering." *Yale Law Journal* 111:1575–1663.

Sega v. Accolade. 977 F.2d 1510 (9th Cir. 1992).

Telegeography. 2000. "Global Internet Primer: Finance." In *Hubs and Spokes: A Telegeography Internet Reader.* Washington, DC: Telegeography. Available at www.telegeography.com/.

United States v. Microsoft Corp., 253 F.3d 34 (D.C. Cir. 2001).

11 Innovation in the Global Economy

For most people it comes as a surprise that almost half of U.S. patents are issued to foreign inventors. In this chapter we turn to why that might make sense, and what we get in return. It is not only the United States that grants patents to foreigners. All major jurisdictions do this, and not just patents. Almost all intellectual property available to domestic inventors is also available to foreign inventors. This is true in most countries.

The most important patenting jurisdictions are Japan, the European Union, and the United States, whose patent offices are respectively the JPO, the EPO, and the USPTO. Collectively, the residents of these three jurisdictions account for only about 13 percent of the world population, and no more than half of the world GDP.[1] Even more disproportionate is the fraction of total patents accounted for by inventors in these jurisdictions. Instead of 13 percent or even half, as we might expect if the countries of the world were symmetric in their innovative capacity, in 2002 inventors from the trilateral block collectively applied for 97 percent, 94 percent, and 88 percent of patents in the JPO, EPO, and the USPTO respectively (EPO, JPO, and USPTO 2002).

Even though all inventors have the same patent rights in each jurisdiction, regardless of their own nationalities, it is not true that the three patent offices issue patents proportionately to, say, GDP or population. Patents are not issued in proportions of 16 percent, 47 percent, and 37 percent in any of the three patent offices, as would reflect relative

---

1.   Because of the problem of purchasing-power parity, it is difficult to compare GDP in the industrialized world with GDP elsewhere. See Heston, Summers, and Aten 2002 for GDP estimates that account for purchasing-power parity. The relative GDPs of Japan, the European Union (including 15 nations in 2002), and the United States are about 18:36:46. The relative populations are about 16:47:36 (European Union in the U.S., 2003).

populations. They deviate in two ways: there is a home bias, and Japanese inventors patent at a disproportionately high rate. In 2002, the USPTO granted 52 percent of its patents to American inventors and only 48 percent to foreign inventors, disproportionately to Japanese. The home bias in the JPO is even greater. The JPO issued 90 percent to Japanese inventors, with 5 percent to Americans and 4 percent to Europeans. The EPO issued 54 percent to European inventors, 25 percent to United States residents, and 17 percent to Japanese (EPO, JPO, and USPTO 2002).

One reason for the home bias might be that innovations in each country are targeted at the domestic market. The Japanese bias might additionally arise from a historical difference between patent systems. Recall that United States and European patents can have many claims. Until a reform in 1988, this was not true in the Japanese system, where there was a single claim per patent. After the reform, the number of claims per patent increased up to fourfold, depending on technology field (see Branstetter and Sakakibara 2001).

For copyrights, there are no administrative data analogous to those available for patents, so it is hard to track the international dimension. This is because there is no application or examination process. Even notification with the symbol © is no longer necessary. To a large extent, international copyrights are automatic, although they might not be enforced.

This chapter turns to how the globalized system arose, why globalization does or does not make sense, and the extent to which it encourages countries to rely on intellectual property incentives instead of, for example, public sponsorship.

11.1   Trade Policy and Treaties

The reciprocal exchange of intellectual property rights is governed by treaties. The earliest large-scale intellectual property treaties were the 1883 Paris Convention on patents and other industrial property, and the 1886 Berne Convention for literary and artistic works. These treaties began with only a few members. Under various revisions, they have remained in effect ever since and now have well over 100 members. Both established the principle of "national treatment of foreign inventors." National treatment is the provision by which national intellectual property rights must be extended to foreign inventors. Within each member country, foreign inventors receive the same rights given to nationals.

The most important modern descendant of the Berne and Paris Conventions is the 1994 agreement on Trade Related Aspects of Intellectual Property Rights (TRIPS), which has over 140 members. Membership in TRIPS is required for membership in the World Trade Organization. The WTO, which governs more than 97 percent of trade, creates trade advantages for its members, binds them to certain limitations on trade tariffs, and creates and enforces obligations to provide certain intellectual property rights. There are important nations that have not yet become part of these treaties, including the former Soviet states.

The principle of national treatment does not specify what subject matters should be protected, but only specifies that whatever protections are given to domestic inventors shall also be extended to inventors in other member states. TRIPS goes beyond the principle of national treatment by also specifying a minimum set of rights that each member state must provide. Until the TRIPS agreement, there were sharp differences in what was protected—for example, many countries did not protect pharmaceuticals.

The trilateral markets are the important markets in which to receive intellectual property rights, mainly because they are large. An inventor in, say, South Korea will find it more profitable to receive intellectual property rights in any or all of those three markets than to protect the intellectual property at home, at least for inventions that are globally useful. In fact, if inventors in a small country like South Korea can be protected in the United States, Europe, and Japan, it is hard to see why the small country would grant domestic intellectual property rights at all. Why not use the three large markets to reward their inventors, without imposing proprietary prices on their own consumers? Inventors and consumers in the large markets would naturally take a dim view of such free riding, and TRIPS forbids it.

The U.S. stance toward free riding has changed with its economic circumstances. In the early days when the U.S. was a small, underdeveloped country, it allowed its nascent printing industry to reproduce British books without paying royalties. Printers did not give up this privilege even after 1789, when the Constitution authorized the federal government to grant intellectual property rights. The federal copyright statute enacted in 1790 in response to lobbying by American authors, especially Noah Webster, provided no protection for foreign authors.

In the next century, the United States refused to join the Berne Convention, which granted reciprocal copyright privileges among all the member states. The official reason was that the United States had different procedures concerning registration and copyright notice, and did not want to conform to world practice. However, this had other benefits as well. Skeptics will notice that U.S. readers continued to dodge royalties on foreign works.

It was not until American authors became popular overseas that they began to favor an agreement with England for reciprocal copyright privileges. Such an agreement was made in 1890 after the publishing houses, seeing a profit opportunity, joined their effort. Although the United States did not join the Berne Convention until 1989, it was a party to other copyright treaties earlier (Beldon and Sampliner 1996–1997; Ryan 1998, 52).

The problem of international piracy has become more acute in the digital age, and American interests have reversed. There is still a copyright conflict between developing countries and developed countries, but now the United States is a developed country that wants to protect its interests. Today, copyright piracy usually concerns software, movies and music on disk, and to some extent textbooks. As soon as the popular Harry Potter movies were released, illicit copies were reportedly selling on the streets of Beijing, even before they had reached most British and American movie houses. These acts of piracy are not a formal government policy against protecting foreign authors, but they have the same effect.

The globalization of intellectual property rights is also tied to trade policy more generally. In the United States, trade policy is governed by the 1974 Trade Act. Among other things, it authorizes the U.S. Trade Representative (USTR) to investigate unfair trade practices and impose trade sanctions on the perpetrators. In 1984, section 301 was amended to say that a failure to protect intellectual property is an unfair practice. This strengthened U.S. copyright and patent lobbies, by giving them a weapon to pressure foreign governments for stronger intellectual property protection without a cumbersome appeal to the international bodies that enforce treaties.

A second amendment in 1988 was equally important. It requires the USTR to produce an annual assessment of piracy, and to announce a list of priority objectives for trade diplomacy that targets specific countries. The process requires the USTR to accept public comment, which gives the intellectual property lobby an automatic platform. They routinely produce "white papers" that the USTR is obligated to read and consider.

An umbrella lobby organization on copyright matters is the International Intellectual Property Alliance (IIPA), which represents various member organizations on behalf of movie, music, and software producers. In the 1980s they produced an estimate of piracy losses that jolted policymakers—$1.3 billion—and that precipitated a round of fierce negotiations with certain targeted countries, in particular, South Korea and China (Ryan 1998, chap. 4). More recently, the Business Software Alliance (2001) reported that the piracy rate is 37 percent of total usage of business software in the world as a whole, with country-specific rates as high as 94 percent in China. Similarly, the International Federation of the Phonographic Industry (IFPI), a lobby organization that collects data on music piracy, estimates that piracy reduces legitimate sales of music CDs by 22.7 percent.

These numbers make for powerful rhetoric, especially when translated into dollar losses. However, it is obviously naive to estimate lost revenue by assuming that each pirated copy would otherwise have been bought at the list price. Although pirated copies probably crowd out some sales, the crowding out is presumably not one to one. In fact, Hui and Png (2003) estimated that piracy reduces revenues by only 6.6 percent worldwide, assuming that industry prices are fixed. This is still substantial, but much less than the loss estimated by industry.

Perhaps the greatest victory of the copyright and patent lobby was to inject intellectual property into the negotiations over the General Agreement on Trade and Tariffs (GATT) in the early 1990s.[2] This was the origin of TRIPS. Going beyond the earlier treaties that established the principle of national treatment, TRIPS established standards of protection that all members must adhere to, including lengths of protection and requirements that certain subject matters must be protected. Such an effort is generally called *harmonization*. For example, TRIPS mandates protections for pharmaceuticals, some bioengineered products, computer chips, and computer software. Disputes about whether members of the treaty are in compliance can be brought to the World Trade Organization, which is the successor to GATT and is also a dispute-resolution body for the rules negotiated in TRIPS.[3]

---

2.   GATT is a multilateral trade agreement that dates back to the mid-twentieth century. Its objective is to avoid mutually destructive trade restrictions and tariffs that might otherwise arise as countries try to protect their own manufacturers. The rules of trade change in rounds of negotiation, the most recent of which was the Uruguay Round.

3.   See Samuelson 1999 for the history of dispute resolution and the policy issues involved.

In addition to TRIPS and other treaties that govern the treatment of foreign inventors and the substance of intellectual property law, there are treaties that coordinate the administrative aspects of running the intellectual property system. It can be expensive for inventors to exercise their worldwide intellectual property rights. For patents, the legal fees and translation costs for an individual application can cost thousands of dollars per country. To avoid this, many countries have unified their application procedures. The Patent Cooperation Treaty of 1970 (amended in 1979 and 1984) provides a unified application procedure for 115 countries, with an optional preliminary examination that gives applicants some confidence that individual countries will approve the application. After the PCT examination is complete, the applicant can route the application to various member countries, with patents issuing according to national laws.

Further coordination for the European community is provided by the 1973 European Patent Convention, which established the European Patent Office. The EPO conducts examinations and issues patents that are interpreted according to the individual laws of the twenty states in which they apply (mostly overlapping with the European Union). An inventor who only seeks protection in Europe can apply directly to the EPO, or can file a PCT patent, which is then routed to the EPO.

The objective of this chapter is to contemplate the economic forces behind and consequences of intellectual property treaties. As already mentioned, national treatment of foreign inventors creates an opportunity for free riding. This can be cured to some extent by harmonizing protections, but many commentators think that the harmonizations of TRIPS went too far.

Given the strength of the intellectual property lobbies in the United States (Ryan 1998), some commentators believe that the USTR was "captured" by them in the TRIPS negotiations and ended up negotiating on their behalf. However, not all domestic interests are aligned with that lobby. User groups such as the Association of Research Libraries generally prefer low prices and free access, whether the protected property is offered by domestic or foreign vendors.

In view of these conflicting interests, what type of intellectual property policies should be viewed as optimal? That is the subject of the next subsection. Is there any sense in which we can infer that the copyright and patent lobbies have overturned the interests of the developed world as a whole? What is the likely consequence of a harmonization effort in which the members of TRIPS negotiate common minimum protections? Would we expect harmonized protections to be stronger than those that would arise if countries chose their policies independently?

11.2   National Treatment and Efficient Protection

Before discussing national treatment further, we introduce the simple model used in the remainder of the chapter. The simple model focuses on product innovations, and we use it to study the policies that best mitigate global deadweight loss while supporting innovation. We then investigate the policies likely to arise in equilibrium among countries, with and without a harmonization effort.

Suppose there are two countries, a, w. The focus will generally be on country a, and w will be interpreted as "the rest of the world." For each of $i = a, w$, assume for simplicity that the market for each new commodity is the same within each country, generating consumers' surplus v^a and v^w when sold at the competitive price. If country w is larger than country a, it is natural to assume that v^w is larger than v^a. Assume, as we did for computer software, that the marginal cost of producing the new commodity is zero.

If an innovation is sold by a monopolist, we can think of v^a (similarly v^w) as divided into three parts: the consumers' surplus that is available under monopoly, mv^a, the profit, πv^a, and the deadweight loss, ℓv^a (see figure 2.2), where $m + \pi + \ell = 1$. Profit and consumers' surplus are assumed to be the same under national treatment whether the innovation is supplied domestically or by a foreign firm.

If inventors in country a can protect their inventions in country w as well as country a, then their per-period profit is $\pi(v^a + v^w)$ instead of πv^a. In fact, with bilateral protection, inventors in *both* countries receive $\pi(v^a + v^w)$. This observation has an important consequence: under a system of national treatment, an inventor's incentives to invent do not depend on where he or she is domiciled, regardless of differences in intellectual property laws—inventors in both countries receive $\pi(v^a + v^w)$. Hence, there are good reasons to think that the efficacy of intellectual property protection cannot be studied by comparing the success of inventors across countries with different systems. Even if there is heterogeneity in intellectual property protections, there is no heterogeneity in firms' incentives.

Inventors in both countries confer externalities on foreign consumers whether or not they receive foreign patent rights, although in different amounts. If an invention in country a is not protected in country w, then it can be supplied competitively in w, generating per-period consumers' surplus v^w. This is what we previously called free riding. If the invention is protected in w, then some consumers' surplus is repatriated to country a as profit in amount πv^w per period. The per-period external benefit to w is then $m v^w$ rather than v^w, reflecting the outflow of profit and deadweight loss.

From country a's perspective, protection in w is unambiguously desirable. Protection allows country a to repatriate some of the external benefit conferred by its inventors. The fact that this imposes a loss on residents of w is of no concern to policymakers in a. However, although it is easy to see why country a would want protection in w, it is not theirs for the taking. Why would policymakers in country w grant national treatment to innovators in a? Wouldn't they be better off free riding?

Indeed they may. Some commentators think that the United States took this view at the founding of the republic, when they decided to protect national authors but not foreign authors. In more recent controversies, Ryan (1998, 80–81) describes how the desire to free ride has sometimes been explicit. In particular, China has argued that local printing and reproduction of Western works provides local jobs as well as cheap access to knowledge, and is therefore an aid to development. Western negotiators have countered that the actual printing or reproduction effort would take place in the developing countries in any case, since that is more efficient, and that copyright holders would not charge the same high royalties that they charge in the West. This may be true, but there is still an advantage to avoiding royalties.

If small or underdeveloped countries do not have inventions that they wish to protect in the large markets, then the large, innovative countries have little leverage to overcome the incentive to free ride. In the GATT negotiations, the incentive to free ride was overcome by linking trading privileges to membership in TRIPS.

We wish to understand the efficiency properties of the intellectual property regime that is likely to arise under national treatment, and also under a harmonization effort. We start by exploring how aggregate deadweight loss depends on lengths of protection in the two countries. Here we will consider two policy variables jointly: the geographic extent of protection, and the length of protection. Of course, when copyright holders or other rightholders ask for a geographic expansion of their rights, they generally do not volunteer for a simultaneous reduction in how long they are protected. The point here is to reason from a global efficiency point of view. Assuming that the goal is to keep the incentives for invention (profit) fixed, is it better to provide geographically expansive rights for a relatively short time, or to provide geographically restricted rights for a longer period?

Perhaps surprisingly, the answer is that the geographic extent of protection does not affect aggregate deadweight loss, provided the length of protection is tailored to keep the incentives for invention fixed. This conclusion depends only on the assumption that the ratio of profit to deadweight loss is the same in both markets, regardless of the relative sizes of the markets. It is another application of the ratio test discussed in chapter 4.

Let T_a, T_w represent the (discounted) lengths of protection in a and w respectively. The total profit that accrues to an inventor by marketing the proprietary product in both a and w is $\pi(v^a T_a + v^w T_w) = \Pi$. The accompanying deadweight loss is $\ell(v^a T_a + v^w T_w)$. Thus, all combinations (T_a, T_w) that provide the same total profit Π also provide the same total deadweight loss, namely, $\ell\Pi/\pi$.

As a consequence, to a first approximation, the controversies over how to protect intellectual property in the international arena are largely about equity or fairness, and not about efficiency in the sense of aggregate deadweight loss. The following three regimes are equally efficient in the sense of generating the same aggregate deadweight loss, provided that patent lives are adjusted so that an inventor's profit is always the same:

1.   Inventors are protected only in their own domestic countries (autarky).
2.   Inventors are protected in all countries, regardless of domicile.
3.   Inventors everywhere in the world are protected in one country, which for most inventors is not their own.

Autarky means that each country protects its own innovators and no others. This was the situation prior to the Paris and Berne Conventions. Under autarky, the inventions of each country become available for competitive supply in other countries—there are huge externalities from innovative countries to foreigners.

Is there anything wrong with this? One possible problem is that there is a limit to how much profit can be collected from a small, domestic market. The maximum profit in market a is $(1/r)\pi v^a$, which is the discounted sum of profit if the profit stream πv^a lasts forever. If v^a is small, such profit may not cover the cost of innovations. Thus, if the world consists of many small nations, an autarkic system of domestic rights will not support very much innovation. In fact, however, the world as we know it has large jurisdictions like Japan, the United States, and Europe. In these countries, autarky is less likely to stifle innovation.

Autarkic protection would seem the natural solution to the international equity/efficiency problem, at least if regional markets are more or less the same size. Under a system of autarkic protections, the externalities that flow among nations are more or less commensurate, and no country should feel less favorably treated than any other country. American inventors may complain that Japanese users do not help pay the cost of American inventions (and vice versa), but American consumers should also be pleased to receive Japanese inventions at competitive prices (and vice versa). The externalities balance out.

Oddly, however, this system of reciprocal externalities is precisely what is excluded by the principle of national treatment. Under a regime of national treatment, an invention that is protected for a domestic inventor must also be protected for a foreign inventor. Autarky is not possible.

Current practice follows the second option for inventions covered by TRIPS. However, it follows the third for certain inventions that are still only protected in a handful of high-protection countries like the United States.

The third option also prevailed prior to TRIPS, when the United States protected several types of knowledge that were not, for the most part, protected elsewhere, even in other developed countries. For example, computer software was protected by copyright in the United States, and the PTO was beginning to patent it, but those protections were either not provided or still being debated elsewhere. Many jurisdictions had no protections for computer chips. For pharmaceuticals, many nations had no protections or only weak protections, undermined by compulsory licensing. The status of bioengineered organisms was similarly asymmetric. Starting in 1980, bioengineered organisms were protectable in the United States but not in most jurisdictions abroad.

Thus, under national treatment, the cost of developing computer software, computer chips, and bioengineered organisms was largely borne by American users and users in other high-protection jurisdictions, whether the developers were domestic or foreign. Consumers and other users in low-protection jurisdictions could receive the benefit of competitive supply without paying to develop the innovations. The harmonization in TRIPS changed that. For example, it extends protection to biologically modified microorganisms, although it stops short of requiring protection for larger organisms like the Harvard oncomouse.

One might have thought on this basis that harmonization would benefit consumers in high-protection jurisdictions by spreading development costs around the world. However, domestic consumers would only have benefited, at least in the short run, if the protection had been shortened. This was never on the table. Instead, the patent and copyright interests sought a geographic expansion without shortening the duration of rights.

From an efficiency point of view, increased innovation might justify the expansion in rights. Indeed, the copyright and patent lobbies did not make their argument purely on grounds of fairness. They also argued that widespread piracy undermined incentives for R&D. This is true almost by definition, but it does not mean that more incentives are necessarily better. As discussed in chapter 4, higher profit might only lead to wasteful rent seeking.

11.3   Country-Level Optimal Protection

In an environment of national treatment, intellectual property rights are no longer just a way to encourage domestic invention. They also become a strategic instrument to affect profit flows among nations. To affect profit flows favorably, each country wants the strongest possible protections in foreign countries, and the weakest possible protections for foreigners in its own domestic market. Holding the total profit $\pi(v^a T_a + v^w T_w)$ fixed, country a prefers $T_a = 0$ and a very large T_w, at least if country w is large enough to support innovation. Deadweight loss to consumers in country a is $\ell v^a T_a$, which obviously increases with T_a. Similarly, deadweight loss increases with T_w in country w.

Previous chapters of this book have discussed efficiency in the sense of aggregating all the costs and benefits of both producers and consumers into a single measure, ignoring the conflicts of interest that can arise between them. Even in a domestic economy, this approach is not entirely defensible. The best justification is that consumers and shareholders are largely the same people. On average, a higher level of consumers' surplus and profit will benefit everyone.

The argument for aggregating costs and benefits is much weaker in the global economy. For that reason, we modify the premise, and assume that domestic policymakers only care about *domestic* consumers' surplus and profit, net of domestic R&D costs. Thus we continue to assume that there are no irresolvable conflicts of interest within domestic borders, but that there are conflicts of interest across borders.

Instead of thinking solely in terms of optimality, we now think in terms of equilibrium. In equilibrium, each country chooses its intellectual property policy optimally for domestic consumers and producers, conditional on what the other country chooses. We first investigate the length of protection that each country would choose independently, and then consider the length of harmonized protection that each country would advocate if it believed that it could impose its choice on both countries.

The *equilibrium with independent choices* (T_a, T_w) has the property that T_a is optimal for country a conditional on the protection T_w in the other country, and vice versa.

To investigate this equilibrium, we make some preliminary observations. Suppose first that all innovations require the same R&D investment cost c. If T_w is long enough so that it covers the cost of innovations, $\pi v^w T_w \geq c$, then country a will not provide any intellectual property rights at all, $T_a = 0$. For country a it is better to rely on protection in country w, and allow its own consumers to benefit from competitive supply rather than proprietary prices. On the other hand, if the protection abroad is not sufficient to cover the costs of innovation, $\pi v^w T_w < c$, then country a will provide the complementary patent life required to cover the cost—that is, T_a such that $\pi(v^w T_w + v^a T_a) = c$, but no more.

Notice that any combination (T_a, T_w) will be an equilibrium if $\pi(v^w T_w + v^a T_a) = c$. If, for historical reasons, country w has strong (lengthy) protections, then country a can exploit that fact by granting lower protections. And of course each country is in the best possible position if it can rely on the other country entirely. The particular combination of protections that arises can easily be a matter of historical accident, and the initial historical accidents can perpetuate inequities.

We now expand the discussion by introducing "one-size-fits-all" intellectual property rights. Countries cannot set different patent lives or copyright durations for different pieces of knowledge. Patents have uniform length, regardless of how much the invention costs to develop.

This aspect implies that countries will find it optimal to set lengths of protection so that it is not cost-effective to invest in all potential innovations.

In the domestic context, the Nordhaus trade-off discussed in chapter 4 was that it is only optimal to lengthen the intellectual property right if the value of the increased innovation outweighs the additional deadweight loss on innovations that would occur even with the shorter intellectual property right. The trade-off is between the marginal gains to innovation and the inframarginal losses due to deadweight loss on innovations that would occur in any case.

In the international context, there is another consideration. When a country lengthens its intellectual property rights, it generates an outflow of profit to foreign inventors. The increase in innovation must be balanced against the increased domestic deadweight loss and the outflow of profit, not only on the newly engendered innovations but also on all the innovations that would have occurred in any case. The consequence is that countries will choose lengths of protection that are shorter than the lengths that maximize aggregated global consumer welfare, and shorter (as we will see) than the lengths they would harmonize on. They do this to stem the outflow of profit.

We will now see more formally why the countries choose protections that are too short. Let $\hat{c}(T_a, T_w)$ be the maximum innovation cost that can be covered by the worldwide intellectual property rights (T_a, T_w), namely,

$$\hat{c}(T_a, T_w) = v^a \pi T_a + v^w \pi T_w \qquad (11.1)$$

When country a increases the length of protection T_a, it increases the number of innovations at the margin, because innovations with cost just greater than $\hat{c}(T_a, T_w)$ will now be forthcoming. The increase in innovations comes not only from country a, but also from country w.

As before, we assume that each innovation has the same market in each country, described by v^a, v^w, but that innovations may have different costs, c. We assume that the costs c of potential innovations in country a are distributed according to a function F such that there are $F(c)$ potential innovations with cost less than or equal to c. Thus, if the highest cost that can be covered with intellectual property is $\hat{c}(T_a, T_w)$, there will be $F(\hat{c}(T_a, T_w))$ innovations in country a. Assume that the costs of potential innovations in country w are distributed the same way, but scaled by a parameter γ. If the highest cost that can be covered with intellectual property is c, there will be $\gamma F(c)$ innovations in country w. Thus country w is more or less innovative than a according to whether $\gamma > 1$ or $\gamma < 1$. With policies (T_a, T_w) in place, there will be $(1 + \gamma)F(\hat{c}(T_a, T_w))$ innovations in countries a and w—that is, all the innovations with $c \leq \hat{c}(T_a, T_w) = \pi(v^a T_a + v^w T_w)$ will be undertaken in both countries.

It is also useful to have notation for the total costs of innovation in the countries, as well for the total numbers of inventions. With policies (T_a, T_w) in place, the cost of the marginal innovation is $\hat{c}(T_a, T_w)$. However, the total cost includes inframarginal innovations as well. Let $Y(c)$ be the total cost of all potential innovations in country a with cost less than or equal to c.[4] This total cost will satisfy $Y(c) < cF(c)$ for each c, since there are $F(c)$ such innovations, and all except the marginal one have cost less than c. Similarly, the cost of all potential innovations in w with cost less than c is $\gamma Y(c)$.

Let $S(\cdot)$ represent aggregate social welfare as a function of (T_a, T_w):

$$S(T_a, T_w) = (1 + \gamma)F(\hat{c}) \sum_{i=a,w} v^i \left(\frac{1}{r} - \ell T_i\right) - (1 + \gamma)Y(\hat{c})$$

where $\hat{c}$ is given by (11.1).

The first term is the discounted consumers' surplus generated by innovations in both countries. There are $(1 + \gamma)F(\hat{c})$ such innovations, since innovators develop all potential innovations with cost less than $\hat{c}(T_a, T_w)$. Regardless of which country created the innovation, the innovation provides consumers' surplus and profit in both countries, for a total of $\sum_{i=a,w} v^i ((1/r) - \ell T_i)$. On any innovation, the total consumers' surplus plus profit in country a is $v^a ((1/r) - \ell T_a)$, namely, the discounted consumers' surplus under competitive supply, v^a/r, minus deadweight loss during the patent life, $v^a \ell T_a$.[5] Symmetrically, the total consumers' surplus plus profit in country w is $v^w ((1/r) - \ell T_w)$. The last term of $S(\cdot)$ represents the total cost of innovation in both countries.

However, neither country will choose its policy to maximize the total social welfare $S(\cdot)$. To characterize the choices of the two countries, focus on country a. The choice of country w can be described symmet-

---

4.   Suppose that the cumulative distribution of costs F has density f. Then the number of innovations with cost less than $\hat{c}$ is $F(\hat{c}) = \int_0^{\hat{c}} f(z)dz$, and those innovations have total cost $Y(\hat{c}) = \int_0^{\hat{c}} zf(z)dz < \hat{c}\int_0^{\hat{c}} f(z)dz = \hat{c}F(\hat{c})$.

5.   Notice that $v^a(1/r - \ell T_a)$ is equal to $v^a(1/r - T_a) + v^a m T_a + v^a \pi T_a$, since $\ell = 1 - m - \pi$. The first term is the consumers' surplus that accrues after the patent expires. The second term is the consumers' surplus at the proprietary price while the intellectual property is protected, and the third term is the profit.

rically, by reversing a and w and recognizing that the number of innovations and cost in w are γ times those in a. Region a's objective function is W^a:

$$W^a(T_a, T_w) = F(\hat{c})v^a\left(\frac{1}{r} - \ell\, T_a\right) + \gamma F(\hat{c})v^a\left(\frac{1}{r} - (\ell + \pi)T_a\right)$$
$$+ F(\hat{c})v^w \pi T_w - Y(\hat{c})$$

(11.2)

where $\hat{c}$ is again given by (11.1). The first term is the consumer and producer benefits in country a that accrue from innovations in a. The second term is the consumer benefits in country a that accrue from innovations in w. The third term is the profit that country a can collect from country w. The fourth term is the cost of country a's innovations.

The benefits of foreign innovations (the second term of (11.2)) do not include profit, which flows out of country a to country w. However, the third term represents the reverse profit flow, from w to a, due to intellectual property rights that domestic innovators in country a are granted in w.

Suppose now that country a contemplates an increase in its length of protection T_a. What are the benefits for the world as a whole, and what are the benefits for country a? First, there will be more innovations in both countries, due to national treatment. When T_a is larger, the cost $\hat{c}(T_a, T_w)$ of the marginal innovation is larger, so there are more innovations. In the social-welfare function $S(\cdot)$, there are more total innovations, since $(1 + \gamma)F(\hat{c})$ goes up, and these innovations create benefits for consumers in both a and w.

However, country a cares only about the benefits and costs that accrue domestically. It vastly undervalues the global benefits by not taking account of the benefits that accrue to consumers and innovators in country w. In fact, the additional profits that accrue to innovators in w weigh directly against country a's domestic interests, since the profits are paid partly by country a's consumers. The increased outflow of profit is not only on the marginal innovations with cost $\hat{c}(T_a, T_w)$ that are brought about by the longer protection, but also on the many innovations with lower cost $c < \hat{c}(T_a, T_w)$ that would be undertaken even with shorter protection. The increase in T^a generates an outflow of profit to country w on all of its innovations, not only the incremental ones that arise from the increase in T_a.

This argument holds not only for country a, but symmetrically for country w. Neither country will have an incentive to support as much innovation as required to maximize aggregate global welfare $S(\cdot)$. This is due to profit flows and because domestic policymakers do not value the benefits created for foreigners. It is important to notice that this result holds even if the countries are completely symmetric, so that the externalities conferred across borders balance out. That is, it holds even if the innovativeness is the same ($\gamma = 1$), the markets are the same ($v^a = v^w$), and the countries start from the same levels of protection $T_a = T_w$.

This demonstrates a misfortune of equilibrium that arises in many economic contexts. If one actor is choosing the socially best policy, the other actor can often exploit that fact by deviating from its own socially best policy in a way that serves its own interests at the expense of the other. Consequently an equilibrium can be worse for both parties than some other outcome they would like to agree on. The best intellectual property policy consists of the (T_a^*, T_w^*) that maximizes $S(\cdot)$. But starting from an optimum (T_a^*, T_w^*), each country, assuming the other country's policy will stay fixed, has an incentive to shorten its protection.

Can this problem be fixed? One of the main achievements of the TRIPS agreement was to set minimum lengths of protections, twenty years in the case of patents. Let T^* be a value such that $S(T^*, T^*) \geq S(T, T)$ for all T—that is, a common patent life that cannot be improved on for the world as a whole. If the countries sign a treaty to protect for T^* years, then neither can shorten its protection even though it would like to. By committing themselves in this way, they are better off than if they were free to change their policies.

When the countries are symmetric, the harmonization problem is easy, because the countries agree on the optimum. Their profit flows are offsetting and their innovations confer equal and reciprocal benefits. A policy that is good for one is also good for the other. However, when the countries are different in size or innovativeness, they may not agree. Even if the lengths of protection (T_a^*, T_w^*) maximize $S(\cdot)$, the social benefits will not fall on the two countries equally. Cross-border profit flows and cross-border spillovers are asymmetric.

Suppose, for example, that country a has a larger market than country w, $v^a > v^w$, but that they have the same innovative capacity, $\gamma = 1$. Would we expect country a to favor longer or shorter harmonized protection T than country w favors?

Notice that this experiment is different from asking, as we did above, what level of protection each country would choose if it could choose its protection independently of the other country. Here, the countries must come to an agreement. Instead of characterizing what each country will "choose" (since the choice is not entirely under its own control), we will characterize what each country would "advocate," if it believed it could win the negotiation so that both countries implemented its preference. We show that country a prefers a longer harmonized protection than country w when

•   The countries are equally innovative but country a has a smaller market.
•   The countries have the same-size markets, but country a is more innovative.

When country a contemplates the common level of protection T that would be best for its own domestic interests, it is asking what level of T maximizes $W^a(T, T)$. Similarly, country w is asking what level of T maximizes $W^w(T, T)$. By inspecting (11.2) and imposing a harmonized outcome, $T_a = T_w = T$, we see that an increase in T has two effects. First, there is a direct effect of increasing the deadweight loss on domestic consumers consuming both foreign and domestic innovations. The deadweight loss imposed on domestic consumers in country a is $v^a \ell T F(\hat{c})(1 + \gamma)$, and in country w is $v^w \ell T F(\hat{c})(1 + \gamma)$. Deadweight loss is smaller in a smaller region—that is, smaller in region a if $v^a < v^w$. This feeds the first bullet point.

Second, an increase in the harmonized length of protection, T, will change the net flow of profit to country a, namely, $F(\hat{c}) v^w \pi T - \gamma F(\hat{c}) v^a \pi T$, which can be either negative or positive. The net flows in the two countries sum to zero, so that one country gains profit and the other loses profit. If the countries are equally innovative ($\gamma = 1$), then an increase in T will increase the net flow of profit to country a if and only if country a is smaller than w. This is again the first bullet point above. But if the sizes of markets are the same ($v^a = v^w$), then an increase in T will increase the net flow of profit to country a if and only if it is more innovative than country w—that is, $\gamma < 1$. This shows the second bullet point above.

Thus, harmonization will not resolve all disagreements. The countries will disagree on the best harmonized protection in a way that still reflects asymmetric externalities.

We conclude this section by comparing the countries' preferences about harmonization to the T^* that maximizes $S(\cdot)$. Recall that if the countries make independent choices, they will choose protections that are too short. Does this deficiency remain when they negotiate to harmonize?

In fact, we have already sorted this out. In the symmetric case, the countries will agree to harmonize on the efficient level of protection that maximizes $S(\cdot)$. Otherwise, the smaller or more innovative country prefers longer-than-optimal protection, while the larger country prefers shorter-than-optimal protection.

In the TRIPS negotiation, the rich industrialized nations such as the United States pushed hard for strengthening intellectual property rights. The rich industrialized nations have both high innovative capacity and large markets. The preceding arguments suggest that it is the innovative capacity, not the size of the market, that caused the large developed countries to be strong advocates of intellectual property. The size of the market cuts the other way. Based on the foregoing arguments, small, very innovative countries should be most enthusiastic about strengthening global intellectual property rights. Switzerland, for example, was a strong advocate.

11.4 National Autonomy and Protected Subject Matters

Although the TRIPS agreement sets minimum lengths of protection and mandates the protection of many types of knowledge, it also leaves scope for national autonomy. For example, although TRIPS requires protection for computer software, it does not require U.S.-style patents for software or that business methods be protected.

Since nations can exercise autonomy in protecting certain subject matters, choosing subject matters is another way to escape the common lengths of protection. Region a can effectively choose $T_a = 0$ by not protecting the subject matter at all. When will it have an incentive to do this? What will a subject-matter harmonization look like?[6]

We can ask the same questions about protected subject matter as we asked for length of protection: If nations choose independently which subject matter to protect, as they did prior to TRIPS, will they protect too much or too little? How will the externalities flow? What will a harmonization effort lead to?

We will answer this question within the framework of a harmonized length of protection. All subject matter protected by patents is protected for twenty years, and similarly for other general-purpose protections like copyright. Within this framework, the problem raised by

6. For a more elaborated version of this discussion see Scotchmer 2004.

independent choices is again free riding. The fear of free riding is illustrated by what happened when the U.S. computer chip manufacturers lobbied Congress for some form of chip protection in the early 1980s. U.S. chip developers such as Intel had failed to get the courts to recognize copyright protection for their semiconductor chips and were uncertain whether patents would be granted. They therefore lobbied Congress for a special act, which became the Semiconductor Chip Protection Act (SCPA) of 1984, to grant them protection against copying ("cloning") of chips. Cloning has been automated and is very cheap compared to the cost of designing a new chip. The potential competition therefore threatened the viability of chip development.

However, protection in the domestic American market would not protect American chip developers from foreign manufacturers who could clone U.S. chips and market the clones abroad. With national treatment, foreign jurisdictions would be in the best of all possible worlds: receiving protection for their own innovators in the large American market, but having a competitive supply of chips in their own markets.

Congress addressed this threat by including a reciprocity requirement in SCPA. Protection was denied to any chip developer whose home jurisdiction did not provide reciprocal protection for American chip makers. Even though SCPA was not part of the patent and copyright systems covered by the Paris and Berne Conventions, the reciprocity provision was controversial because it flouted the well-established principle of national treatment. (In 1996, the European Union retaliated in a directive calling on the member states to enact sui generis protection for databases. They included a provision that database providers domiciled in nonmember jurisdictions like the United States would not be protected unless the nonmember jurisdictions provided similar database protection.)

For subject matters protected by patent or copyright, it is not possible under the Paris and Berne Conventions to provide stronger protection than required by TRIPS unless it is provided symmetrically to both domestic and foreign inventors. As illustrated by this example, that puts jurisdictions in a bind. On the one hand, inventors may need protection to cover their costs, but on the other hand, no jurisdiction wants to provide that protection unilaterally. If any jurisdiction provides it unilaterally, then the other jurisdictions have an incentive to free ride.

We now make these arguments more formally. Assume, as before, that each innovation has a market size v^a in country a and v^w in country w. The harmonized length of intellectual property protection is T.

We will now group subject matters in terms of the cost c: some are cheap to develop, and others are expensive. For simplicity, assume that $v^a < v^w$ (the indices a and w can be reversed to consider the other case), and consider four types of subject matter, defined by the following conditions on their cost c:

Case I $c \leq \pi v^a T < \pi v^w T$
Case II $\pi v^a T < c \leq \pi v^w T$
Case III $\pi v^a T < \pi v^w T < c \leq \pi T(v^a + v^w)$
Case IV $\pi T(v^a + v^w) < c$

In case I, protection in either jurisdiction is sufficient to cover cost. With independent choices, there are two equilibria: one in which the subject matter is protected in the smaller market, a, as is efficient, and the other in which the subject matter is protected in w, which generates more deadweight loss.

In case II, the only equilibrium is where the subject matter is protected in w, and that is efficient.

In case III, there are two equilibria. In one equilibrium, the subject matter is protected in neither country. Conditional on seeing that there is no protection in w, there is no reason for country a to provide protection, since protection would be ineffective, and vice versa. In the other equilibrium, the subject matter is protected in both countries.

In case IV, protection would be ineffective even if it were bilateral.

Case III illustrates a coordination problem that can arise. If bilateral protection is required in order to cover costs, then independent choices may lead to no protection at all. Conditional on country w not protecting the subject matter, country a sees no reason to protect it because unilateral protection would be ineffective in any case. Harmonization can fix this coordination problem. If the countries sit down at a bargaining table, they will presumably agree that bilateral protection is better than none.

Harmonization can also fix the equity problem that arises when the outcome would be protection in a single market, as in cases I and II. Of course, the free-riding jurisdiction will oppose this harmonization. Fixing the equity problem with harmonized bilateral protection is a second-best solution, since it leads to high prices in both jurisdictions and deadweight loss. Two other solutions would be to (1) relax the principle of national treatment and allow each jurisdiction to protect only its own inventors (the countries would then confer externalities symmetrically on each other); and (2) allow different subject matters to be protected for lengths of time that reflect their costs. (For low-cost subject matters, the length of protection would be shortened so that the relevant inequality would be the third one instead of the first or second, and then bilateral protection would be no less efficient than unilateral protection.)

Neither solution is likely to be proposed. National treatment is solidly entrenched. And tailoring length to cost is essentially impossible on a case-by-case basis, since cost is impossible to verify (see chapter 2). It might be possible to cleave off certain subject matters that are known to be particularly low cost on average, but that would require sui generis forms of protection, rather than the one-size-fits-all regimes of patent and copyright.

11.5   Intellectual Property and the Public Domain

The foregoing arguments assume that, absent an effective intellectual property regime, innovation will not take place. That supposition ignores the large role played by the public sector in R&D spending. As pointed out in chapter 8, public spending accounts for between one-quarter and one-half of R&D spending almost everywhere in the industrialized world, and mostly closer to half. We now consider how the preceding arguments must be modified if an alternative to effective intellectual property protection is public sponsorship rather than a dearth of innovation.

As stressed in chapter 2, public sponsorship has a natural advantage over intellectual property incentives. Public sponsors can fund R&D out of general revenue and then put the resulting knowledge in the public domain, thus reducing deadweight loss. If we think that intellectual property is a better incentive system, it is either because we value the fact that everyone who helps pay for the innovation does so voluntarily, or because public sponsorship introduces some kind of inefficiency that is worse than deadweight loss.

In the international arena, private incentives can have another advantage for regional taxpayers. Public sponsors are unlikely to marshal public funds for R&D investments whose benefits lie largely outside their own borders. In contrast, intellectual property rights abroad can allow investors to reclaim some of this external benefit as profit. As a consequence, public sponsors may not support innovations that the private sector would support, even if the public sector is much more efficient in avoiding deadweight loss.

If an innovation is in the public domain, the per-period benefit that it confers in country a is v^a. It is reasonable to suppose that a public sponsor will only fund a project for the public domain if it generates domestic benefits $(1/r)v^a$ that are greater than the cost. It also generates benefits $(1/r)v^w$ abroad, but these are of no concern to policymakers in a. If the innovation is protected in both countries, the profit is $\pi(v^a T_a + v^w T_w)$. It can easily happen that for some innovation with cost c, $(v^a T_a + v^w T_w)\pi > c > (1/r)v^a$. Even though the cost of the invention is greater than $(1/r)v^a$, so that a public sponsor would not undertake the investment, the investment would be undertaken by a private investor in order to collect profit.

For innovations likely to be supported by the public, the possibility of public sponsorship will change our notion of which subject matters should be protected by intellectual property. If inventions will be publicly sponsored rather than lost in the absence of protection, the argument for intellectual property is weaker. However, even within this modified framework, the previous results hold. It is still true that the countries will choose too little protection if they choose independently, will strengthen protections if they have an opportunity to harmonize, and will generally disagree. One country will favor protection that is too strong, and the other will favor protection that is too weak.

In keeping with a common view of the public sector, assume that publicly sponsored research is more costly than private research. Thus, if the private cost of a development effort is c, the public cost is kc, $k > 1$. We now interpret F as describing the distribution of costs within a given subject matter.

The following questions arise: (1) When is intellectual property more efficient than public sponsorship in the sense that global deadweight loss is less than the cost disadvantage of the public sector? (2) Will independent choices of subject matter coincide with what is efficient? (3) What is the likely outcome of a harmonization effort?

It is useful to write down the conditions under which country a would prefer to protect the subject matter, assuming that otherwise public sponsors would step in. Conditions (11.3) and (11.4) are useful in understanding what happens with independent choices, and (11.5) is useful in understanding the countries' incentives to harmonize. Again let $\hat{c}(T, T)$ defined by (11.1) represent the maximum R&D cost that could be covered by the profit available in both markets, where T is the harmonized length of protection. The three conditions that follow apply under three different assumptions about country w's policy.

Assuming that country w does not protect a subject matter, country a will protect it if

$$v^a \ell T(1+\gamma)F(v^a\pi T) + v^a\pi T\gamma F(v^a\pi T) < (k-1)Y(v^a\pi T) \qquad (11.3)$$

Assuming that country w protects the subject matter, country a will protect it if

$$v^a \ell T(1+\gamma)F(\hat{c}) + v^a\pi T\gamma F(\hat{c}) - v^w\pi TF(\hat{c}) + v^w\pi TF(v^w\pi T) < (k-1)(Y(\hat{c}) - Y(v^w\pi T)) \qquad (11.4)$$

Finally, assuming that the choice is between harmonized bilateral protection for (given) length T and no protection in either country, country a will favor bilateral protection of the subject matter if

$$v^a \ell T(1+\gamma)F(\hat{c}) + v^a\pi T\gamma F(\hat{c}) - v^w\pi TF(\hat{c}) < (k-1)Y(\hat{c}) \qquad (11.5)$$

In each inequality, the right-hand side is the saving in R&D costs that would result from protection of the subject matter in country a instead of public sponsorship, and the left-hand side is the deadweight loss and net loss in profit. If the cost saving outweighs the deadweight loss and net outflow of profit, so the inequality holds, the country will protect the subject matter.

The inequalities (11.4) and (11.5) can hold even if $k = 1$, so that the private sector has no cost advantage over the public sector. In a purely domestic context, the case of $k = 1$ would be a clear case for public sponsorship, since public sponsorship avoids deadweight loss. But in the international context, profit flows can make intellectual property an attractive domestic policy despite the deadweight loss.

The most important observation, arising directly from a comparison of (11.4) with (11.5), is that a harmonization effort is likely to restrict the public domain relative to what would happen with independent choices. Whenever (11.4) is satisfied, (11.5) is also satisfied, but not vice versa. This implies that the countries will advocate stronger protections (more protected subject matter) if they know they will get reciprocity than if they must make independent decisions. Countries will agree to harmonized protections that either country would drop if given the right to do that.

Consider what country a gains by dropping the subject matter unilaterally. With a unilateral defection, country a stems the flow of profit to inventors in country w. A bilateral reduction in protection would also deprive country a of the profit it earns in country w, and this is the difference. If both must happen simultaneously, country a will be more keen to keep the protection.

Of course these arguments do not reveal whether protection of the subject matter is globally efficient or inefficient, but only that independent choices are more likely to leave inventions in the public domain. The condition under which bilateral protection is efficient, in the sense of minimizing global deadweight loss net of R&D costs, is

$$\ell T\left[\sum_{i=a,w} v^i\right](1+\gamma)F(\hat{c}) \le (k-1)(1+\gamma)Y(\hat{c}) \tag{11.6}$$

Unlike (11.3) through (11.5), this comparison of deadweight loss to cost inefficiency does not contain profit flows.

To compare the efficient outcome with independent choices, take the marginal case, where (11.6) holds with equality. Then, with independent choices, at most one country will protect the subject matter, and it is possible that neither will. For example, in the symmetric case ($v^a = v^w$ and $\gamma = 1$), if (11.6) holds with equality, then neither (11.3) nor (11.4) holds, so that the equilibrium with independent choices will be that neither country protects the subject matter, even though protection would be efficient.

Now consider harmonization. If we add the inequality (11.5) and its mirror image for country w, switching the superscripts a and w, and recognizing that the number of innovations and cost in w are γ times those in a, the inequality (11.6) is precisely what we get. It follows that, if (11.6) holds with equality, then either (11.5) holds or its mirror image for w holds. One country will favor harmonized bilateral protection and the other will oppose it, except in the perfectly symmetric case where they agree. Although the countries generally disagree, their preferences bracket what would be efficient. We can also see from (11.5) that the disagreement will take the following form:

- If the countries have the same market size, but country w is more innovative than country a, in the sense that $\gamma > 1$, then country w will favor bilateral protection of the subject matter whenever country a favors it, but not vice versa.

- If the countries are equally innovative ($\gamma = 1$), but country w has a smaller market than country a($v^a > v^w$), then country w will favor bilateral protection of the subject matter whenever country a favors it, but not vice versa.

11.6   National Autonomy and Trade Rules

When the intellectual property covers a good sold in the market, as discussed in the previous three subsections, any unauthorized use is an infringement and can be stopped. Unauthorized imports ("parallel imports") can be stopped at the border. As a consequence, intellectual property can be protected in some but not all countries. There is a large measure of national autonomy in protections, at least where TRIPS is silent.

This is not necessarily true of intellectual property that protects inventions other than consumer goods. Differences in national rules can sometimes be arbitraged so that national autonomy is undermined (Samuelson 2004). Several examples follow.

The first example concerns research tools. A research tool is knowledge, perhaps in the form of an instrument or chemical structure, that aids a researcher in developing further knowledge, but it is not typically embodied in the further product once it is developed or in the process of manufacturing the product. In biotechnology, the research tool may be a technique for combining genetic material in bacteria that will then produce useful proteins. Once the bacterium exists, the research tool is no longer required, and there is no evidence in the bacteria that it was used. In computer programming, the research or development tool may be an automated way to generate boilerplate code that is required for routine operations. Once the code exists, there may be no evidence that it was developed with the tool.

Research tools are problematic for several reasons, even in the domestic arena. One is philosophical. Research tools may be examples of knowledge in which investment is mostly uncontroversial, and for which the benefits are widespread. Using the arguments in chapter 2, they are therefore good candidates to be publicly sponsored and put in the public domain.

Another problem has to do with enforcement. Even in the domestic arena, it is difficult to verify that a protein-producing bacterium was developed with the unauthorized use of a research tool. If infringements cannot be detected, the intellectual property cannot be enforced.

The enforcement problem is compounded in the international arena by ambiguities in trade rules that keep derived products out. Trade rules treat the importation of proprietary products, and products produced with proprietary processes, differently than products developed with proprietary research tools. In the case of products, provenance does not matter, since unauthorized sale or use is an infringement. Prior to the Process Patent Amendments Act of 1988, which added section 271(g) to the Patent Act, there was no law prohibiting the importation of products made abroad with infringing processes. That was an untenable situation, since it created incentives to manufacture products offshore, to avoid paying royalties when the products were imported. Section 271(g) remedied that problem for process patents but makes no mention of research tools. Since the research tool is not required to manufacture the product—development and manufacture are different things—there is no presumption that 271(g) applies.

If there are jurisdictions where a particular research tool is not protected, use of the research tool may be pushed offshore. Adding insult to injury, products developed with the research tool could then, absent clear and enforceable trade rules, be proprietary in all jurisdictions where such products are protected, without obliging the seller to pay royalties to the developer of the research tool. In the extreme case, this would deprive the research tool of its commercial value even in the country where it was invented, a situation that is hard to distinguish from not having protection at all.

The second example concerns efforts to enable price discrimination. As chapter 2 pointed out, price discrimination can serve the interests of both consumers and producers. The difficulty of price discrimination is in finding the submarkets where customers with similar willingness to pay are clustered, and preventing resale from low-priced market segments to high-priced segments.

In the international arena, the market is segmented automatically to the extent that willingness to pay is determined by culture and income. The movie industry has developed a clever means of exploiting this segmentation by coding DVD players and DVD movies with country codes. A movie can only be played on a DVD player if the country code matches. This prevents movies priced for the Asian market from being resold to play on American machines.

Country codes are a form of encryption, and they can be circumvented. In the United States, such circumvention is illegal under the DMCA (see chapter 7). However, its legality elsewhere is still being debated. If it is not illegal to reverse engineer the country code in, say, Finland, clever technologists can undermine the content providers' attempt at price discrimination by doing so, and then arbitrage the low-priced and high-priced markets. This will put upward pressure on price in markets where the content providers would otherwise charge a lower price.

These international arbitrage opportunities have the consequence that intellectual property protections are automatically harmonized, usually toward the least protective regime. National autonomy will be hard to preserve in any meaningful way.

11.7   Externalities and International Cooperation

Since the public has no means to recoup cross-border external benefits that arise from innovations that it puts in the public domain, the large amount of public research is perhaps surprising. Large public research programs are mainly undertaken by large industrialized countries competing, among other things, for prestige. Still, prestige may be a thin thread on which to hang the justification for a public R&D program.

A natural way to overcome externalities is joint funding. In fact, there are several impressive examples, mostly involving big science, where blocks of countries have coordinated their research spending for mutual benefit. Several European countries collaborated on a particle accelerator called CERN, located in Switzerland, which is an important nuclear research facility for European physicists and is also used by Americans. Another such research facility is the International Space Station, which is mostly funded by the United States but also has major contributions from Russia and other countries. Finally, the Canada-France-Hawaii telescope, located in Hawaii, shows how international cooperation extends to even relatively small-scale facilities.

Cooperation can also occur implicitly and without common facilities. Since 1945, governments have understood that current fossil-fuel and nuclear-energy technologies cannot meet society's demand for electricity indefinitely. By contrast, a successful fusion technology would generate essentially limitless energy from an isotope, deuterium, found in seawater. Governments in the United States, Europe, Russia, and Japan have all invested heavily to solve this problem. Interestingly, different countries tend to pursue different technical strategies (see Maurer and Scotchmer 2004). This has presumably limited duplication and facilitated an aggregate investment that no single country could afford.

Despite these successes of international cooperation, the area of cooperation with perhaps the highest payoff, pharmaceuticals, remains firmly in private hands.

11.8   Conclusion

The notion of an optimal incentive strucuture must be reinterpreted for the international context. In a domestic context, it is natural to define an optimal incentive mechanism as one that maximizes the sum of benefits that accrue to consumers and innovators, recognizing that innovators must receive benefits in order to discover new knowledge. In the international arena, domestic policymaking is influenced by profit flows. Stronger protection at home increases the profit flow to foreigners, and stronger protection abroad bolsters the profit flow to domestic innovators.

From an overall global point of view, profit flows are merely transfers, but they nevertheless have an important impact on domestic policymaking. No country's domestic calculation of an optimal policy will accord with the policy that is optimal from the point of view of maximizing the sum of global benefits. We concluded that when countries must provide national treatment of foreign inventors but make independent choices about the length of protection or the subject matters covered, their domestic interests are best served by choosing protections that are shorter or cover fewer subject matters than would be optimal from a global perspective. This is directly because of the profit flows. Harmonization will generally strengthen protection.

Profit flows are affected by the relative sizes of domestic markets and by the relative sizes of the countries' innovative capacities. We showed that the countries' bargaining positions in the international negotiations over harmonization will likely reflect these two aspects. Countries with smaller markets should favor stronger protections, as should countries with more innovative capacity. This seems to have been broadly true in the TRIPS negotiation.

Much of this book has been concerned with the proper balance between public funding of R&D and sponsorship by the private sector under a system of intellectual property rights. The international arena tilts the balance toward privatization, because intellectual property protection allows some spillovers to be repatriated to the innovating country. It is hard to see why domestic public sponsors would devote public funds to a project unless domestic benefits outweigh the costs. However, there are many worthy projects for which worldwide benefits outweigh the costs, even if domestic benefits do not, especially in a small country. Intellectual property incentives can often overcome this problem. Under a system of reciprocal national treatment, foreign users of a protected innovation will be taxed through proprietary pricing, so that some of the benefits conferred abroad can partially be repatriated.

If, as this line of reasoning suggests, worldwide innovation policies have shifted inefficiently away from public sponsorship and toward the private sector, then the culprit probably lies in a dearth of international efforts to coordinate and commit to public spending on R&D. There are no international organizations for public spending that are analogous to the TRIPS negotation for intellectual property rights.

References and Further Reading

Alston, J. 2002. "Spillovers." *Australian Journal of Agricultural and Resource Economics* 46:315–346.

Aoki, R., and T. J. Prusa. 1993. "International Standards for Intellectual Property Rights and R&D Incentives." *Journal of International Economics* 35:251–273.

Bagwell, K., and R. W. Staiger. 1999. "An Economic Theory of GATT." *American Economic Review* 89:215–248.

Bender, T., and D. Sampliner. 1996–1997. "Poets, Pirates and the Creation of American Literature." *NYU Journal of International Law and Politics* 29:255–270.

Boettiger, S., E. VanDusen, G. D. Graff, P. G. Pardey, and B. D. Wright. Forthcoming. "Intellectual Property Rights for Plant Biotechnology: International Aspects." In P. Christou and H. Klee, eds., *Handbook of Plant Biotechnology.* New York: Wiley.

Branstetter, L., and M. Sakakibara. 2001. "Do Stronger Patents Induce More Unnovation? Evidence from the 1988 Japanese Patent Law Reforms." *RAND Journal of Economics* 32:77–100.

Bromberg, J. L. 1983. *Fusion: Science, Politics, and the Invention of a New Energy Source.* Cambridge: MIT Press.

Business Software Alliance. 2001. "Sixth Annual Global Piracy Study." Available at www.bsa.org/usa/press/newsreleases//2001-05-21.566.phtml and at www.bsa.org/resources/2001-05-21.55.pdf.

Chin, J., and G. Grossman. 1990. "Intellectual Property Rights and North-South Trade." In R. W. Jones and A. O. Krueger, eds., *The Political Economy of International Trade: Essays in Honor Robert E. Baldwin,* 90–107. Cambridge, MA: Basil Blackwell.

Deardorff, A. 1992. "Welfare Effects of Global Patent Protection." *Economica* 59:35–51.

Dixit, A., G. Grossman, and E. Helpman. 1997. "Common Agency and Coordination: General Theory and Application to Government Policy Making." *Journal of Political Economy* 105:752–769.

European Patent Office. 2002a. "Facts and figures 2002." Available at www.european-patent-office.org/epo/facts_figures/facts2001/pdf/facts_figures_01.pdf.

European Patent Office. 2002b. "Trilateral Statistical Reports 2001." Available at www.european-patent-office.org/tws/tsr_2001/index.php.

European Patent Office, Japanese Patent Office, and United States Patent Office. 2002. "Trilateral Statistical Report 2002 edition." Available at www.european-patent-office.org/tws/tsr_2002/.

European Union in the U.S. 2003. "European Union and World Trade. Basic Statistics on European Union Trade for Years 2001 and 2002. Comparison with the United States, Japan and Regional Trading Areas." Available at www.eurunion.org/profile/EUUSStats.pdf.

Grossman, G., and E. Lai. 2001. "International Protection of Intellectual Property." Mimeograph. Princeton, NJ: Princeton University.

Helpman, E. 1993. "Innovation, Imitation and Intellectual Property Rights." *Econometrica* 30:27–47.

Heston, A., R. Summers, and B. Aten. 2002. *Penn World Table Version 6.1.* Philadelphia: Center for International Comparisons at the University of Pennsylvania (CICUP). Available at pwt.econ.upenn.edu/aboutpwt.html.

Hui, K.-L., and I. Png. 2003. "Piracy and the Legitimate Demand for Recorded Music." *Contributions to Economic Analysis and Policy* 2:Article 11.

Lanjouw, J. O., and I. M. Cockburn. 2001. "New Pills for Poor People? Evidence after GATT." *World Development* 29:265–289.

Maskus, K. 1998. "The International Regulation of Intellectual Property." *Weltwirtschaftliches Archiv* 134:186–208.

Maskus, K. 2000. *Intellectual Property Rights in the Global Economy.* Washington, DC: Institute for International Economics.

Maskus, K. 2001. "Canadian Patent Policy in the North American Context." Paper presented at the conference "Intellectual Property and Innovation in the Knowledge Based Economy," Industry Canada and University of Toronto Law School, Toronto.

Maurer, S., and S. Scotchmer. 2004. "Procuring Knowledge." In G. Libecap, ed., *Advances in the Study of Entrepreneurship, Innovation and Growth*, 1–31. Amsterdam: JAI Press.

McCalman, P. 2001. "Reaping What You Sow: An Empirical Analysis of International Patent Harmonization." *Journal of International Economics* 55:161–185.

Moschini, G. 2003. "Intellectual Property Rights and the World Trade Organization: Retrospect and Prospects." Paper presented at the conference "Agricultural Policy Reform and the STO: Where Are We Heading?," Iowa State University, Department Agricultural Economics.

National Fusion Science Energy. 1998. "Fusion Innovations: A Report from ICC98." Available at www.fusionscience.org/ICC98/ICC98_Sum.pdf.

Reichman, J. H. 1997. "From Free Riders to Fair Folowers: Global Competition under the Trips Agreement." *International Law and Politics* 29:11–93.

Ryan, M. P. 1998. *Knowledge Diplomacy*. Washington, DC: Brookings Institution Press.

Samuelson, P. 1999. "Challenges for the World Intellectual Property Organization and the Trade-Related Aspects of Intellectual Property Rights Council in Regulating Intellectual Property Rights in the Information Age." *European Intellectual Property Review* 11:578–591.

Samuelson, P. 2004. "Intellectual Property Arbitrage: How Foreign Rules Affect Domestic Protections." *University of Chicago Law Review* 71:223–339.

Scotchmer, S. 2004. "The Political Economy of Intellectual Property Treaties." *Journal of Law, Economics and Organizations* 20:415–437.

Stern, S., M. E. Porter, and J. L. Furman. 2002. "The Determinants of National Innovative Capacity." Working Paper 7876. Cambridge, MA: National Bureau of Economic Research.

Watal, J. 1998. "The Trips Agreement and Developing Countries–Strong, Weak or Balanced Protection." *Journal of World Intellectual Property* 1:281–307.

World Intellectual Property Organization. 2002. "Basic Facts about the Patent Cooperation Treaty." WIPO Publication Number 433(E). Available at www.wipo.org/pct/en.

World Trade Organization. 2002a. *Agreement on Trade-Related Aspects of Intellectual Property Rights*. Available at www.wto.org/english/tratop_e/trips_e/_agm0_e.htm.

World Trade Organization. 2002b. "In Brief." Available at www.wto.org/english/thewto_e/whatis_e/inbrief_e/inbr02_e.htm.

Index